D07713889

Sustainability Education

Sustainability Education

Perspectives and Practice across Higher Education

Edited by
Paula Jones, David Selby and Stephen Sterling

earthscan
publishing for a sustainable future

London • Washington, DC

First published in 2010 by Earthscan

Copyright © Paula Jones, David Selby and Stephen Sterling, 2010

Earthscan Ltd, Dunstan House, 14a St Cross Street, London EC1N 8XA, UK
Earthscan LLC, 1616 P Street, NW, Washington DC 20036, USA
Earthscan publishes in association with the International Institute for Environment and Development

For more information on Earthscan publications, see www.earthscan.co.uk or write to earthinfo@earthscan.co.uk

ISBN: 978-1-84407-877-6 hardback
ISBN: 978-1-84407-878-3 paperback

Typeset by MapSet Ltd, Gateshead, UK
Cover design by Rob Watts

A catalogue record for this book is available from the British Library

Library of Congress Cataloging-in-Publication Data

Sustainability education : perspectives and practice across higher education / edited by Paula Jones, David Selby, and Stephen Sterling.
    p. cm.
    Includes bibliographical references and index.
    ISBN 978-1-84407-877-6 (hardback) – ISBN 978-1-84407878-3 (pbk.) 1. Education, Higher–I. Jones, Paula. II. Selby, David, Dr. III. Sterling, Stephen R.
    LC65.S87 2010
    338.43378–dc22

                                                                2010000827

At Earthscan we strive to minimize our environmental impacts and carbon footprint through reducing waste, recycling and offsetting our CO$_2$ emissions, including those created through publication of this book. For more details of our environmental policy, see www.earthscan.co.uk.

Printed and bound in the UK by TJ International, an ISO 14001 accredited company. The paper used is FSC-certified and the inks are vegetable based.

Mixed Sources
Product group from well-managed forests and other controlled sources
www.fsc.org   Cert no. SGS-COC-2482
© 1996 Forest Stewardship Council

Contents

List of Figures, Tables and Boxes

Figures

Tables

Boxes

Acknowledgements

We would like to thank all those who have contributed to making this book possible. In particular, we would like to thank the authors for their time, energy and patience in researching and writing their chapters. We would also like to thank members of the Centre for Sustainable Futures at the University of Plymouth for their support and the Higher Education Academy subject centres who collaborated in this project.

Preface

The idea for this book arose from discussions in 2008 centring on the response of the higher education sector to the increasingly insistent sustainability agenda, particularly with regard to teaching and learning. The Centre for Sustainable Futures at the University of Plymouth, working with the UK Higher Education Academy Education for Sustainable Development Project, wanted to use both its own and the Project's experience to frame a book that would help answer one of the most intractable but important questions: how can disciplines 'embed' sustainability into their theory and practice in a way that is consistent with the huge challenges that sustainability-related issues present – and will continue to present – to graduates?

The Centre has been working to catalyse organizational change towards sustainability at the University of Plymouth, including curriculum development and reorientation, while the Academy Project exists to help institutions and subject communities to develop curricula and pedagogy that will give students the skills and knowledge to live and work sustainably. The experience of both initiatives, and of other actors in the field, is that interest in sustainability education, or education for sustainable development, is growing remarkably in higher education, both within the UK and internationally. Yet while increasing numbers of policy-makers, senior managers and academics are convinced of its importance, understanding of its implications for policy and practice is much less well developed. Although universities are grappling with developing sustainability policies and many are making real progress in greening their campuses, the challenge of transforming curricula and teaching and learning practices remains great.

One means of addressing both interest and resistances – whether academic or institutional – is by demonstrating the disciplinary potential and benefits accruing from infusing sustainability concepts, issues and case studies into learning and teaching, in terms of the quality of student motivation and learning, teacher satisfaction and opportunities for innovative and active learning. The book was developed with this in mind. Written by academics at Plymouth, contributors from Academy subject centres and beyond, it attempts to comprehensively review the current state of play. It discusses the potential contribution different disciplines can make to the emerging response of higher education to the sustainability agenda, seen against the background of increasing interest within higher educa-

tion and public expectation of the sector in this regard, both nationally and internationally.

The chapters present discussion, case studies and reports of ongoing work
and debates and point the way to future developments. They indicate that, in
practice, the range of challenges and opportunities that sustainability presents has
a resonance across different disciplines, so we hope readers will be tempted to
look outside their areas, not least in the interests of interdisciplinary perspectives
and potentials, which many contributors touch on.

We also hope this book will be of interest to theorists and practitioners alike,
and that it will appeal to academics, students, policy-makers and senior managers
seeking to navigate a growing sustainability tide in higher education and help
them take it further – in the interests of all our futures.

Paula Jones, David Selby and Stephen Sterling
Plymouth
January 2010

Foreword

Sustainability education in higher education: Perspectives and practices across the curriculum

Peter Blaze Corcoran

The nature of sustainability, and the prospect of unsustainability, require a fundamental change of epistemology, and therefore of education. Changes are necessary in curricula, pedagogy, policy and institutional structures. Stephen Sterling has argued elsewhere for 'the necessary transformation of higher education towards the integrative and more whole state implied by a systemic view of sustainability in education and society' (2004). But how do we achieve such a transformation? Now, several years into the effort to reimagine higher education for sustainability, we see as much as ever the academy's stubborn resistance to change. It is clear that we have failed to *transform* either higher education or society. Yet, we have begun to *reform* it. Around the world, we see the earnest and critical work of students, scholars and administrators embedding sustainability across the higher education curriculum. This book gives us hope that systemic sustainability education is possible.

Even as higher education fails to put its house in ecological order, sustainability has become the metanarrative of our time – while at the same time sustainability has become a diminishing prospect. This puts the future of the beauty and bounty of life on Earth, as it has evolved over four billion or more years, and of human life, as we have known it for hundreds of thousands of years, in jeopardy. The social world, too, is in agony. Our efforts to eradicate or even to alleviate poverty are a massive failure. Undemocratic systems and lack of peace abound. The UN Development Programme's Millennium Development Goals go unmet. Climate change talks collapse even as the climate systems on which life on

Earth utterly depends collapse. One must ask how can higher education *not* respond to the challenge of sustainability?

The editors successfully make the case for higher education's moral responsibility to respond and review the history of its efforts to do so, including interdisciplinarity, international perspectives and pedagogy. They offer salient analyses and compelling examples of how we *can* respond. The book is based on the sound thesis that academic resistance and inhibition can be overcome by infusing sustainability concepts, issues and case studies into the disciplines.

Approaching the possibility of change through disciplines is intelligent and practical. The editors also wisely select several fields that are not traditional academic disciplines. This helps us challenge our ingrained conceptions of disciplinarity and helps us see wider possibilities. Loyalty among academicians to disciplines has been primary; the structure of the disciplines provides valuable ways of knowing but has limited our ability to generate knowledge, and learning, in other ways. The contributors to this thoughtful book know how to work across these boundaries. In this way, they make a much-needed contribution to moving education for sustainability beyond the immediate community of scholars who have been concerned with it, thus broadening involvement across the academic terrain.

They are previewing how higher education might look in years to come as they demonstrate ways in which we can overcome disciplinary barriers and meet institutional and systemic challenges. The University of Plymouth's Centre for Sustainable Futures and the Higher Education Academy's Education for Sustainable Development Project deserve credit for supporting this important, widened participation.

The struggle to overcome institutional inertia and disciplinary traditions is widely shared throughout the global university culture. This means that the hard work of these editors and authors is broadly applicable – as so much of the innovative higher education work in the UK has been. Because the chapters are thoughtful and serious of purpose, they demonstrate effectively how the work must be done – idea by idea, field by field. Sustainability education as presented here is promising. It offers motivation and imaginative possibilities for engaging in change. These scholars have reason to be confident that their contribution has meaning and international significance for higher education – and for society.

Peter Blaze Corcoran
Professor of Environmental Studies and Environmental Education
Director of the Center for Environmental and Sustainability Education
College of Arts & Sciences
Florida Gulf Coast University

References

Sterling, S. (2004) 'Higher education, sustainability, and the role of systemic learning', in Corcoran, P. B. and Wals, A. E. J. (eds) *Higher Education and the Challenge of Sustainability: Problematics, Promise, and Practice*, Kluwer Academic Publishers, Dordrecht, pp47–70

UN Development Programme (undated) *Millennium Development Goals*, available at www.undp.org/mdg, accessed 2 February 2010

List of Acronyms and Abbreviations

(All UK-specific unless otherwise stated)

AEU	Association of European Universities
AHRC	Arts and Humanities Research Council
AISHE	Auditing Instrument for Sustainability in Higher Education
ASC	Academy for Sustainable Communities
BAN	Basel Action Network
BASW	British Association of Social Workers
BELP	'Beyond Leather Patches' project
CBA	cost–benefit analysis
CDP	Community Development Project
CEBE	Centre for Education in the Built Environment
CEO	Chief Executive Officer
CETL	Centre of Excellence in Teaching and Learning
CFO	Chief Financial Officer
CIOB	Chartered Institute of Building
COPERNICUS	Cooperation Programme in Europe for Research on Nature and Industry through Coordinated University Studies
CRE	Conference of European Rectors of European Universities
C-SCAIPE	Centre for Sustainable Communities Achieved through Integrated Professional Education
CSF	Centre for Sustainable Futures (at University of Plymouth)
CSR	Corporate Social Responsibility
DCSF	Department for Children, Schools and Families
DEFRA	Department for Environment, Food and Rural Affairs
DESD	(UN) Decade of Education for Sustainable Development
DfES	Department for Education and Skills (now DCSF)
DoH	Department of Health
DHO	The Dutch National Network for Sustainable Development in Higher Education Curricula
DIUS	Department for Universities, Innovation and Skills
EC	European Community
EfS	Education for Sustainability
EC	Engineering Council
EngSC	(HEA) Engineering Subject Centre

ES3	earth science, environmental sciences and environmental studies
ESD	Education for Sustainable Development
EWB-UK	Engineers Without Borders UK
FIDH	*Fédération Internationale des ligues des Droits de l'Homme* (International Federation for Human Rights)
GDP	gross domestic product
GEES	geography, earth and environmental sciences
GIS	geographic information systems
HE	higher education
HEA	Higher Education Academy
HEFCE	Higher Education Funding Council for England
HEI	higher education institution
HEPS	Higher Education Partnership for Sustainability
HKU	University of Hong Kong
IAU	International Association of Universities
IBL	inquiry-based learning
ICE	Institution of Civil Engineers
ICUS	Industry through Coordinated University Studies
IJSHE	*International Journal of Sustainability in Higher Education*
iLand	Interdisciplinary Laboratory for Art, Nature and Dance
ISEW	index of sustainable economic welfare
ITT	initial teacher training
MD	Managing Director
MeCCSA	Media, Communication and Cultural Studies Association
MESA	Mainstreaming Environment and Sustainability in African Universities
NERC	Natural Environmental Research Council
NGO	non-governmental organization
NHS	National Health Service
NHSSDH	NHS Sustainable Development Unit
NMC	Nursing and Midwifery Council
NSF	(US) National Science Foundation
Ofsted	Office for Standards in Education
PBL	problem-based learning
PRS	(Subject Centre for) Philosophical and Religious Studies
QAA	Quality Assurance Agency for Higher Education
QCA	Qualifications and Curriculum Authority
RAE	Research Assessment Exercise
RAEng	Royal Academy of Engineering
RBC	Rose Bruford College
RCE	Regional Centre of Expertise on ESD
RESTDL	(MSc in) Renewable Energy Systems Technology by Distance Learning
RICS	Royal Institution of Chartered Surveyors

RMIT	Royal Melbourne Institute of Technology
RTPI	Royal Town Planning Institute
SASS	system for appraising the sustainability of structures
SCUDD	Standing Conference of University Drama Departments
SD	sustainable development
SDN	Sustainable Design Network
SHA	Strategic Health Authority
SUNY	State University of New York
TIE	Theatre in Education
TRE	*Theologische Realenzyklopädie (Band 30)*
TSL	transformative sustainability learning
UCAS	University and College Admissions Service
UCL	University College London
UKCLE	UK Centre for Legal Education
ULSF	University Leaders for a Sustainable Future
UNCED	UN Conference on Environment and Development
UNEP	UN Environment Programme
UNESCO	UN Educational, Scientific and Cultural Organization
UN FCCC	UN Framework Convention on Climate Change
UWE	University of the West of England
VP	Visiting Professor (RAEng)
WCC	World Council of Churches
WCED	World Commission on Environment and Development
WRI	World Resources Institute

Chapter 1

Introduction[1]

Paula Jones, David Selby and Stephen Sterling

The international background

In their call for the education of 'earth-literate leaders', Martin and Jucker (2005, pp19, 21) note that most of the 100 or so world leaders attending the World Summit for Sustainable Development in Johannesburg in 2002 who collectively and conspicuously 'failed to rise to the challenge of sustainability' had 'a higher degree from some of the world's most prestigious universities'. Recalling David Orr's oft-cited observation that the threat to the planet is largely 'the results of work by people with BAs, BSs, LLBs, MBAs and PhDs' (1994, p7), Martin and Jucker go on to raise serious questions about the world's universities as they educate future generations of professionals. 'Why is it so rare', they ask (2005, p21), 'that we encounter in our leaders the qualities needed to enable sustainability: humility, respect for all forms of life and future generations, precaution and wisdom, the capacity to think systemically and challenge unethical actions? And, more worryingly on the basis of current performance, what hope of improvement is there for future leaders?'

An earlier gathering of world leaders, the UN Conference on Environment and Development Rio de Janeiro, 1992 (UNCED), had been influential in linking the challenge of sustainability to education and learning. *Agenda 21*, the programme of action emerging from the conference, identified school-age to adult education as 'critical for promoting sustainable development and improving the capacity of people to address environmental and development issues', floating but hardly consolidating the idea that countries 'could support university and other tertiary activities and networks' (UNCED, 1992, pp265–266).

A far less tentative role for the tertiary sector was evident 12 years later in the planning for the UN Decade of Education for Sustainable Development

(DESD), 2005–14, for which the UN Educational, Scientific and Cultural Organization (UNESCO) became the lead international agency. Higher education was designated as having 'a particular role to play' during the decade:

> *Universities must function as places of research and learning for sustainable development... Higher education should also provide leadership by practicing what they teach through sustainable purchasing, investments and facilities that are integrated with teaching and learning... Higher education should emphasize experiential, inquiry-based, problem-solving, interdisciplinary systems approaches and critical thinking. Curricula need to be developed, including content, materials and tools such as case studies and identification of best practices. (UNESCO, 2004, pp22–23)*

In fulfilling that role, universities – like all other formal, non-formal and informal education providers – were enjoined by those framing the decade to promote the following 'underlying values':

- Respect for the dignity and human rights of all people throughout the world and a commitment to social and economic justice for all.
- Respect for the human rights of future generations and a commitment to intergenerational responsibility.
- Respect and care for the greater community of life in all its diversity, which involves the protection and restoration of the Earth's ecosystems.
- Respect for cultural diversity and a commitment to build locally and globally a culture of tolerance, non-violence and peace (UNESCO, 2004, p14).

Education for sustainable development (ESD) at all educational institutions, including universities, was, according to UNESCO, to demonstrate a range of key features. It was to be interdisciplinary and holistic, and so embedded across the whole curriculum; explicitly values driven, with the values 'examined, debated, tested and applied'; built around critical thinking and problem solving, and so confidence building in the face of the dilemmas and challenges of sustainable development; multi-method and participatory, applying different pedagogies and fostering cooperative learning and decision-making between teachers and learners; and locally relevant and grounded in local languages and cultures (UNESCO, 2004, p16).

Internationally, university alliances, consortia and networks have promoted commitment on the part of higher education institutions to a sustainability ethic. In 1990, the US-based University Leaders for a Sustainable Future (ULSF) convened a meeting of university presidents, chancellors and rectors to share their concerns about the state of the world and to create a document spelling out the actions that institutions for higher education needed to take to play their part in forging a sustainable future. The resultant ten-point action plan, *The Talloires Declaration* (ULSF, 1994), was the outcome. Among the action points, prominent areas to be addressed were identified as curricula, teaching and learning. Signatories of the *Declaration* commit to establishing programmes for 'environmentally responsible citizenship', to teaching 'environmental literacy to all undergraduate, graduate, and professional students', and to developing 'interdisciplinary approaches to curricula, research initiatives, operations, and outreach activities'. As of October 2009, the *Declaration* carried the signature of the presidents, chancellors or rectors of some 390 universities in 52 countries around the world.

The *Talloires Declaration* furnished an international model that has inspired declarations from other university consortia. At the ninth International Association of Universities' (IAU) Round Table in 1993 in Kyoto, Japan, delegates adopted the *Kyoto Declaration on Sustainable Development* (IAU, 1993), agreeing to develop university capacity to teach, research and take action according to 'sustainable development principles, to increase environmental literacy, and to enhance the understanding of environmental ethics within the university and with the public at large'. At the time of writing, IAU has 1200 member institutions, all endorsing the Declaration by dint of their membership.[2] In 1994, the Conference of European Rectors (CRE) of European Universities, the predecessor of the Association of European Universities (AEU), promulgated *The University Charter for Sustainable Development* through its COPERNICUS programme (CO-operation Programme in Europe for Research on Nature and Industry through Coordinated University Studies). Like *The Talloires Declaration*, the *Charter* (CRE-COPERNICUS, 1994) emphasizes the importance of embedding sustainability in university curricula, teaching and learning:

> Universities shall incorporate an environmental perspective in all their work and set up environmental education programmes involving both teachers and researchers as well as students – all of whom should be exposed to the global challenges of environment and development, irrespective of their field of study... Universities shall encourage interdisciplinary and collaborative education and research programmes related to sustainable development as part of the institution's central mission.

As of the time of writing, some 305 European university heads from 37 countries have signed the *Charter* (UNESCO, 2009a).

This impetus was further strengthened by the *Bonn Declaration*, which emerged from the UNESCO World Conference on ESD, held in Bonn, Germany in March 2009. The *Declaration* urged stakeholders to 'mobilise the core functions of universities: teaching, research and community engagement to strengthen global and local knowledge of ESD ... and develop model projects that can respond to the complexity and urgency of ESD' (UNESCO, 2009b, p4).

Given such a significant upsurge in declared commitment to sustainability-related policy and practice at tertiary level, including a commitment to transforming curricula, teaching and learning, is the philosophical and rhetorical embrace being matched by concrete action at national and institution-specific levels?

The national and institutional foreground

In January 2005, the Higher Education Funding Council for England (HEFCE) issued a consultation document, *Sustainable Development in Higher Education* (HEFCE, 2005a), offering a vision and strategy whereby the Council could support higher education's contribution to sustainable development. Recognizing that fostering awareness of the world and understandings of complex economic, social and environmental processes 'have long characterized good learning and teaching in higher education', the document went on to say that 'few students graduate with an understanding of how to make a specific contribution to future social and economic development *in a sustainable way*' (HEFCE, 2005a, p7; italics in original). Its vision of higher education's sustainability contribution then went on to include developing 'curricula, pedagogy and extra-curricular activities that enable students to develop the values, skills and knowledge to contribute to sustainable development' within a wider context of sustainability-related institutional change (HEFCE, 2005a, p8).

The document met with a withering response from Peter Knight, then Vice-Chancellor of the University of Central England. 'It is one of the most pernicious and dangerous circulars ever to be issued. It represents the final assault on the last remaining freedom of universities... The issue here is not whether sustainable development is a good or bad idea. It is about the basic rights and responsibilities of universities, and the need to safeguard academic freedom. It is not the job of universities to promote a particular orthodoxy; it is their role to educate students to examine critically policies, ideas, concepts and systems, then make up their own minds' (Knight, 2005).

Resultant sensitivities over non-intrusion into the affairs of notionally independent tertiary institutions led HEFCE to mollify its advocacy of sustainability-related curricula. It tiptoed along the 'fine, but important, dividing line between offering support to the HE sector, and attempting to steer it in a particular way' (Sterling and Scott, 2008, p389). The organization's follow-up document acknowledges that the consultation had elicited 'negative comment' on its curricular proposals, states its 'wish to help institutions to find their own way forward in relation to this agenda,' but then restates its opinion that 'the greatest contribution higher education has to make to sustainable development is by enabling students to develop new values, skills and knowledge' in which cause it expresses itself ready to engage with a 'range of groups' (HEFCE, 2005b, pp1, 3, 5, 28). In a subsequent consultation round leading to an updated strategic statement and action plan, the Council retained its 'hands-off' stance on curricula, teaching and learning, more or less confining itself to a 'sharing of good practice' role, while reiterating its view regarding education's 'greatest contribution' to sustainable development (HEFCE, 2008; HEFCE, 2009).

The absence of a bold legitimizing catalyst for sustainability-related curriculum development in higher education in England did not seem to augur well for curricular change of any significance at the institutional level, especially given the experience of the earlier Higher Education Partnership for Sustainability

(HEPS), which ran from 2000 to 2003. The partnership, coordinated by the non-governmental organization Forum for the Future, involved 18 universities in estates management and curricular aspects of sustainable development (Parkin et al, 2004). A self-professed top-down approach entailing institutional buy-in by senior university administrators but, in some cases drawing in sustainability 'champions' at participating institutions, HEPS was considered to have had 'a moderate and positive impact' helping move the sustainability agenda forward and bringing coordination and coherence to disparate initiatives (SQW, undated, i–v). Its provision of a 'curriculum toolkit' for curriculum content and pedagogical development notwithstanding, HEPS, fell short in terms of influencing curricula, even though it made significant progress in applying sustainable principles to estates management. As Forum for the Future acknowledges:

Most partners identified integrating sustainable development into the curriculum as a priority during their opening sustainability reviews. Putting this into practice proved to be much harder, and it has been one of the disappointments of HEPS that the very purpose of a university – teaching and learning – should end up being one of the least developed by the partnership (Parkin et al, 2004, p29).

For Sterling and Scott, the disparity between environmental management and curriculum development progress is easily explained. 'Environmental managers,' they write (2008, pp389–90), 'have to take the university's environment seriously. It's their job, there is a clear legal and regulatory framework within which they have to act, and clear financial incentives to do so. Academics, however, don't *have* to take SD [sustainable development] seriously, except to the extent that there is accreditation pressure, or that they are interested, or that, perhaps, students demand it. Moreover, they usually resent being told what their job entails… In most cases, "campus greening" is advancing more strongly than the more intractable area of curriculum change' (Sterling and Scott, 2008, pp389–390; italics in original).

A similar picture emerges from Australia of universities moving ahead with greening their campuses while sustainability-related curriculum and pedagogical development drags its heels (Noonan and Thomas, 2004; Lang et al, 2006, p46). 'Consequently, apart from the occasional course/subject that is often an elective, most tertiary students have few opportunities to participate in education for sustainability within their disciplines' (Lang et al, p46). Although several Australian institutions have signed *The Talloires Declaration*, Thomas (2004, p33) finds 'little indication that their curricula have been changed to include sustainability education'. The experience of his own institution, the Royal Melbourne Institute of Technology (RMIT), he reports, is one in which enthusiastic conviction and vision on the part of individual academic staff is not enough to effect programmatic change (Thomas, 2004, p33).

Returning to England (before revisiting Australia), we find that the vacuum left by HEFCE's reluctance to deal the curriculum card strongly has been to some extent filled by the ESD Project of the Higher Education Academy (HEA). The Academy is a UK-wide organization funded by HEFCE and its sister funding councils in Scotland and Wales dedicated to enhancing the student learning experience. It works with higher education institutions and through 24 discipline-based subject centres at different universities. The ESD Project was established as a 'special theme' in the Academy's overall programme in 2005 with a remit 'to help institutions and subject communities develop curricula and pedagogy that will give students the skills and knowledge to live and work sustainably' (cited in Sterling and Witham, 2008, p401). Its first endeavour was to commission a team to examine the state of the art in sustainability-related curricula, teaching and learning, primarily in disciplinary contexts, by gathering data from 18 of the 24 subject centres. The published outcome, *Sustainable Development in Higher Education: Current Practice and Future Developments* (Dawe et al, 2005) reports minority but widening engagement with ESD, and identifies potential for, as well as inhibitors of, further and more widespread curriculum development and change. Since 2005, by means of small grants and mini-grants, research, network-ing events and national conferences (Sterling and Witham, 2008, pp402–406), the Project has promoted and disseminated path-finding disciplinary-based sustainability curriculum development, examples of which are featured in seven of the chapters of this book (Chapters 6, 9, 10, 11, 12, 16 and 17).

In the UK, the Universities of Bradford and Plymouth have been to the fore in taking a more comprehensive and structured approach to sustainability-related curriculum development. In 2006, Bradford launched a strategic initiative known as Ecoversity with the object of embedding sustainable development 'across the operations and culture of the University' and within the 'living and learning experience of all students'. A HEFCE Strategic Development Fund Grant in 2007 provided the resources for staffing and support structures to realize this vision (Hopkinson et al, 2008, p440). The UNESCO DESD's underlying values and implementation features, as described earlier, provided the framework for the initiative, being deemed particularly appropriate for an institution in a strongly multicultural context (Hopkinson et al, 2008, p442). During 2006, a pilot ESD curriculum review project of four programmes in pharmacy, midwifery, civil engineering and business administration had been undertaken, using a methodol-ogy based on documentation review and interviews with staff and students to ascertain the degree of alignment between the programmes and the UNESCO framework. It was concluded that the programmes had 'clear content, assessment and learning approaches ...entirely consistent with ESD (as framed by UNESCO) but are not explicitly recognized or presented as such by the programme leaders' (Hopkinson et al, 2008, p444). Encouraged by this finding, Ecoversity determined to adopt a more strategic approach. The HEFCE grant and the appointment of a Director of ESD followed, as did the identification of 'academic ESD pioneers' for each of the University's seven schools. The role of the pioneers was 'to complete a comprehensive and systematic curriculum review (as in the pilot) and develop three-year action plans for embedding ESD in the curriculum of all programmes. Guidelines for incorporating ESD requirements

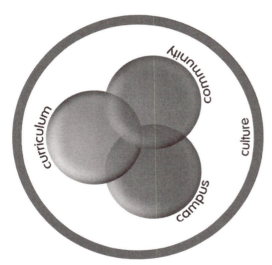

Figure 1.1 *The '4C' model*

into course approval and review processes were devised concurrently with the development of school action plans (Hopkinson et al, 2008, pp444–445).

In 2004, the University of Plymouth was awarded a five-year Centre for Excellence in Teaching and Learning – Education for Sustainable Development (CETL ESD) by HEFCE for the period 2005–2010 (Dyer et al, 2006). The Centre for Sustainable Futures (CSF), as it came to be known, similarly adopted a systematic and systemic approach to sustainability-related curriculum development. At the whole university level, the Centre facilitated a 'wide and deep' consultation in developing a University Sustainability Policy and Action Plan based on an holistic '4C' model in which Curriculum, Campus, Community and (institutional) Culture are seen as mutually enfolded and complementary foci of the sustainability university (see Figure 1.1). In this way, learning programmes encompass the exploration of campus, community partnerships and initiatives, and university culture from a sustainability perspective, while student experiential and action research can be directed towards campus, community and institutional cultural change. The Policy and Action Plans embrace an holistic notion of sustainability that, while taking the environment as fundamental, melds together economic, health, social justice and other humanitarian concerns (Selby, 2009, p103). At faculty and school level, CSF employed a Fellowship scheme to bring about systematic curriculum development. Some 45 Centre Fellows were bought out from 7 of the university's academic faculties and 13 of its 18 schools, Fellows and their heads of school committing to taking forward sustainability-related curriculum development and providing associated continuing professional development for academic staff. The Centre Fellows also committed to taking initiatives to further the University-wide sustainability agenda (Selby, 2009, p104).

Their curriculum development involved the infusion of sustainability concepts, themes and case studies into established (undergraduate and postgraduate) modules and programmes and/or the development of new sustainability-related modules and programmes – Centre Fellows being encouraged to make interdisciplinary links wherever possible given the multidimensional nature of sustainability (Selby, 2009, p104). Five of the chapters in this book are written or co-written by one-time CSF Fellows (Chapters 6, 7, 8, 13 and 17). Given academic and disciplinary barriers and resistance to the embedding of sustainable development in curricula, as touched on earlier and discussed further below, CSF developed a smorgasbord of curriculum frameworks, skills and concept lists, indicative syllabus content lists, assessment criteria and innovative assessment modes, all customizable by discipline, to support curriculum innovation. To pre-empt the objection of there being little space in a crowded academic curriculum to incorporate sustainability content, and working on the principle that 'something is better than nothing', so-called 'podules' were developed by the Centre; that is, materials allowing for time-economic injections of sustainability-related materials into class sessions (Sterling et al, 2008).

A smaller-scale systematic approach to embedding sustainability in curricula, beginning from the bottom up but supported by a state government grant, has been attempted at RMIT. The Beyond Leather Patches (BELP) project was 'developed to provide an effective and practical approach for integrating the broad concepts of sustainability into a wide range of university programs' (Lang et al, 2006, p55). Building on a ten-year history of small-scale curriculum development initiatives, BELP provided a 'supported and facilitated process' for academics in three disciplinary areas to engage with the theory of sustainability education, creating ownership of the change process by developing an understanding of the relationship of sustainability to their discipline and its professional practice. Following a curriculum audit and survey of staff attitudes, a workshop series helped academics shape their own vision of sustainability and identify the nature of the support needed to transform their own teaching. In this, they were supported by a web resource explaining the general theory behind sustainability education practice, case studies of good practice, and information and links to sustainability concepts and tools. BELP led to the revision of 16 courses in line with sustainability precepts and principles (Lang et al, 2006, p55–56).

Towards sustainability curricula in higher education: inhibiting and enabling conditions

Drawing on experiences of sustainability-related curriculum and pedagogical development at universities and colleges, what appear to be the principal inhibitors to wider and deeper curriculum change, and what approaches or factors might pre-empt or circumvent each inhibitor to create the conditions allowing change?

Principal inhibitor I

Academic staff, jealously guarding their academic freedom, see education for sustainable development as an imposition, something not commensurate with their discipline or student expectations of their discipline. Steeped in their specialism, they are uncomfortable about the interdisciplinary teaching for which the multi-dimensional concept of sustainability calls. They see no rewards or career advancement in sustainability curriculum innovation.

In response to this, enabling approaches include the following:

- Conveying sustainability as a contested and unfolding idea around which debate and discussion by staff and students alike is encouraged and, even if and when identified as an institutional priority, welcoming of contrary and subversive opinion (Gray-Donald and Selby, 2004, p204).
- Utilizing the process benefits of vagueness, while still being ready to offer a succinct definition of sustainability for those new to it who need a 'recipe'. As Wals and Bawden aver, vagueness in defining ESD 'has enormous canvassing and heuristic capacity if it is systematically used as a starting point or operational device to exchange views and ideas. These ongoing discussions may generate fruitful working hypotheses for the concrete formulation of curricula, study programmes, subject matter content and didactical arrangements' (Wals and Bawden, 2005, p38).
- Offering an holistic explanation of sustainability that, while grounded in environmental concern, brings into play the dimensions of culture, economy, ethics, health, peace and conflict, science and technology, and social justice, thus enabling those who see sustainability as exclusively or primarily 'environmental' to more readily discern the connections with their discipline (Gray-Donald and Selby, 2004, p205).
- Nurturing an interdisciplinary ethos by creating arenas and spaces (working groups, seminars, communities of interest) in which sustainability can be a 'strange attractor', bringing together academics of different disciplines to explore 'similarities within differences and differences within similarities around a nebulous but common set of sustainability values' (Gray-Donald and Selby, 2004, p205).
- Engaging students in sustainability advocacy and change processes.
- Ensuring, enlisting and flagging up-front senior management or top-down support for sustainability initiatives, including the personal involvement of some key senior staff. Using the legitimization so created to develop and enact a strategy for structured and systematic curriculum development, galvanizing sustainability 'champions' to make a bottom-up contribution to change through enthusiastic advocacy, role modelling and otherwise influencing peers. Building tangible and intangible rewards into the process.
- Making the process invitational rather than impositional, dialogic rather than prescriptive, participative rather than directive.

Principal inhibitor 2

Academic staff, both converts and contrarians, consider themselves as lacking the knowledge and skills, expertise and experience to implement sustainability-related teaching and learning. Enabling approaches might include:

- Providing whole university and discipline-specific staff development opportunities (avoiding the often-deskilling one-off event and opting for a cumulative, reinforcing approach), helping academics develop sustainability understandings and giving opportunities to apply their learning to existing and possible new courses (Noonan and Thomas, 2004, p74). According to Rowe (2002, pp86–87), 'professional development opportunities for faculty seem to be a key component for success'.

- Providing print or electronic manuals, case studies of good practice and collections of teaching and learning activities, and creating an electronic forum in which peers can share successful (and not so successful) experiences of sustainability-related teaching and learning.

- Establishing school-based resource people with a track record of sustainability education to whom colleagues can turn for advice and guidance.

- Pointing academic staff in the direction of externally available curriculum development growth points for their discipline, such as those at other higher education institutions, or (in the UK) a network such as the HEA ESD Project and the Academy Subject Centres.

Principal inhibitor 3

Academics and administrators hold that the ethos of the institution is not favourable for successful integration of sustainability across the teaching and learning programmes of the institution. Enabling approaches could then be:

- Developing an overarching institutional commitment through a consultative process, enshrining it in policy and supporting it with a strategic action plan for sustainability, in which curriculum, teaching and learning are linked to the institution's campus and community-related sustainability goals and attendant initiatives.

- Establishing a high-level and highly visible coordinating and monitoring body for sustainability, representing a multiplicity of interests and with open lines of communication to senior management.

- Having the university or college sign up to an internationally known framework and alliance for sustainability, such as that provided by *The Talloires Declaration*, and value statements such as the *Earth Charter* (Miller and Westra, 2002, pp9–16).

- Celebrating success through newsletters, electronic media and events and by instituting a formal recognition and reward system.

- Employing external stimuli to foster change (Sterling and Scott, 2008, p389), and not least external funding for sustainability-related change initiatives as is the case at the Universities of Bradford and Plymouth (large funding) and RMIT (small funding). Grants in aid of sustainability-oriented change add force and momentum to change efforts and help shift the institutional ethos.

Drawing insights from a survey of academics' views of conditions held to be important for the successful implementation of ESD at tertiary level, de la Harpe and Thomas (2009, p82) summarize factors held most likely to secure academic buy-in and achieve successful curriculum change outcomes:

A core group of staff would be identified to work together to lead and oversee the curriculum development and change initiative and to convince others that change is necessary. Key and influential staff would be specifically chosen to include a range of staff involved in curriculum change. They would be charged to work together to form a powerful guiding coalition to ensure that direction and momentum are sustained. They would also work with others to ensure that a vision was agreed to collaboratively or that a project or programme brief was developed to guide the intended change. Sufficient resources would be identified and set aside for project development. A clear implementation strategy would be developed, and most important, resources would be specifically allocated to support implementation activities. Identifying staff professional development needs and providing appropriate and relevant activities, located as close as possible to the change initiative, would also be needed. To embed the change into institutional processes or the way things get done around here', administrative systems and structures, as well as individual work roles, would be openly discussed, agreed and modified. Finally, a monitoring programme to assess the degree to which the desired change has occurred would be put in place, and small successes would be communicated often and rewarded along the way. It would certainly not involve a top-down management-led approach to change (italics in original).

What is clear from positive work in this area over recent years is that the 'embedding' of ESD is as much about organizational and institutional learning as it is student learning, and that both arenas of learning are involved and interdependent (Brooks and Ryan, 2008). This process of change is further evidenced by the subsequent chapters of this book, to which we now turn.

About this book

Working with an holistic interpretation of sustainability (i.e. as embracing cultural, environmental, health, peace, social justice, scientific and technological dimensions), prospective contributors to this volume were invited to review and critically and creatively reflect on sustainability-related curricula, teaching and learning in their discipline in response to the following questions:

- What does a critical appraisal of the state of the art of sustainability-related curriculum, teaching and learning in your disciplinary field reveal (strengths, weaknesses, lacunae)?

- What windows of opportunity are there within your disciplinary field for embedding sustainability in curriculum, teaching and learning? How would the disciplinary field benefit from a further embedding? How would sustainability-related education in general benefit from a more thoroughgoing embrace by your field?

- What obstacles and constraints do you discern as impeding the take-up of sustainability-related concepts, ideas and cases in your disciplinary field? How are they being or might they be circumvented?

- What, if anything, is sustainability bringing to the discipline in terms of innovative pedagogies?

A total of 28 authors took up the challenge and their work is presented over 13 chapters (Chapters 5 to 17). The book does not cover all academic subjects where sustainability already has or might in the future have a place. For instance, architecture, design and science, where much is happening in terms of sustainability-related curriculum development, do not feature. Rather than seeking to be comprehensive (an impossible task anyway!) the editors were more interested in providing an eclectic demonstration of the art of the possible, especially in subjects that might not, at first glance, seem to offer sustainability potential.

The earlier chapters of the book are given over to exploring scene setting. The editors explore the potential for and appropriateness of addressing the complexity and uncertainty surrounding sustainability through interdisciplinary approaches. They note the gap in higher education institutions between an often fulsome rhetoric of interdisciplinarity and its rather limited manifestation in programme offerings. As many contributors intimate, sustainability and interdisciplinarity are seen as having a hand-in-glove relationship but one that is much more in evidence in research than in teaching. There follows a chapter by Debby Cotton and Jennie Winter drawing on recent research at the University of Plymouth into ways that academics incorporate sustainability into curricula (finding no correlation between subject area and the belief of staff as to its relevance to their discipline) and academics' understandings of sustainability pedagogies. An overview of the kinds of teaching method deemed appropriate for delivering sustainability curricula is offered. Arjen Wals and John Blewitt next explore international trends and developments in education for sustainability, drawing in particular on European and African experience. 'The question of the place of sustainability in the curriculum of higher education,' they note, 'is slowly shifting from one of campus greening and curriculum integration to one of innovation and systemic change in the whole university system,' something both explicit and implicit in our earlier reflections on inhibitors and enabling approaches to institutional change.

The chapters on discipline-specific curricula and pedagogical development begin with Delyse Springett's account of bringing critical perspectives to bear in courses on sustainability and business in New Zealand and Hong Kong. Brian

Chalkley, Jennifer Blumhof and Kristín Vala Ragnarsdóttir argue for both the centrality of education for sustainability in geography, earth and environmental science (GEES) curricula and for an anchoring role for these subjects in taking forward sustainability-related curriculum developments in the higher education sector. Benny Goodman and Janet Richardson point out the panoply of public health pronouncements in the UK legitimizing the inclusion of climate change education and education for sustainability in nursing curricula but identify the workforce planning nature of these curricula as an obstacle to such inclusion. They draw from leading-edge nursing curricula at the University of Plymouth to flag up what can be achieved.

Tracey Varnava, Jason Lowther and Simon Payne demonstrate the 'special relationship' between law and sustainable development and, hence, the huge potential for addressing sustainability through the law curriculum. They also acknowledge the challenges and obstacles to be faced in integrating sustainability into law curricula before closing with a case study of how sustainability and legal education have been melded together at the University of Plymouth's School of Law. Explaining that sustainability has been seen as a somewhat 'awkward fit' in performing arts education, Paul Kleiman offers a tour de force demonstration of how dance, drama and music have a centrally creative role to play in conveying ideas, values and attitudes, and so fostering social action for sustainability. Simon Steiner, meanwhile, took upon himself the Herculean task of seeking out and coordinating contributions on engineering education for a sustainable future from academics across the UK so as to demonstrate the width and depth of sustainability curriculum development in the field.

Debbie Flint explores environmental sustainability in media, communications and cultural studies, making the case that a critical decoding and deconstruction of the media and an understanding of the cultural institutions of society is vital for the sustainability-savvy graduate. Katja Stuerzenhofecker, Rebecca O'Loughlin and Simon Smith then make a case for a mutually beneficial confluence of sustainability and theology in the curriculum. A critical understanding of the role of humanity in relation to creation, they argue, gives rise to deep ethical questions with potential to offer alternative visions of the future inspiring action at personal, grassroots and institutional levels. They also argue that theology's affinity with transformative pedagogies of an inclusive, transformational, empowering and democratic nature can only make a beneficial contribution to the maturation of a sustainability pedagogy. Like Benny Goodman and Janet Richardson, social work academics Andy Whiteford, Viv Horton, Diane Garrard, Deirdre Ford and Avril Butler demonstrate that it is possible to meet national professional requirements while promoting global awareness and sustainability practices through degree courses. Case studies of their pedagogical practice, community practice learning, community development projects and international partnerships are offered.

Judi Farren Bradley, Sarah Sayce and Amanda Lewis take the reader into the field of built environment education, arguing that sustainability offers an essential paradigm shift for the field if its graduates are 'to envision and deliver the built environment needed to support a low-carbon economy servicing sustainable communities'. Anthony Plumridge maintains that economics includes concepts and methodologies that are relevant to sustainability but that it is late in their studies that undergraduates meet sustainability and only then in specialist courses. His chapter suggests how sustainability might become embedded in earlier, general economics courses. For John Canning, the fields of languages, linguistics and area studies offer fascinating and rich potential for studying sustainability through modalities such as 'ecocriticism' (an 'interdisciplinary approach to the study of nature, environment and culture'), intercultural exchanges, ecolinguistics (the study of the relationship between language and the environment), language death studies (concerning the loss of inherited knowledge, including ecological wisdom, through the death of a language) and study abroad. The final disciplinary contribution is from the field of education, specifically teacher training. Robert Cook, Roger Cutting and Denise Summers make a strong case for teacher training that enables schools at the very least to 'become public information beacons for the basic values of sustainability', but also to be places and spaces where radical values such as self-reliance, economic localization, frugality and communalism are entertained and explored in the pursuit of a sustainable future. No better vision of the influence of university spilling out into the community could be offered to end this overview.

The book concludes with a brief reflective endpiece.

References

Brooks, C. and Ryan, A. (2008) 'ESD: Strategic consultations among English HEIs', www.heacademy.ac.uk/projects/detail/esd/esd_EnglishHEIs, accessed 31 March 2010

CRE-COPERNICUS (1994) *The University Charter for Sustainable Development*, CRE, Geneva, www.iisd.org/educate/declarat/coper.htm, accessed 7 October 2009

Dawe, G., Jucker, R. and Martin, S. (2005) *Sustainable Development in Higher Education: Current Practice and Future Developments*, HEA, York www.heacademy.ac.uk/assets/York/documents/ourwork/tla/sustainability/sustdevinHEfinalreport.pdf, accessed 23 January 2010

de la Harpe, B. and Thomas, I. (2009) 'Curriculum change in universities: Conditions that facilitate education for sustainable development', *Journal of Education for Sustainable Development*, vol 3, no 1, pp75–85

Dyer, A., Selby, D. and Chalkley, B. (2006) 'A Centre for Excellence in Education for Sustainable Development', *Journal of Geography in Higher Education*, vol 30, no 2, pp307–312

Gray-Donald, J. and Selby, D. (2004) 'Through the (not so) green door: University campus greening and curriculum change', *Ekistics*, vol 71, no.s 427–429, pp203–212

HEFCE (2005a) *Sustainable Development in Higher Education: Consultation on a Support Strategy and Action Plan*, HEFCE, Bristol

HEFCE (2005b) *Sustainable Development in Higher Education: Strategy and Action Plan*, HEFCE, Bristol

HEFCE (2008) *Sustainable Development in Higher Education: Consultation on 2008 Update to Strategic Statement and Action Plan*, HEFCE, Bristol

HEFCE (2009) *Sustainable Development in Higher Education: 2008 Update to Strategic Statement and Action Plan*, HEFCE, Bristol, www.hefce.ac.uk/pubs/hefce/2009/09_03/09_03.pdf, accessed 3 February 2010

Hopkinson, P., Hughes, P. and Layer, G. (2008) 'Sustainable graduates: Linking formal, informal and campus curricula to embed education for sustainable development in the student learning experience', *Environmental Education Research*, vol 14, no 4, pp435–454

IAU (1993) *Kyoto Declaration on Sustainable Development*, www.unesco.org/iau/sd/sd_dkyoto.html, accessed 7 October 2009

Knight, P. (2005) 'Unsustainable developments', *The Guardian*, 8 February, www.guardian.co.uk/education/2005/feb/08/highereducation.administration, accessed 7 October 2009

Lang, J., Thomas, I. and Wilson, A. (2006) 'Education for sustainability in Australian universities: Where is the action?', *Australian Journal of Environmental Education*, vol 22, no 2, pp45–58

Martin, S. and Jucker, R. (2005) 'Educating earth-literate leaders', *Journal of Geography in Higher Education*, vol 29, no 1, pp19–29

Miller, P. and Westra, L. (2002) *Just Ecological Integrity: The Ethics of Maintaining Planetary Life*, Rowman & Littlefield, Lanham MD

Noonan, D. and Thomas, I. (2004) 'Greening universities in Australia: Progress and possibilities', *Australian Journal of Environmental Education*, vol 20, no 2, pp67–79

Orr, D. (1994) *Earth in Mind: In Education, Environment, and the Human Prospect*, Island Press, Washington DC

Parkin, S., Johnstom, A., Brookes, F. and Buckland, H. (2004) *On Course for Sustainability: Report of the Higher Education Partnership for Sustainability 2000–2003*, Forum for the Future, London

Rowe, D. (2002) 'Environmental literacy and sustainability as core requirements: success stories and models', In Filho, W. L. (ed) *Teaching Sustainability at Universities: Towards Curriculum Greening*, Peter Lang, Frankfurt, pp79–104

Selby, D. (2009) 'Towards the sustainability university: The Centre for Sustainable Futures, University of Plymouth', *Journal of Education for Sustainable Development*, vol 3, no 1, pp103–106

SQW Ltd (undated) *Specialist Review and Evaluation of the Higher Education Partnership for Sustainability (HEPS) Partnership*, SQW Ltd, Cambridge

Sterling, S. with Burkill, S., Kagawa, F. and Shoenborn, P. (2008) *Sowing Seeds: How to Make Your Module a Bit More Sustainability Oriented*, CSF, University of Plymouth, http://csf.plymouth.ac.uk/?q=node/585, accessed 8 October 2009

Sterling, S. and Scott, W. (2008) 'Higher education and ESD in England: A critical commentary on recent initiatives', *Environmental Education Research*, vol 14, no 4, pp386–398

Sterling, S. and Witham, H. (2008) 'Pushing the boundaries: The work of the Higher Education Academy's ESD Project', *Environmental Education Research*, vol 14, no 4, pp399–412

Thomas, I. (2004) 'Sustainability in tertiary curricula: What is stopping it happening?', *International Journal of Sustainability in Higher Education*, vol 5, no 1, pp33–47

UNCED (1992) *Agenda 21: Programme of Action for Sustainable Development*, UN Department of Public Information, New York NY

UNESCO (2009a) *Education for Sustainable Development: United Nations Decade (2005–2014)*, UNESCO, Paris, http://portal.unesco.org/education/en/ev.php-

URL_ID=34756&URL_DO=DO_TOPIC&URL_SECTION=201.html, accessed 7 October 2009

UNESCO (2009b) *Bonn Declaration*, www.esd-world-conference-2009.org/fileadmin/download/News/BonnDeclarationFinalFR.pdf, accessed 12 October 2009

UNESCO (2004) *United Nations Decade of Education for Sustainable Development (2005–2014: Draft International Implementation Scheme*, UNESCO, Paris

ULSF (1990) 'The Talloires Declaration: 10 Point Action Plan', www.ulsf.org/programs_talloires_td.html, accessed 7 October 2009

Wals, A.E.J. and Bawden, R. (2005) 'Integrating sustainability into agricultural education: Dealing with complexity, uncertainty and diverging worldviews', in Wals, A.E.J. (ed), *Curriculum Innovations in Higher Agricultural Education*, Reed Business Information, The Hague, pp21–57

Notes

1   The authors would like to thank Joanna Blake, Research Assistant at the Centre for Sustainable Futures, University of Plymouth, for undertaking the data collection required for writing the introduction.

2   Personal communication from Director, Membership and Programme Development, International Association of Universities, 8 October 2009.

Chapter 2

More than the Sum of their Parts? Interdisciplinarity and Sustainability

Paula Jones, David Selby and Stephen Sterling

Introduction

How far does sustainability inevitably require an interdisciplinary approach to inquiry and education? Is there any necessary relationship between sustainability and interdisciplinarity? If there is, can higher education respond sufficiently to the challenge this represents, not least to discipline-based structures? And if so, how?

This chapter seeks to clarify the relationship between sustainability and interdisciplinarity, review the literature and draw conclusions from some recent research based on case studies. It also attempts to suggest ways forward as the sector seeks to grapple with the implications of sustainability for teaching and learning. (It does not, however, cover interdisciplinary research: while such research may often encourage interdisciplinary teaching, it opens up areas beyond the scope of this chapter.)

The best place to start is not in the university, but the real world. The Bonn Declaration, an outcome of the UNESCO World Conference on Education for Sustainable Development (ESD), held in Bonn, Germany in March 2009, states that:

A decade into the 21st century, the world faces substantial, complex and interlinked development and lifestyle challenges and problems.

Going back some four decades, an integrative view was strongly advocated by the Club of Rome's influential *Limits to Growth* study (Meadows et al, 1972). This recognized the reality of what was later termed by the Club 'the world problematique' (Peccei, 1982; King and Schneider, 1992). This 'problematique' is the set of closely interconnected problems – political, economic, social, cultural, psychological, technological and environmental – that characterize our times and which, according to Peccei, cannot be dealt with separately because of their systemic nature and therefore fail to respond to non-systemic, non-integrative approaches.

Similarly, the World Commission on Environment and Development (WCED)'s Brundtland Report of 1987 – which introduced the notion of 'sustainable development' on the international stage – saw interconnectivity as a starting principle. Hence, it stated:

> Until recently, the planet was a large world in which human activities and their effects were neatly compartmentalised within nations, within sectors (energy, agriculture, trade), and within broad areas of concern (environmental, social). These compartments have begun to dissolve. This applies in particular to the various global "crises" that have seized public concern ... These are not separate crises: an environmental crisis, a development crisis, an energy crisis. They are all one (WCED, 1987, p4).

On the next page we read that 'ecology and economy are becoming ever more interwoven – locally, regionally, nationally, and globally – into a seamless net of causes and effects' (WCED, 1987, p5). Particularly since the Brundtland Report, the interrelationship between issues thematically, spatially and temporally has gained increasing attention. For example, Clayton and Radcliffe (1996, p11) state that 'environmental questions are inextricably interlinked with social, economic and cultural values', while Gunderson and Holling (2002, p21) state that 'the expanding influence of human activity intensifies coupling between people and systems of nature so that neither can be understood in isolation'. The key issue then is the adequacy of the match between the real world and the ways through which it is understood. The catch here, perhaps, is that while human and natural systems can be and are studied in isolation, from a sustainability point of view, setting strong conceptual boundaries around such systems reduces or impedes what might be termed a more holistic understanding and perspective. Significantly then, sustainability challenges the tradition of reductionist epistemology which is reflected in the disciplinary basis of many higher education structures, policies and practices. As Schmidt suggests (2008, p58): 'Disciplinary reduction is undercomplex and hence cannot cope with real-world problems because such problems are too new, complex, wicked, hybrid, or too risky (for instance environmental/global change problems).'

This realization has been with us for some years, for example, Gross (1971, p353) suggests that in the context of interdependency, 'increasing specialization makes all problems more difficult ... The more able, honoured and highly valued expert is the one who works within an increasingly narrow sphere and who has great difficulty in communicating with other experts as well as laymen'. Around the same time, one of the original members of the Club of Rome, the scientist Eric Jantsch, was arguing the case for inter- and transdisciplinarity as fundamental organizing principles for universities, the purpose of which was, in his view, enhancing society's capability for self-renewal. For Jantsch, the achievement of interdisciplinarity in itself is not enough; rather it has to be understood as a teleological and normative concept: 'we must ask, *interdisciplinarity to what end*' (Jantsch, 1972, p10, author's italics). He conceived of inter- and transdisciplinarity as higher-level inquiry and organization, going beyond the limits of single disciplines, which he saw as being essentially empirical and pragmatic pursuits rather than normative and purposive. For Jantsch, the inter- and transdisciplinary university was a necessary ideal. Nearly four decades later, progress is still limited. While there is evidence of increasing interest in more integrative understanding and holistic management of problems in policy-making, echoed by more interest in promoting interdisciplinary research, teaching and learning in universities (Natural Environmental Research Council [NERC], 2009; HEFCE, 2009), interdisciplinarity seems to be 'everywhere and nowhere' (Schmidt, 2008, p54). It is 'in vogue in science, society and economy', but the term 'is quite misty, foggy and shadowy' (Schmidt, 2008, p56). Similarly, Julie Klein (one of the leading theorists in the field) says 'interdisciplinarity is a concept of wide appeal [but] is also one of wide confusion' (Klein, 1990, p11).

To address this situation, it may be helpful to explore the philosophical, definitional, motivational and practical dimensions of interdisciplinarity. These aspects are reviewed below, starting with a brief discussion of the relationship between sustainability and interdisciplinarity.

Linking sustainable development and interdisciplinarity

As sustainability issues rise further up the national and international agendas – reflected in media reports almost every day – the systemic links between (say) energy consumption, climate change, loss of biodiversity and poverty become more evident and the need for multiple perspectives and integrative approaches to issues becomes more accepted, as reflected in the common parlance (if not the practice) of 'joined-up thinking' and 'joined-up policy'.

For the purposes of this chapter, we can say sustainability represents a condition or set of conditions whereby human and natural systems can continue indefinitely in a state of mutual well-being, security and survival. In other words, it has primarily ontological and normative dimensions. Interdisciplinarity on the other hand is an approach to knowledge and inquiry, and has both epistemological and methodological qualities. In sum, sustainability presents an overarching and complex socio-economic–ecological context wherein interdisciplinarity – as a putative holistic mode of understanding, organization of knowledge and inquiry – seems appropriate. The relationship might thus be represented as in Figure 2.1.

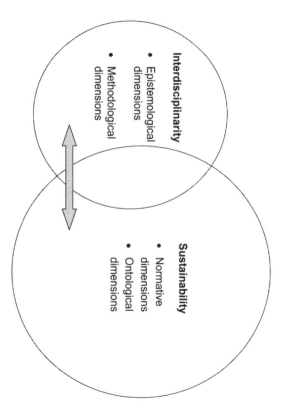

Interdisciplinarity

- Epistemological dimensions
- Methodological dimensions

Sustainability

- Normative dimensions
- Ontological dimensions

Figure 2.1 *Suggested relationship between interdisciplinarity and sustainability*

The logic of interdisciplinary approaches to sustainability issues derives from a broad consensus that such issues cannot be sufficiently understood in isolation. Hence, Donella Meadows suggests:

> The world is a complex, interconnected, finite, ecological–social–psycho-logical–economic system. We treat it as if it were not, as if it were divisible, separable, simple, and infinite. Our persistent, intractable, global problems arise directly from this mismatch (Meadows, 1982, p101).

At a deeper level of analysis, Gregory Bateson suggests that the nexus of issues that face us have a perceptual or epistemological root, believing that the 'massive aggregation of threats to man and ecological systems arises out of errors of thought at deep and partly unconscious levels' (Bateson, 1972, p463). The argument here is that an ingrained dualistic and compartmentalizing mindset is maladaptive in a world that is deeply and systemically interconnected. Dale and Newman (2005, p352) echo a body of literature in stating that 'human societies and ecological systems are so interconnected that they are co-adaptive, reacting to each other and to previous interactions and reactions in a network of feedbacks', and therefore approaches to sustainable development education, 'must be complex, transdisciplinary and broad'.

Similarly, Becker et al (1997, p37) propose that 'the different (social, economic, political, cultural etc.) dimensions of sustainability (and their relation-ship to the environment), set up the task of overcoming the limitations imposed by the fragmentation and segmentation of social scientific knowledge'.

In short, there appears to be an emerging consensus that sustainability issues cannot be sufficiently understood or addressed without a primary recognition of *interrelationship*, and therefore also an assumption of the need for interdisciplinary approaches. Yet typically, educational structures and practices are widely characterized by disciplinary compartmentalization (Godemann, 2008).

Against this background, there have been calls for more interdisciplinarity in higher education (HE). A report from the UK New Economics Foundation argues that the problems we face at local and global scales require HE to equip its learners 'with the knowledge, skills and understanding to pioneer innovative and creative responses to achieving wider economic, social and environmental well-being' (Steuer and Marks, 2008, p12). Internationally, the G8 University Summit held in Japan in 2008 issued a *Sapporo Sustainability Summit Declaration*, which states:

Universities have a critical role to play in educating future generations, disseminating information about sustainability, and particularly by training leaders with the skills to solve regional and local problems from a global and interdisciplinary perspective (G8 University Summit, 2008).

In the USA, there is a strong tradition of interdisciplinarity evidenced by the liberal arts movement. Much of the recent research and scholarship around the topic is therefore US-based. In the UK, the position is less positive with evidence of a gap between rhetoric that favours interdisciplinarity and actual practice. A research paper on the status of sustainable development in HE in England, commissioned by the Higher Education Funding Council for England (HEFCE) as a 'strategic review', noted that 'it is quite clear that the whole question of interdisciplinary working, its opportunities and its difficulties, looms large in the minds of those who wish to promote sustainable development' (Policy Studies Institute et al, 2008, p30), while the same review recommended to HEFCE that 'Detailed consideration should be given to measures to facilitate interdisciplinarity in course design and teaching' (Policy Studies et al, 2008, p35).

According to Chettiparamb (2007, p1), 'the drive for interdisciplinarity is encouraged both through the Higher Education Academy (HEA) and the Research Councils',[1,2] and HEFCE's recent sustainable development policy paper (HEFCE, 2009, p25) notes the need to encourage further interdisciplinary research 'of relevance to major world challenges'. However, while interest in interdisciplinarity is common in sustainability discourse, the reverse is not necessarily true: many of those advocating interdisciplinarity do so in response to the limits of what they see as overspecialization, and may have no particular interest in the broader context of sustainability (as reflected in Figure 2.1). One might imagine that for writers like Jantsch, however, the spheres of interest shown in Figure 2.1 virtually coincide. Meanwhile, we turn to the meanings and interests attached to disciplinarity and forms of interdisciplinarity.

Disciplinarity and multi-, inter- and transdisciplinarity

While the term 'interdisciplinarity' is often used loosely to mean any approach that goes beyond a single discipline, many writers distinguish between different states of interdisciplinarity. It is perhaps helpful to first look at disciplinarity itself.

The term 'discipline' derives from the Latin *disciplina* (instruction) from the root *discere* (to learn). According to Arum (2004), 'discipline' has been used since the Middle Ages to represent a way of ordering knowledge for teaching and learning. Arum sees disciplines as 'thought domains' that are 'quasi stable, partially integrated, semi-autonomous intellectual conveniences consisting of problems, theories, and methods of investigation' (Arum, 2004, p380). They are quasi stable, he suggests, because of constant revision, they are partially integrated because they are characterized by core and peripheral fields as well as highly specialized sub-fields, and semi-autonomous through 'ambiguous boundaries' (Arum, 2004, p380). Chettiparamb, in an extensive literature review, notes that disciplines are not static but variable 'by virtue of enterprise and fragmentation and recombination in time', yet they 'still possess and retain characteristics that make them identifiable as disciplines' (2007, p7).

Disciplines form the 'organising framework' in higher education (Selby, 2006, p57), as reflected in the structures of faculties and schools. The survival and continuing strength of disciplines as the dominant *modus operandi* might be explained by looking at the arguments in favour of disciplines. Chettiparamb's review points to such arguments as the role of disciplines in the production of knowledge, the maintenance of rigour and thoroughness, the development of skills and knowledge necessary for society and the labour market, as well as their 'internal role' in providing academics with a framework for their professional engagement, advancement and identity. A further factor relating to the resilience of disciplines may be – interpreted in Kuhnian terms (Kuhn, 1962) – the strength and maintenance of disciplinary intellectual paradigms.

At the same time, disciplinarity is subject to critique and debate. Chettiparamb's review points to a number of such arguments:

- Disciplines tend to restrict what is perceived as relevant and therefore can draw their boundaries too narrowly.
- The desire for and practice of continuity can restrict innovation and creativity.
- Deep engagement with a discipline can limit reflexivity.
- A lack of engagement with real-world problems.
- A lack of engagement with other disciplines.
- 'Heresy' and critical questioning of norms – which might be the source of innovation – may be suppressed.

The emergence of interdisciplinarity may be seen as a response to the perceived shortcomings of disciplinarity. Philosophically, according to Schmidt, interdisciplinarity is an 'integration instrument', the basic goal of which is to 'obtain a synthesis and restore what is thought be lost'. It is 'a means to regain a presupposed unity from the (obvious) plurality of disciplines' (Schmidt, 2008, p56). As Klein (1990, p11) claims, 'All interdisciplinary activities are rooted in the ideas of unity and synthesis, evoking a common epistemology of convergence'. This urge is not new: Klein later notes that, 'the underlying concepts of interdisciplinarity – breadth and general knowledge, integration and synthesis – are ancient' (2004, p2), while elsewhere she states that 'the modern system of disciplinarity is little more than a century old' (Klein, 2006, p10). Also with an eye to historic precedence, the biologist E.O. Wilson advocates what he calls 'consilience' – or the unity of knowledge – claiming that, 'the greatest enterprise of the mind has always been and always will be the attempted linkage of the sciences and humanities' (Wilson, 1999, p5).

However, further to this desire for greater unity, Schmidt discerns a second driver motivating interdisciplinarity, which is as a means to address complex problems of society. A deeper – and essentially epistemological – argument arises from the idea that bounded, distinct and non-relating bodies of knowledge as reflected in disciplinary structures are no longer appropriate for a world characterized by complexity and rapid change. Wilson (1999, p6) maintains that 'The ongoing fragmentation of knowledge and resulting chaos in philosophy are not reflections of the real world but artefacts of scholarship'. Some go further and argue that reductive understanding informing policy and actions in the real world contributes to problems (Bawden, 2005; Meadows, 1982; Chapman, 2002). For example, Bohm states:

it is not an accident that our fragmentary form of thought is leading to such a wide range of crises, social, political, economic, psychological, etc. in the individual and in society as a whole (Bohm, 1980, p16).

Bawden suggests that '"disciplinary successes" have involved high levels of abstraction resulting in deductive conclusions, which are generalized to the real world with little awareness of the dangerous consequences of doing so' (2005, p121). More optimistically, Klein detects an historical shift taking place from a position characterized by stability, consistent realities, boundary formation, and compartmentalization, towards a more dynamic picture:

Images of boundary crossing and cross-fertilisation are superseding images of disciplinary depth and compartmentalization. Isolated modes of work are being supplanted by affiliations, coalitions and alliances. And older values of control, mastery and expertise are being reformulated as dialogue, interaction and negotiation (Klein, 2004, p3; author's emphasis).

This argument, which resonates with the ideas of post-normal science (Funtowicz and Ravetz, 2008), has radical implications, according to Klein, for 'the nature of knowledge, the structure of the university, the character of problem solving, the dialogue between science and humanities, and the theoretical relationship of complexity and interdisciplinarity (Klein, 2004, p2). Yet not all perceptions and practices of interdisciplinarity either spring from or manifest such a radical view. Klein and Newell (1997, p393) define interdisciplinarity as 'a process of answering a question, solving a problem, or addressing a topic that is too broad or complex to be dealt with adequately by a single discipline or profession'. While this definition might be broadly accepted, it is clear from the literature that interdisciplinarity is widely interpreted, reflecting, in Salter and Hearn's words, differing levels of 'challenge to the limitations or premises of the prevailing organization of knowledge or its representation in an institutionally recognized form' (1996, p43).

These differing levels are reflected in a number of typologies that seek to make sense of the proliferation both of terms and practices relating to interdisciplinarity. For example, Lattuca's 2001 research with academics gives rise to the classification of four types of interdisciplinarity:

- **Informed** – where a discipline is intentionally informed by other disciplines; say, in relation to teaching a particular course.
- **Synthetic** – a linking of disciplines, for example, theories and concepts, through courses or research, yet where the integrity of the contributing disciplines remains.
- **Transdisciplinary** – where courses or research questions cross disciplines and theories and concepts are tested across disciplines.
- **Conceptual** – areas that have no disciplinary basis and are new intellectual territory.

Building on this model, Rhoten et al (2006, p3) suggest 'interdisciplinary education' is:

> *a mode of curriculum design and instruction in which individual faculty or teams identify, evaluate, and integrate information, data, techniques, tools, perspectives, concepts, and or theories from two or more disciplines or bodies of knowledge to advance students' capacity to understand issues, address problems, appraise explanations, and create new approaches and solutions that extend beyond the scope of a single discipline or area of instruction.*

The literature largely recognizes 'multidisciplinarity' as being the least integrated form of interdisciplinarity, whereby disciplines might work together cooperatively but without sharing ideas, assumptions and methodologies and without being influenced or changed by the other. As Klein (1990, p56) states, 'it is essentially *additive*, not *integrative*' (author's italics). A less common term, 'pluridisciplinarity', refers to the juxtaposition of disciplines that have some linkage (for example, different languages in language studies), described by Selby (2006, p58) as 'contiguous' or 'proximate' interdisciplinary, whereas a multidisciplinary approach brings together apparently unrelated disciplines (Organization for Economic Co-operation and Development [OECD], 1972). 'Interdisciplinarity' is normally understood to indicate disciplines working collaboratively, sharing their insights and methods in an attempt to go beyond their own boundaries to address whatever issue or question that concerns them, which perhaps conforms more to Lattuca's 'transdisciplinary' category. In university settings, Klein (2006, p14) opines that transdisciplinary approaches are reflected in 'new comprehensive frameworks that transcend the narrow scope of disciplinary worldviews through an overarching synthesis, such as general systems, policy sciences, feminism, cultural critique, and ecology and sustainability', which echoes Lattuca's 'conceptual' category.

The notion of interdisciplinarity has wide appeal. However, Klein relates research indicating that too often, so-called interdisciplinary projects are developed that are poorly thought through. Fazenda (in Klein 2006, p12) is quoted as saying: 'In the name of interdisciplinarity, established routines are condemned and abandoned, and slogans, nicknames, and working hypotheses are created which many times are improvised and ill-considered'. Meaning is complicated by people using particular terms differently and/or interchangeably, or claiming interdisciplinarity for practices that others might deem as not deserving the appellation. Hence Klein (1990, p56) notes: 'Most purportedly interdisciplinary activities are multidisciplinary or pluridisciplinary'. Clearly, the use of the term 'interdisciplinarity' in an initiative is no guarantee of innovation and quality, although both might be claimed.

Sustainability, interdisciplinarity and pedagogy

As already outlined, a major driver for more interdisciplinary approaches to teaching and learning is the sustainability agenda. It is argued that the complex nature of sustainability-related issues requires commensurate approaches to knowledge, research, teaching and learning. As Klein (2004, p4) states:

Arising from environments characterized by turbulence and uncertainty, complex problems are typically value-laden, open-ended, multidimensional, ambiguous, and unstable. Labelled 'wicked' and 'messy', they resist being tamed, bounded or managed by classical problem-solving approaches.

Funtowicz and Ravetz add:

These new problems are characteristic of 'complex systems'. These are not necessarily complicated; they involve interrelated subsystems at a variety of scale levels and of a variety of kinds. Thus we now know that every technology is embedded in its societal and natural contexts, and that 'nature' itself is shaped by its interactions with humanity. In such complex systems, there can be no single privileged point of view for measurement, analysis and evaluation (2008).

In this context, Becker et al (1997, p37) argue that 'attempts to cope with the complexity of issues raised by sustainability cannot simply aim at adding some new pieces to an already existing knowledge base'. Rather, they argue for a 'paradigm shift towards a new knowledge base' characterized by 'practices of integration'. While this might sound radical to some, Klein (2004) argues that the convergence of interdisciplinarity and complexity should be seen as part of the larger cultural shift of postmodernism, whereby national, political and cultural boundaries have become more permeable. This includes 'a reversal of the differentiating, classificatory dynamic of modernity and increasing hybridization of cultural categories, identities, and previous certainties'. All have undergone 'de-differentiation, de-insulation, and hybridization. All boundaries are at risk' (Klein 2004, p8).

This kind of argument implies that approaches to knowledge have no choice but to engage with such shifts, and question boundaries. Not least because, as Selby argues, ESD embraces 'aesthetic, cultural, ecological, economic, environmental, ethical, philosophical, political, scientific, social, spiritual, and technological' dimensions (2006, p57). Godemann suggests that ESD in HE requires not only the acquisition and generation of knowledge, but the ability to reflect on the effects and complexity of behaviour and decisions in a future-oriented and global framework of responsibility. 'This new knowledge', she writes, 'is structured in a fundamentally different way necessitating academic curricula and academic cultures which cross disciplinary boundaries' (Godemann 2008, p626). Meanwhile, Gough and Scott (2007, p167) argue:

The significance of sustainable development for higher education ... is the potential that it has, not as a specialism with departments of economics, or environmental science or sociology or politics, but as a fresh and necessary challenge to the way that ideas are classified into economics, environmental science, politics and so on. Unfortunately, this potential is lost if sustainable development is allowed itself to become an academic specialism (authors' italics).

This raises profound questions about the relationship between disciplines and interdisciplinarity. While some see interdisciplinarity as a necessary and desirable *alternative* to disciplinarity – implying a kind of epistemological evolutionary step – others see interdisciplinarity as necessarily relying on disciplinarity, that is, as a foundation through which a *complementary* interdisciplinarity can be achieved. According to the literature, the kinds of interdisciplinarity that emerge in practice partly depend on the kind of problem at issue and on how it is perceived. Hence Kelly (1996) makes a distinction between the *narrow* integration of disciplines, as when focusing on specific problems, and *wide* interdisciplinarity, sharing epistemological or metaphysical positions across disciplines when faced with value-laden issues. One might argue that sustainability requires both kinds of interdisciplinarity, given the range of issues that it encompasses, but that wide interdisciplinarity is often most appropriate to the multifaceted and value-laden nature of many sustainability issues.

Apart from the apparent necessity and relevance of interdisciplinarity to a changing and complex real world, there appear to be a number of practical factors that favour this approach. A major multinational study of interdisciplinarity in HE carried out by the OECD in 1972 reviewed the motives behind engagement with interdisciplinarity. For students, these included enhancing their ability to adjust to shifting job markets, develop new career paths, sense the relevance of their subjects and develop more flexible skills. For teachers, motives for engagement included finding solutions to problems of growing specialization, working towards common goals, opening up new fields of knowledge and breaking down divisions between university and society (OECD, 1972).

However, interdisciplinarity raises significant challenges to established norms, not least with regard to pedagogy. According to Klein (2006, p15) while integration is the primary goal of an interdisciplinary approach to teaching (referring to schools, although there are parallels with HE), 'there is no unique interdisciplinary pedagogy'. However, research indicates that teachers seeking to advance interdisciplinarity tend towards 'innovative approaches that promote dialogue and community, problem posing and problem solving, and critical thinking'. She continues by stating that the following approaches, strategies and activities are often reported:

Team teaching and team planning; collaborative learning and learning communities; clustered and linked courses; core seminars; theme or problem focus in courses; proactive attention to integration and synthesis; models of interdisciplinary and integrative process; theories and methods from interdisciplinary fields; projects and case studies; dyads, triads and small groups for discussion; game and role playing; inquiry and discovery-based learning; learning portfolios; experiential and service learning, internships and fieldwork; residential living-learning experiences (2006, p15).

The literature shows that interdisciplinarity is often inevitably associated with a constructivist pedagogy. As an integrative approach to knowledge making is intended, students are engaged in meaning making, not least by weaving different modes of thinking from two or more disciplines. At the same time, the focus inevitably shifts towards a more student-centred model of teaching and learning. Interdisciplinarity does not just imply a change of method, then, but also of methodology and philosophy, which challenge the pedagogic norms of disciplinarity. Hence, Klein (2006, p16) notes a 'philosophical' shift from 'transmitting prior notions of a unified view of commonly held knowledge and relationships between existing fields to the creation of new integrative concepts, pedagogy, models, structures, systems and principles, as well as the learner's capacity to perceive new relationships'. This is borne out in practice. For example, commenting on the experience of a team-taught undergraduate unit in Sustainable Development at the University of Bristol, the teaching team states:

> *When different contributors presented together, listening to each other and responding, there was a tangible benefit for contributors and students compared with the normal teaching mode where one person produces a multidisciplinary overview with all the wrinkles apparently 'ironed out'* (Hoare et al, 2008, p479).

Issues of implementation

It is clear from research that putting interdisciplinarity into practice presents a range of significant challenges. The 2008 HEFCE *Strategic Review of Sustainable Development in Higher Education in England*, which surveyed practice across the sector, offered this analysis regarding obstacles to interdisciplinary teaching:

- 'The focus on cost centres for purposes of financial administration.
- The continuing disciplinary basis of Research Council funding.
- The Research Assessment Exercise (RAE) categories, which tend to create difficulties for interdisciplinary research, and so HE institutions (HEIs) may prefer to appoint staff with a single-discipline focus. This then has consequences for what is taught. (The RAE is used as a basis for research grant allocation.)
- Particular issues around integrating the social aspects of sustainability into natural science-based courses.
- Much interdisciplinary work is reported in "grey literature" or in relatively low-status journals. This is in part because interdisciplinary journals tend to have lower status. Hence academics may prefer to focus elsewhere.' (Policy Studies Institute et al, 2008, p31)

Furthermore, the review states:

> *The achievement of interdisciplinarity in teaching presents serious challenges, although examples of innovative good practice do exist. Barriers extend well beyond issues of conservatism among disciplinary practitioners and touch upon much wider matters of management and governance in the sector* (Policy Studies Institute et al, 2008, p35).

These points might be summarized as relating to issues of governance, structures, finance/resources, status and 'culture clash' between disciplines. The OECD study reports on the difficulties of interdisciplinary teaching under the headings 'Rigidity of institutional structures', 'Rigidity of people and disciplines' and 'Lack of facilities'. Of these, personal issues appear particularly important, the report suggesting that:

Interdisciplinarity is first and foremost a state of mind requiring each person to have an attitude that combines humility with open mindedness and curiosity, a willingness to engage in dialogue and, hence the capacity for assimilation and synthesis (OECD, 1972, p192).

Similarly, Godemann (2008, p637) suggests that academics need to be able to look beyond boundaries, be capable of self-reflexivity, able to engage in knowledge integration and take on new ideas. Yet interdisciplinarity is often viewed with suspicion, scepticism and reluctance, not least by those who view career prospects and rewards as lying within their known, disciplinary areas. Chettiparamb remarks that the challenges identified in the OECD report in 1972 'can still be thought of as largely defining the current situation in UK academia' (Chettiparamb, 2007, p37). Similarly, Sterling et al note that from the time of the Toyne review of HE's response to the environmental agenda in 1993 through to the HEFCE policy on sustainable development of 2005, the area of curriculum change 'has been and continues to be the most difficult aspect of the HE response to the sustainability agenda as regards its implementation, particularly if the intention is to address this holistically and with regard to interdisciplinary' (Sterling et al, 2008, p400).

Godemann (2008, p626) suggests 'the structure of universities remains highly specialized and is not oriented towards cooperation and conjoint inter-institutional work ... Confined to the existing structures of knowledge generation and transmission, universities find it difficult to do justice to contemporary problems'. HEFCE's Strategic Review (Policy Studies Institute 2008, p74) indicates that while 'Much has been learned in recent years about how to stimulate successful interdisciplinary work in teaching and research ... the continuing predominance of disciplinary structures in both HEIs and the RAE presents ongoing challenges in persuading academics to make the investment of their time and career in pursuing an interdisciplinary path'.

Such issues surrounding implementation were echoed in discussions held by the UK HEA ESD Project, in partnership with the Academy Interdisciplinary Project. The initiative was based on a perceived need, shared by a number of Academy Subject Centres, for greater understanding of and dialogue on the relationship between ESD and interdisciplinarity, not least between academics working in specific disciplines and those working in broader multidisciplinary contexts. A series of three 'interdisciplinary meetings' were held at the Universities of Leeds, York and Birmingham respectively between 2006 and early 2007 to:

- support dialogue between academics in relation to the intellectual and pedagogical issues surrounding interdisciplinarity and ESD;
- provide a forum for academics to develop their understanding of the ways in which they might work with the parameters and principles of interdisciplinary ESD;

- inform the strategic agenda for the Academy ESD Project on the issues at stake in the intersections of ESD, sustainability and interdisciplinarity.

The debate involved 27 participants over the course of the three meetings, representing a wide range of academic backgrounds: architecture, engineering, design, bioscience, environmental sciences, geography, development studies, anthropology, philosophy, politics, history, archaeology, psychology, education and religious studies. Every member of the group had an active teaching and/or research engagement with issues of sustainability, and an orientation towards interdisciplinary working, and many had expertise in more than one discipline. Hence, the meetings presented a 'sounding board' of opinions from academics engaged in debate and practice in this area. A detailed report by the debate's facilitators (Brooks and Ryan, 2008) reflects the complexities of both the interrelationship of ESD and interdisciplinarity and the issues surrounding implementation. Findings and discussion points include:

- An agreement to view 'sustainability' as a 'threshold concept' whose richness and importance disallowed final definitions (p5).
- An interdisciplinary approach combining human, economic and scientific analysis is a necessity for ESD (p9).
- An opportunistic approach to potential synergies with other disciplines is required of disciplines (p11).
- Questions about whether ESD suffuses institutional strategies or supplants them, serving as a catalyst for new priorities (p13).
- A focus less in terms of content and towards pedagogies supporting skills development – critical thinking and reflexive, democratized and experiential learning – and the relevance of this to students' skills development and links to employability (p13).
- Linking skills to 'service' and notions of social responsibility and global citizenship can be attractive in terms of recruitment (p15).
- Values are critical – reflected in a tension between the ethical and scientific dimensions of ESD – and remain a crucial issue for personal and pedagogic practice (p14).
- A sense that students entering HE are generally ill-prepared for interdisciplinarity and therefore potential for interdisciplinary ESD at postgraduate level is likely to be greater (p16).
- The need for further persuasion and change at organizational and sectoral levels. 'Inspired leadership' is required, but an entrepreneurial spirit is also called for among interested academics, working with appropriate businesses, professional bodies and employers to influence senior management and curriculum design (pp16–17).
- Linking to employability and skills agendas is a pragmatic approach to organizational change towards ESD, as is linking to the movement towards flexible and distance learning, short courses and professional training (p18).

- A significant interest in extending the responsibilities of HE and its personnel to include public issues in their remit more openly, including potential to harness a culture of enterprise towards sustainability (p23).

Brooks and Ryan (2008, p5) suggest that the discussion meeting findings 'are in many ways congruent with the broader aims of skills and employability agendas of particular interest to those responsible for HE recruitment and programme provision'.

The HEA discussion meetings suggested a number of strategies for implementation including:

- Specialist interdisciplinary ESD centres in HEIs, coordinating input from all departments.
- Making ESD values inherent in all programmes, via assessment techniques, for example.
- Compulsory ESD modules common to all programmes in an HEI.
- ESD as a strategic corporate commitment and/or collegiate ethos.
- Implicit ESD or the 'hidden classroom', not made explicit as 'ESD' in course outlines (Brooks and Ryan, 2008, p13).

Selby (2006) makes a distinction between pragmatic infusionist approaches, whereby disciplines work with sustainability concepts within existing parameters, and more ambitious interdisciplinary and transdisciplinary approaches, suggesting a number of pathways through which sustainability can be addressed practically.

In sum, a literature review presents a picture of rising socio-economic–ecological challenges, characterized by complex problems requiring multifaceted and interdisciplinary approaches to policy; and a rich discourse on the nature of interdisciplinarity, yet a gap between interdisciplinarity rhetoric and practice given the continuing strength of disciplinary thinking and structures. These factors also tend to be reflected at an institutional level, as was largely borne out by research by the Centre for Sustainable Futures (CSF) (Blake et al, 2009).

Case studies

From 2008 to 2009, the University of Plymouth's CSF carried out research on the implementation of interdisciplinary and sustainability at three UK HEIs and one each in South Africa and Australia, using questionnaires and interviews with key staff. The case studies were developed as part of the *Occasional Paper* on which this chapter is based (Blake et al, 2009). The case studies comprised:

- The Postgraduate Training Programme in Sustainable Engineering, Graduate School of Engineering, University of Strathclyde, Scotland.
- First-year undergraduate course in Sustainability, Society and the Environment, School of Global Studies, Social Science and Planning, Faculty of Portfolio of Design and Social Context, RMIT, Australia.

- MSc in Human Ecology, Centre for Human Ecology; in partnership with the Department of Geography and Sociology, Faculty of Law, Arts and Social Sciences, University of Strathclyde.
- BSc/MA in Sustainable Development, School of Geography and Geosciences, University of St Andrews, Scotland.
- Cross-faculty elective module programme Environmental Awareness, Techniques and Training, University of the Western Cape, South Africa.

The CSF paper looks in some detail at each of these initiatives, drawing out the differences and similarities in how each sought to establish, develop and gain credibility and support for their interdisciplinary programme. Some of the conclusions emerging from this study are outlined below.

The paper also reviews progress at the University of Plymouth, where interdisciplinarity is endorsed in the *University of Plymouth Research and Innovation Strategy 2009–2012 (2009)* and by the *University of Plymouth Sustainability Policy*, (2008), while the *University of Plymouth Teaching and Learning Strategy 2009–2012 (2009)* implies promotion of the interdisciplinary components of teaching and learning by broadly describing 'co-learning, active participation and mutual respect' as a basis for the teaching and learning (p3) and includes sustainability education as one of the ten key themes across all disciplines. However, the issue here now is to develop greater synergy between these policies, and also between policy and practice in developing interdisciplinary teaching and learning.

Overview and analysis

A key point arising from the research that CSF undertook is the relationship between sustainability and interdisciplinarity. As noted earlier, neither is necessarily linked to the other: sustainability and sustainable development can be and are studied and approached from within distinct disciplines, while interdisciplinarity as an approach to knowledge and pedagogy need not be centred on sustainability. However, it is clear that, given so many issues associated with sustainability are complex, multifaceted and unbounded (for example, resource use and availability, equity and justice, social cohesion and community well-being, ecological integrity, economic viability, uncertain futures, local and global policy responses and so on), single disciplines seem insufficiently well equipped to encompass and handle them alone.

Against this background, disciplines *informed* by other disciplines and disciplines working towards *interdisciplinary* arrangements are increasingly likely be in evidence. In some institutions, there may be sufficient flexibility to allow experiments with 'true' *transdisciplinarity*, as defined earlier. While sustainability and interdisciplinarity may not always be found together in higher education, many sustainability theorists and practitioners (including all the key actors in the case studies) see some expression of interdisciplinarity as necessary to achieve multiple perspectives, insights and understanding on sustainability issues – not least because these are often seen to be characterised by 'wicked' rather than simple and contained problems. A further driver in this direction is the interest amongst employers for graduates who possess 'soft skills' and flexibility in their understanding and approach to issues (Andrews and Higson, 2008). Furthermore, the increasing profile of sustainability amongst policy-makers and the public is reflected in interdisciplinary research agendas in higher education, and it follows that there could well be corresponding pressure for teaching and learning policy and practice to follow suit in terms of embracing interdisciplinarity.

However, it is clear from the literature review and case studies above that the institutionalization of interdisciplinarity – whether or not it is oriented towards sustainability – is not at all simple. Not least, the holistic and cross-cutting modes of organization and inquiry do not sit easily with disciplinary structures, as evidenced by all the case studies. Success depends on many factors, including the energy and vision of the protagonists, the response of students and colleagues, the level of support and resources from senior managers, the degree of institutional flexibility with regard to inter-school and inter-faculty money transfers for teaching work done by academics outside of their home school or faculty, and the level of integration envisaged.

All initiatives detailed in the case studies above are required by organizational structures to sit within a school and faculty. Respondents at RMIT and St Andrews in particular emphasized the point that space to manoeuvre across disciplines is hampered by the necessary bias of traditional allegiances – the Faculty of Arts and Humanities, the Faculty of Science and so forth. Where interdisciplinarity is attempted within a faculty, and where similar disciplines work together, the initiative may be easier to develop and sustain. For example, the engineering-related disciplines appear to converge with relative ease at Strathclyde. However, adding the social aspects of sustainability into the mix has proved a significant challenge.

The case study of the Centre for Human Ecology provides an interesting example. Its work was legitimated by its much larger, former partner institution (the University of Strathclyde), but its relative freedom allowed experimentation with alternative pedagogies that many sustainability educators advocate. At the same time, interest shown by Strathclyde and by other 'host' institutions in the programmes reviewed in the case studies indicates the potential of small scale innovation to affect the wider institution: this is particularly well illustrated by St Andrews. It may be that the potential for mainstream change towards interdisciplinarity and sustainability is – inevitably – engendered first on the margins of conventional policy and practice before it has a chance of more widespread influence.

At the same time, making progress is hampered by a lack of consensus about both the meaning and implications of terms. The case studies display a broad spectrum of responses, ranging from key actors making no attempt to define interdisciplinarity to a thoroughly debated and succinct typology. This finding echoes a key point from Brooks and Ryan with regard to sustainability: 'an agreement to view "sustainability" as a "threshold concept" whose richness and importance disallowed final definitions' (Brooks and Ryan, 2008, p5).

What is clear from this research is that there is no easy formula for developing interdisciplinary programmes around sustainability. In most cases, and in the case studies reviewed here, it has been a matter of growing an idea in conditions that have then been proved to be more or less fertile. For the future, the growth of interdisciplinary curricula linked to sustainability will depend on a willingness on the part of policy-makers and academics to design interdisciplinary approaches into their teaching and learning policies and practices, so that some of the common struggles to assert the identity and logistics of interdisciplinarity are eased, and the benefits to academics and students of working in this way are more quickly apparent and realized.

Conclusion

While there is expertise and experience in interdisciplinary in HEIs it still appears on the margins of the mainstream, which remains dominated by discipline-based practices and structures. Initiatives that link sustainability and interdisciplinarity are rarer still. Embedding interdisciplinarity into the policies, practices and culture of HEIs is difficult because it challenges cultural and structural norms; yet, where it is done well, it affords a renewal of pedagogy and stimulus to learning and a boost to collaboration and cross-fertilization that benefits the host institution – both internally and in terms of its reputation.

Given that sustainability-related issues are increasingly evident and pressing, and that addressing sustainability in the real world often demands interdisciplinary approaches, it is safe to assume that HEIs seeking to innovate in a changing world will need to pay increasing attention to interdisciplinarity and sustainability and their interrelationship, and further, seek links with other agendas that may be driving the institution.

Although there are some signs of this with regard to research directions, where funding and research councils are increasing support for interdisciplinarity, there is a danger that similarly oriented teaching and learning will fall behind any such movement. However, viewed as an opportunity rather than as a problem, interdisciplinarity across the curriculum can offer renewal, the development of extended communities of practice and the critical engagement of academe with the community, around key issues of social, economic and ecological change that (should) concern both (Fear et al, 2006). Indeed, Klein believes that interdisciplinarity is a key to universities rethinking their purposes and practices at a fundamental level – echoing Jantsch's ideas of some decades earlier:

Ultimately, interdisciplinarity raises the most fundamental question of all. What is the purpose of education? In its highest form, interdisciplinarity is not a finite set of skills, a simple add-on, or an adjustment in the schedule. The ultimate goal is to reconstruct what is taught and how it is taught (Klein, 2006, p16).

Put like this, the coming together of interdisciplinarity and sustainability would certainly be more than the sum of their parts; it would be a radical reorientation of higher education, resonant with the calls of the UN Decade of Education for Sustainable Development (DESD) and the Bonn Declaration for the reorientation of education towards a more sustainable world.

References

Andrews, J. and Higson, H. (2008) 'Graduate employability, "Soft Skills" versus "Hard" business knowledge: A European study', *Higher Education in Europe*, vol 33, no 4, 2008, pp411–422

Arum, J. (2004) 'Concepts of interdisciplinarity: Configurations of knowledge and action', *Human Relations*, April 2004, vol 57, no 4, pp379–412

Bateson, G. (1972) *Steps to an Ecology of Mind*, Chandler, San Francisco CA

Bawden, R. (2005) 'Stepping Stones for Curriculum Development', In Wals, A.E.J. (ed), *Curriculum Innovations in Higher Agricultural Education*, Elsevier Overheid, The Hague, pp117–128

Becker, E., Jahn, T., Stiess, I. and Wehling, P. (1997) *Sustainability, A Cross-Disciplinary Concept for Social Transformations*, Management of Social Transformation Policy Papers 6, UNESCO, Paris

Blake, J., Sterling, S. and Kagawa, F. (2009) *Getting it Together: Interdisciplinarity and Sustainability in the Higher Education Institution*, Occasional Paper 3, CSF, University of Plymouth

Bohm, D. (1980) *Wholeness and the Implicate Order*, Ark Paperbacks, London

Brooks, C. and Ryan, A. (2008) *Education for Sustainable Development: Strategic Consultations Among English HEIs*, Report for the HEA ESD Project, available at www.heacademy.ac.uk/assets/York/documents/ourwork/sustainability/esd_EnglishHEIs.pdf, accessed 1 June 2009

Chapman, J. (2002) *System Failure: Why Governments Must Learn to Think Differently*, Demos, London

Chettiparamb, A. (2007) *Interdisciplinarity: A Literature Review*, The HEA Interdisciplinary Teaching and Learning Group, Subject Centre for Languages, Linguistics and Area Studies, University of Southampton

Clayton, A. and Radcliffe, N. (1996) *Sustainability – A Systems Approach*, Earthscan Publications, London

Dale, A. and Newman, L. (2005) 'Sustainable development, education and literacy', *International Journal of Sustainability in Higher Education*, vol 6, no 4, pp351–362

Fear, F., Rosaen, C., Bawden, R. and Foster-Fishman, P. (2006) *Coming to Critical Engagement*, University Press of America, Lanham MD

Funtowicz, S. and Ravetz, J. (2008) *Post-Normal Science*, available at www.eoearth.org/article/Post-Normal_Science, accessed 1 June 2009

G8 Summit (2008) *Sapporo Sustainability Declaration*, available at http://g8u-summit.jp/english/ssd/index.html, accessed 1 June 2009

Godemann, J. (2008) 'Knowledge integration: A key challenge for transdisciplinary cooperation', *Environmental Education Research*, vol 14, no 6, pp625–641

Gough, S. and Scott, W. (2007) *Higher Education and Sustainable Development – Paradox and Possibility*, Routledge, London

Gross, B. (1971) 'Management strategy for economic and social development', *Policy Science*, no 2, no 4, pp339–371

Gunderson, L. and Holling, C. (2002) *Panarchy – Understanding Transformations in Human and Natural Systems*, Island Press, Washington DC

HEFCE (2005) *Sustainable Development in Higher Education: Strategic Statement and Action Plan*, HEFCE, Bristol

HEFCE (2009) *Sustainable Development in Higher Education: 2008 Update to Strategic Statement and Action Plan*, HEFCE, Bristol, available at www.hefce.ac.uk/pubs/hefce/2009/09_03/#exec, accessed 3 February 2010

Hoare, A., Cornell, S., Bertram, C., Gallagher, K., Heslop, S., Lieven, N., MacLeod, C., Morgan, J., Pickering, A., Wells, S. and Willmore. C. (2008) 'Teaching against the grain: Multi-disciplinary teamwork effectively delivers a successful undergraduate unit in sustainable development', *Environmental Education Research*, vol 14, no 4, pp469–481

Jantsch, E. (1972) 'Inter- and transdisciplinary university: A systems approach to education and innovation', *Higher Education*, vol 1, no 1, pp7–37

Kelly, J. (1996) 'Wide and Narrow Interdisciplinary', *Journal of General Education*, vol 45, no 2, pp95–113

Klein, J.T. (1990) *Interdisciplinarity: History, Theory and Practice*, Wayne State University Press, Detroit MI

Klein, J.T. (2004) *Interdisciplinarity and Complexity: An Evolving Relationship*, E:CO vol 6, nos 1–2, pp2–10

Klein, J.T. (2006) 'A platform for a shared discourse of interdisciplinary education', *Journal of Social Science Education*, vol 5, no 2, pp10–18

Klein, J.T. and Newell, W. (1997) 'Advancing Interdisciplinary Studies', in Gaff, J. and Ratcliff, J. (eds), *Handbook of the Undergraduate Curriculum*, Jossey-Bass, San Francisco, pp393–415

King, A. and Schneider, B. (1992) *The First Global Revolution*, Simon and Schuster, London

Kuhn, T. (1962) *The Structure of Scientific Revolutions*, University of Chicago Press, Chicago IL

Lattuca, L. (2001) *Creating Interdisciplinarity: Interdisciplinary Research and Teaching Among College and University Faculty*, Vanderbilt University Press, Nashville TN

Meadows, D.H., Meadows, D.L. and Randers, J. (1972) *The Limits to Growth*, Potomac Associates, New York and Pan Books, London; republished 1994

Meadows, D.H. (1982) 'Whole Earth Models and Systems', *The CoEvolution Quarterly*, Summer 1982, pp98–108

NERC (2009) *Living with Environmental Change*, available at www.nerc.ac.uk/research/programmes/lwec/aims.asp, accessed 29 September 2009

OECD (1972) *Interdisciplinarity: Problems of Teaching and Research in Universities*, OECD, Paris

Peccei, A. (1982) *One Hundred Pages for the Future*, Futura, London

Policy Studies Institute, PA Consulting Group and Centre for Research in Education and the Environment (2008) *Strategic Review of Sustainable Development in Higher Education in England*, HEFCE, London, available at www.hefce.ac.uk/pubs/rdreports/2008/rd03_08, accessed 1 June 2009

Rhoten, D., Mansilla, V., Chun, M. and Klein, J.T. (2006) *Interdisciplinary Education at Liberal Arts Institutions*, Teagle Foundation White Paper, New York NY

Salter, L. and Hearn, A. (1996) *Outside the Lines: Issues in Interdisciplinary Research*, McGill–Queen's University Press, Montreal

Selby, D. (2006) 'The catalyst that is sustainability: Bringing permeability to disciplinary boundaries', *Planet*, no 17, 57–59, GEES, University of Plymouth

Schmidt, J. (2008) 'Towards a philosophy of interdisciplinarity – An attempt to provide a classification and clarification', *Poiesis Praxis*, vol 5 pp53–69

Sterling, S. and Witham, H. (2008) 'Pushing the boundaries: The work of the Higher Education Academy's ESD Project', *Environmental Education Research*, vol 14, no 4, pp399–412

Steuer, N. and Marks, N. (2008) *University Challenge: Towards a Well-being Approach to Quality in Higher Education*, New Economics Foundation, London

UNESCO (2009) Bonn Declaration, available at www.esd-world-conference-2009.org/fileadmin/download/News/BonnDeclarationFinalFR.pdf, accessed 12 October 2009

University of Plymouth (2008) *University of Plymouth Sustainability Policy*, available at http://csf.plymouth.ac.uk/?q=policy, accessed 13 October 2009

University of Plymouth (2009) *University of Plymouth Research and Innovation Strategy 2009–2012 (April 2009)*. University of Plymouth

University of Plymouth (2009) *University of Plymouth Teaching and Learning Strategy 2009–2012*. University of Plymouth

WCED (1987) *Our Common Future: The Report of the World Commission on Environment and Development* ['The Brundtland Report'], Oxford University Press, Oxford, available at www.un-documents.net/wced-ocf.htm, accessed 29 January 2010

Wilson, E.O. (1999) *Consilience: The Unity of Knowledge*, Abacus, London

Notes

1   As well as providing general support for interdisciplinarity, the HEA set up an Interdisciplinarity Teaching and Learning Group in 2005. For further information, please visit: www.heacademy.ac.uk/ourwork/networks/itlg

2   There are currently seven research councils in the UK. For further information, visit: www.rcuk.ac.uk/aboutrcs/default.htm

Chapter 3

'It's Not Just Bits of Paper and Light Bulbs': A Review of Sustainability Pedagogies and Their Potential for Use in Higher Education

Debby Cotton and Jennie Winter

Sustainable development is a way of thinking about how we organize our lives and work – including our education system – so that we don't destroy our most precious resource, the planet ... It must be much more than recycling bottles or giving money to charity. It is about thinking and working in a profoundly different way (Department for Education and Skills [DfES], 2006, p6).

Introduction

In 2005, the UK Government published its sustainable development (SD) strategy *Securing the Future*, which endorses education as a major vehicle for raising awareness and building a skills base for sustainability. This document promotes sustainability literacy as a core competency for graduates and professionals in the workplace, and encourages universities and colleges to 'raise the profile of sustainability literacy in all curricula' (Department for Environment, Food and Rural Affairs [DEFRA], 2005, p151). The HEFCE also produced an SD strategy and action plan in 2005 that endorsed ESD, followed up by a strategic review three years later (HEFCE, 2008). These strategies were updated in 2009, in the light of consultation with the HE sector, culminating in a document that identified higher education as 'a major contributor to society's efforts to achieve sustainability – through the skills and knowledge that its graduates learn and put into practice' (HEFCE, 2009, p3). Among other things, the HE sector is encouraged to 'develop curricula and pedagogy that will give students the skills and knowledge to live and work sustainably' (HEFCE, 2009, p21). Here, then, is clear support at a national strategic level for sustainability pedagogies in UK HEIs.

This emphasis is reflected in some parts of the academic literature by authors who view higher education as offering an unrivalled opportunity to provide leadership on sustainability: 'Given what academics know about the current ecological condition of the planet, there is an obligation for universities to become leaders in the movement to prevent global ecological collapse' (Moore, 2005, p326). Increasingly, sustainability is being seen as an integral, cross-cutting theme in HE, rather than being consigned to specific parts of the curriculum such as environmental science and geography (Haigh, 2005). Viewed as an institution-wide issue, sustainability has the potential to become 'a gateway to a different view of curriculum, of pedagogy, of organizational change, of policy and particularly of ethos' (Sterling, 2004, p50), drawing together campus changes, curriculum development and pedagogic reform. This reflects a move away from the conception of ESD as embedding prescribed, pre-defined content into curricula towards an understanding of sustainability as a different way of thinking and of teaching. Recent research has investigated the extent of this conception among university lecturers and the impact of changing pedagogies instead of – or as well as – the content of university programmes (see Cotton et al, 2007 and 2009). The findings suggest that there is considerable support for utilizing innovative pedagogies to teach sustainability.

Despite the strategic developments and conceptual advances that have occurred in ESD, development of HE curricula and pedagogies in practical terms has been 'patchy' at best (Dawe et al, 2005, p4). The HEFCE strategic review in 2008 observed 'very disparate ESD activity across the sector', and much of the activity in HE has thus far been focused on campus greening rather than on pedagogic reform (SQW Ltd, 2006). Moving towards an increased emphasis on sustainability offers a profound challenge to all systems of education, but perhaps especially to HE. Some in the sector remain sceptical about incorporating sustainability into the curriculum. Fears about indoctrination that inhibited the introduction of environmental education in schools have resurfaced in the light of the current interest in sustainability and still haunt the ESD agenda. One vociferous opponent has been Peter Knight, who writes:

> [The HEFCE SD strategy] is one of the most pernicious and dangerous circulars ever to be issued. It represents the final assault on the last remaining freedom of universities ... It is not the job of universities to promote a particular political orthodoxy (Knight, 2005).

Responses such as this have led some to comment that 'the higher education sector is one of the hardest sectors in which to institutionalize sustainability' (Junyent and de Ciurana, 2008, p764).

Even where individual tutors are committed to the inclusion of sustainability, other factors may make it difficult for them to implement its principles in their teaching. For example, the complexity and lack of clarity around the terms 'sustainability' and 'sustainable development' inhibit ESD teaching innovation by many in academia. Scott and Gough (2003, p2) describe sustainable development as 'a set of contested ideas rather than a settled issue', so its inclusion in the curriculum is an ongoing challenge. Although it might be argued that the controversial nature of such issues offers fertile opportunities for the use of exciting and innovative pedagogies – and indeed sustainability appears to invite interactive, discursive teaching methods – the dominant pedagogy in HE is lecturing, generally favouring one-way transmission of information. Furthermore, the interdisciplinary nature of sustainability requires a change in mindset for academics, who are generally accustomed to working within clearly defined disciplinary boundaries.

Nonetheless, despite these constraints there are a large number of alternative pedagogies that have been used successfully in both secondary and higher education and which will be reviewed in this chapter. There is also increasing evidence to suggest that 'in general, good sustainable development pedagogy is often simply good pedagogy' (HEFCE, 2008, p34); thus it is potentially an attractive option for HE practitioners and fits well with a broader move towards more constructivist, learner-centred approaches in HE (Biggs, 1999).

Sustainability pedagogies

Sustainability pedagogies have emerged from an initial focus on environmental education compartmentalized as *about*, *in* and *for* the environment. Education *about* the environment focuses on declarative knowledge and provides the learner with information about environmental systems and issues using approaches designed to investigate and discover. Education *in* the environment capitalizes on the environment as a real-world resource for enquiry and discovery that can enhance the learning process and challenge traditional understandings of meta-cognition. Education *for* the environment conceptualizes the transformative (and contentious) component of environmental education. It requires the development of a 'personal environmental ethic'; the values and attitudes that motivate behavioural change in favour of the environment (Palmer and Neal, 1994, p19). From these beginnings, alternative pedagogic approaches have emerged, promoting inclusive forms of communicating knowledge based primarily on dialogue and experience (Scott and Gough, 2003) that have remained a central feature through the movement away from the traditional interests of environmental education towards the wider concept of ESD.

There are a number of general principles regarding sustainability pedagogies including participatory and inclusive education processes, transdisciplinary cooperation, experiential learning and the use of environment and community as learning resources; all of which involve student-centred and interactive enquiry-

Table 3.1 *Integration of sustainability in HE*

Integration of sustainability within higher education implies shifts

From	To
Transmissive learning	Learning through discovery
Teacher-centred approach	Learner-centred approach
Individual learning	Collaborative learning
Learning dominated by theory	Praxis-oriented learning linking theory and experience
Focus on accumulating knowledge and a content orientation	Focus on self-regulative learning and a real issues orientation
Emphasis on cognitive objectives only	Cognitive, affective, and skills-related objectives
Institutional, staff-based teaching/learning	Learning with staff but also with and from outsiders
Low-level cognitive learning	Higher-level cognitive learning

Source: Sterling, 2004:58; adapted from Van den Bor et al, 2000

based approaches to teaching and learning (Fien, 2006; Rasmussen, 2008; Sterling, 2004). It is clear that many of the core principles of integrating sustainability into HE require substantial shifts in thinking and practice that may be out of reach of the individual lecturer and more challenging for some disciplines than others (see Table 3.1).

The difficulty of negotiating transformative changes to curricula – which are themselves within the boundaries of a wider (and largely traditional and conservative) educational system – has been raised by Sterling (2001). However, recent research (Cotton et al, 2007 and 2009), carried out with the the University of Plymouth's CSF, shows that academics in a wide range of disciplines are making changes to their teaching to incorporate sustainability into the content of their curricula, despite highly variable institutional support for such activities. What is perhaps more difficult is promoting the changes in pedagogies that sustainability seems to require. Tilbury (2007, p119) notes that, 'more and more we are seeing the word sustainability being added to the titles of programs, projects, activities, departments or units – however, few have actually been redesigned to address new social learning approaches'. This is perhaps simply because the pressures on HE militate against such changes – the increasing marketization of HE on a mass scale make participatory, collaborative approaches problematic. However, there may be wider impediments at work: previous research has identified lack of curriculum time, perceived irrelevance of sustainability to some disciplines (see Box 3.1) and lack of a shared understanding of the terminology as barriers to the growth of sustainability pedagogies (see Dawe et al, 2005, for a discussion of some of the issues).

Why do we need different pedagogies for sustainability?

The need for different approaches for teaching about sustainability (and previously environmental education) has been under discussion for some time and is

Box 3.1 Is sustainability relevant to your discipline?

Much of the literature on integrating environmental or sustainability issues into higher education focuses on campus greening alongside the possibilities for incorporating sustainability-related knowledge into relevant subject areas (e.g. Heinz Family Foundation, 1995). However, recent research by the University of Plymouth has investigated the ways and extent to which academics incorporate sustainability across all parts of the curriculum, as well as exploring their understanding of sustainability pedagogies (Cotton et al, 2007 and 2009). Throughout this chapter, we will draw on interviews and analysis undertaken as part of this research to illustrate key points.

The Plymouth research findings suggest that although there might appear more plentiful opportunities for incorporating sustainability into teaching in certain disciplines (such as environmental science or geography), there is no obvious correlation between subject area and the belief of staff that sustainability is relevant to their discipline. It seems that tutors who are personally committed to sustainability are likely to see it as relevant to their teaching irrespective of what discipline they work in:

So with most of the things you do, issues of energy conservation and efficiency and therefore the whole broad issues of sustainability crop up (lecturer in engineering).

On the surface you would think, occupational therapy is about recruiting people for the health profession, primarily; what has that to do with sustainable development? And yet if you look at … all the resources that are required to get them qualified, it does have an impact on sustainability (lecturer in health).

It does fit in the history of the EU stuff that I teach so I will probably expand it there a little bit (lecturer in humanities).

This research on sustainability suggests that there is potential for its inclusion in all curriculum areas – but only if lecturers can be persuaded that it is important to do so. To some degree, this provides a specific example of a more general rule which is that a lecturer's prior knowledge and beliefs about a subject influence the way in which the subject is presented to students (Prosser and Trigwell, 1999).

often linked with the potentially controversial nature of environmental or sustainability issues. However, research on how to teach controversial issues reveals a far from straightforward situation. It has long been assumed that a neutral or balanced perspective is required to avoid indoctrination of vulnerable students, and this belief is still held by many teachers in secondary and tertiary education. For example, research in England (Oulton et al, 2004, p415) suggests that school teachers identify three underpinning beliefs about teaching controversial issues. These are:

- a focus on rationality, reasoning and sticking to the facts;
- presenting a balanced view;
- teacher neutrality.

All three of these underpinning beliefs, however, are problematic if investigated further. For example, the facts relating to sustainability may be less than clear and depend significantly on the values of the individual describing them. An understanding of the transitory nature of facts, of knowledge and of what can be known undermines this position particularly strongly in the research-led environment of HE. Moreover, the notions of maintaining neutrality and balance may be constrained by a number of practical limitations including: premature consensus, entrenched positions or apathy on the part of students involved in discussion; inadvertent projection of the teachers' views while attempting to convey a neutral position (see Box 3.2 on the hidden curriculum); and reduction of complex arguments to dichotomies and polarized positions in an effort to provide balance. Oulton et al (2004) offer a range of possible suggestions for the tutor, including:

- helping students to distinguish between sound and unsound reasoning, developing a respect for evidence and open-mindedness;
- being open about the fact that true balance is an unachievable goal, but helping students develop 'a critical awareness of bias and make this one of the central learning objectives' (p 417);
- declaring their own position explicitly so that students can be aware of potential bias in the teaching.

These approaches potentially offer an attractive proposition for higher education across the disciplines, drawing as they do on notions of logic, reasoning and criticality. Alongside an attempt to incorporate sustainability content into the curriculum, it is perhaps helpful to think in terms of developing the knowledge and skills of sustainability literacy – these would include open-mindedness and critical awareness of bias. A set of key questions might help to scaffold students' critical thinking skills in terms of issues such as:

- Where did this information or view come from?
- Who provided it?
- How are they funded?
- Whose interests do they represent?
- What values are they expressing (explicitly or covertly)?
- What evidence do they present?
- Do they evaluate it?

These questions could be utilized in a range of different contexts to explore the basis of decision-making, including decisions on sustainability issues, as appropriate. In this way, ESD is viewed as a different lens through which to view the discipline that focuses on the implications for economy, environment and society, rather than an imposed set of constructs and beliefs.

Box 3.2 The hidden curriculum

Aside from overt impacts on students' views of sustainability, which might be attributed to curriculum and pedagogy, it is clear that students will also be affected by what is known as 'the hidden curriculum' (Jackson, 1968, pp10–33). This incorporates the messages sent by an individual tutor or an institution to students, often unconsciously and covertly, about how they ought to think and behave. A key way in which the hidden curriculum is made manifest is through the ethos and values of the institution. These might be illustrated by the extent of recycling facility provision and green travel plans, or by student engagement in decision-making and democratic processes. There is also potential, the Plymouth research suggests, for individual lecturers' personal beliefs to influence both the content and structure of the curriculum:

As lecturers we have viewpoints that we share with our students in many ways, probably more complexly than just teaching about it. Very simple comments that you slip in, in a lecture, about saving trees for instance ... I think that tutors actually influence students in ways well beyond the classroom or the subject ... by choosing texts and cultural products which, while possibly commenting on their structure or contextualization, also provide pawns for discussing issues of sustainability, which is actually what people do all the time (lecturer in art).

This lecturer suggests that comments in a lecture or use of resources may send messages about the tutor's underlying values. A surprising finding of our research on ESD in HE was the extent to which lecturers talked about sustainability 'creeping' into the curriculum through informal or subconscious means such as this (Cotton et al, 2009). Research in schools also indicates that it is extremely difficult to maintain a neutral position when teaching about controversial issues such as those pertaining to sustainability. A detailed analysis of classroom discussions on environmental topics reveals that the teacher's viewpoint was expressed covertly (and often unintentionally) via control of participants' turns in discussion and use of rhetorical questions to indicate disagreement (Cotton, 2006).

While it is impossible to avoid such unconscious messages to students, a critical awareness of the different ways in which the hidden curriculum might be at work both within and beyond the classroom is essential to understanding the impact of teaching about sustainability. Encouraging student participation in classes, and in making decisions on assessment and other academic issues, is one way in which lecturers can model good practice to set the tone for sustainability in higher education.

What kinds of teaching methods have been advocated for sustainability?

The literature includes a wide range of suggestions for appropriate approaches to teaching about sustainability and also for specific teaching methods. Underlying many of these approaches is support for active, experiential learning, interdisciplinarity and use of the local (and regional) environment for educational purposes. Potential learning approaches are *participative inquiry/action research*, where students investigate an issue which is of importance to them personally (Tilbury, 2007); *transformative sustainability learning* (TSL), where tutors attempt to use the three domains of learning – cognitive, psychomotor and affective, or head, hands and heart as they have been described – to engage students in a transformative educational experience (Sipos et al, 2008); and *action competence*, where students are encouraged to envisage alternatives and solutions to unsustainable practices (Breiting and Mogensen, 1999).

Specific teaching strategies advocated for environmental education or ESD include those listed below (examples of how some of these are used in practice are given in Box 3.3). It is likely that utilizing a range of these strategies would be most appropriate.

Role-plays and simulations

Role-plays have long been recommended for teaching about environmental issues and sustainability, although there is a surprising lack of evidence in terms of effective outcomes (Oulton et al, 2004). Potential advantages of role-plays are that they provide an opportunity for students to gain an in-depth understanding of another person's perspective and to empathize with others; disadvantages are the amount of time and organization required to enable effective role-playing and the difficulties of managing the role-play, particularly with large groups. Role-plays are used rarely in university education, possibly because of the practical difficulties or because the pedagogy is poorly aligned with the learning culture of HE.

Group discussions

Group discussions were frequently mentioned by both school teachers and lecturers when asked to describe an appropriate pedagogy for sustainability (Cotton, 2006, Cotton et al, 2007). The use of a discussion may be an attempt to counteract the risk of the tutor taking a transmissive or authoritarian approach, thereby enabling students to discuss their own and others' views. Discussions potentially enable a range of perspectives to be aired, but they may be confrontational and prove difficult to control, especially if the topic is a controversial one. The tutor needs to be able to encourage listening and self-reflection rather than argument and should be clear about their own role in the discussion (see Box 3.2 for some of the difficulties of neutrality as a tutor position). Structured questions to scaffold students' learning may be helpful, as may explicit meta-cognitive instructions as to the purpose of the discussion and the rules of engagement. Without such guidance, many students – accustomed to the transmissive nature of much of their educational experience – may be uncertain how to respond.

Stimulus activities

A stimulus activity might involve watching a video or looking at photos, poems or newspaper extracts to initiate reflection or discussion (Oulton et al, 2004). Students may even be involved in producing their own work such as photos taken around the campus to stimulate a discussion on campus greening. Use of videos or externally-produced documents potentially enables the tutor to bring in a wide range of viewpoints for critical analysis, and this approach is feasible even with very large groups.

Debates

Debates in which two groups of students put forward opposing arguments on an issue are often recommended as a method of teaching about sustainability since they encourage students to gather information about the topic and develop an argument. However, they can become confrontational and students may be discouraged from engaging or empathizing with others' views. Authors such as Oulton et al specifically warn against asking students to vote on an issue as this may lead to them making up their minds too soon, hardening their attitudes and leaving them feeling committed to the stance that they have taken (Oulton et al, 2004).

Critical incidents

The use of critical incidents to teach about sustainability is described in a paper by Nott and Wellington. Students are given an example and asked what they would do, what they could do and what they should do (Nott and Wellington, 1995). This allows them to consider their personal perspectives and actions in the light of a moral or ethical stance. The approach can also be used with groups to promote awareness about multiple perspectives on sustainability.

Case studies

Another popular choice of pedagogy for teaching about sustainability described by lecturers in our research was the case study approach. Tutors described using case studies to bring ESD into areas of the curriculum that had not traditionally involved a clear focus on sustainability (Cotton et al, 2009), and to provide students with an holistic view of an issue. Case studies enable students to investigate issues that affect their local area, to work with private enterprises and community groups and to work together in finding solutions to local issues. They may take a variety of forms, but one possible approach is to place strong emphasis on 'reflection, research, participation and action' (Junyent and de Ciurana, 2008, p769).

Reflexive accounts

Considering their own position in relation to new knowledge about sustainability can help students understand how individual actions contribute to sustainability. Although contentious in HE (Knight, 2005), behaviour change is a cross-cutting priority of the UK sustainable development strategy (DEFRA, 2005) and education is identified as a core vehicle for achieving this. Therefore, pedagogies that provide opportunities for students to reflect on personal roles, attitudes and responsibilities in relation to a range of sustainability issues are potentially advantageous.

Personal development planning (PDP)

PDP has been embedded in UK HE since 2000 (Quality Assurance Agency for Higher Education [QAA], 2000). 'PDP is a structured and supported process undertaken by a learner to reflect upon their own learning, performance and/or achievement and to plan for their personal, educational and career development. It is an inclusive process, open to all learners, in all HE provision settings, and at all levels' (QAA, 2009, p3). PDP can provide an opportunity for students to learn about and reflect on sustainability (John Forster Associates, 2006). Sustainability literacy may be a set of skills, development of which is encouraged throughout the student experience of HE and recorded through the PDP process. Students may also be able to integrate relevant informal learning activities and volunteering into the PDP record.

Critical reading and writing

Reading and writing are often downplayed in favour of more interactive pedagogies. However, these are important social practices and the key to progressing sustainability and literacy. Stibbe suggests students can gain from deconstructing destructive, alternative or counter-discourses to identify the possible motivation of the author. They may also be able to envisage alternative futures, and write a contrasting account based on a differing set of values (Stibbe, 2008).

Problem-based learning

Problem-based learning is an iterative learning process that can be used to teach a whole range of subject matter. In the context of ESD, a sustainability-related issue may be identified and students asked to research this to generate a body of knowledge. They can then develop a vision of alternative actions and potential solutions to the problem, which they use to devise a plan of action. The action may then be carried out, followed by a period of reflection and evaluation. This process can be extremely useful because it promotes both the conceptual and practical aspects of sustainability literacy. Brunetti et al (2003) describe a specific example of the use of problem-based learning to teach about social, economic and environmental sustainability issues.

Fieldwork

Fieldwork is an example of experiential pedagogy that can influence students' emotions (Sivek, 2002) and help develop the critical thinking skills so essential to understanding the complexity of sustainability (Jones, 2003; Scott and Gough, 2003). Fieldwork for sustainability can be based on issues in the local community and environs, linking theory to real-world examples (Hope, 2009), which can help students to understand multiple stakeholder perspectives in situ. There is also evidence that outdoor experience is an important precursor to understanding sustainability (Palmer and Suggate, 1996) and that fieldwork promotes broader benefits for learning by encouraging active and reflective learning among students (Hope, 2009).

Box 3.3 Examples of sustainability pedagogies in practice

Role plays

Through role-playing is the way forward. I often ask the room if any of them have a feeling on this ... and then I'll flip their role. So for the ones who say I don't think fishing should kill dolphins, I'll make them research on the side of the fishermen. So instead of leaving them with their preconceived idea, stick them in the other one. So I say, "Right, you guys are going to be the environmental lobby, you'll be the industry lobby and in both cases one will lead and the other will defend." So when the conservationists are leading, the industry will defend, and [the others] will be the audience. And at the end of that discussion, see which one they think is going to get the public's vote (lecturer in marine science).

Discussions

I feel in some ways education should equip young people to be able to make up their own minds about their futures... I think there is an interesting thing about how we view excess at the moment, which is worth having a discussion with students about. In some ways I think they get mixed messages; on the one hand, I think they get the kind of Pepsi Max society – it's all possible. There is this sort of idea of choice; and on the other hand, they possibly run into some surprising constraints if they choose to do some other things ... that's why I think we need to keep an impartial position (lecturer in media).

Stimulus activities

I do encourage critical thinking. So I will present an article to the student. This is a very old article from the Ecologist on recycling and reuse, which you can tell is something I feel very strongly about. I think anybody who really thinks for two minutes about recycling has to ask questions. I think the more in favour of recycling you are the more questions are going to come up. So I would use this article with them, which does have questions of sustainability in it, because ultimately it is promoting a culture of durability, as opposed to a culture of throughput and reprocessing. It's obviously not my remit to actually teach sustainability. But I prefer to use texts with some kind of ethical value (lecturer in business).

Case studies

We are doing some teaching on a project called Ecohouse looking at ecological development... It is like a design project where students are given a plot and design buildings on that site and look at things such as energy use and their aim is to build something that is sustainable. The site is near the railway and in an area that has social problems and it's interesting to see the students take on things and not just looking at the environmental issues (lecturer in engineering).

Modelling good practice

I think at a personal level there is a huge amount we can do, and I've always felt that in the position where you have a teacher and students ... you set an example, it's not just what you say; it's what you are. And if you stand up in front of a group of students and say you should be going by public transport and every evening you go out to your car and drive home... Students are very perceptive, and they understand this (lecturer in health).

Modelling good practice

Despite the focus here on teaching strategies, the importance of learning taking place implicitly through the hidden curriculum (see Box 3.2) and outside the classroom should not be underestimated. In our research, many lecturers talked of reducing paper (by provision of online resources, for example) and turning lights out at the end of a teaching session, and it is clear that students will react cynically to any indication that the lecturers' expressed views conflict with their own behaviour. Moreover, the role of higher education as a transformative experience could, and perhaps *should*, go well beyond turning off lights and providing recycling facilities:

> *Social education for me is a big part of the university. It is not just coming out with a degree, it is how you change and what your values are when you finish. I think there is so much to sustainable development for me in the University of Plymouth that is not just about bits of paper and light bulbs (lecturer in health).*

Potential for future development of sustainability pedagogies in HE

Looking at the pedagogies advocated above, it is immediately obvious that many of these approaches require a significant amount of prior preparation, as well as small groups and a reasonable time allocation. The barriers to engaging in such teaching approaches in the constraints of the current HE system should not be underestimated.

However, it is also clear that if students are to be given the opportunity to reflect seriously on sustainability issues, time needs to be made available within the curriculum for serious exploration and discussion. To provide a successful learning environment that encompasses sustainability, both students and lecturers should feel free to express their views in a supportive environment, but one where self-reflection and change of viewpoint is encouraged. As a general rule, students should be encouraged to evaluate critically any information provided, to identify potential sources of bias and to reflect on their own views and prejudices to help them make decisions about complex issues both within and beyond the sustainability debate.

If the use of sustainability pedagogies is to become more widespread, then those lecturers who are already committed to sustainability principles will need support and resources to enable them to develop their teaching along these lines. For those who are yet to be convinced, an understanding of the potential of sustainability pedagogies to form part of a wider move towards student-centred, active learning approaches may act as an incentive.

Pedagogies that help students develop critical thinking skills also provide an important contribution to the wider skills sector. The link between skills for sustainable development and the needs of the economy to provide a sustainable future has only recently been made (DfES, 2003); however, skills for sustainable development are fast becoming viewed as a 'vital national asset' (DfES, 2003, p8) with the potential to enhance social mobility and tackle exclusion as well as achieve economic objectives. Although this may be more easily accommodated in vocational degrees, the profile of employability skills continues to rise throughout academia and may provide a useful framework for including sustainability literacy in subjects where its relevance is not clear-cut. In all cases, there is an undoubted need for professional development to embed, value and reward good (sustainability) pedagogic practice and to enable lecturers to engage with new ways of thinking about teaching and learning in HE.

A further requirement is what has been described as 'space for pedagogical transformation' – the creation of 'spaces on campus where transformative and transdisciplinary learning is supported and encouraged' (Moore, 2005, p337). This should include physical space to support the development of more student-centred, collaborative (and interdisciplinary) approaches, a space where reflection can take place, and where project or action planning can occur. It should be innovative, exciting, technology-rich and, crucially, flexible in terms of lighting, seating and presentation areas to encourage lecturers to consider variation in modes of working and interacting with students – in contrast to the formal teacher-focused pedagogy which is encouraged by the traditional stepped lecture theatre.

E-learning contexts can also provide a space for sustainability-related learning to occur. Online forums can provide a suitable environment for constructing discussions and debates and enable participants to cross disciplinary boundaries by offering a neutral space for students and staff from different subject areas. Online modules about sustainability can be used as an aid by lecturers with little experience of sustainable development.

The perception of students as consumers, together with the marketization of HE, has further consequences for sustainability. Students may be reticent to sign up to courses that feature sustainability, not viewing it as applicable to their personal or career trajectories. If the sustainability of teaching methods is considered in its broadest sense then key selling points for courses such as foreign field trips would need to be reconsidered, which may have adverse impacts on course recruitment. A lecturer in our Plymouth study, for instance, noted the reluctance of students to become involved in sustainability activities, despite their underlying concerns:

I've spoken to a lot of students at a personal level about what they feel about sustainability, and I believe many are extremely concerned about the situation that they perceive we're in and would like to do something if they felt it was going to be worth their while. So while there's a reluctance perhaps at the moment to commit themselves, I think if they could see why something was being put forward or suggested, then I believe they would become involved (lecturer in health).

However, Sterling and Scott (2007) identify ways in which student demand can put pressure on academics to include sustainability in their courses, and the HEFCE's 2008 review notes that 'There is a clear niche in the academic market-place for institutions that wish to champion sustainability …' (p35). In this way, pressure from both staff and students may combine to move this agenda forward.

References

Biggs, J. (1999) *Teaching for Quality Learning at University*, Society for Research in Higher Education and Open University Press, Buckingham

Breiting, S. and Mogensen, F. (1999) 'Action competence and environmental education', *Cambridge Journal of Education*, vol 29, no 3, pp349–353

Brunetti, A.J., Petrell, R.J. and Sawada, B. (2003) 'SEEDing sustainability: Team project-based learning enhances awareness of sustainability at the University of British Columbia, Canada', *International Journal of Sustainability in Higher Education*, vol 4, no 3, pp210–217

Cotton, D.R.E. (2006) 'Teaching controversial environmental issues: Neutrality and balance in the reality of the classroom', *Educational Research*, vol 48, no 2, pp223–241

Cotton, D.R.E., Warren, M.F., Maiboroda, O. and Bailey, I. (2007) 'Sustainable development, higher education and pedagogy: A study of lecturers' beliefs and attitudes', *Environmental Education Research*, vol 13, no 5, pp579–597

Cotton, D., Bailey, I., Warren, M. and Bissell, S. (2009) 'Revolutions and second-best solutions: Education for sustainable development in higher education', *Studies in Higher Education*, vol 34, no 7

Dawe, G., Jucker, R. and Martin, S. (2005) *Sustainable Development in Higher Education: Current Practice and Future Developments*, HEA, York www.heacademy.ac.uk/assets/York/documents/ourwork/tla/sustainability/sustdevinHEfinalreport.pdf Accessed 6 March 2009

DEFRA (2005) *Securing the Future: The UK Government Sustainable Development Strategy*, The Stationery Office, London, available at www.defra.gov.uk/sustainable/government/publications/uk-strategy/documents/SecFut_complete.pdf, accessed 6 March 2009

DfES (2003) *White Paper Twenty-First Century Skills: Realising Our Potential. Individuals, Employers, Nation*, HM Treasury: Department of Trade and Industry, London

DfES (2006) *Sustainable Schools for Pupils, Communities and the Environment: Government Response to the Consultation on the Sustainable Schools Strategy*, available at http://publications.teachernet.gov.uk/default.aspx?PageFunction=productdetails&PageMode=publications&ProductId=DFES-04294-2006, accessed 6 March 2009

Fien, J. (2006) *Education for Sustainable Development: A Perspective for Schools*, Raja Roy Singh Lecture, 10th Asian Programme of Educational Innovation for Development International Conference, Bangkok, Thailand, 6–8 December 2006, available at www.unescobkk.org/education/apeid/apeid-international-conference/10-th-apeid-international-conference/speakers-and-speeches/john-fien/raja-roy-singh-lecture/, accessed 23 June 2009

Haigh, M. (2005) 'Greening the university curriculum: Appraising an international movement', *Journal of Geography in Higher Education*, vol 29, no 1, pp31–48

HEFCE (2005) *Sustainable Development in Higher Education: Strategic Statement and Action Plan*, HEFCE, Bristol

HEFCE (2008) *Strategic Review of Sustainable Development in Higher Education in England*, HEFCE, Bristol, available at www.hefce.ac.uk/pubs/rdreports/2008/rd03_08, accessed 6 March 2009

HEFCE (2009) *Sustainable Development in Higher Education: 2008 Update to Strategic Statement and Action Plan*, HEFCE, Bristol, available at www.hefce.ac.uk/pubs/hefce/2009/09_03/09_03.pdf, accessed 3 February 2010

Heinz Family Foundation (1995) *Blueprint for a Green Campus: The Campus Earth Summit Initiatives for Higher Education*, Pittsburgh PA

Hope, M. (2009) 'The importance of direct experience: A philosophical defense of field-work in human geography', *Journal of Geography in Higher Education*, vol 33, no 2, pp169–182

Jackson, P.W. (1968) *Life in Classrooms*, Holt, Rinehart and Winston, New York NY

John Forster Associates (2006) *Embedding Sustainability into the Curriculum of Scotland's Universities and Colleges*, available at www.sfc.ac.uk/reports_publications/reports_publications.aspx?Search=john%20forster&Type=Reports%20and%20publications&Sector=-1, accessed 22 February 2010

Jones, V. (2003) *Young People and the Circulation of Academic Knowledges*, Department of Geography, University of Aberystwyth

Junyent, M. and de Ciurana, A.M.G (2008) 'Education for sustainability in university studies: A model for reorienting the curriculum', *British Educational Research Journal*, vol 34, no 6, pp763–782

Knight, P. (2005) 'Unsustainable developments', *The Guardian*, 8 February, available at www.guardian.co.uk/education/2005/feb/08/highereducation.administration, accessed 6 March 2009

Moore, J. (2005) 'Seven recommendations for creating sustainability education at the university level: A guide for change agents', *International Journal of Sustainability in Higher Education*, vol 6, no 4, pp326–339

Nott, M. and Wellington, J. (1995) 'Critical incidents in the science classroom and the nature of science', *School Science Review*, vol 76, no 276, pp41–46

Oulton, C., Dillon, J. and Grace, M. (2004) 'Reconceptualising the teaching of controversial issues', *International Journal of Science Education*, vol 26, no 4, pp411–423

Palmer, J. and Neal, P. (1994) *The Handbook of Environmental Education*, Routledge, London

Palmer, J. and Suggate, J. (1996) 'Influences and experiences affecting pro-environmental behaviour of educators', *Environmental Education Research*, vol 2, no 1, pp109–121

Prosser, M. and Trigwell, K. (1999) *Understanding Learning and Teaching: The Experience in Higher Education*, The Society for Research into Higher Education and Open University Press, Buckingham

QAA (2000) *Policy Statement on a Progress File for Higher Education*, available at www.qaa.ac.uk/academicinfrastructure/progressFiles/archive/policystatement/default.asp, accessed 23 June 2009

QAA (2009) *Policy Development Planning: Guidance for Institutional Policy and Practice in Higher Education*, available at www.qaa.ac.uk/academicinfrastructure/progressfiles/guidelines/pdp/pdpguide.pdf, accessed 23 June 2009

Rasmussen, H. (2008) *The Earth Charter and the Educative Principles of Sustainability*, Earth Charter International, available at www.cartadellaterra.org/media/File/PROGETTI_E_PERCORSI/terra%20che%20cura/intervento%20henriette.pdf.pdf, accessed 23 June 2009

Scott, W. and Gough, S. (2003) *Sustainable Development and Learning: Framing the Issues*, Routledge, London

Sipos, Y., Battisti, B. and Grimm, K. (2008) 'Achieving transformative sustainability learning: Engaging head, hands and heart', *International Journal of Sustainability in Higher Education*, vol 9, no 1, pp68–86

Sivek, D.J. (2002) 'Environmental sensitivity among Wisconsin high school students', *Environmental Education Research*, vol 8, no 2, pp155–170

SQW Ltd (2006) *Specialist Review and Evaluation of the Higher Education Partnership for Sustainability (HEPS) Programme*, available at www.hefce.ac.uk/Pubs/rdreports/2006/rd08_06/, accessed 6 March 2009

Sterling, S. (2001) *Sustainable Education: Re-visioning Learning and Change*, Green Books, Dartington

Sterling, S. (2004) 'An analysis of the development of sustainability education internationally: Evolution, interpretation and transformative potential' in Blewitt, J. and Cullingford, C. (eds) *The Sustainability Curriculum: The Challenge of Higher Education*, Earthscan, London, pp43–62

Sterling, S. and Scott, W. (2007) England contribution, *First International Meeting on Implementation of Education for Sustainable Development for Higher Education Institutes*, 8–9 February 2007, Amsterdam, available at www.eauc.org.uk/first_international_meeting_on_implementation_of_e, accessed 10 March 2008

Stibbe, A. (2008) 'Words and worlds: New directions for sustainability literacy', *Language and Ecology*, vol 2, no 3, pp1–10

Tilbury, D. (2007) 'Monitoring and evaluation during the UN decade of education for sustainable development', *The Journal of Education for Sustainable Development*, vol 1, no 2, pp239–254

Van den Bor, W., Holen, P., Wals, A. and Filho, W. (2000) *Integrating Concepts of Sustainability into Education for Agriculture and Rural Development*, Peter Lang, Frankfurt

Chapter 4

Third-wave Sustainability in Higher Education: Some (Inter)national Trends and Developments

Arjen E.J. Wals and John Blewitt

Introduction

Conventional wisdom holds that all education is good, and the more of it one has, the better… The truth is that without significant precautions, [it] can equip people merely to be more effective vandals of the Earth (Orr, 2004, p6).

Sustainability is not just another issue to be added to an overcrowded curriculum, but a gateway to a different view of curriculum, of pedagogy, of organizational change, of policy and particularly of ethos. At the same time, the effect of patterns of unsustainability on our current and future prospects is so pressing that the response of higher education should not be predicated only on the 'integration of sustainability' into higher education, because this invites a limited, adaptive, response… We need to see the relationship the other way around – that is, the necessary transformation of higher education towards the integrative and more whole state implied by a systemic view of sustainability in education and society (Sterling, 2004, p50).

In this chapter, we will highlight what we call examples of 'third-wave' sustainability in higher education from outside the UK.[1] Third-wave sustainability in HE refers to a university's attempt to re-orient teaching, learning, research and university–community relationships in such a way that sustainability becomes an emergent property of its core activities. We do so by teasing out some didactic and pedagogic stepping stones for re-orienting teaching and learning towards sustainability. We will draw on exemplary initiatives from Europe, North America and Africa. First, we will provide a brief sketch of the evolution of sustainability in HE.

Sustainability in HE is no longer novel. Across the globe, national, regional and trans-regional networks for what might be termed sustainable HE have been set up, the number of international meetings and networks focusing on this area continues to grow, and several declarations on sustainability in HE have been signed in the past ten or so years by university provosts, deans and rectors. Earlier, in 1990, *The Talloires Declaration* became the first official statement made by university administrators of a commitment to environmental sustainability in higher education. The *Declaration* is a ten-point action plan for incorporating sustainability and environmental literacy into teaching, research, operations and outreach at colleges and universities. It has since been signed by more than 350 university presidents and chancellors in over 40 countries (ULSF, 1990). At a more concrete level, the *Tufts CLEAN!* initiative from Tufts University's Environmental Center in the USA became one of the first university attempts to reduce the environmental impact of a higher education institution (Hammond Creighton, 1998).

The integration of 'environment' – in many ways a predecessor of 'sustainability' – into the HE curriculum in Western education can be traced back to the 1970s and 1980s, when pressing environmental issues led to the rise of such fields as environmental engineering and environmental studies. However, the emergence of 'environment' in HE hardly resulted in the rethinking of teaching and learning, even though some environmental studies programmes called for an integrated approach and/or a more problem-based curriculum. Since the late 1990s, declarations and commitments on sustainability in higher education have been numerous and ambitious (see Table 4.1), but the gap between rhetoric and reality is equally striking. Bekessy et al (2007), for instance, provide some evidence that non-binding declarations rarely influence a university's sustainability practices.

Whereas such declarations tend to be oriented towards 'Northern' or 'Western' HEIs, more recent declarations and cooperative agreements between universities also involve institutions in other parts of the world (UN Environment Programme [UNEP], 2008).

Perhaps the most visible changes and commitments lie in HEIs' efforts to reduce their ecological footprint by improving environmental management of their estates. An analysis[2] of the *International Journal of Sustainability in Higher Education* (*IJSHE*) reveals that during the first nine years of its publication (i.e. up to 2009), the overwhelming majority of articles focus on issues such as environmental management, university greening and reducing a university's ecological footprint (see Table 4.2). In the more recent volumes there are more articles on pedagogy, learning, instruction, community outreach and partner-

Table 4.1 Common principles of sustainability in HE declarations

Declaration[3]	Moral obligation	Public outreach	Sustainable physical operations	Ecological literacy	Development of interdisciplinary curriculum	Encouragement of sustainable research	Partnership with government, NGOs and industry	Inter-university cooperation
1990 – Talloires	×	×	×	×	×	×	×	×
1991 – Halifax	×	×	×	×			×	×
1993 – Kyoto	×	×	×	×		×	×	×
1994 – Swansea	×	×	×	×		×		×
1997 – COPERNICUS	×	×		×		×	×	
2000 – Lüneburg	×	×			(×)	×	×	×

Note: Blank = Not addressed; × = addressed; (×) = partially addressed.
Source: Wright, 2004, p13

ships. Not surprisingly, earlier volumes contained more articles on the meaning of sustainability and SD and the integration of sustainability into disciplines such as chemistry, engineering, architecture, natural resource management, accounting and industrial design. Indeed, many natural scientists continue to argue that the lack of precision in the concept of sustainability remains a distinct problem. Schultz, Brand, Kopfmuller and Ott from Berlin's Wuppertal Institute for Climate, Environment and Energy insist that it is the responsibility of science to build a coherent theory of SD. Only a strong theoretical and normative conception of sustainability, based on an 'enlightened anthropocentrism', can really provide the necessary clarity that will allow progress to be scientifically measured and thus inform politics and the policy-making process effectively. They believe a sound theory will offset the confusion and diffuseness of much public debate and (mis)understanding (Schultz et al, 2008, p477).

The more fundamental challenge of re-orienting teaching, learning and research in a way that will lead to new mental models and competencies appears more problematic. Firmly established empirical and analytical frameworks are invariably reductionist and mechanistic and have come to characterize 'higher' education. Although the sector is notoriously resistant to change, we are currently witnessing the emergence of a 'third wave' of sustainability in HE, following the environmental and greening the campus waves. This third wave focuses precisely on the teaching and learning implications of sustainability; it resonates with Stephen Sterling's observation that the nature of sustainability requires a fundamental change of epistemology, and therefore, of both education and learning. He writes that 'the process of sustainable development or sustainable living is essentially one of learning, while the context of learning is essentially that of sustainability' (Sterling, 2004, p52). The analysis of *IJSHE* articles does reveal 31

Table 4.2 *Thematic focus of articles published in first nine volumes of IJSHE*

Area	No of articles	%
Environmental management/ecological footprint/campus greening	44	25
Integrating sustainability in existing disciplines	31	17
Pedagogy, learning and instruction	31	17
Philosophy/principles/concepts	19	11
Community outreach/partnerships	15	8
Policy/organizational learning/institutional commitment	15	8
Course development/curriculum	7	4
Auditing, assessment, quality assurance	10	6
Research	3	2
Competencies, professional development	3	2
Total[4]	178	100

that discuss alternative forms of teaching and learning that tend to be associated with re-orientation towards sustainability.

Learning and instruction approaches and methods featured in these include:

- interdisciplinary learning, project-based learning;
- gaming, computer simulations, distance learning;
- back-casting, case studies, policy laboratories;
- problem-based learning, bootstrapping, values education;
- ecological footprint analysis, transdisciplinary learning;
- experiential approaches, reflective journal writing.

Later in this chapter, we will focus in on third-wave sustainability. Before doing so, however, we will address some regional flavours or trends from North America, continental Europe and Africa. These flavours and trends not only help us understand the different manifestations of sustainability in higher education that are 'learning-based', they also point out some important regional differences.

Regional trends

The *IJSHE* analysis reveals that most internationally reported research on sustainability in HE stems from Europe and North America (Table 4.3), which may possibly be a consequence of the geographical make-up of the editorial board and/or the geographical pattern of institutional subscriptions.

Indeed, by far the most (reported) research on sustainability and case studies in HE originate in Europe or North America, although some fascinating work is also being carried out in Asia, Oceania, Latin America and Africa, where there is a strong interest in the transformative processes of capacity building, poverty reduction and health promotion (Wals, 2009). To illustrate this we have included in this section some of the work that is being done in the Mainstreaming Environment and Sustainability in African Universities (MESA) partnership.

Table 4.3 *Geographical focus of articles published in first nine volumes of IJSHE*

Region	No of articles
North America	38
Europe	32
Asia	8
Oceania	14
Africa	3
Latin America & Caribbean	5
Total[3]	100

It should also be noted that some regional developments have received some encouragement through the formation of Regional Centres of Expertise (RCEs) after negotiations for the Fifth Ministerial Environment for Europe Conference, which took place in Kiev in 2003 (Mochizuki and Fadeeva, 2008). In 2005 in Nagoya, Japan, at a conference celebrating the Asia-Pacific launch of the UN DESD, the UN University (UNU) announced the formation of seven Regional Centres of Expertise on ESD involving collaboration and cooperation between HEIs and other formal and non-formal educational providers (Elias, 2006). By June 2009, the number of RCEs had increased to 62, with centres in Africa, North America, Asia, Europe and the Middle East, although there was just one in Latin America (Curitiba-Parana). The impetus behind this initiative has been the desire to stimulate action, the creation of vertical partnerships (i.e. between different levels of government) and horizontal partnerships (i.e. between different local stakeholders), and opening up stakeholders to dialogue and change to remedy the deficiencies in globally dominant unsustainable education systems. The overall aim is to establish local and regional knowledge bases that are both culturally sensitive and relevant to their areas that can in a relatively short period establish vibrant and effective communities of practice (Fadeeva, 2007). The pedagogic emphasis is on knowledge creation through active, contextually grounded learning, although the most common barriers and obstacles RCEs face are ignorance of ESD principles and the institutional compartmentalization of teaching and research in disciplinary silos and industrial era mindsets (Mochizuki and Fadeeva, 2008). Many RCEs are fostering action research as a means of establishing new learning spaces and opportunities (Mochizuki and Fadeeva, 2008).

North America

Based on an analysis of the 38 *IJSHE* articles that address developments in the USA and/or Canada, it is clear that a vast majority of them focus on 'greening the campus', improving environmental management and reducing ecological footprints, often looking for ways to minimize the environmental impact and negative social impacts of a university's operations such as food services, purchasing, mobility, energy, waste, student housing and so on. These articles frequently discuss ways of including students and staff in generating and implementing new sustainable practices. Students often find that their campus is becoming part of their formal and informal learning environment, with projects exploring green building design, social and mental well-being, waste reduction and renewable energy generation (Savanick et al, 2008). An example of this might be the environmental technology centre at Sonoma State University that fosters a 'pedagogy of place' (Rohwedder, 2004) or the energy-efficient 'building that teaches' at Brown University (Fickes, 2002). Many universities in the USA are seeking certification from the Green Building Council's Leadership in Energy and Environmental Design (LEED) scheme (US Green Building Council, 2009).

Generally, however, HE in North America has not been redesigned in a way that transcends the physical aspects and changes the DNA of the university. David Orr, Professor of Environmental Studies and Politics at Oberlin College, has done pioneering work in this area at his own institution over the years, but not without some administrative resistance (Orr, 2006). However, many universities do have a strong community outreach focus that increasingly addresses sustainability issues, such as Emory University's sustainability initiative (Emory University, 2008) or Ithaca College's community outreach programme (Ithaca College, 2007). M'Gonigle and Starke (2006) write of the University of Victoria in British Columbia becoming a key driver of sustainability in the provincial capital itself by involving the whole of the community.

Europe

In continental Europe, progress in integrating sustainability in HE has been variable but rarely spectacular. In Spain, for instance, the biggest handicap to progress is the common and residual resistance to change at HEIs and a high degree of inconsistency in decision-making processes in curriculum design and innovation (Benayas et al, 2007). For example, the experience of mainstreaming environmental goals in the Technical University of Catalonia's overall strategic planning has increased the level of 'greening' but has not incorporated sustainable development in the redesign of specific curriculum programmes (Benayas et al, 2007). For some practitioners, opportunities and hopes for significant change are anticipated with the consolidation of the Bologna Process, as this leads to a major overhaul of what tend to be rather rigid and historically grounded structures by creating a European Higher Education Area. By contrast, in Sweden, a 2006 amendment to the Higher Education Act (SFS, 1992) charged universities to promote sustainable development in all their activities. This legislative amendment greatly aided the formation and development of the RCE in the Skane region in the south of Sweden (Axelsson et al, 2008) showing the importance of government in furthering sustainability in HE. More generally, the concept of SD has generally focused on ecological sustainability, but it is slowly being widened to encompass social, economic and cultural dimensions (Djuberg et al, 2007). Centres promoting education, research and cooperation both within a university and alongside local, regional, national and international actors have been established at several universities, although most institutions report that they are still in the initial stages of integrating sustainability into their curricula (Axelsson et al, 2008).

In Belgium, sustainability is not a structural part of the curriculum (Rottiers, 2007). Here, heavy emphasis is placed on environmental management. The *EcoCampus initiative* – set up and supported by the Flemish Government – encourages, rewards and assists HEIs in Flanders in moving towards environmental sustainability and sound operational and management practices (Rottiers, 2007).

The concept of SD can be found in many courses in German universities, but as the 'UNI 21' study published by the Federal Ministry of Education and Research (BMBF, 2004) makes clear, this has occurred as a result of action and initiatives emerging from individual HEIs themselves. Germany has an educational system whose responsibility is devolved to the individual states, making a nationally unified strategy for integrating sustainability into HEIs quite challenging. An interesting phenomenon in the German context is the emergence of 'Gestaltungskompetenz' as a concept to help articulate the qualities, competencies and attributes learners need to develop when engaging with sustainability issues. Gestaltungskompetenz is sometimes described as the forward-looking ability 'to modify and model the future of the societies in which you live, participating actively in the spirit of sustainable development' (De Haan, 2006, p22). Although rather vague, this definition is nonetheless consistent with a number of key characteristics of SD that are likely to become increasingly evident as Gestaltungskompetenz is rolled out across the German education system. As the *Report of the Federal Government on Education for Sustainable Development* noted, 'the need for Gestaltungskompetenz can be substantiated in terms of education theory and at a pedagogic level using the principle of sustainable development' (BMBF, 2002, p14). A national ESD pilot programme took place between 1999 and 2004, but it has yet to be fully implemented in every state. A fuller definition is provided by the Quality and Competences Working Groups of the Transfer-21 programme (Transfer-21, 2006, p12):

Gestaltungskompetenz describes pupils' abilities to apply knowledge on sustainable development and to identify problems of non-sustainable development. This means they are able to draw conclusions from studies into the present or future in the areas of ecological, economic and social development in their varying relations of interdependence, and take decisions on the basis of these conclusions, understand these decisions and apply them individually, as part of a community and politically in order to further sustainable development processes.

Thus, Gestaltungskompetenz aims to fashion an historical, systems-orientated and largely holistic framework for understanding and action. There are elements of similarity with both deep ecology and critical cultural theory in framework design and application, with specific acknowledgement of the importance of mediation, dialogue and social participation; but it also seems that a more incisive recognition of, and engagement with, the dangers and negative consequences of societal power relationships, conflict, inequality and ideology is required. The pilot ESD programme that ran until 2004 has yet to be fully implemented in every state. In the context of sustainability, elements of Gestaltungskompetenz include:

- competence to think in a forward-looking manner, to deal with uncertainty and with predictions, expectations and plans for the future;
- competence to work in an interdisciplinary manner;
- competence to achieve open-minded perception, trans-cultural understanding and cooperation;
- participatory competence;
- planning and implementation competence;
- ability to feel empathy, sympathy and solidarity;
- competence to motivate oneself and others;
- competence to reflect in a distanced manner on individual and cultural concepts (Michelsen and Adomssent, 2007, p22).

In the Netherlands, the Dutch Foundation for Sustainable Development in Higher Education (DHO) was established in 1998 and within ten years was exerting significant influence on almost every HEI in the country. The DHO aims to develop learning opportunities, innovative learning environments and methodologies in HE that enable individuals to develop competence in sustainable development (DHO, 2009). More specifically, DHO aims to stimulate such opportunities for all students at institutes of higher learning in the Netherlands to enable them to gain:

- insight into the concept of sustainable development;
- insight into what their discipline can contribute to sustainable development;
- the competence to collaborate with representatives of other disciplines;
- the competence to develop strategies to work on sustainable development in their future careers (DHO, 2009).

DHO has six main projects to integrate SD into HE.

1   *North–South*: interdisciplinary, intercultural student projects on SD in Asia, Africa and Latin America.
2   *Challenging experts*: integrating SD into various disciplines.
3   "*Auditing Instrument for Sustainability in Higher Education*" (AISHE): see Box 4.1
4   *Charter for Universities of Professional Education*: system of granting and support to integrate sustainable development in colleges.
5   *Transdisciplinary education*: in the transdisciplinary education model, students research SD together with various stakeholders.
6   *Past, present and futures*: future-embedded education in SD.

Box 4.1 Auditing Instrument for Sustainability in Higher Education (AISHE)

Although many universities want to integrate SD as a theme into education, many of them do not know how to do it in practice. By examining all aspects of the curriculum using AISHE, a list of at least 20 substantial targets will be produced to refocus the curriculum towards sustainable development. The AISHE procedure is as follows:

- A faculty or study board, dean or coordinator decides to audit a study programme.
- At least one coordinator or study manager, ten teachers and three students are committed to attend the full audit.
- A full audit takes two meetings of half a day, two separate days or one full day.
- During the first meeting, the AISHE consultants explain the audit and afterwards all participants fill in a list of 20 criteria.
- During the second 'consensus' meeting, all personal scores are discussed.
- The first step of the second meeting is to reach consensus on the present situation with respect to SD, the second step is to explore the desired situation and formulate action actions for improvement.
- At the end of the meeting, three to five items are selected as priorities.
- All results of the meeting are entered directly into the AISHE software tool and the results are accessible through clear, comprehensible diagrams.
- Universities may receive the Certificate for Sustainability in Higher Education.

Besides the minimum audit, the AISHE team offers a few extra options. Quite often, participants do not have a clear idea about SD, so a few meetings on the basic principles are recommended before the first audit takes place. After an audit, the AISHE team can offer extra tools to support the implementation of the plans put forward during the process. Another audit of the curriculum is highly recommended after about one or two years to take note of the results achieved.

Source: Roorda 2004 and DHO, 2009

Sustainable development has been integrated into the Dutch and Flemish accreditation system. This means that there is a set of criteria against which degree programmes can be assessed and recognized for their efforts to promote SD. In general it is the more professionally orientated universities, the former polytechnics, rather than the more academic and research-intensive institutions, that have made most progress in integrating sustainability into curricula (Wals, 2007b). In the Russian Federation, where the HE system includes 129 universities and covers a huge landmass, there has been a general shift away from general environmental education to ESD. Geography has played a leading role, not least because it can act as a bridge between the natural and human sciences and because there is an academic heritage of nature management derived from the work of the Soviet scientist, David L. Armand within the discipline; Armand's 1964 book *For Us and*

For Our Grandchildren prefigures much that is found in the seminal Brundtland Report. The Moscow State University is taking a leading role in advancing sustainability in Russian higher education with Kasimov et al writing:

> Ideas of sustainable development are being incorporated into many disciplines and courses by the method of so-called 'embedded education'; the material in existing courses is used to provide a vehicle for teaching the ideas of sustainable development and is subsequently built up into independent educational blocks or courses in sustainable development
>
> (Kasimov et al, 2005, p57).

Africa[5]

In Africa, the MESA partnership programme was established in 2004 with the support of UNESCO and UNEP. It aims to create a mechanism and supportive structure for universities to respond to environmental, SD and climate change challenges confronting the continent, emphasizing that African universities have been engaged in a long and complex struggle to establish themselves as knowledge generators and disseminators, as partners of the state and communities and as critical voices of and in society (UNEP, 2008). MESA refers to Mahmood Mamdani and other African intellectuals who suggest that to continue with this project does not simply involve an 'adoption' of institutional rhetoric on SD, or development of new structures and projects in universities but a deeper engagement with the remaining institutional legacies of colonialism (and neo-colonialism) in Africa (Okolie, 2003). This includes an examination of the current institutional form of the university itself, and contemporary trends to marketize and privatize university services in society. It, therefore, involves a broader postcolonial intellectual project of reconceptualizing African universities, their relationship to democracy and the societies, cultures and environments in which they are embedded (UNEP, 2006a and 2006b).

Priorities for renewing higher education in Africa include: the transformation of African universities into 'development universities' that respond to local and regional needs while also enhancing the continent's competitiveness in the global knowledge economy; the positioning of the continent's universities as partners and resources for regional cooperation and integration; and the mobilization of all stakeholders in a concerted effort to share responsibilities and create synergies in the universities' renewal (UNEP, 2008).

The MESA partnership holds that mainstreaming SD encompasses all three core functions of a university: teaching, research and community engagement, and also includes management and extramural partnerships. Mainstreaming environment and sustainability concerns is value-based, involving transformative learning processes and new ways of engagement that are oriented towards change at institutional and societal levels (UNEP 2008). Mainstreaming cannot be prescriptive and so requires a participatory process of co-definition as to what can or ought to be integrated and how this might best be done in different universities, countries and other institutional frameworks.

In 2004, a baseline study commissioned by UNEP found that in most African universities the subject of the environment is still mainly taught as a separate course (25 per cent) or as a fringe aspect of a limited number of disciplines such as ecology, hydrology, climatology or geography, with the main interest being in the sciences (30 per cent). Few teacher training, law, engineering or humanities faculties had integrated environment and SD issues. Only around 5 per cent of universities had a special institutional framework (such as a centre, institute or school) addressing the interdisciplinary nature of environment and sustainability issues (UNEP, 2006b).

Significantly, the focus of the MESA partnership lies in creating more systemic changes in the way universities are organized, the way they connect with the wider community and the primary processes they support rather than on reducing their ecological footprints or improving their environmental management practices. This is reflected in the partnership's future priorities, which include more capacity-building initiatives such as leadership, curriculum change, community engagement and research. A stronger systems approach also needs to be developed to support systemic changes so innovations do not overly depend on individual efforts. University leaders need to become more involved and sub-regional networks are also required to provide for more localized, networked interactions, as well as stronger integration with university policy systems. According to Akpezi Ogbuigwe, UNEP's Nairobi-based Head of Environmental Education, progress is being made – by mid-2009, there were at least 50 university courses that had been revised in the direction of including or considering SD, while the MESA network included 200 academics from 65 universities across 32 African countries. Other outcomes, she reports, include changes in research, curriculum and teaching practice, networking among different countries, increased engagement with e-learning, a systematic approach to change initiatives in universities supported by MESA, and business–university–community partnerships (Gower, 2009).

Transformative learning

Although the above regional reviews are at best snapshots, they do suggest that the interest in sustainability in HE is becoming more mainstream but also that most involved are looking for the kind of engagement with sustainability that transcends adding it on to an overcrowded curriculum or the 'efficient environmental management' of universities' infrastructure. There appears to be a common search for what an existentially relevant and meaningful engagement with sustainability might be in a regional context.

Perhaps sustainability in HE can best be regarded as both the product of continual collaborative development and as an engaging creative process involving a variety of participants. Moving towards sustainability as a learning process has until now received less attention than various concepts of sustainability predetermined and taught by experts (Wals and Jickling, 2002; Jickling and Wals,

2008). Although scientists such as Schultz et al (2008) may call for a single strict definition, this would be to deny the concept's inherent multi-dimensionality and the need for it to adapt to and with the world as we make it

One question must be raised, though: how can academia help develop collective agency, personal capabilities and capacities that generate positive but perhaps unforeseen outcomes? This is related to determining the kind of competence required to contribute to sustainability, and academia's role in developing such competence among all its staff and students. We agree with Raven and Stephenson (2001) here that competence in this context does not refer to getting the job done effectively – after all, there is no consensus about what 'the' job entails – but rather to making an effective contribution to society by going beyond mental and disciplinary boundaries, structural barriers and physical borders, as well as by influencing the systems in which the competence is developed. From this perspective, sustainability can, at the institutional level, be viewed as a catalyst for systemic institutional and organizational change.

Third-wave sustainability in HE above all means the creation of space for transformative learning: learning that helps people transcend the 'given', the 'ordinary' and the often 'routine ways of doing' to create a new dynamic and alternative ways of seeing and doing. Space is needed for:

- alternative paths of development;
- participation minimally distorted by power relations;
- pluralism, cultural diversity and minority perspectives;
- dialogue and deep consensus, but also for respectful disagreement and differences;
- autonomous and deviant thinking;
- self-determination;
- contextual differences (Wals and Heymann, 2004; Wals, 2007a).

Perhaps, in referring again to the German notion of Gestaltungskompetenz, an essential quality that needs to be developed in students and staff alike is the ability to look at the world as it unfolds from multiple vantage points. A phrase we might introduce is 'Gestaltswitching' – the switching between different mindsets. In the context of sustainability, we need to be able to switch back and forth between disciplinary perspectives, time perspectives (past–present–future), space perspectives (local–regional–global), cultural perspectives and perhaps even between human and other or more-than-human perspectives. This Gestaltswitching requires again the creation of space for pluralism and diversity in both research and teaching, as well as the blurring of the boundaries between science and society. The result indeed might be referred to as transformative learning that also allows for transdisciplinary, transgeographical, transtemporal, trans-species and transcultural learning (Wals, 2006; Blewitt, 2008).

An example of this might be an Austrian regional planning project showing that success in transdisciplinary cooperation can be enhanced by the early participation of non-academics in the project and by the creation of an effective structure for networking, communication, joint decision-making and responsibility for and ownership of ideas during the process (Muhar et al, 2006). This requires time and 'dialogic space'. Evaluating this case, Muhar et al write:

> To create dialogue space for a transdisciplinary process, it is necessary that all participants realize that they do not need "the others" but rather "us all" as equal partners with different expertise. Furthermore, it is essential to give space for different perspectives – using, developing and reflecting specific methodological and research frameworks (researchers and students), learning as a preparation for future occupation or profession (students), or to find answers for everyday life challenges (actors). All participants need to reflect their own role in this process. Providing space for this reflection is a key factor in initiating transdisciplinarity (p306).

Barth et al (2007) in turn stress the importance of blurring the boundaries between formal and informal learning in this respect, concluding that to develop and acquire 'sustainability competencies' at a higher level involves a variety of contexts enabling both formal and informal learning. It is therefore necessary for universities to nurture a learning culture that allows interaction, engagement and an interplay of perspectives extending beyond the walls of the academy (Barth et al, 2007; Holden et al, 2008). Likewise, research on adult environmental education in Thailand and elsewhere shows that similar success and effectiveness depends on respect for, and integration of, local knowledge with professional or academic knowledge and expertise, and appropriately resourced local authority structures that enable participation, planning, problem-solving and social learning (Fien et al, 2002).

Recent international statements and declarations on sustainability in higher education are beginning to reflect this turn towards transformative, cross-boundary learning (see Box 4.2 for an example). Yet these statements are often generated by what we might call the pedagogic backbone of an institution, which tends to be rather weak. As a result, the theories and lessons derived from pedagogues and pedagogical research have not, as yet, significantly informed the practices of other academic faculty members, who are unattuned to sustainability. As Svanstrom et al (2008) remind us, the educators must themselves be educated:

> [What] must not be forgotten [is] the need to provide capacity building for the educators. They need to be knowledgeable in sustainability and in education for SD, otherwise they will not weave SD into their courses with the appropriate teaching methodologies. In order for this to happen, teachers must also be given the appropriate resources as well as other incentives, which may challenge traditional educational structures and reward systems (p349).

Gambini (2006) suggests that resistance in the academy often mirrors or articulates wider cultural resistance to, and suspicion of, sustainability in society.

Box 4.2 Excerpts from the section on higher education in The Gothenburg Declaration on ESD

HEIs need to become open ESD centres and hubs

HEIs can become ESD interfaces between the local and the global community, addressing local sustainability issues but also using global networks to take advantage of perspectives and expertise grounded in contexts elsewhere. HEI expertise in both ESD and SD needs to be easily accessible to all members of society. This expertise needs to be globally and openly accessible, through for instance open-source internet-based platforms, to allow for scientists, community groups and individual citizens from around the world to contribute to and benefit from this new kind of research. Mechanisms need to be in place that allow all members of society to contribute to the continuous advancement of (E)SD expertise.

HEIs need to develop knowledge and education that penetrates through and transcends disciplines, space, time and cultures

Our search for a more sustainable world requires a spirit of innovation and cutting-edge knowledge that can deal with the kind of complexity, uncertainty and risks that characterize SD challenges. HEIs should be challenged to advance systemic thinking by examining connections, relationships and interdependencies. Simultaneously, HEIs should research, develop and introduce new forms of learning that can help people understand and engage in SD. Hence, adequate and robust theories as well as practices of learning and change need to be developed, researched and shared by multidisciplinary teams.

HEIs need to contribute to the development of (E)SD-competence in all, both in and outside the higher education community

HEIs have a key role to play in capacity building and competence development for (E)SD through courses, professional development programmes, community outreach activities and post-initial education and training, in both the public and private sector. Developing this role could help various groups in society become more competent in exploring the sustainability dimensions of their personal and professional lives. HEIs should provide resources for all members of the university community who can be considered SD-change agents and for those who wish to pursue careers in ESD in or outside the university structure.

Source: Holmberg et al, 2008

Consequently, there is probably a need to go beyond the recognition of differing perspectives expressed in international declarations, affirmations, pedagogic research and theorizing. Changes in the wider society, in cultures more generally, are required; and here, the transformative role for primary and secondary educators, community workers, media professionals, vocational trainers, cultural heritage workers and many others is of supreme importance. There needs to be an understanding that learning for sustainability involves recognizing the affordances

---

Box 4.3 Recommendation on sustainability research in The Gothenburg Declaration on ESD

Support sustainability research

National and transnational research programmes on SD should be supported with structural funding that is not dependent on private funding. Such structural funding should be tailored towards research programmes that explicitly emphasize transdisciplinary research focusing on SD-related issues. This research, supported by a wide range of methodologies both old and new, would not only focus on a better understanding of sustainability but also on forms of governance, management, community engagement and citizen participation. Researchers seeking to make a career in this emerging field need to be supported by their home institutions. Such support also means that publishing in niche journals that may not have Institute for Scientific Information status but provide a platform for integrated research on SD and ESD issues should be actively supported. HEIs should create special appointments for those who specialize in sustainability-oriented research.

Source: Holmberg et al, 2008

---

offered throughout the social world, throughout the course of life and the social environment in which such learning takes place (Blewitt, 2006).

Transformative learning and research

Having privileged the transformative learning aspect of sustainability in HE, we now turn to the important role of research and the relationship between research and teaching. It is clear that there is a need to rethink both the meaning of 'research' and the relationship between research, teaching and learning when viewing sustainability as a normative process. There are early signs of changes in this direction. The journal *Environmental Education Research* recently devoted an entire issue to the topic of 'Sustainability in Higher Education Research' (*Environmental Education Research*, 2008). In the USA, the National Science Foundation (NSF) is now using the term 'transformative research' to refer to 'research that has the capacity to revolutionize existing fields, create new subfields, cause paradigm shifts, support discovery and lead to radically new technologies' (NSF, 2007). *The Gothenburg Declaration* has a special recommendation on 'research' in higher education (Table 8) calling for structural funding, transdisciplinary methodologies, interprofessional and citizen engagement publishing in journals that support both SD and ESD issues and the appointment of specialist staff able to undertake effective sustainability-orientated research (Ottosson and Samuelsson, 2008). The Ahmebadad Declaration of the fourth International Conference on Environmental Education in 2007 also urges governments and national research bodies to 'integrate emancipatory, participatory and other forms of transformative research approaches into international, national and institutional research agendas' (UNESCO, 2007, p11).

Conclusion

The question of sustainability's place in HE curricula is slowly shifting from one of campus greening and curriculum integration to one of innovation and systemic change across the whole university. With this shift, space emerges for transformative learning and research emphasizing 'learning and research for knowing, doing and, indeed, being' (Wals and Bawden, 2000), echoing in some ways the 1996 Delors Report on lifelong learning, which speaks of learning to do, to be, to know and to live together. The resulting third-wave sustainability requires permeability between disciplines, the university and wider community and between cultures, along with the competence to integrate, connect, confront and, as much as possible, reconcile multiple ways of looking at the world.

To create pathways towards such systemic redesign will require healthy opportunism, such as taking advantage of current trends in education (competence-based education) and society (the rise of corporate social responsibility and the green economy, increased concern about global warming and so on), but also a healthy dose of creativity (building unlikely partnerships and coalitions, creating space for innovation) and risk-taking at all levels (teachers, researchers, management, higher education policy and others). For instance, it makes sense to advocate 'sustainability competence' and to develop ways of fashioning such competence. Conceptualizing and applying sustainability competence can become a useful exercise in embedding sustainability in many bachelors and masters degrees, which in turn requires a parallel process of reconceptualizing teaching, learning and research and reconfiguring university–community relationships.

At present, most universities are too often still advancing the kind of thinking, teaching and research that leads to unsustainability and ignoring alternative ways of knowing and being, that are not rooted in Western (scientific) traditions. As HE becomes globalized, globalization needs to be contested politically in the academy. As the Indian scholar M.G. Jackson (2003) argues, the ideological dominance of globalization, together with its corollary, a Westernized model of HE practice, must itself be challenged in that globalization and internationalization are inexplicably linked with a notion of progress that is tied to Western notions of economic development, growth and the fiduciary interests of corporate business. Additionally, Jackson argues that the idea of progress is entirely Western and lacks deep historical or cultural roots in non-Western societies. The need, then, is perhaps to de-Westernize higher education.

Despite the early signs of a transition in some parts of the academic community, sustainability is still by and large largely external to the HE student, academic faculty member and administrator. Too often, 'sustainable development' is just another course or research project as expendable as anything else if it does not pay its way. To overcome this, we academics need to reshape deeply entrenched routines, structures and practices by taking advantage of the privileged position universities have in our society. We need to confront our own assumptions and probably stand outside our systems to gain a clearer view of how this necessary systemic change can occur.

References

Armand, D.L. (1964) *For Us and Our Grandchildren*, Mysl, Moscow [in Russian]

Axelsson, H., Sonesson, K. and Wickenberg, P. (2008) 'Why and how do universities work for sustainability in higher education (HE)?', *IJSHE*, vol 9, no 4, pp469–478

Barth, M., Godemann, J., Rieckmann, M. and Stoltenberg, U. (2007) 'Developing key competencies for sustainable development in higher education', *IJSHE*, vol 8 no 4, pp416–430

Bekessy, S.A., Samson, K., Clarkson, R.E. (2007) 'The failure of non-binding declarations to achieve university sustainability: A need for accountability', *IJSHE*, vol 8, no 3, pp301–316

Benayas, J., Alba, D., Ferrer, D. and Buckland, H. (2007) 'Education for sustainable development strategies in Spanish universities', in Wals, A.E.J (ed, 2007b), pp5–7

Blewitt, J. (2006) *The Ecology Of Learning: Sustainability, Lifelong Learning and Everyday Life*, Earthscan, London

Blewitt, J. (2008) *Understanding Sustainable Development*, Earthscan, London

BMBF (2002) *Report of the Federal Government on Education for Sustainable Development*. Bundesministerium für Bildung und Forschung, Bonn

BMBF (2004) *UNI 21 – Hochschulbildung für eine nachhaltige Entwicklung [UNI 21 – University Education for Sustainable Development]*, Bundesministerium für Bildung und Forschung, Berlin

De Haan, G. (2006) 'The BLK "21" programme in Germany: a 'Gestaltungskompetenz'-based model for education for sustainable development', *Environmental Education Research*, vol 12, no 1, pp19–32

Delors, J. (1996) *Learning: The Treasure Within*, UNESCO, Paris

DHO (2009) homepage www.dho.nl, accessed 27 August 2009

Djuberg, M., Wilenus, M. and Sammalisto, S. (2007) 'Education for sustainable development in Swedish universities', in Wals, A.E.J. (ed; 2007b), pp 9–14

Elias, D. (2006) 'UNESCO's approach to implementing the Decade of Education for Sustainable Development (DESD) in Asia and the Pacific', *Australian Journal of Environmental Education*, vol 22, no 1, pp273–75

Emory University (2008) *Sustainability Initiatives*, www.sustainability.emory.edu, accessed 27 August 2009

Environmental Education Research (2008) 'Special issue: Sustainability in higher education research', vol 14, no 6

Fadeeva, Z. (2007) 'From centre of excellence to regional centre of expertise: Regional centres of expertise on education for sustainable development', In Wals, A.E.J. (ed; 2007a), pp245–264

Fickes, M. (2002) 'Campus buildings that teach lessons', *College Planning and Management*, vol 5, no 3, pp14–18

Fien, J., Ratanachai, C., Umaporn, M. and Suwannatchote, S. (2002) 'Participatory planning as environmental adult education: A case study of local environmental governance in Thailand', *Applied Environmental Education & Communication*, vol 1, no 4, pp255–262

Gambini, B. (2006) 'Cultural assumptions against sustainability: An international survey', *Journal of Geography in Higher Education*, vol 30, no 2, pp263–279

Gower, P. (2009) 'African universities' united response to climate change', *Mail & Guardian Online* 24 June, available at www.mg.co.za/article/2009-06-24-african-universities-united-response-to-climate-change, accessed 3 August 2009

Hammond Creighton, S. (1998) *Greening the Ivory Tower: Improving the Environmental Track Record of Universities, Colleges, and Other Institutions*, MIT Press, Boston MA

Holden, M., Elverum, D., Nesbit, S., Robinson, J., Yen, D. and Moore, J. (2008) 'Learning teaching in the sustainability classroom', *Ecological Economics*, vol 64, no 3, pp521–533

Holmberg, J., Lotz-Sistka, H., Samuelsson, B., Wals, A.E.J. and Wright, T. (2008) 'Specific recommendations on integrating ESD in higher education', In Ottosson, P. and Samuelsson, B. (eds), pp43–48

Ithaca College (2007) *Community Outreach*, available at www.ithaca.edu/sustainability/ outreach.php, accessed 27 August 2009

Jackson, M. G. (2003) 'Internationalising the university curriculum', *Journal of Geography in Higher Education*, vol 27, no 3, pp325–340

Jickling, B. and Wals, A.E.J. (2008) 'Globalization and environmental education: Looking beyond sustainable development', *Journal of Curriculum Studies*, vol 40, no 1, pp1–21

Kasimov, N.S., Malkhazova, S.M. and Romanova, E.P. (2005) 'Environmental education for sustainable development in Russia', *Journal of Geography in Higher Education*, vol 29, no 1, pp49–59

M'Gonigle, M. and Starke, J. (2006) *Planet U: Sustaining the World, Reinventing the University*, New Society Publishers, Gabriola Island

Michelsen, G. and Adomssent, M. (2007) 'Education for sustainable development strategies in German universities', In Wals, A.E.J. (ed: 2007b), pp 21–24

Mochizuki, Y. and Fadeeva, Z. (2008) 'Regional centres of expertise on education for sustainable development (RCEs): An overview', *IJSHE*, vol 9, no 4, pp369–381

Muhar, A., Vilsmaier, U., Glanzer, M. and Freyer, B. (2006) 'Initiating transdisciplinarity in academic case study teaching experiences from a regional development project in Salzburg, Austria', *IJSHE*, vol 7, no 3, pp293–308

US NSF (2007) 'National Science Board approves NSF plan to emphasize transformative research', available at www.nsf.gov/news/news_summ.jsp?cntn_id=109853, accessed 3 August 2009

Okolie, A.C. (2003) 'Producing knowledge for sustainable development in Africa: Implications for higher education', *Higher Education*, vol 46, no 2, pp235–260

Orr, D. (2004) *Earth in Mind: On Education, Environment, and the Human Prospect*, Island Press, Washington DC

Orr, D. (2006) *Design on the Edge: The Making of a High-Performance Building*, MIT Press, Cambridge MA

Ottosson, P. and Samuelsson, B. (eds) (2008) *The Gothenburg Recommendations on Education for Sustainable Development*, Chalmers University and Gothenburg University, Gothenburg; adopted as *The Gothenburg Declaration on 12 November 2008* in Gothenburg's Centre for Environment and Sustainability

Raven, J. and Stephenson, J. (2001) *Competence in the Learning Society*, Peter Lang Publishers, New York NY

Rohwedder, R. (2004) 'A pedagogy of place: The environmental technology center at Sonoma State University', In Corcoran, P.B. and Wals, A.E.J. (eds), *Higher Education and the Challenge of Sustainability: Problematics, Promise, and Practice*, Kluwer Academic Press, Dordrecht, pp293–305

Rottiers, I. (2007) 'Education for sustainable development strategies in Belgium universities', In Wals, 2007b, pp18–19

Roorda, N. (2004) 'Policy development for sustainability in higher education – Results of AISHE audits', In Corcoran, P.B. and Wals, A.E.J. (eds), *Higher Education and the Challenge of Sustainability: Problematics, Promise, and Practice*, Kluwer Academic Press,

Dordrecht, 2004, pp305–318

Savanick, S, Strong, R. and Manning, C. (2008) 'Explicitly linking pedagogy and facilities to campus sustainability: Lessons from Carleton College and the University of Minnesota', *Environmental Education Research*, vol 14, no 6, pp667–679

SFS (1992) Högskolelagen [The Higher Education Act] [Revised SFS 1992:1434, valid from 1 February 2006)

Schultz, J., Brand, F., Kopfmuller, J. and Ott, K. (2008) 'Building a "theory of sustainable development": Two salient conceptions within the German discourse', *International Journal of Environment and Sustainable Development*, vol 7, no 4, pp465–482

Sterling, S. (2004) 'Higher education, sustainability, and the role of systemic learning', In Corcoran, P.B. and Wals, A.E.J. (eds), *Higher Education and the Challenge of Sustainability: Problematics, Promise, and Practice*, Kluwer Academic Press, Dordrecht, pp47–70

Svanstrom, M., Lozano-Garcia, F.J. and Rowe, D. (2008) 'Learning outcomes for sustainable development in higher education', *IJSHE*, vol 9, no 3, pp339–351

Transfer-21. (2006) 'Developing quality at "ESD Schools" quality areas, principles & criteria', Freie Universität Berlin, available at www.bne-portal.de/coremedia/generator/unesco/en/04_ The_20UN_20Decade_20in_20Germany/06_ Publications_20and_20documents/Transfer_2021_20_20Developing_20 Quality_20at_20ESD_20Schools.pdf, accessed 27 August 2009

UNEP (2006a) *Africa Environment Outlook: Our environment, OurWealth*, UNEP, Nairobi

UNEP (2006b) *Education for Sustainable Development Innovations for African Universities*, UNEP, Nairobi, available at www.unep.org/training, accessed 23 June 2009

UNEP (2008) *Mainstreaming Environment and Sustainability in African Universities Partnership: Report on supporting universities to respond to environmental, sustainable development and climate change challenges*, UNEP, Nairobi

UNESCO (2007) *The Ahmedabad Declaration:A Call for Action*, Key outcome of the 4th International Conference on Environmental Education, Ahmedabad, India, November, available at www.unescobkk.org/fileadmin/user_upload/esd/documents/desd/ Final_20Recommendations.pdf, accessed 22 June 2009

ULSF (1990) *The Talloires Declaration*, available at www.ulsf.org/programs_talloires.html, accessed 3 August 2009

US Green Building Council (2009) Homepage www.usgbc.org, accessed 27 August 2009

Wals, A.E.J. (2006) 'The end of ESD… the beginning of transformative learning: Emphasizing the "E" in ESD', In Cantell, M. (ed), *Proceedings of the Seminar on Education for Sustainable Development*, Helsinki, 15 February 2006, Finnish UNESCO Commission, Helsinki, pp41–58

Wals, A.E.J. (2009) *Learning for a Sustainable World: Review of Contexts and Structures for Education for Sustainable Development – DESD M&E report*, UNESCO, Paris

Wals, A.E.J. and Bawden, R. (2000) *Integrating Sustainability into Agricultural Education: Dealing with Complexity, Uncertainty and Diverging Worldviews*, ICA, Ghent

Wals, A.E.J. and Jickling, B. (2002) '"Sustainability" in higher education: From double-think and newspeak to critical thinking and meaningful learning', *Higher Education Policy*, vol 15, no 2, pp121–131

Wals, A.E.J. and Heymann, F.V. (2004) 'Learning on the edge: Exploring the change potential of conflict in social learning for sustainable living', In Wenden, A. (ed), *Working toward a Culture of Peace and Social Sustainability*, SUNY Press, Albany NY

Wals, A.E.J. (ed) (2007a) *Social Learning Towards a Sustainable World*, Wageningen Academic Publishers, Wageningen

Wals, A.E.J. (ed) (2007b) *From Cosmetic Reform to Meaningful Integration: Implementing Education for Sustainable Development in Higher Education Institutes: The State of Affairs in Six European Countries*, International Meeting on Implementation of Education for Sustainable Development, Amsterdam, December 2007, DHO

Wright, T. (2004) 'The evolution of sustainability declarations in higher education', In Corcoran, P.B. and Wals, A.E.J. (eds), *Higher Education and the Challenge of Sustainability: Problematics, Promise, and Practice*, Kluwer Academic Press, Dordrecht

Notes

1   As most chapters in this volume contain a UK perspective, we have intentionally omitted the UK from this chapter.

2   Analysis was based on a quick scan of the journal's online tables of contents and the listed keywords for each article. A few articles that did not explicitly focus on sustainability in higher education were not included.

3   Declarations can be accessed online at:

Talloires: www.ulsf.org/programs_talloires.html

Halifax: www.iisd.org/educate/declarat/halifax.htm

Kyoto: www.unesco.org/iau/sd/sd_dkyoto.html

Swansea: www.iisd.org/educate/declarat/swansea.htm

COPERNICUS: www.unece.org/env/esd/information/COPERNICUS%20Guidelines.pdf

Lüneburg: http://portal.unesco.org/education/en/files/37585/11038209883LuneburgDeclaration.pdf/LuneburgDeclaration.pdf

4   Only articles that explicitly disclosed their geographical focus in the title and/or the articles' keywords have been included.

5   This section is based on the 2008 UNEP report on MESA Partnership support for universities in responding to environmental, sustainable development and climate change challenges (see References, UNEP, 2008).

Chapter 5

Education for Sustainability in the Business Studies Curriculum: Ideological Struggle

Delyse Springett

Ideological struggle as a basis for discourse

The concepts of sustainability and sustainable development (SD) have had a rocky ride trying to make it into the mainstream academic discourse of business studies. They have been described as 'the strangers at the door' (Springett and Kearins, 2001, p213). While business schools have generally not been averse to embracing new theories, programmes, courses and 'student markets', it has been harder for programmes about sustainability to become accepted, particularly if these are driven by a critical perspective. This chapter addresses the ideological struggle that education for sustainability in the business studies curriculum represents. To combine theory with praxis, a brief overview is provided of the principles and practices employed, the critical perspectives promoted and the pedagogical choices made for two postgraduate courses on business and sustainability. One of these was taught at Massey University in New Zealand from 1994 to 2006; the other has been taught at the University of Hong Kong (HKU) since 2005.

While theory, principles and recommendations for the practice of environmental education have been in place since the 1970s, it was the Brundtland Report (WCED, 1987) that helped to drive the turn to 'education for sustainable development' (ESD) and 'education for sustainability' (EfS). Ecologists and educators alike had concerns about the 'dangerous liaison' (Sachs, 1991, p252) between environment and economic growth that the Report's definition of 'sustainable *development*' rested on. Sustainable development was seen as the progeny of the management paradigm that had captured nature (*The Ecologist*, 1993). Harvey (1996), for example, notes that the WCED's framing of the concept was ultimately more about preserving a particular social order than preservation of nature. The goal of many educators consequently became 'education for *sustainability*'. At the same time, a stronger theoretical focus on critical and political education was proposed to prepare teachers and learners for an active role as agents of change for the environment and society (Robottom, 1992; Fien, 1993; Huckle and Sterling, 1996; Huckle, 1996). The approaches advocated for EfS have been ones that are holistic and interdisciplinary, multidisciplinary or transdisciplinary. Pedagogical choices that engage teachers and learners in action research and methods of learning have been advocated since these provide for experiential learning and help to create democratic learning contexts. Best regarded as a paradigm rather than a set of methods, the action methods approach gives students a higher degree of control over their own learning and provides a basis for responsible decision-making.[1] The role of the teacher who combines action methods with an approach based in critical theory is akin to Gramsci's classification of the 'organic' intellectual. The goal is to enable people to see the world in a new way through active participation in practical life (Gramsci, 1971).[2]

It has been noted (Gladwin et al, 1995; Springett and Kearins, 2001; Springett, 2005) that, after the Brundtland Report, business organizations and business leaders moved more quickly towards shaping the discourse of sustainability and sustainable development than did the higher education sector. Business has also tended to use the terms indiscriminately, as though they were synonymous (Springett, 2006b). The Brundtland Report did not eschew 'growth', giving business a place to stand in the environmental debate. This resulted in an alternative orthodoxy of 'eco-modernism' or 'greener-business-as-usual' – what Levy (1997, p126) calls 'political sustainability'. The World Business Council for Sustainable Development (WBCSD) and the International Chamber of Commerce (ICC) provided some of the earliest accounts of 'sustainable development', attempting to assert control over the language and practice of the concept (ICC, 1991; Schmidheiny, 1992; Willums and Golüke, 1992). The WBCSD coined the concept of 'eco-efficiency' (Schmidheiny, 1992). This construction has come to characterize much of the debate since the early 1990s, helping to drive out competing discourses about sustainability by steadfastly ignoring or appropriating them (Kearns and Springett, 2003, p191). Such business accounts have rarely risen above a discussion of principles of environmental management; nor do they envisage a significant change in values, core technologies or organizational shape. The eco-modernist narrative has generally disregarded the critical view that the structural basis of *un*sustainability is traceable to the means of production and consumption. Eco-efficiency promotes a benign paradigm of more 'management' (Springett, 2006b, p53) while ignoring the fact that much of management orthodoxy is antithetical to core radical themes of SD. At the same time, this swift assumption of leadership underlines that business is generally not subject to the inertia that can characterize higher education (Springett and Kearins, 2001), making business appear 'proactive'. Consultants and business leaders who have led some of the discourse (Elkington, 1994; 1997; Hawken, 1993; Hawken et al, 1999; Anderson, 1998) have generally failed to challenge the political and structural limitations of the concept. Levy (1997, p138) has seen this as an attempt to control 'the meaning of greening'. Much of the discourse about 'eco-efficiency', 'eco-modernism' or 'green business' has been dismissed by Newton and Harte (1997, p75) as 'green kitsch' or 'free-market environmentalism' (1997, p92). The issue that is assiduously avoided by the 'green business' promoters is the fact that sustainability calls for fundamental change to many of the structures promoted in modern capitalism.

The tertiary education sector, as 'conscience and critic' of society, might have been expected to take the leadership role in the discourse about business and sustainability. Nowhere has that challenge proved more problematic than in the business studies curriculum (Roome, 1994; Gladwin et al, 1995; Forum for the Future, 1998; World Resources Institute [WRI], 1998; WRI and the Aspen Institute, 1999; Springett and Kearins, 2001; Kearins and Springett, 2003; Springett, 2005). Yet it might be argued that there is no more important disciplinary platform for sustainability studies if our corporate leaders and managers of the future are to become agents of the turn towards sustainability, a role that has sometimes been claimed for them (Hawken, 1993). Furthermore, the influence that business has on broader societal thinking and planning through its hegemonic coalition with government and other elites (Levy, 1997) also reinforces the argument that EfS should be integral to the business studies curriculum.

Instead, it has long represented a key 'silence', a null curriculum of issues that do not have a voice. At the heart of this silence is the ideological struggle between the orthodox business model that is based upon growth and the paradigm of change that sustainability requires. In addition, an approach to EfS that is robust enough to drive teaching about business and sustainability calls for a critical theorization, and therein lies the crux of another problem. Critical perspectives on sustainability and SD reveal the theoretical underpinnings of corporate rationality that have played a part in relegating environmental and social issues to the level of 'externalities'.

Nevertheless, the 1990s saw the emergence from business educators of a trenchant critique of management theory and practice, based in critical theory (see, for example, Willmott, 1984; 1994; Alvesson and Willmott, 1996; Alvesson and Deetz, 1996; 2000). Initially, few of these early critics paid more than lip service to SD as a crucial part of the critical turn they were advocating: it still represented a 'gap' in the emerging critical analysis. However, the dichotomy between 'greener management' and the fundamental change that sustainability demands has been highlighted by other critical management theorists who have developed their own discourse of business and SD (Hajer, 1995; Levy, 1997; Newton and Harte, 1997; Springett, 2006a; 2006b; 2006c).

Introducing structural issues and the politics of sustainability into the business studies curriculum itself has remained problematic. While the rhetoric of eco-modernism and incremental change readily assumed a place, described by Newton and Harte (1997, p90) as 'MBA-quality eco-wrap', a radical critical perspective has not been common. The business discourse has focused on 'management' of the SD agenda (Springett, 2006b, p53). There are also political difficulties and possible career consequences for business educators who promote a critical agenda (Springett and Kearins, 2001). Academics have to seek publication opportunities in top-tier journals; they must compete for promotion and research funding; and forays outside their disciplinary boundaries represent risky moves. While questions of *why* and *how* we might develop such a curriculum are discussed, there has been relatively little evidence of praxis. Sometimes, the focus of successful programmes has been on 'executive' education rather than the core curriculum of business studies (Wheeler et al, 2005), or on an international partnership for teaching a 'global MBA' (Roome, 2005) through faculties in different countries. However, these are programmes that sit somewhat to the side of the core business studies curriculum: they have been developed by 'self-made' business and environment champions.

A critical perspective on sustainability presents an ideological struggle that strikes at the 'legitimacy' and legacy of orthodox management theory (Springett and Kearins, 2001). Like sustainability itself, such a perspective steps outside mainstream orthodoxy. It also results in a chicken-and-egg dilemma, posing the question of how business educators themselves are to gain preparation for teaching critical perspectives on business and sustainability. EfS that 'makes a difference' requires a critical theorization to frame the goals, structure, curriculum content and pedagogical choices made, as well as to shape the overall process of planning and action, monitoring and reflection (Springett, 2005). The process itself becomes a critical inquiry in its own right that explores the complexities and implications of sustainability and takes account of the economic, political, cultural, technical, social and environmental forces that foster or impede its goals (see Huckle, 1996). The Wuppertal Institute's 'prism of sustainability' (Spangenberg, 1995, see Figure 5.1) introduces the 'institutional imperative' of sustainability that takes us beyond the 'triple bottom line' (Elkington, 1997). It focuses attention on questions of equity, burden-sharing and democracy.

While a critical curriculum theorization is openly ideological, that is not to say the intention is to co-opt students to a particular perspective. Instead, the goals are emancipatory and intended to foster a healthy scepticism as well as the habit of critical inquiry that *prevents* such capture. It involves learners in thinking through both personal and broader societal issues. The intention is to 'hold a mirror to the world and show it as it is and as it has produced and shaped its own nature' (O'Connor, 1998, p52). It requires that we listen to voices that are seldom empowered and hear perspectives on sustainability and SD that do not solely reflect the views of management (Springett and Foster, 2005). It is, then, 'political' in intent, not claiming the supposed 'neutrality' of the orthodox curriculum that helps to reinforce societal hegemony in order to maintain the values and ideology of dominant social groups (Apple, 1979; Fien, 1993; Huckle, 1996; O'Connor, 1998; Springett, 2005). It does not perpetuate a 'sanitized' picture of

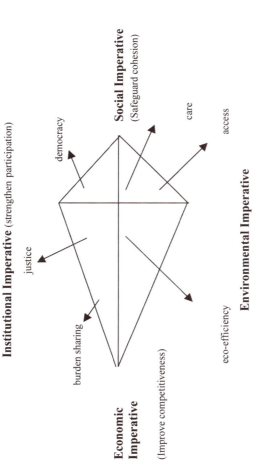

Figure 5.1 *The Wuppertal prism of sustainability*

Source: Spangenberg, 1995

the world (Willmott, 1994). However, it is necessary to clarify, in keeping with Faubion's summary of Foucault's political stance, 'that "left" values neither prohibit one from being anti-communist nor compel the desire for revolution' (Faubion, 1994, pxiv).

The 'problem' of introducing a critical agenda of sustainability is, of course, wider than the business curriculum. It is grounded in the increasingly reductionist turn the broader HE agenda has taken, characterized by competition and market-driven values (Capra, 1983; Trainer, 1990; Orr, 1992; Huckle, 1996) and following rather than challenging the 'rationality' of the dominant social paradigm (Sterling, 1996). Beder (1997) has demonstrated how the corporate assault on environmentalism has had its implications for the formal curriculum, and has reminded us recently (Beder, 2009) that the corporate attempt to control our worldviews begins not at tertiary level but in the corporate capture of childhood. Ralston Saul (1997) suggests that HE has abandoned the field of free enquiry and teaching people to *think* in order to pursue corporate sponsorship and focus on vocational training for the workforce. Consequently, Dobers et al (2008, p212) conclude that it is important 'to reframe and analyse the role of universities in a broader socio-cultural and historical perspective' if universities are to be agents in the paradigm shift to sustainability.

Some thoughts on introducing a critical theorization

It ain't necessarily so … (Gershwin, 1935)

Some of the reasons for employing a critical perspective in business education for sustainability, and the scepticism this can invite, have already been referred to. The goal is to emancipate students' capacity to engage in critical inquiry, including their reflections on the course itself, its content and delivery. Students have grown up in a climate that the corporate public relations machine has helped to create. EfS has a role in presenting values and worldviews that help them question the world as they know it (Springett, 2005). Consequently, we have to be clear about the aims and objectives of the course. In my own work, the goal is not to teach a course 'about' critical theory per se, nor is it to produce 'critical theorists'. Instead, a kit of common-sense tools is provided for looking at the world as we find it, helping to hold up the 'mirror' of critical theory that, as O'Connor (1998) has noted, shows the contingent nature of the world as we know it.

My introduction to critical perspectives starts with an overview of what that perspective sets out to do and includes the following areas for discussion:

- A critical perspective does not accept things at face value. Taken-for-granted beliefs are to be challenged: they are contingent, have been constructed and can change.
- Questions are asked about who 'constructed' things the way they are and why. Who benefits from this and who loses? What are the impacts for nature and for people?
- Who holds the power to maintain the status quo? How do they attain and maintain that power?
- How are others persuaded to accept their perspective or ideology?
- What happens to an 'alternative' agenda such as sustainable development? How might the agenda become appropriated, accommodated, normalized or 'hijacked'?

My experience is that such perspectives are not introduced to students without some resistance on their part. 'Dissonance' can readily replace 'harmony' (Sayer, 1984, p231), which adds to the texture of the dialectical learning process and starts the critical inquiry. Concepts from critical theory are introduced as a toolkit that we can choose to employ:

- 'Power': What is power? Who holds power? How is it used in the sustainability debate?
- Asymmetric power relations and how these relate to that debate.
- The exposure of exploitation, repression and unfairness.
- 'Domination' and 'hegemony': the ways in which power may become legitimated or naturalized and what this means.

- The concept of 'false consciousness': the ways in which we may consent to domination and hegemony and accept taken-for-granted ideologies without realizing we are doing so.

- 'Accommodation', 'appropriation' and 'normalization' of competing discourses such as the sustainability discourse.

- The exploration of 'silences' or 'gaps' in the discourse: what is not 'up for discussion' may be even more important than what is.

- The 'constructed' nature of people, institutions and concepts: things did not 'just happen', they are contingent and can change.

The goal of introducing these concepts is to foster the habit of 'critique', to encourage student reflexivity and employ action methods as a means of extending and reinforcing the learning (Springett and Kearins, 2001; Kearins and Springett, 2003; Springett, 2005).

At the same time, the perceived 'negativity' of the critical perspective must be taken into account. It is important to discuss this with students, since the goal is not to leave them feeling helpless or daunted. Giroux (1988) warns that critical perspectives may have the disabling effect of convincing people that they have insufficient agency to influence the way things are or to become agents of change. More recently, Thomas (2007) has expressed concern that EfS may have the unintended effect of reducing student inclination to act on personal beliefs. Consequently, it is important to use a 'language of possibility' (Fien, 1993, p10; Huckle, 1996, p106) and to discuss how an understanding of critical concepts can help to develop human potential for emancipation, autonomy and independence of thought and will. Along with this goes a willingness to accept responsibility, to acquire knowledge and to develop the capacity to make informed choices. In the courses taught at Massey University and at HKU, it leads to the discussion of 'agency', that is, the willingness and ability to act, to be effective and to 'make a difference'.

Praxis: Educating for 'Business and Sustainability'

The curriculum content for both of the courses discussed here begins and ends with values – students' clarification of their own values, understanding the changes in values and worldviews that have led to the sustainability dilemma and envisioning the values that may help to overcome the crisis. This focus is made more effective by the action methods that are described here which also provide a level of experiential learning that empowers students, giving them some control over their learning.

The courses share the same theorization, goals and pedagogical methods, and have been evaluated by students, as well as the formal university systems, over a long period, from 1994 to the present. Both courses set out to problematize the concepts of 'sustainability' and 'sustainable development' and examine the contested ways in which they are framed and the reasons for this. The approach is different from 'green management' courses, which tend to focus on 'issues' and 'solutions' but do not explore the genealogy and politics of these 'symptoms' of the ecological and social problematic.

The first course, Massey University's 'Business and Sustainability', has been described in some detail in earlier papers (Springett and Kearins, 2001; Kearins and Springett, 2003; Springett, 2005) and is referred to briefly here. Developed in 1994 and taught until 2006, it established the following goals for my teaching:

- To provide a critical understanding of the forces establishing the environment, sustainability and SD as important issues for business by examining the social, political and economic context of the discourse.
- To assist students in gaining an understanding of how the theory, principles and practice of management might incorporate the issues of sustainability.
- To help students understand the paradigm shift required for business to become sustainable, including changes at the structural and institutional levels.
- To prepare students for a change-agent role in order to assist business organizations in making that paradigm shift.

Both courses draw on a wide range of readings to emphasize the interdisciplinary nature of the study and to introduce a discursive approach. The institutional roots of the environmental problematic are explored from the time of the scientific and industrial revolutions to the present. This reveals the social, political and economic dimensions of the problem and the associated cultural, spiritual and intellectual implications of changing worldviews. Focusing on the institutional imperative of SD helps students to become aware of functions of business, government and international institutions that have been harmful to the environment and people, but which they may previously have seen as taken-for-granted forces for good. The genealogy of the environmental debate and the discourses of sustainability, SD and eco-modernism are examined through a critical lens. The purpose is to clarify disparate discourses that have tended to become conflated and to identify the causes of the contestation over who defines 'sustainable development'. Problematization of SD reveals the danger of the discourse of sustainability becoming normalized from a 'strong' discourse that is political and progressive and that views SD as a force for democracy, to a 'weak' discourse that seeks to maintain functional, mainstream positions that focus on sustainable *growth*. The competing dimensions shown in Table 5.1 have proved useful as a basis for this discussion. They underline what is required for the discourse of SD to move towards that of sustainability.

The business sector's response to the pressure for sustainable business is examined from the basic practice of environmental management to more sophisticated corporate involvement in sustainability reporting. The relationship between 'sustainability' initiatives and public relations is explored, as is the values shift that would be required for real change to take place. In New Zealand, the ability to involve speakers from business in the course has provided students with

Table 5.1 A 'weak–strong' continuum of sustainable development

WEAK SUSTAINABLE DEVELOPMENT	STRONG SUSTAINABLE DEVELOPMENT
Functional, mainstream positions	Political, progressive positions
Sustainable growth'	Sustainable development
The narrative of management (and management of the narrative)	The discourse of sustainable development and democracy/inclusivity
'Triple bottom line'	Structural and institutional change
Eco-efficiency (WBCSD)	Social and environmental justice
'political sustainability' ("business-as-usual")	'sustainability'
'Symbolic' politics	Political change

Source: Based on Springett, 2003a

the opportunity to critique and understand business positions. It has also helped them consider the challenges for managers who may wish to be more proactive but who currently have little capacity for progressive agency in their work.

Students in the HKU course are a mixture of internal and external students, ranging in age from their early 20s to mid–50s. Most are from Hong Kong, but some are from mainland China and several international students come from, for example, North America, the UK and Europe. The external students are already in employment, some in middle to senior management positions. The goals of the course reflect those of the Massey University course and these are presented to and discussed with the students along with a 'roadmap' for the course (see Box 5.1). The new 'challenge' has been to present the nucleus of the Massey University course, its critical perspective, discursive approach and pedagogical style in a concentrated programme extending over one weekend. It might have been tempting to revert to lecturing and abandon action methods of teaching and learning. However, these methods have actually made for a more intensive learning experience: students have more control over their learning and consequently more interest in it.

Box 5.1 HKU course structure ('roadmap')

Session One: Values for Sustainability and Critical Perspectives
Session Two: The Sustainable Development Debate: Problematizing a
                Contested Concept
Session Three: Critiquing the 'Business Case' for Sustainable Development
Session Four: Learning in Action: Focus on You

Pedagogical methods: learning in action

Pre-course preparation

Student involvement begins well before the teaching component. This underlines the responsibility they hold for their own learning, but is also dictated by the short timeframe. Students are provided with all course materials and clear guidelines about the level of action learning that will take place. Prior engagement with the readings is ensured by selecting seminal articles as the basis for student reviews, which are carried out in pairs, presented orally in class and form part of the overall assessment for the course.

There are other tasks to be completed in self-selected groups before the course begins. The major project is a group assignment with a choice of two set topics or an alternative selected by students. They choose their groups and topic before the course so that they can then examine the topic through the 'lens' of course content and process. The assignment also requires a level of action research, such as interviewing relevant commentators. Students form different groups again for class debates that involve everyone. The debate topics are provided in advance, as are the debating ground rules.

Introducing the course

Seminar-style teaching is the basis of the course, but action methods start immediately with an exercise in which students introduce themselves. The aims of every session are presented and discussed with students before it begins and each session concludes with an informal evaluation: 'The most important thing I gained from this session was ....'; or, 'One thing this session made me think about was ....' This helps to establish the climate for employing action methods and makes for a democratic learning context.

Another pre-course activity is to supply students with an exercise for measuring their 'ecological footprint'. Early in the first session, students and the course director take their places on a 'continuum' across the room according to the size of their footprint. They discuss these and the lifestyle and consumption habits they represent, setting themselves goals for the future. The continuum is a clarifying and decision-making tool that can be used at any point in the course to explore or resolve issues.

Clarifying needs and wants

The ecological footprint exercise leads to another activity in which students consider their 'needs' and then distinguish between 'needs' and 'wants'. This generally leads to robust debate. Using Maslow's hierarchy of needs (Maslow, 1943), the class discusses the meaning of the levels on that hierarchy and where their own expressed needs and wants fit. Foucault's concept of 'self-construction' is introduced – how 'one must take responsibility for inventing or producing oneself' (Foucault, 1984, pp39–42). The 'needs hierarchy' generates discussion about self-actualization, agency, goals for the future and the students' capacity to become agents of change. They also discuss challenges they may face as agents of change, as well as the possible downside of the concept of 'self-actualization', recalling the warnings by Bandura (2007) and others that selfish individualism represents a cause of social and environmental unsustainability.

Reviews

Generally, students have read the selected texts thoughtfully, prepared sophisticated slide presentations for the class and searched the library and/or internet for other papers on the topic to provide comparisons between different perspectives. They choose different styles of presentation, sometimes using role-play and frequently incorporating challenges for the course director and the class. In 2008, the students decided to distribute hard copies of the reviews to each member of the class as additional resources.

Debates

The debates are interspersed with the rest of the course process, as are the oral reviews of articles. This means that the 'leadership' of the course constantly flows between course director and students. In 2008, this resulted in one student commenting: 'I didn't expect it to be like this. I've realized – we ARE the course. The students are the course.' Because of the need for students to maintain 'face', the time allowed for preparation of the debates and reviews is never skimped and, consequently, these are conducted with considerable gusto and good humour. The rules for the debates are 'relaxed', compared with normal debating procedure, to ensure that each member of the group is involved. The focus here and with the reviews and other techniques is to ensure that reticent members of the class or those who do not have a confident command of English become involved.

Role-play

A role-play takes place between the course director and groups of students representing three key industrial sectors in Hong Kong. These 'companies' are to decide whether they will take part in a survey of corporate environmental and social responsibility, using the survey instrument that I have administered to New Zealand companies since 1999. Students form their groups, select their sector, receive a copy of the survey questionnaire and choose role cards for chief executive officer (CEO), managing director (MD), chief financial officer (CFO), environmental manager, women's representative, union representative, worker and so on. The fact that high-level meetings including workers and others of similarly lowly status would be a rarity is not overlooked, and never better demonstrated than in 2008 when an actual CEO played the part of the 'worker' and explained that he had never been invited to a meeting before and didn't dare speak! This exposed in action the asymmetric power relations that generally characterize the workplace. The role-play encourages students to think about the level of progressive agency that managers and other workers actually possess. As most of them are already in the workplace, they understand that major shifts in corporate values and goals are not easy to implement, and they start to employ some of the concepts from critical theory to understand why change is difficult to initiate. The course director engages with each group as the 'consultant' who approached the environmental manager with the invitation to participate in the survey and facilitates the group discussions.

Major assignment

An element of action research is carried into the major assignment, where possible. This is not easy for a group of people who are mostly in the workplace and studying part-time. Nevertheless, the students generally manage to pose some of the key questions of their assignment task to participants in the corporate workplace, in government authorities, in non-governmental organizations (NGOs) or the general community and comment on the responses received.

Student reflexivity and course evaluation

Student evaluation of the process and content of the course, its philosophical underpinnings, the methods employed and the course director's style, as well as reflections on their own learning and development, are important aspects of the course and encouraged at each stage. Students generally comment on the open style of interaction and the strong involvement they themselves have in the process. The concepts from critical theory that are examined are complex: student evaluation is vital for understanding whether these concepts are conveyed clearly. In fact, students readily become engaged in the 'critical' underpinnings of the course and comment on the fact that they are beginning to look at things differently. They remark on the unusually high level of involvement they experience in the course and enjoy the parts of the course that they drive themselves. The informal evaluations sought at the end of each session help to develop their confidence in providing feedback that is not intended to 'give teacher what she wants to hear'. It enables them to comment, without inhibition, on the reflexivity they are experiencing.

Thomas (2005) has underlined the importance of educators understanding whether their students perceive the agenda of sustainability as having legitimacy. In the two courses discussed here, a more formal evaluation instrument is introduced at the end of the course that is completed anonymously and seeks to establish whether that level of legitimacy is being met. Students rate aspects of the course on Likert scales and then provide qualitative feedback on other key aspects of the course and its presentation. Open-ended questions for qualitative responses seek to understand which topics most or least interested students and the reasons for this. Comments are invited about their own development and understanding as a result of taking the course and the reasons why they would or would not recommend it to others. This feedback helps to keep fresh the goals of student engagement, reflexivity and action and their 'legitimizing' of the course (Springett, 2005). Comments have included:

- 'We exchange opinions through discussion, debates and it is effective.'

- (Most interesting topics) 'Critical theory. It is absolutely important for this programme. The readings were extremely significant to our field of study.'

- 'Stimulating, challenging, applicable … Don't expect to walk out of this class without a sense of urgency, ambition and a burning desire to make a difference!'

- 'Interesting and insightful. I like the way you teach us how to think about the issues of SD rather than just tell us the facts and problems.'

- 'Great readings. The course puts things into perspective – very important. Good discussions with the director and other students.'

- 'Group activities enable us to express what we think and also enhance connection with real situations.'

- 'You can learn new concepts by debating, role-playing and discussion, which allowed me to learn it less painfully.'

- 'Makes students think about their contribution towards sustainable development and realize it's not that simple an issue to resolve.'

- 'Very good practice of applying what we have learned and to use it in the class.'

Concluding comments

The importance of bringing critical perspectives into the literature on business and sustainability has been emphasized for well over a decade (Welford, 1998; Redclift, 1999; Becker, 1999; Springett, 2003b; Kallio and Markkanen, 2003; Cerin, 2004; Kallio, 2004). The fact that relatively little progress has been made in the area has been tracked by Ählström et al (2007), who analysed the content of articles on the environmental management discourse that appeared over six years in the journal *Business Strategy and the Environment*.[3] Critical perspectives had been advocated in the journal since 1998, but Ählström et al discovered that the articles generally followed a positivist paradigm: papers with a critical perspective were in the minority.

Members of the business discipline itself have led the critique on the dearth of EfS in the curriculum. Gladwin et al (1995) critiqued the prestigious Academy of Management and its Review[4] for not providing more leadership, a challenge that the Academy has since embraced. The Association to Advance Collegiate Schools of Business recently introduced its own six Principles for Responsible Management Education.[5] This initiative represents some leadership and progress, but, as Levy has commented, the approach taken cannot be termed 'critical' (Levy, 2009, personal communication).

One salutary insight emerged from research conducted with corporate managers in New Zealand (Springett, 2003b; 2004). They started to note, even to complain, that their education had lacked any introduction to the principles of sustainability or SD. They called for more and better EfS in formal tertiary education as well as in professional and on-the-job training (Springett, 2004, p18), including the education of board members to ensure that sustainability becomes central to the governance of companies. This could be perceived as the tertiary sector ignoring an important 'market' – one that Wheeler et al (2005) and Roome (2005) have identified. At the same time, more universities are engaging with the idea of a 'sustainable university' (see, for example, Dobers et al, 2008) and, as this concept takes hold and becomes, perhaps, a part of university 'branding' (market values being something we are not likely to abandon soon), the spotlight will fall on those areas of the curriculum and research programmes that do not endorse sustainability. However, that is not to assume that critical approaches will readily follow.

This chapter has discussed one person's attempt to introduce critical perspectives into courses on business and sustainability, and to be frank in exposing the praxis that emerges from the theorization. The attempt is made to 'practise what I teach': participatory and democratic discourse and a preparation for life are the goals of the course (Springett, 2005). This invites student contestation that promotes a discourse that is more dialectical, empowering and emancipatory in its aims. As students become more 'sceptical', they begin to recognize that, 'After they've been told for a while, stories can turn into politics, into our institutions, and it is important that they seem *just the way things are, and the way they have to go on being.*' (Kureishi, 2003, p4; emphasis added). They begin to understand that there is hegemonic power over which 'stories' are perpetuated, and that the narratives they may have taken for granted '*ain't necessarily so*'. They begin to perceive themselves as having a role as agents striving for a theoretical reorganization of dominant narratives so that these 'stories' come to reflect greater social and environmental sustainability.

References

Alvesson, M. and Deetz, S. (1996) 'Critical theory and postmodernism approaches to organizational studies', in Clegg, S.R., Hardy, C. and Nord, W.R. (eds), *Handbook of Organization Studies*, Sage, London, pp91–217

Alvesson, M. and Deetz, S. (2000) *Doing Critical Management Research*, Sage, London

Alvesson, M. and Willmott, H. (1996) *Making Sense of Management: A Critical Introduction*, Sage, London

Anderson, R. (1998) *Mid-Course Correction – Toward a Sustainable Enterprise: The Interface Model*, Pereginzilla Press, Atlanta GA

Apple, M.W. (1979) *Ideology and Curriculum*, Routledge and Kegan Paul, London

Bandura, A. (2007) 'Impeding ecological sustainability through selective moral disengagement', *International Journal of Innovation and Sustainable Development*, vol 2, no 1, pp8–35

Becker, E. (1999) 'Fostering transdisciplinary research into sustainability in an age of globalization: A short political epilogue', In Becker, E. and Jahn, T. (eds), *Sustainability and the Social Sciences: A Cross-Disciplinary Approach to Integrating Environmental Considerations into Theoretical Reorientation*, Zed, London, pp59–73

Beder, S. (1997) *Global Spin: The Corporate Assault on Environmentalism*, Scribe Publications, Melbourne

Beder, S. (2009) *This Little Kiddy Went to Market: The Corporate Capture of Childhood*, University of New South Wales Press, Sydney

Capra, F. (1983) *The Turning Point: Science, Society and the Rising Culture*, Wildwood House, London

Cerin, P. (2004) *Turning Corporate Behaviour into Sustainability: Challenges of Environmental Strategies in Industry*, PhD thesis, The Royal Institute of Technology, Stockholm

Dobers, P., Linderström, M. and Mobjörk, M. (2008) 'Institutional entrepreneurship in an academic organization: Sustainability at Mälardalen University', *International Journal of Innovation and Sustainable Development*, vol 3, nos 3–4, pp201–216

Elkington, J. (1994) 'Towards the sustainable corporation: Win–win–win business strategies for sustainable development', *California Management Review*, vol 36, no 2, pp90–100

Elkington, J. (1997) *Cannibals with Forks: The Triple Bottom Line of 21st Century Business*, Capstone, Oxford

Faubion, J.D. (ed.) (1994) *Essential Works of Foucault, 1954-1984; Volume Three – Power*. Trans. R. Hurley and others. Allen Lane/The Penguin Press, London

Fien, J. (1993) *Education for the Environment: Critical Curriculum Theorising and Environmental Education*, Deakin University, Melbourne

Forum for the Future and DETR (1998) *Business Curriculum Audit*

Foucault, M. (1984) *The Care of the Self*, Pantheon, New York NY

Gershwin, G. (1935) 'It ain't necessarily so…', In *Porgy and Bess*

Giroux, H.A. (1988) *Teachers as Intellectuals: Towards a Critical Pedagogy of Learning*, South Bergin and Garvey, Hadley MA

Gladwin, T., Kennelly, J. and Krause, T.-S. (1995) 'Shifting paradigms for sustainable development: Implications for management theory and research', *Academy of Management Review*, vol 20, no 4, pp874–907

Gramsci, A. (1971) *Selections from the Prison Notebooks of Antonio Gramsci* (ed. and trans. Derek Boothman, 1995), Lawrence and Wishart, London

Hajer, M. (1995) *The Politics of Environmental Discourse: Ecological Modernization and the Policy Process*, Clarendon Press, Oxford

Harvey, D. (1996) *Justice, Nature and the Geography of Difference*, Blackwell, Cambridge MA

Hawken, P. (1993) *The Ecology of Commerce: How Business Can Save the Planet*, Harper Collins, New York NY

Hawken, P., Lovins, A. and Lovins, L.H. (1999) *Natural Capitalism: Creating the Next Industrial Revolution*, Little, Brown and Company, Boston MA, New York NY and London

Huckle, J. (1996) 'Realizing sustainability in changing times', In Huckle, J. and Sterling, S. (eds) *Education for Sustainability*, Earthscan, London, pp105–119

ICC (1991) *Business Charter for Sustainable Development: Principles for Environmental Management*, ICC, Paris

Kallio, T.J. (2004) *Greening Organizational Studies – A Critical Reflection*. Turku School of Economics and Business Administration Series Discussion and Working Papers, no 8

Kallio, T.J. and Markkanen, P. (2003) 'Ten years after Gladwin's plea for organizational theory: Where are we now? Some critical remarks', 11th International Conference of the Greening of Industry Network Conference, San Francisco CA, October

Kearins, K. and Springett, D.V. (2003) 'Educating for sustainability: Developing critical skills', *Journal of Management Education*, vol 27, no 2, pp188–204

Kureishi, H. (2003) 'Loose tongues and liberty', *Guardian Review*, 7 June, pp4–6

Levy, D.L. (1997) 'Environmental management as political sustainability', *Organisation and Environment*, vol 10, no 2, pp126–147

Maslow, A. (1943) 'A theory of human motivation', *Psychological Review*, vol 50, no 4, pp370–396

Newton, T. and Harte, G. (1997) 'Green business: Technicist kitsch?', *Journal of Management Studies*, vol 34, no 1, pp75–98

O'Connor, J. (1998) *Natural Causes: Essays on Ecological Marxism*, Guilford, New York NY

Orr, D. (1992) *Ecological Literacy: Education and the Transition to a Post-Modern World*, SUNY Press, Albany NY

Ralston Saul, J. (1997) *The Unconscious Civilisation*, Free Press, New York NY

Redclift, M. (1999) 'Sustainability and sociology: Northern preoccupations', in E. Becker and T. Jahn (eds) *Sustainability and the Social Sciences: A Cross-Disciplinary Approach to Integrating Environmental Considerations into Theoretical Reorientation*, Zed, London, pp59–73

Robottom, I. (1992) *Environmental Education: Practice and Possibility*, Deakin University, Melbourne

Roome, N.J. (1994) *Environmental Responsibility: An Agenda for Higher and Further Education – Management and Business*, Pluto, London

Roome, N.J. (2005) 'Teaching sustainability in a global MBA: Insights from the OneMBA', *Business Strategy and the Environment*, vol 14, no 3, pp160–171

Sayer, A. (1984) *Method in Social Science*, Hutchinson, London

Sachs, W. (1991) 'Environment and development: The story of a dangerous liaison', *The Ecologist*, vol 21, no 6, pp252–257

Schmidheiny, S. (1992) *Changing Course: A Global Business Perspective on Development and the Environment*, MIT, Cambridge MA

Spangenberg, J.H. (1995) 'The Linkage of Economy, Environment and Social Organization in the Concept of Sustainability'. In Spangenberg, J.H. (ed), *Roundtable Discussions on Sustainable Production and Consumption in Europe*, UNEP/Regional Office for Europe, Geneva, pp49–56

Springett, D.V. and Kearins, K. (2001) 'Gaining legitimacy: Sustainable development in business school curricula', *Sustainable Development Journal*, vol 9, no 4, pp213–221

Springett, D.V. (2003a) *Corporate Conceptions of Sustainable Development in New Zealand: A Critical Analysis*, PhD thesis, Durham University.

Springett, D.V. (2003b) 'Business conceptions of sustainable development: A perspective from critical theory', *Business Strategy and the Environment*, vol 12, issue 2, pp71–86

Springett, D.V. (2004) 'Contesting "the business case" for sustainable development: A New Zealand perspective', *Partnerships for Sustainability: The 12th International Conference of the Greening of Industry Network*, Hong Kong, November

Springett, D.V. (2005) 'Education for sustainability in the business studies curriculum: A call for a critical agenda', *Business Strategy and the Environment*, vol 14, no 3, pp146–159

Springett, D.V. and Foster, A.B. (2005) 'Whom is sustainable development *for?* Deliberative democracy and the role of unions', *Sustainable Development*, vol 13, issue 5, pp271–281

Springett, D.V. (2006a) 'Contesting the business case for sustainable development: A New Zealand perspective', in Welford, R., Hills, P. and Young, W. (eds), *Partnerships for Sustainable Development: Perspectives from the Asia-Pacific Region*, HKU, pp33–52

Springett, D.V. (2006b) 'Managing the narrative of sustainable development: "Discipline" of an "inefficient" concept', *International Journal of Green Economics*, vol 1, nos 1–2, pp50–67

Springett, D.V. (2006c) 'Structural limits to sustainable development: Managers and progressive agency', *International Journal of Innovation and Sustainable Development*, vol 1, no 1, pp127–152

Sterling, S. (1996) 'Education in change', In Huckle, J. and Sterling, S. (eds), *Education for Sustainability*, Earthscan, London, pp18–39

The Ecologist (1993) *Whose Common Future?* Earthscan, London

Thomas, T. (2005) 'Are business students buying it? A theoretical framework for measuring attitudes toward the legitimacy of environmental sustainability', *Business Strategy and the Environment*, vol 14, no 3, pp186–197

Thomas, T. (2007) 'Educating for sustainability: A double-edged sword?', *International Journal of Innovation and Sustainable Development*, vol 2, nos 3–4, pp453–465

Trainer, T. (1990) 'Towards an ecological philosophy of education', *Discourse*, vol 10, no 2, pp92–117

WCED (1987) *Our Common Future: The Report of the World Commission on Environment and Development*, Oxford University Press, Oxford

Welford, R. (1998) 'Corporate environmental management, technology and sustainable development: Postmodern perspectives and the need for a critical research agenda', Editorial, *Business Strategy and the Environment*, vol 7, no 1, pp1–12

Wheeler, D., Zohar, A. and Hart, S. (2005) 'Educating senior executives in a novel strategic paradigm: Early experiences of the Sustainable Enterprise Academy', *Business and the Environment*, vol 14, no 3, pp172–185

Willmott, H. (1984) 'Images and ideals of managerial work: A critical examination of conceptual and empirical accounts', *Journal of Management Studies*, vol 21, no 3, pp349–368

Willmott, H. (1994) 'Management education: Provocation to a debate', *Management Learning*, vol 25, no 1, pp105–36

Willums, J.-O. and Golüke, U. (1992) *From Ideas to Action: Business and Sustainable Development, The ICC Report on the Greening of Enterprise 1992*, ICC and Ad Notam Gyldendal

World Resources Institute (1998) *Grey Pinstripes with Green Ties: MBA Programmes Where Environment Matters*, WRI, Washington DC

World Resources Institute and The Aspen Institute (1999) *Beyond Grey Pinstripes: Preparing MBAs for Social and Environmental Stewardship*, WRI/The Aspen Institute, Washington DC

Ählström, J., Macquet, M. and Richter, U. (2007) 'The lack of a critical perspective in environmental management research: Distortion in the scientific discourse', *Business Strategy and the Environment*, vol 18, no 5, pp334–346

Notes

1   For an introduction to action research and action methods, see Norton, L.S. (2008) *Action Research in Teaching and Learning: A Practical Guide to Conducting Pedagogical Research in Universities*, Routledge, London.

2   In Gramsci's classification of intellectuals into 'traditional' and 'organic', the former are seen as 'functionaries' with close allegiance to their own tradition and craft, practis-

ing under what they believe to be a rhetoric of autonomy. 'Organic' intellectuals, on the other hand, enable people, through the provision of an alternative ideological framework, possibly to resolve dual consciousness by seeing the world in a new way. Levy (1997) suggests that business school academics are in danger of acting as Gramsci's 'traditional intellectuals' by propagating the theories and practices that support the dominant paradigm.

3   *Business Strategy and the Environment* www3.interscience.wiley.com/journal/5329/home

4   Academy of Management, www.aomonline.org

5   The six principles of the Association's approach focus on: Purpose, Values, Method, Research, Partnership and Dialogue, www.aacsb.edu

Chapter 6

Geography, Earth and Environmental Sciences: A Suitable Home for ESD?

Brian Chalkley, Jennifer Blumhof and
Kristín Vala Ragnarsdóttir

Introduction

Geography, earth and environmental Sciences (GEES) are HE disciplines that already engage with Education for Sustainable Development (ESD). All three GEES subjects share a well-established focus on the Earth, its resources and environments. In this sense SD can be considered 'natural territory' for GEES, and indeed the rise of the sustainability agenda is perhaps one factor encouraging the three disciplines to work more closely together. The GEES disciplines have certainly played a leading role in promoting and supporting ESD in the UK's HEA, the principal national body for enhancing the student learning experience.

Although this natural alignment between the GEES subjects and ESD rests principally on their subject content, and especially their focus on the environment, pedagogy also plays a part. ESD is characterized by a strong commitment to deep learning (Warburton, 2003, p45), which the GEES disciplines demonstrate particularly effectively through their extensive use of field and laboratory work – such experiential approaches being especially useful in promoting learning that lasts.

A major purpose of this book is, of course, to illustrate that a very wide range of disciplines have the potential to produce sustainability-literate graduates and thereby to make a useful contribution to the ESD agenda, as also argued by Roberts and Roberts (2007). Nonetheless, it is widely assumed in HEIs that the GEES disciplines have a special responsibility in this area: they are thus expected to play a leading role in the 'greening' of HE. Two principal questions running through this chapter are, therefore, how far the GEES disciplines are in fact playing this leading role, and how far they have adjusted their curricula to exploit the natural advantage they possess in this increasingly important area. As we shall see, there are significant differences of approach between the three GEES disciplines, so this chapter looks briefly at each one in turn before closing with some overarching comments and suggestions.

Geography and the place of ESD

On the basis of what geographers write about the nature and scope of their discipline, we can safely say that most see geography as a natural home for teaching and research on sustainability (Bednarz, 2006). Certainly the study of society's relationships with the environment has traditionally occupied a central position in the discipline and has often been considered its principal hallmark. In the UK, the QAA for Higher Education has produced benchmark statements for all the main disciplines, which offer guidelines on curriculum content. The opening statement of the geography benchmark is:

> *Geography occupies a distinctive place in the world of learning, offering an integrated study of the complex, reciprocal relationships between human societies and the physical components of the earth (QAA, 2007a, p1).*

The next paragraph goes on to refer to the many HE geography courses that 'deal explicitly with human–environment relations and sustainable development, building on the role of geography in schools as the main discussion platform for environmental concerns' (QAA, 2007a, p1). The UK schools inspectorate OFSTED has also made clear that it expects geography to take the lead in environmental and sustainability-related education among young people (OFSTED, 2008).

This close alignment between geography and ESD is reinforced by the unusual breadth of the discipline and its emphasis on synthesis and holistic thinking. An informed approach to sustainability demands joining things up and bringing together a wide range of considerations – economic, social, political, ecological and physical. It is precisely this kind of synthesis to which geography lays claim (QAA, 2007a) and which arguably distinguishes it from many other disciplines that have a more narrow or even exclusive focus on analysis. The breadth of geography's canvas is indeed striking, with HE students often being asked to study an apparently eclectic mix of subjects that can span both palaeo-ecology and urban policy, glaciation and tourism. While this diversity can raise questions about the discipline's coherence, a well-balanced geographical education gives students an understanding of both physical and social processes and of how to investigate the interconnection between them in a rounded way.

There is also a value to ESD in the strength of geography's international perspective. It is a discipline with global reach, and this too aligns well with ESD's requirement to view the planet as a whole and to be aware of the interconnectedness between places. The QAA's geography benchmark refers several times to the concept of scale and to the subject's concern with understanding physical and human processes at a variety of scales from the local to the global – an idea which echoes the exhortation of many environmentalists to 'think global, act local' (QAA, 2007a).

ESD also requires a commitment to long-term thinking and being conscious of our inheritance from generations past and our obligations to generations still to come. Geography shares this interest in change and the temporal scale. Through short- and medium-term projections, geographers express their interest in future environments, while historical and physical geographers in particular emphasize the importance of learning lessons from the study of past environments and landscapes.

Geography's general alignment with ESD is, not surprisingly, reflected in the work of individual UK university geography departments and their curricula. At first-year level, for example, it is common to find modules in topics such as Geography and Environment (Royal Holloway, London), People and Environment (University of Manchester) and Global Environmental Issues (University of Brighton and King's College, London). At later stages, one finds more specialized modules such as Global Climate Change (University of Durham), Environmental Change, Society and Nature: Actions and Interactions (University of Bristol), Towards Sustainable Cities (University of Leeds), Rural Change and Sustainability (University of Nottingham) and Atmospheric Pollution (University of Hull). The University of Bristol set up an award-winning interdisciplinary course in 2007, led from its School of Geographical Sciences, entitled Sustainable Development; this outlines SD perspectives from science (geographical and earth sciences), humanities (philosophy and history), social science (geography and economics) and engineering (civil engineering) disciplines.

Further evidence of geography's leading engagement with ESD is provided in the recently published major collection of articles edited by Chalkley et al (2009). This wide-ranging volume is designed to celebrate the UN DESD 2005–2014 and the academic background of many of its contributors illustrates very clearly the special position that geography occupies in the community of ESD academics. The discipline's role is also illustrated by the work of authors such as Pearson et al (2005), Summers et al (2004) and Wellens et al (2006), who illustrate its focus on social–environmental relationships through a range of different approaches to teaching. Geography's prominent position in the ESD landscape is also evidenced in the schools sector as well as in HE. Both the Geographical Association[1] (the professional body for the schools sector) and the Royal Geographical Society[2] (which has more of an HE emphasis) have been active in the ESD arena, not least in promoting conferences, workshops and staff development.

Moreover, as indicated earlier, geography's alignment with ESD is also underlined in terms of pedagogy. It is, of course, difficult to measure or quantify precisely the differences between disciplines in their approaches to teaching, but geographers would argue that their discipline has an especially strong record of pedagogic innovation, student-centred methods and experiential learning. Geography, and indeed the other GEES disciplines, commonly use a wide range of teaching and learning approaches including projects, debates, simulations, case studies drawn from the world of employment, seminars, tutorials, workshops, laboratory classes, computer-aided learning and resource-based learning. Geography's pedagogic achievements are evidenced, for example, by the high level of geographers' success in terms of the award of UK National Teaching Fellowships and in the HE Academy's Senior Fellowships,[3,4] where no fewer than 4 of the first 14 awards, given for outstanding contributions to HE teaching, went to geographers. This kind of success points to the subject's commitment to innovative, interactive and participatory approaches to learning, as further illustrated by literally hundreds of articles published in the *Journal of Geography in Higher Education*,[5] one of the leading and longest-established international journals in subject-based pedagogy. In the UK, it is also relevant to note the work of the Centre for Excellence in Active Learning which is based at the University of Gloucestershire and is headed by geographers. The Centre and the University have each made significant contributions to ESD pedagogy, both in geography and more widely (Roberts and Roberts, 2007), especially through their commitment to experiential forms of learning.

In recent years, geography has like many other HE disciplines sought to strengthen its commitment not only to ESD but also to preparing graduates for the world of work (Gedye and Chalkley, 2006), and there are early signs of the subject recognizing the growth of 'green' business practices and job opportunities. At the University of Plymouth, for example, second-year geography students have been asked to explore the corporate social responsibility (CSR) policies of major companies and to assess their efficacy. In this way, students engage with corporate documentation while sharpening their critical faculties and immersing themselves in the practicalities of how organizations are seeking to become (or at least appear!) more sustainable.

It would, however, be misleading to imagine that geography as a discipline is entirely synonymous with ESD. It has other academic interests and traditions, particularly the study of places and of spatial distributions. There have been periods when regional (or place) geography has been out of fashion, but several degree programmes continue to offer modules with titles such as Rural Development in Latin America (University of Aberdeen) or Southern Africa (University of Plymouth). Moreover, the spatial analysis theme has been strengthened by the increased importance and sophistication of geographic information systems (GIS) and automated cartography.

It is interesting also to note, as does Bednarz (2006), that geography does not yet seem to have taken major steps to reinforce and intensify its traditional teaching interests in society–environment relationships. Instead, areas such as cultural geography have been in the ascendancy. There are signs of geography programmes responding to the climate change agenda, particularly through the provision of optional modules in this area (as at the University of Plymouth), but the study of energy resources (once a significant curriculum component) is today relatively invisible. It seems that, at present, geographers are only partially exploiting their natural advantage in the ESD arena: this sense of unfulfilled potential is considered further in the closing parts of this chapter.

Environmental science

Perhaps as much or even more than geography, environmental science can claim to be the discipline that underpins SD and which carries out essential research. Environmental scientists have taken the lead in promoting SD strategies and initiatives in HEIs. They have also led ESD initiatives at a national and international level through their work, for example, with the GEES HEA Subject Centre (GEES, 2009a), where they have played a significant role in the preparation of staff development teaching resources. Nevertheless, ESD for environmental scientists is also somewhat controversial, particularly when it shifts from 'neutral science' into what is perceived to be a more evangelical sphere – although of course, this idea of neutrality is also contested! Emphasizing the place of the discipline, James Longhurst states that:

Environmental science is the potential guardian of sustainability in higher education and beyond, as it, uniquely, has the capacity and intellectual reputation to define the environmental limits within which all sustainability decisions need to be made (Longhurst, 2008).

To cite some UK examples in support of this claim, the Environment Team at the University of Hertfordshire was set up by academics from the Division of Environmental Sciences. Some of the universities with top environmental performance (such as energy use) designated by People and Planet (e.g. the Universities of Gloucestershire, Plymouth and the West of England) had their initiatives promoted and supported by, among academics of other disciplines, their in-house environmental scientists (People and Planet, 2008). The People and Planet Green League is a ranking of UK HEIs based on their sustainability practice and is compiled by a student campaign group. The Sustainable Development open first year module at the University of Bristol was sparked from the University's Environment Office through their advisory team of academics.

Leading-edge research into SD is undertaken, for example, by the University of Surrey's Centre for Environmental Strategy (University of Surrey, 2009). The School of Environmental Sciences at the University of East Anglia was rated 'double 5★', in the most recent RAE,[6] the highest possible research ranking (University of East Anglia, 2009). The University of Lancaster Environment Centre cites work on sustainable agriculture, energy and water management among its areas of expertise (University of Lancaster, 2009). Environmental scientists also co-developed and ran workshops on ESD for GEES academics across the UK, including an audit tool that allows departments to assess their current provision, accessible via the GEES Subject Centre website (GEES, 2009b).

Environmental science is a relatively new discipline, and like SD is evolving with a variety of definitions, but at its core it is the systematic study of the environment. The environment includes the natural world as well as the 'built' or technological, social, cultural, political and economic worlds that we inhabit. Elements of environmental science may focus to a greater or lesser extent on these varying aspects of the environment, but the science is highly interdisciplinary, integrating knowledge from many fields to move towards an holistic understanding of issues and problems. These attributes are all highlighted in the subject benchmark statement for earth science, environmental sciences and environmental studies (ES3) published in 2000 and updated in 2007 (QAA, 2007b). Formal environmental science education in UK HEIs has been developing over 40 years:

> *The pervasive and unique role environmental science plays in higher education has evolved from a relatively modern movement, questioning, analysing and evaluating our influence on, and relation with, the environment. A number of universities and former polytechnics lay claim to establishing some of the earliest environmental programmes. These include East Anglia, Hertfordshire, Lancaster, Plymouth, Southampton, Stirling and Sunderland* (Blumhof and Holmes 2008, p4).

With reference to curriculum and teaching approaches, the panel of academics who worked on the subject benchmark statement for ES3 reports that degree programmes in environmental science typically involve the following:

- A systems approach to understanding the processes operating in the lithosphere, cryosphere, hydrosphere, atmosphere and biosphere, and the perturbations of these systems by extraterrestrial influences.
- The scientific study of surface and near-surface physical, chemical, biological and anthropogenic processes operating on the Earth.
- The history of the Earth in the context of the period of human occupancy.
- The monitoring and management of natural and human-induced environmental changes.
- Scientific examination of the implications of sustainability and sustainable development (QAA, 2007b).

It is this that gives substance to the claim for environmental science being the underpinning science for understanding SD. On ES3 teaching, the panel reported on the following key attributes:

- An holistic, multidisciplinary and interdisciplinary approach.
- The integration of fieldwork, experimental and theoretical investigations.

- Quantitative and qualitative approaches to acquiring and interpreting data.
- Examination of the exploration for, and exploitation of, physical and biological resources.
- Examination of the implications of sustainability and sustainable development (QAA, 2007b).

It is in the last point that sustainability and SD are particularly referred to, making the implicit explicit.

The early concerns of the discipline, supported both by scientific work and polemical writings, focused on resource depletion. The idea of SD emerged in the 1980s and was crystallized in the oft-quoted Brundtland Report (WCED, 1987). The focus here was very much on humanity and the way people interact with each other and the natural environment. To understand SD as defined by Brundtland – improving the quality of life for present generations in a way that does not damage or destroy the resource base and development potential for future generations – an understanding of environmental science is needed. Effective measures for environmental/resource management and conservation require a sound knowledge of environmental processes and systems.

Nonetheless, there are some environmental scientists who argue that the concept of SD is peripheral to what they do. In fact, some take an even stronger line and argue that SD is a quasi-political or even spiritual or religious ideology, about which environmental science should remain strictly neutral. If one were to pursue this more sceptical view, using the term SD in course publicity literature or in programme or module titles could be considered a marketing ploy to encourage students to apply (Magnier, 2006).

The original version of the subject benchmark statement for ES3, published in 2000, had a brief reference to sustainability, but in the revised edition in 2007 the panel agreed that there should be 'a greater emphasis on sustainability with particular emphasis on the environmental context of sustainability' (QAA, 2007, piv). There was considerable debate in both the 2000 and 2007 panels, and views covered the spectrum from neutral science to 'green' dogma. Nevertheless, the imperatives in society were clearly changing, with the scientific paradigm moving towards agreement on the magnitude and dangers of human impacts on the natural environment. As Blumhof and Holmes report:

It is now apparent that across government, industry, the media and society as a whole concern for the environment is once again moving up the policy agenda. Research carried out by a generation of diverse professionals, which include environmental scientists, is revealing the multiplicity of impacts of human activity on resources and natural systems. These professions depend upon higher educational institutions to provide high-quality graduates who are able to link many aspects of science and society together in order to tackle environmental issues (Blumhof and Holmes, 2008, p4).

In *Mapping the Environmental Landscape* (2008), Blumhof and Holmes look at the state of the environmental science as an HE subject, including the role of SD. The aim of their project is, in phase one, to map the complex landscape of formal environmental science provision in HE over time by investigating recent provision from a number of perspectives. Statistical data were interrogated and surveys conducted with environmental science providers (lecturers and programme leaders) and environmental science professionals on SD. In answer to the question 'What do you think the key issues will be for HE provision of environmental science?', respondents thought that there would be an increased awareness of sustainability (Blumhof and Holmes, 2008, p16). Use was also made of the report by John Baines on the current agenda of sustainability in UK HE curricula (Baines, 2006), particularly with reference to professional development and the relevance of ESD to the world of work.

Phase two of Blumhof and Holmes's project, ongoing at the time of writing, involves a panel of HE environmental science providers interrogating the survey findings to examine the trends and issues (including the role of SD) identified in phase one, and to make recommendations for the direction of the discipline and further study. This work is being led by the Committee of Heads of Environmental Sciences[7] and supported by the HEA Subject Centre for GEES and the Institution of Environmental Sciences.[8] The Committee of Heads is the collective voice of environmental sciences and related programmes in higher and further education in the UK and at present has 32 member departments. The Institution is a UK charitable organization that promotes and raises public awareness of environmental science by supporting professional scientists and academics working in this arena.

It has previously been argued that the knowledge and skills intrinsic to understanding sustainable development are deeply embedded in environmental science. Nevertheless, it is useful to see how overtly SD is articulated in environmental science degree programmes. In a small research project by Blumhof and Davis (2008), a representative sample of 11 old and new UK universities was surveyed.[9] There were 18 undergraduate programmes with environmental science in the title and 5 masters programmes. Only one institution had an undergraduate programme called Sustainable Development and there were three masters programmes with 'sustainable development' in the title. Of 90 modules, 14 had 'sustainable' in their titles, some of these being shared across a number of programmes. From a review of the content of the programmes, it was apparent that the knowledge and skills underpinning SD were firmly embedded in them (Blumhof and Davis 2008), including the study of society–environment relationships and the means of investigating environmental issues and problems. It is doubtful whether any other HE discipline fully matches this level of engagement and these survey results therefore confirm the substantial contribution that environmental science is making.

Sustainability education in earth sciences

For the earth sciences – formerly referred to as geology and including natural resources, petrology, mineralogy, crystallography, hydrogeology and atmospheric and climate science – ESD offers special opportunities and poses some difficult challenges. The opportunities self-evidently derive from the discipline's focus in both research and teaching on Earth's processes. Certainly geologists and those in related fields would consider an understanding of such processes to be fundamental in underpinning and informing policy discussions in key areas such as climate change and energy resources. Indeed, climate and energy are both widely considered as major (and related) parts of the sustainability agenda, and both are areas where earth science can make significant contributions.

The challenge for earth scientists is that their discipline can also easily be portrayed as part of the problem as well as part of the answer. Traditionally, many students with an earth science or geology training have found employment in mining and resource extraction industries, in particular in the oil and gas sector (Muttitt, 2003). Their technical expertise has been vital in the identification and exploitation of the Earth's natural resources. From the early days of the industrial revolution, it was apparent that there could be unwelcome by-products from such exploitation such as health problems and air and water pollution, but these negative effects were generally seen by society as localized and a relatively small price to pay for the related economic prosperity and growth.

In the modern era, however, earth scientists and the international community have recognized that environmental problems are no longer only local in scale, but increasingly have a global reach. Pollution, for example, is transported in the atmosphere and leaves polar bears with a high body burden of polychlorinated biphenyls (PCBx) and mercury. Burning fossil fuels was largely unquestioned until it became apparent that using the atmosphere for the waste disposal of carbon dioxide is contributing to the greenhouse effect and changing the Earth's climate. It is thus no longer sufficient to describe the problems: we also need solutions so we can live sustainably on the planet.

But how far along are earth sciences curricula in including ESD? This subject has not been much explored in the ESD literature. However, a recent paper by Jones et al (2008) found that there is a perceived incompatibility between ESD and the geosciences that could discourage the further embedding of ESD in such degree programmes. This is based on a survey of academic staff and students in the School of Earth, Ocean and Environmental Sciences at the University of Plymouth. One lecturer surveyed stated that there is a conflict of interest because of the mutual exclusivity of ESD and student career aspirations: in training a geologist one important end occupation is in the oil industry, which by definition is not very sustainable. More positively, the study also found that messages from industry and professional bodies that accredit courses have recently changed and are giving more priority to sustainability, but that the academic community is being slow to recognize this because they are insufficiently aware of this shift in direction. Jones et al (2008) conclude that there is general support for embedding of ESD in the curriculum, but it is not clear to the lecturers how this might be done. The academics expressed concern that embedding ESD in degree programmes might lead to reductions in the amount of teaching time available for other aspects of the subject.

For society as a whole, we can describe the journey towards environmental sustainability as a four-step process, involving using fewer resources (Ragnarsdóttir, 2008), improving environmental management, adopting a whole life-cycle perspective (including product disposal) and ultimately learning to simulate the effectiveness of natural systems that are inherently sustainable. This process is named by McDonough and Braungart (2002) as *Cradle to Cradle*, where every industrial step does not produce waste but rather 'food' for nature or another industrial process, and the production does not pollute the environment. Such necessary changes in how we use the Earth's resources clearly demand parallel changes in earth science education including a greater emphasis on conservation. In the UK, small but significant shifts in this direction have been evident for some time. For example, Imperial College London was a pioneer in putting together undergraduate and MSc programmes on environmental issues in the 1970s. Other pioneering developments have included the University of Bristol's degree in Environmental Geoscience, and Edinburgh and St Andrews, which both have a Sustainability Institute. These developments point to the fact that, despite constraints and tensions, earth science is showing signs of responding to the ESD agenda.

Synopsis

Early adopters of ESD discussed in the sections above represent an encouraging trend, but more generally what is needed is a paradigm shift across GEES and indeed other disciplines too. Instead of HE being mostly or only a preparation for economic life (i.e. a job), it becomes a broader education for sustainable societies and communities, including a sustainable or steady-state economy and sustainable ecology. Rather than HE being largely confined to instruction and transmission, it becomes much more a participative, dynamic, active learning process, based on generating knowledge and meaning in context and on real-world problem solving (Sterling 2001 and 2003).

This chapter has shown that by virtue of their subject matter, content and pedagogy, the GEES disciplines have a long-established interest in ESD and in the broader field of society–environment relationships. In all three disciplines, there are signs that staff departments and programmes have begun to identify and seize the opportunities for capitalizing on this 'natural advantage'. However, the pace of change is slower than might have been expected and many GEES degree curricula do not yet give sufficient prominence to the sustainability agenda. Perhaps the focus on the 2008 RAE and the lack of clear staff incentives to engage with ESD are part of the explanation, as is (particularly in earth science) a reluctance among some 'hard science' academics to engage with social and political issues.

In assessing the current status of ESD in the GEES disciplines, it may be helpful to adopt the generic framework used by Sterling (2003), which defines three levels of ESD engagement; namely education *about* sustainability, education *for* sustainability and, ultimately, education *as* sustainability. Education *about* sustainability focuses simply on knowledge of sustainability issues (such as climate change and natural resource depletion). Education *for* sustainability has a commitment to help students with the understanding, expertise and values to enable them to make a positive contribution to change. In education *as* sustainability, the learning process itself adopts the principles of sustainability and emphasizes holism, systems thinking, dialogue, citizenship, cross-cultural empathy and, most importantly, interdisciplinarity. Based on the authors' collective experience of working in the ESD field, and on GEES degree curricula, conferences and publications (e.g. Jones, et al 2008, Chalkley et al, 2009) and on the QAA benchmark statements (2007), our judgement is that, although almost all GEES departments are now engaged in education *about* sustainability to varying extents, there has not yet been a sufficiently substantial shift towards the more holistic levels of engagement implied in education *for* and *as* sustainability. One course entitled Sustainable Futures that could have been classified at this level was taught for a single year (2007–2008) at the University of Bristol but was cancelled after the lecturer left (although it is now being taught in Iceland). This illustrates the way in which sustainability teaching, especially in earth science, can depend on one or two key individuals and is therefore vulnerable to staffing changes.

The reasons for the still modest pace of change are not hard to find and are no doubt shared with many other disciplines. They include the sense of tension between academic objectivity and any ideological commitment to the 'green' agenda, a fear that teaching more ESD could be at the expense of other, established, subject content, and the practical and timetabling difficulties that can complicate and frustrate attempts at interdisciplinary teaching and cross-departmental collaboration. Moreover, most GEES academics (and this is probably true of other disciplines too) are not familiar with the concept of education as sustainability; they instead perceive ESD as being about curriculum content rather than the process of teaching and learning (Jones et al, 2008, p348).

In addition, there are some GEES-specific obstacles, the most conspicuous example being geology's relationship with the oil and mining industries. Some academics might also be anxious about ESD as a challenge to the flying involved in long-haul fieldwork, which in recent years has become a prominent component of many GEES curricula – also, one that staff and students enjoy and that is thought to assist student recruitment (McGuiness and Simm, 2005). Moreover, GEES academics must be careful not to claim too much for their subjects. Although it is clear that environmental sustainability enjoys a natural home in the GEES subjects, the case is overall probably less convincing with respect to social sustainability, for example, and issues relating to areas such as social justice, equity, peace, health and well-being. Some prominent human geographers, most notably David Harvey (1973), have, of course, written seminal works in these kinds of fields, but not always from a sustainability standpoint. And taking the GEES disciplines as a whole, their main contribution is clearly strongest in the physical environment arena and less, for example, in the social or indeed the technological aspects of ESD.

However, alongside these constraints and tensions, it is important also to highlight the benefits that the GEES disciplines could derive from a stronger focus on ESD. First among these is the chance to shed the disciplines' somewhat traditional and conservative image, which in recent years has tended to result in a largely static level of student recruitment. ESD provides the GEES disciplines with an opportunity through teaching and research to demonstrate the subjects' modernity and their relevance to what are arguably the greatest challenges of the 21st century. We can design and deliver 'degrees that matter' (Rappaport and Creighton, 2007; Parker and Wade, 2008). Moreover, ESD enables GEES to demonstrate the disciplines' relevance not only in term of local and global citizenship but increasingly also in terms of jobs and employability. In the case of geography, for example, many prospective students have in the past probably been put off by a perception that, unless they wanted to go into teaching or town planning, a degree in geography might bring only limited career benefits. This perception, always unfair, can now increasingly be challenged by the fact that employers in the private, public and voluntary sectors are keen to advertise their green credentials and operate in more sustainable ways. A recent survey found that over half of UK graduate employers (54 per cent) are now looking to employ candidates who can demonstrate expertise in sustainability and CSR (Cade, 2008, p15). There is, of course, a long way still to go, but the employability and sustainability agendas are starting to converge. This is good news for the GEES subjects and indeed for other disciplines that are sufficiently far-sighted and responsive to recognize the opportunities that ESD can offer.

For the GEES disciplines, ESD can be used to provide a springboard for change that could advertise their contemporary relevance, help recruit students and provide career openings for graduates. These benefits will not, however, materialize automatically; they will need to be worked for through active investment in change. This chapter has highlighted evidence that the changes needed are now under way, but that they are happening unevenly and at too slow a pace. The argument is not that the GEES disciplines should adopt an exclusive focus on ESD and abandon their other traditions and perspectives, but rather that they should respond positively and imaginatively to the special opportunities that ESD presents. This would bring significant benefits, not only to the GEES disciplines and their staff and students but also to HE as a whole. The GEES subjects, working with other disciplines, have the potential to provide academic leadership in the ESD field, because of their subject matter and their breadth, and their potential for working across academic boundaries. That these opportunities should be taken is vital for the health and vitality of the GEES disciplines – and also for advancing the sustainability agenda more widely across HE.

References

Baines, J. (2006) *Integrating Sustainable Development Principles into Professional Practice: Initial Training Requirements for Environmental Scientists*, Report for GEES Subject Centre

Bednarz, R.S. (2006) 'Environmental research and education in US geography', *Journal of Geography in Higher Education*, vol 30, no 2, pp 237–250

Blumhof, J. and Davis, Y. (2008) 'Research into the sustainable development content of environmental programmes' (Unpublished data)

Blumhof, J. and Holmes, P. (2008) *Mapping the Environmental Landscape: An Investigation into the State of the Environmental Science Subject in Higher Education*, Committee for Heads of Environmental Sciences, Institution of Environmental Sciences and GEES Subject Centre, London

Cade, A. (2008) *Employable Graduates for Responsible Employers*, available at www.heacademy.ac.uk/assets/York/documents/ourwork/tla/sustainability/EmployableGraduates2008.pdf, accessed 12 October 2009

Chalkley, B., Haigh, M. and Higgitt, D. (eds) (2009) *Education for Sustainable Development: Papers in Honour of the United Nations Decade of Education for Sustainable Development (2005–2014)*, Routledge, London

Gedye, S. and Chalkley, B. (2006) *Employability in the GEES Curriculum*, GEES Subject Centre, University of Plymouth

GEES Subject Centre (2009a) www.gees.ac.uk, accessed 21 September 2009

GEES Subject Centre (2009b) *DepartmentalWorkshops*, available at www.gees.ac.uk/events/workshops/workshops.htm, accessed 29 September 2009

Harvey, D. (1973) *Social Justice and the City*, Arnold, London

Jones, P., Trier, C.J. and Richards, J.P. (2008) 'Embedding education for sustainable development in higher education: A case study examining common challenges and opportunities for undergraduate programmes' *International Journal of Education Research*, vol 47, pp341–350

Longhurst, J. (2008) *Committee Heads of Environmental Sciences Annual General Meeting and Conference Proceedings, 23 June 2008*, The Committee Heads of Environmental Sciences, London

Magnier, K. (2006) 'Sustainability as a troublesome concept in the GEES disciplines', *Planet*, vol 17, December, pp32–33

McDonough, W. and Braungart, M. (2002) *Cradle to Cradle : Remaking the Way We Make Things*, North Point Press, New York NY

McGuiness, M. and Simm, D. (2005) 'Going global? Long-haul fieldwork in undergraduate geography', *Journal of Geography in Higher Education*, vol 29, no 2, pp241–253

Muttit, G. (2003) *Degrees of Capture; Universities, the Oil Industry and Climate Change*, New Economics Foundation, Corporate Watch and Platform, London

OFSTED (2008) *Geography in Schools: Changing Practice*, OFSTED, London

Parker, J. and Wade, R. (2008) *Journeys Around Education for Sustainability*, London South Bank University

Pearson, S., Honeywood, S. and O'Toole, M. (2005) 'Not yet learning for sustainability: The challenge of environmental education in a university', *International Research in Geographical and Environmental Education*, vol 14, no 3, pp173–186

People and Planet (2008) *The Green League for Environmental Performance*, available at http://peopleandplanet.org/gogreen/greenleague2008, accessed 21 September 2009

QAA (2007a) *Geography* (subject benchmark statement), QAA, Gloucester, available at www.qaa.ac.uk/academicinfrastructure/benchmark/statements/Geography.pdf, accessed 3 February 2010

QAA (2007b) *Earth Sciences, Environmental Sciences and Environmental Studies* (subject benchmark statement), QAA, Gloucester, available at www.qaa.ac.uk/academicinfrastructure/benchmark/statements/EarthSciences.pdf, accessed 3 February 2010

Ragnarsdóttir, K.V. (2008) 'Rare metals becoming rarer', *Nature Geoscience*, vol 1, pp720–721

Rappaport, A. and Creighton, S.H. (2007) *Degrees that Matter: Climate Change and the University*, MIT Press, Cambridge MA

Roberts, C. and Roberts, J. (eds) (2007) *Greener by Degrees: Exploring Sustainability through Higher Education Curricula*, Centre for Active Learning, University of Gloucestershire, available at http://resources.glos.ac.uk/ceal/resources/greenerbyde-grees, accessed 4 February 2010

Sterling, S. (2001) *Sustainable Education. Re-visioning Learning and Change*, Schumacher Briefing 6, Green Books, Dartington

Sterling, S. (2003) *Whole Systems Thinking as a Basis for Paradigm Change in Education: Explorations in the Context of Sustainability*, PhD. thesis, University of Bath, available at www.bath.ac.uk/cree/sterling.htm

Summers, M., Corney, G. and Childs, A. (2004) 'Student teachers' conceptions of sustainable development: The starting-points of geographers and scientists', *Educational Research*, vol 46, no 2, pp163–182

University of East Anglia (2009) *Environmental Sciences*, available at www.uea.ac.uk/env, accessed 21 September 2009

University of Lancaster (2009) *The Lancaster Environment Centre: LEC and its Research*, available at www.lec.lancs.ac.uk/research, accessed 21 September 2009

University of Surrey (2009) *Centre for Environmental Strategy*, available at www.ces-surrey.org.uk, accessed 21 September 2009

Warburton, K. (2003) 'Deep learning and education for sustainability', *IJSHE*, vol 4, no 1, pp44–56

WCED (1987) *Our Common Future: The Report of the World Commission on Environment and Development* ['The Brundtland Report'], Oxford University Press, Oxford, available at www.un-documents.net/wced-ocf.htm, accessed 29 January 2010

Wellens, J., Berardi, A., Chalkley, B., Chambers, B., Healey, R. and Monk, J. (2006) 'Teaching geography for social transformation', *Journal of Geography in Higher Education*, vol 30, no 1, pp117–131

Notes

1   The Geographical Association is a UK-based organization, run by a board of trustees. It has charitable status and its members organize many events across the UK. www.geography.org.uk

2   The Royal Geographical Society is the learned society and professional body for geography: The Society was established in 1890 to advance geography and support its practitioners. www.rgs.org/HomePage.htm

3   The National Teaching Fellowships Scheme is applicable to those working in England and Northern Ireland. It is funded by the HEFCE and by the Department for

Employment and Learning in Northern Ireland, and administered by the HEA on their behalf. www.heacademy.ac.uk/ourwork/professional/ntfs

4   HEA Senior Fellowships are awarded in recognition of outstanding achievement and contribution to teaching and learning, available at. www.heacademy.ac.uk/ourwork/supportingindividuals/professionalrecognition?tabInd ex=2&#tab3

5   The *Journal of Geography in Higher Education*, available at www.tandf.co.uk/journals/carfax/03098265.html

6   The RAE is carried out around every five years on behalf of the four UK higher education funding councils to evaluate the quality of research undertaken by HEIs.

7   Committee of Heads of Environmental Sciences www.ches.org.uk

8   Institution of Environmental Sciences www.ies-uk.org.uk

9   In the UK today, the term 'old universities' is used to refer to those institutions that have from foundation been known as universities, while 'new universities' refer to former polytechnics that were given university status in 1992 under the then Conservative Government.

Chapter 7

Climate Change, Sustainability and Health in UK Higher Education: The Challenges for Nursing

Benny Goodman and Janet Richardson

Introduction

Climate change is the biggest global health threat of the 21st century.
(Costello et al, 2009, p1693)

We accept that there is a potential crisis for the continued health of individuals and populations, and that this crisis is linked to anthropogenic climate change (Hansen et al, 2007; World Health Organization [WHO], 2009; Costello et al, 2009) and to unsustainable patterns of living based on inappropriate economic models (Abdallah et al, 2009, Jackson 2009, Meadows et al, 2005). This crisis is deep-seated and has the potential to negatively affect the health and well-being of everyone on Earth (McMichael and Powles, 1999; UK Department of Health [DH], 2008a and 2008b; British Medical Association [BMA], 2008; Costello et al, 2009). In addition, the current economic system and the lifestyles it sustains has created this crisis and will be radically altered by it (Abdallah et al, 2009; Meadows et al, 2005; Naess, 2006; Newman, 2006; Jackson 2009; Orr 2004; Sinclair, 2009).

Nursing has long considered itself to be about promoting health, not just that of individuals but, by extension, that of society generally. The UK's professional body for nursing, the Nursing and Midwifery Council (NMC), states that for nurse education:

> *In keeping with the orientation towards holistic care, the emphasis must be one that avoids a narrow disease-orientated perspective and instead encompasses a health promotion and health education perspective* (NMC, 2004, p14).

The NMC is the body responsible for consulting on and publishing standards that underpin programmes of education leading to registration as a nurse. Therefore, any programme of Education for Sustainability (EfS) and climate change has to meet NMC standards. Given the threat to public health (and the NMC's emphasis on holistic care, health promotion and health education), it follows that nurse education should include an emphasis on climate change and sustainability. In this chapter, we will argue that there needs to be a *further* shift within nurse education from an individualistic and biomedical (i.e. disease-orientated) model towards a more radical *ecocentric* model (Kleffel, 1996 and 2004; Wells 2004); the term *ecocentric* will be explained below. In addition, nurse education should also address objectives other than just the immediate vocational and professional needs of the UK's National Health Service (NHS) workforce.

As it stands, there is insufficient explicit nursing response to EfS and climate change at UK universities, and this needs addressing with some urgency.

We will also argue that there is a sustainability–climate change–health triad that needs to be explicitly addressed in pre-registration nurse education; furthermore, we will discuss NHS public health concerns with climate change, sustainability and health, given that public health is at the core of nursing curricula. We will then go on to discuss obstacles and constraints impeding the take-up of ideas and concepts of sustainability. Following that, we will discuss opportunities for curriculum development and illustrate the potential for embedding climate change and sustainability in nursing in HE. We will then share some examples of current and developing nurse education practice. Finally, we will ask what still needs to be done.

At the outset, we must acknowledge that this discussion – given the current context of nurse education – aims to raise awareness of the issues for nursing rather than be a full discussion of sustainable pedagogy.

The sustainability–climate change–health triad

In the UK, the HE sector has taken over the education of a nursing workforce at pre-registration level from the NHS, but the Health Service still purchases and provides training for its qualified nursing workforce, often in partnership with universities. The drivers for pre-registration curricular frameworks and content largely come from the NMC and also from the DH. The NMC sets standards for universities to follow, publishing outcomes that all students must achieve before they can progress from level 4 (year one or 'common foundation programme', which equates to an HE certificate) and from levels 5 and 6 (foundation degree and bachelors degree with honours) onto the register.

The NHS is *the* important purchaser of education from the HE sector, and therefore many nursing courses will reflect the needs of the NHS as well as DH priorities. Therefore if the NMC, the NHS and the DH do not explicitly drive climate change and sustainability into nursing curricula and do not state that nurses need skills, knowledge and competencies to address the issues as part of nursing practice, it is left to university nursing faculties and others to do so. However, it is not clear that UK nursing faculties have done this explicitly.

Before considering the extent to which climate change and sustainability have featured in recent documentation underpinning nurse education and future visions of the role of the nurse (and whether it should feature more), we need to make the link between climate change, sustainability and health.

Climate change is primarily the result of increasing carbon dioxide emissions from fossil fuel energy consumption (Intergovernmental Panel on Climate Change [IPCC], 2007). It is arguable that unsustainable economics (and lifestyles based on current economic structures) also contribute to this process (Abdallah et al, 2009; Jackson, 2009; Meadows et al, 2005; Naess, 2006; Newman, 2006; Sinclair, 2009). Thus sustainable living cannot be achieved without addressing the issues of carbon emissions and climate change. Health at both the level of the individual and whole populations is based on sustainable living and on mitigating and adapting to climate change (McMichael and Powles, 1999; DH, 2008a and 2008b; BMA, 2008; Costello et al, 2009).

Sustainable living entails ensuring that current patterns of consumption and lifestyles do not endanger the physical and non-physical resource base for the coming generations (WCED, 1987; Sinclair, 2009). In addition to healthy genes, human health is based on the fundamentals of physical environment (clean air, clean water, sufficient food and safe waste disposal) and also on good psycho–social–political environments (e.g. low unemployment and absence of military conflict). We would also argue that a sense of aesthetics and the need to ask what constitutes human happiness cannot be ignored when assessing human health. Climate change threatens health because it jeopardizes both the physical environment and the psycho–social–political environment – the latter, for example, will assume increasing importance as clean water becomes a scarce commodity and replaces oil as a source for conflict (Nilekani, 2007). Environmental pollutants, radioactivity and toxins also affect the health of current generations (see, for example, Dhara and Dhara, 2002), and of future generations by increasing the likelihood of passing on genetic defects.

Climate change mitigation and adaptation and sustainability have become important for and accepted by business (Bali Communiqué, 2007), the UK Government (DEFRA, 2008), education (CSF, 2007; the HEA, 2009) and UK healthcare (DH, 2008a; NHS Sustainable Development Unit [NHSSDU], 2008). The implications for human existence, as currently enjoyed in the developed West, are potentially so serious that there is an urgent need to address issues in education. The human experience of climate change raises at least one potential dividing line between the West and the developing world concerning the question of equity of response and justice. The developing world is currently experiencing the results of past practice in the developed world (Ramesh, 2008), while others argue that the burden for tackling climate change must be borne by those responsible for it (*New Internationalist*, 2009). Climate change is likely to force those not conversant with sustainability to engage with it, and there should be an urgent recognition that health relies on both sustainable living *and* addressing climate change.

Thus, the sustainability–climate change–health triad is a useful conceptual model to underpin educational development in nursing. We will now outline the concerns of the NHS and other UK public health bodies.

The NHS and public health

The NHS continues to exacerbate climate change, with recent estimates suggesting that it is responsible for 5 per cent of the road transport emissions in the UK and that in total it emits around 1 million tonnes of carbon each year (O'Dowd, 2007; Mayor, 2008). The consequences of climate change are likely to lead to an increased demand on emergency and health services (Maryon-Davis et al, 2007). Nichols et al (2009) carried out a systematic review and thematic analysis of the literature on climate change and health and provide a comprehensive summary of the health effects of climate change. They found major strategies and policies focusing on mitigation and adaptation, but one other significant discovery was the gap between policy and action: within the published literature there was very little evidence of policy implementation or of action and good practice.

It has been suggested that the responsibility of healthcare practitioners to protect and promote public health should be extended to working to prevent climate change (Gill et al, 2007). Meanwhile, a potentially significant contribution to focus NHS action on climate change is the establishment of the NHS Sustainable Development Unit (NHSSDU) and the recent launch of the NHS *Carbon Reduction Strategy for England* (NHSSDU, 2008).

Other positive developments include the UK Public Health Association strategies for promoting health and SD (Public Health Association, 2007). The Association is an independent voluntary organization, formed by health professionals to unite the public health movement in the UK. The Climate and Health Council,[1] meanwhile, was established by health professionals as a not-for-profit international organization aimed at mobilizing health professionals globally to take action to limit climate change and its effects on human health; it also forms part of a registered charity, Knowledge into Action. In 2008, the UK Faculty of Public Health, a body of public health professionals, published a document outlining action that can be taken at organizational and individual levels (UK Faculty of Public Health, 2008), which was closely followed by publication of the DH guidance document on the health impact of climate change (DH, 2008b).

Additionally, the *British Medical Journal* has set up a Carbon Council aimed at 'harnessing the intelligence and imagination of health professionals to expedite the transition to a low-carbon world' (Stott and Godlee, 2006). There have also been calls for health professionals to make attempts to reduce the carbon footprint of attending medical conferences by considering virtual alternatives to physical meetings (Roberts and Godlee, 2007). Public health bodies' focus on climate change therefore forms a context within which both the NHS and nursing operate.

Nurse education curriculum development: obstacles and constraints

The main barriers to changing the nurse education curriculum can be summarized as follows:

- Instrumental/vocational training orientation to meet local, regional and national NHS needs.
- Approaches to health and illness are individualistic and biomedical.
- There is a lack of specific leadership on climate change and sustainability in both professional nursing and nursing in higher education.

First, the instrumental/vocational training orientation for nursing workforce development to meet local and regional NHS needs does not explicitly discuss climate change or sustainability, despite the public health and DH policy context. As noted earlier, nurse education curriculum development responds mainly to the demands of the NHS (via Strategic Health Authorities [SHAs] and Primary Care Trusts[PCTs]) and the DH, as well as the NMC. The overall context of nursing education is, in the main, producing an NHS workforce. For example, DH documents such as *Working Together, Learning Together* (2001), *Skilled for Health* (2002), *Knowledge and Skills Framework* (2004a), *Modernising Nursing Careers* (2006a) and *Framing the Nursing and Midwifery Contribution: Driving up the Quality of Care* (2008c) have to be taken on board by education staff in the HE sector as well as NHS training departments. These developments do not expressly address the sustainability–climate change–health triad. However, they leave some scope for interpretation. For example, one aspect of the NHS *Knowledge and Skills Framework* is entitled 'Promotion of health and well-being and prevention of adverse effects on health and well-being'. An examination of the detail reveals that climate change and sustainability could easily be used to illustrate achievement in this field.

Thus, under 'Examples for application' in the *Knowledge and Skills Framework*, an educational or training programme or policy objective for NHS workers could focus on the 'broader aspects of the environment that affect people's lives and their health and well-being (e.g. housing, transport, education, employment)' (DH, 2004a, p103). These are all aspects easily illustrated by the link between sustainable living and healthy living; sustainable transport such as cycling brings health benefits as well as carbon reduction.

The goals or *outcomes* for nurse education are clear – that is, achievement of skills and competencies as laid down by the NMC and the DH. However, there may be some room as regards *process*. By 'process' we mean *how* (i.e. the pedagogy) by which one reaches the goal or outcome. This is not prescribed in any detail by the NMC and so universities have a degree of freedom in this. Process pedagogy could address personal development and education for social change but it has to vie for curricular space alongside the achievement of nursing practice learning *outcomes* and demonstration of competence in practical clinical skills. Climate change and sustainability issues do not at first glance seem to fit into this easily, unless addressed through the lens of public health as discussed above.

This situation might be explained by an interpretation of current nursing curricula as based on four competing ideologies (Scrimshaw, 1983) and a confusion of 'cleverness' for 'intelligence' by curriculum designers (Orr, 2004). This suggests that we need to analyse who has the power and influence to drive curricula in certain directions, and also what we think a curriculum is *for*. The four competing ideologies are as follows:

1 *Instrumentalism* – 'This stresses the utility and relevance of training to the existing social and economic order, which may itself be static or changing. This is education for a purpose and arguably the dominant ideology in professional nurse education (Quinn and Hughes, 2007). An instrumental curriculum may be designed to meet current NHS and DH needs for a skilled nursing workforce who are equipped for a specific purpose. The policy context for nurse workforce development may include a health orientation (e.g. DH, 2004b) model in nursing and health care practice (Griffiths, 1998; Castledine, 2005; Limoges, 2007) even for those with a public health role (Poulton et al, 2000; Cameron and Christie, 2007).

  Instrumentalism of this nature could be an example of Orr's (2004) 'cleverness'. We may create practitioners who are 'clever', defined by particularly narrow (workforce) purposes, but fail to equip them with the 'intelligence' to question the purpose of practice in the first place.

2 *Liberal humanism* – This maintains education is a good in and of itself, it does not have to lead to qualifications for skills and careers. This ideology could foster 'intelligence' because it seeks to understand the difference between know-how and 'know-why' (Orr, 2004). In the health context, this would seek to address the appropriateness of expensive technological and pharmacological solutions to health issues rather than learning how to blindly apply them.

3 *Progressivism* – Challenge, shaping and changing personal identity, concern with personal growth and development of the self as well as of communities are the tenets of this ideology.

4   *Reconstructivism* – This emphasizes that education has a role in equipping learners for social roles, changing power structures and challenging orthodoxy; it is education for social change.

Similarly, Sterling (2001, p25) states that the function or roles of education can be:

1   to replicate society, culture and citizenship – the socialization function;
2   to train for employment – the vocational function;
3   to develop the individual – the liberal function;
4   to encourage a fairer society and a better world – the transformative function.

Within the frame of either Sterling's or the 'competing ideologies' typology, designers of nursing curricula will have an explicit or implicit ideology or function in mind, on which they base their curriculum models, perhaps emphasizing one tendency at the expense of others.

We argue that 'instrumentalism' and the 'vocational function' are implicitly dominant in nursing curriculum design and that these current visions of the roles of nurses, especially in the hospital sector, largely exclude sustainability and climate change. This is due to the perceived need for education to prepare nurses for specific clinical, technical or biomedical roles. Thus there is an underlying drive for education to meet outcomes that have been narrowly defined (e.g. by SHAs) and may not address climate change and sustainability, *despite the public health context.*

The second obstacle is an individualistic and biomedical approach to health and illness. A biomedical approach (see, for example, Newell 2000; Greenhill and Greenhill, 2009) would emphasize knowledge and skills that address analysis of physiological and anatomical dysfunction, management of illness and disease and disease patterns, the search for treatments and cures and a focus on the individual patient. Although developments of the model (Greaves and Evans, 2000) have challenged this simplistic view, for example, by drawing attention to the emotional needs of patients, it arguably remains highly influential in nursing curricula, as Castledine (2005, p419) suggests:

There is a great deal of evidence to suggest that the biomedical model has, and continues to be, the model on which many nurses base their practice.
Research studies in nursing have frequently reported that nurses view their patients as physical beings with medical problems to solve, rather than nursing and healing patients' wider personal and individual problems.

This is compounded by post-registration education where it is at least arguable that 'training' to meet local (i.e. SHA) service needs, which exclude analysis of sustainable health and climate change, are prioritized. This may result in no demand for courses and modules on understanding and analysing global inter-connectedness, environment and health because they may seem too academic and irrelevant to nursing in the NHS.

The third issue is a lack of leadership in some quarters. Implementing policies for education and action on health and climate change requires strong leadership by national nursing organizations (for example, the NMC and the Royal College of Nursing in the UK), government health departments and universities. In addition, leadership could come from health service providers such as SHAs, which are the part of the NHS in England responsible for developing strategies for local health services and ensuring high-quality performance. They manage the NHS locally and are a key link between the DH and the NHS. They also ensure that national priorities are integrated into local plans. Given the emphasis on carbon reduction and sustainability at a national level in the UK and the increasing number of good examples to draw on, SHAs are well placed to provide direction on sustainability and efforts to mitigate and adapt to the effects of climate change. However, it appears that many SHAs in England have yet to embrace sustainability or integrate preparations for climate change and energy vulnerability into their organizational strategies (Richardson et al, 2009). PCTs in England are responsible for commissioning a comprehensive and equitable range of services across all service sectors and directly provide care and services such as health promotion. A number of PCTs recognize the impacts that climate change may have on the health of populations and have responded by making commitments to implement policies in regard to SD and climate change (Nichols et al, 2009). PCT action on climate change includes the implementation of green travel plans, efforts to conserve resources, reduce waste and recycle. Both SHAs and PCTs are in key positions to influence policies and practices to mitigate and adapt to the impact of climate change and energy vulnerability, and also to promote sustainable communities.

The DH has clearly stated that sustainability and carbon reduction applies to the NHS (DH, 2006b and 2008d). However, the wider sustainability and climate change discourse internationally and in UK public health has *not* driven nursing workforce development in the direction of explicitly addressing climate change and sustainability as part of clinical nursing practice. Again, we suggest an individualistic, biomedical approach to health, a vocational focus and a lack of leadership in nursing combine to prevent this.

Despite this, the NHS and public health discourse offers a sound basis for nurse education. Public health is core to nursing curricula and therefore there is no need to argue for its inclusion. Exploring health issues through the lens of public health is a totally legitimate sphere of education for nursing professionals, and the insights and resources being developed by all public health professions will provide both resources and an underpinning educational driver.

Leadership in HE is being shown through the HEA's[2] ESD Project. Dawe et al (2005) identify 14 subject centres that are addressing sustainability concepts and also host online sustainability resources for teaching and learning. The coverage of disciplines ranges from art design and media to sociology, anthropology and politics. However, nursing, although part of the Health Sciences and Practice Subject Centre, appears not to have a strong presence or output in terms of educational practice.

Dawe et al (2005) argue that their research shows that progress towards ESD might appear patchy and limited in some important disciplines, with nursing (we would add) offering an example of little or no engagement.

In addition to the work of the HEA, leadership for sustainability and health is emerging with the formal establishment in 2009 of the Institute of Sustainability, Health and the Environment (ISHE),[3] which is based at the University of the West of England. ISHE aims to be a research and knowledge exchange institute providing for the integration of evidence-based, cross-disciplinary understanding on health and sustainability.

Opportunities in nursing education

Next, we will outline opportunities for nurse education to embrace sustainability and discuss the need for leadership from nursing bodies to do so.

The concept of sustainable literacy (Stibbe, 2009) emphasizes ideas such as the interconnectedness of people and planet, and 'being in the world' whereby people have the 'ability to think about the self in interconnection and interdependence with the surrounding world' (Danvers; cited in Stibbe, 2009, p185), along with the 'systems thinking' ability 'to recognise and analyse interconnectedness between and within systems' (Strachan; cited in Stibbe, 2009, p84).

Both 'being in the world' and 'systems thinking' are concepts that are congruent with nursing theory that focuses on holistic care (Ham-Yin, 1993; Sarkis and Skoner, 1987). McEvoy and Duffy (2008, p414) argue:

Nursing is indeed holistic in nature, as the nursing profession has traditionally viewed the person as a whole, concerned with the interrelationship of body, mind and spirit, promoting psychological and physiological well-being as well as fostering socio-cultural relationships in an ever-changing economic environment of care.

Although not an uncontested philosophy in nursing (Woods, 1998; Castledine 2005), holism may provide a way of thinking that emphasizes 'interrelationships' and 'interconnectedness'. Holistic nursing aims to address the patient's physical, mental, emotional and spiritual care needs and is sometimes referred to as 'whole person' care (Kitson, 2004). Wright (2008, p26) argues:

There is much more to holism than 'whole person' care – its true meaning connects each of us to the universe

– and thus emphasizes that nursing care moves beyond the individual to take in the connections that such an individual has with the biosphere. Implicit in this view is the assumption that health and illness cannot be taken out of the environmental context in which the individual lives.

Nurse educators will be familiar with the need to move students beyond an individualistic biomedical model that sees the biological individual as a system in itself disconnected from the environment. However, what needs emphasizing in nurse education to a greater extent is the inclusion of the wider physical and natural environment in the conception of holism (i.e. an 'ecocentric' paradigm, as described below), so that a biomedical approach supports rather than dominates our understandings of health and illness.

We argue that holistic nursing should address the environmental, biophysical, social and cognitive/emotional domains of existence to clarify what health and the goal of nursing action may mean. Nursing models (e.g. Roper et al, 1985) do highlight this holistic approach, but the focus is on the individual rather than the socio-political and the environment (Wells, 2004).

Kleffel (1996, p1) discusses three paradigms for nursing:

1   The egocentric paradigm is grounded in the person and is based on the assumption that what is good for the individual is good for society.
2   The homocentric paradigm is grounded in society and reflects the utilitarian ethic of the greatest good for the greatest number of people.
3   The ecocentric paradigm is grounded in the cosmos, and the environment is considered whole, living and interconnected.

Kleffel also argues that: 'Historically, nurses have adhered primarily to the egocentric paradigm and to a lesser extent to the homocentric paradigm' (1996, p1).

We argue that a nurse's daily clinical activity will involve individuals, but nursing also has to address the social (and public health) level. Nursing often focuses on restoring ill *individuals* back to health (Castledine, 2005), and nursing assessment and intervention are usually at the individual (egocentric) level, but with some attempt to take into account the psycho-social domain. However, to fully address this, nursing may have to shift further from an individual philosophy (egocentric) to a biospherical (ecocentric) philosophy. According to Rowe (1987):

> *ecocentrism is a philosophy that recognizes that the ecosphere, rather than any individual organism, is the source and support of all life and as such advises a holistic and ecocentric approach to government, industry, and the individual.*

This perspective begins from a macroscopic view that takes in all that exists on Earth, explicitly accepting the value of *all* things, animate *and* inanimate. Again there is the idea of the 'interconnectedness' of humanity and the physical environment, supporting the idea that human health cannot be separated from environmental health.

What is missing from current NMC education criteria are explicit attempts to embed ecocentrism and the sustainability–climate change–health triad. If more widely understood and adopted, ecocentrism (as a paradigm for nursing) would address this. Kirk (2002) argues that for nursing, there has been little research and few scholarly papers have debated these issues. This may result in a poor knowledge base on which to empower or challenge nursing students, practitioners and academics. Kirk also reports findings from a small survey of senior nursing academics in the UK, concluding that the 'nursing profession generally is not sufficiently aware of global environmental issues' (2002, p69).

Thus, it may be hypothesized (and extrapolated from this comment) that nursing *students* are ill equipped to make any connections between sustainability, climate change and health. Kagawa's survey (2007) of students' views was conducted at a UK HEI and therefore provides support for this hypothesis.

More recently than Kirk – and taking an international view – Hunt (2006, p572) has argued:

As far as nursing professional organisations are concerned, my quick survey in June 2006 of the web-based policy documents of the International Council of Nurses (ICN), the American Nurses Association (ANA), the UK's Royal College of Nursing (RCN) and the Japanese Nursing Association (JNA) showed an almost total absence of any acknowledgement, let alone engagement with the issue [of climate change]. It is time to change this situation.

However, this was before the seminal IPCC report (2007). To update Kirk's (2002) and Hunt's (2006) comments, we undertook a brief analysis of some key UK nursing and health documents (e.g. Longley et al, 2007, Basford and Kershaw, 2008) and position statements from UK nursing organizations such as the NMC and the RCN. The RCN is now addressing the link between sustainability, climate change and health by, for example, agreeing to support the UK government's target of an 80 per cent reduction in carbon emissions by 2050, and has joined a coalition of organizations to tackle poverty and climate change. The NMC is carrying out a review (2008–2009) of its standards; these underpin nurse education in the UK but the current standards (NMC, 2004) do not explicitly mention climate change or sustainability.

The ICN, a federation of national nursing associations, has published a position statement on *Nurses, Climate Change and Health* (2008), which states:

ICN acknowledges climate change as an important issue for the nursing profession, particularly in light of the impact on people's health and nursing's shared responsibility to sustain and protect the natural environment from depletion, pollution, degradation and destruction (p1).

In addition, the ANA has published a resolution on the *Global Climate Challenge* (2008), the Royal College of Nursing, Australia, (a position statement, *Nurses, Health and the Environment* (1998) and the Canadian Nurses Association a background paper on *The Role of Nurses in Addressing Climate Change*. There are very many other national nursing organizations across the globe, but it is not known how many others, if any, have published position statements linking health and the environment.

Neither nursing philosophy on its own nor an emerging awareness to the health threats posed by climate change will be sufficient to provide a full understanding of the issues. EfS will necessitate drawing on a wide range of disciplines; nursing education already does so (biology, sociology, psychology and physiology, for instance), widening disciplinary horizons as such is not new. But the challenge would be to further draw from other disciplines such as philosophy to address ideas such as speciesism (Ryder, 1973; Singer, 1975). An examination of speciesism, whereby we assign a lesser value to beings merely because of their membership of a different species, could help challenge fundamental assumptions about the superiority of human beings.

As regards pedagogy, there may be a congruence between that in nursing education and that associated with sustainability education. Key ESD precepts and principles include participation, community engagement, collaboration, openness to different perspectives and worldviews, transparency, diversity, thinking alternatively and laterally, action in partnership, futures thinking and visualization and nature-connectedness (CSE, 2009; Stibbe, 2009). We may argue that learning processes should mirror or enshrine those precepts and principles. Therefore, participatory, experiential and action-oriented learning allied to in-community contexts for learning that move away from transmissive forms of teaching are foundational for sustainability and could also be so for nursing education. However, an emphasis on the acquisition of clinical skills and the technical vocational nature of nursing education may militate against this.

Nurse education has frequently been claimed (Quinn and Hughes, 2007, for example) as being based on adult learning theory or 'andragogy' (Knowles, 1984), the main principles of which are:

1   *Self-concept* – As a person matures their self concept moves from one of being a dependent personality towards one of being a self-directed human being.

2   *Experience* – As a person matures they accumulate a growing reservoir of experience that becomes an increasing resource for learning.

3   *Readiness to learn* – As a person matures their readiness to learn becomes oriented increasingly to the developmental tasks of their social roles.

4   *Orientation to learning* – As a person matures their time perspective changes from one of postponed application of knowledge to immediacy of application, and accordingly their orientation toward learning shifts from one of subject-centredness to one of problem-centredness.

5   *Motivation to learn* – As a person matures the motivation to learn is internalized (Knowles, 1984, p12).

Andragogy is in opposition to didactic (transmissive) 'chalk and talk' teaching; it accesses the students' experience and knowledge, values that experience and assumes a motivation to learn, with the student taking as much of a lead as the teacher. However, whether students of nursing see it the same way is debatable. Norrie and Dalby, for instance, argue from a study of 555 students in an under-graduate nursing programme that:

there is no evidence that students gain more of the characteristics of andragogy as they progress… There is some evidence that students become less willing to take on responsibility for their learning (Norrie and Dalby, 2007, p319).

Theoretically, the learning precepts and principles outlined above would not be alien to many nurse educators. In practice, however, nurse educators may wish to reflect on the context of nurse education and consider whether Knowles's theory is manifest in reality. The same argument applies to any application of sustainabil-ity pedagogies. Unless students are enabled to take responsibility for their learning (and do so) they will depend on received wisdom and be shaped rather than be shapers of their futures.

Sustainability concepts and ideas hold a great deal of potential that has yet to be realized in nursing. Concepts such as interconnectedness would resonate well with education staff but the main barrier would seem to be the need to produce a skilled workforce for the NHS. Until the NHS moves beyond seeing climate change and carbon reduction in terms of its estates and energy use and until nursing more fully adopts a public health stance on the issue, education will be shaped by clinicians' and the NMC's need to see clinical skills demonstrated in the workplace at the expense of sustainability.

Nurse education could embed the idea of 'ecological literacy' (Orr, 1991) into curricula and pedagogical strategies. Orr argues this involves asking the question 'What then?' (Orr, 1991, p85) while achieving a technical, scientific and disciplinary mastery. It is not enough, for example, to be literate, or be skilled in information technology or clinical examination. Students must be encouraged to make and understand the connections between how the Earth works and their everyday lives. This orientation to learning ought, Orr implies, to be embedded across the disciplines. This is even more imperative in nursing because a proper understanding of health must include understanding, for example, how we get and maintain clean water. An interesting idea Orr also puts forward is that of 'place', (2004, p125), education currently being too 'indoors'. Space prevents fuller discussion of this concept, but it involves a concern about the disconnection between people and ecology in our educational environ-ments, bounded as we are by steel, glass, concrete and flickering computer screens.

Sustainability in the nursing curriculum

Given the dearth of an explicit nursing response to sustainability, both profession-ally and in HE, actual examples of EfS and climate change education are difficult

Box 7.1 Potential ideas for curricula in pre-registration nursing programmes (levels 4, 5 and 6) leading to qualifications and entry onto the nursing register

Biology modules

- Introduce a common heritage and shared chemistry of living things.
- Discuss evolutionary conservation of some genes, compare homeostasis in the body with the concept of planetary homeostasis.

Pathology modules in nursing programmes

- Epidemiology of diseases such as HIV and bird flu.
- Role of migrations and travel in spread of disease.
- Discussion of the documented effects of lifestyle changes on health to give an insight into changes now happening in our own population. For example, increasing rates of skin cancer due to popularity of sunbathing.
- Discussions about possible effects of climate change on disease distributions (e.g. malaria).

Nursing practice modules

- Investigation of what happens to clinical waste – how it contributes to climate change through being burnt or added to landfill.
- Investigation of whether tap water can be used for wound irrigation rather than sterile containers of 0.9 per cent saline (bringing in toxicity, impact of manufacture and transport of plastic containers and their disposal).
- Discussion of the pros and cons of electronic vs paper records in nursing practice – carbon dioxide emissions, data storage, paper manufacture and disposal, security and so on.

to come by. However, as a direct response to the development of the CSF, the University of Plymouth's Faculty of Health has begun to address sustainability in its nursing curricula. It is fair to say that without CSF input and support, the examples shown in Boxes 7.1 to 7.3 may not have addressed climate change and sustainability so readily. The work was facilitated by some fellowships offered to members of Faculty to begin the development of this work.

Recognizing that there is little of an ecocentric paradigm underpinning curricula, we may still be able to design modules and courses by using one or more of three approaches that have been suggested (CSF, 2009) to engage students with concepts of sustainability during their university courses. Briefly, these can be described as the 'infusion' model (sustainability issues are woven into existing curriculum), the 'generic' model (a generally available framework module is customized by individual disciplines) and the 'common' model (a common cross-disciplinary sustainability module is available as an option for all students).

Box 7.2. A module example for infusing sustainability into the curriculum

This module is offered to registered nurses and other health professionals as part of continuing professional development.

Module title: Public Health: Promoting health through policy.

Level 5. University of Plymouth. BSc Community Specialist Public Health programme, BSc Health Studies.

Module aims

The module aims to develop students' critical awareness of broad political and public health frameworks driving processes of health needs assessment and health promotion, thereby enabling them to promote the health of individuals, groups and communities in an empowering and ethical manner.

Learning outcome 1: Discussion of contemporary policy and public health frameworks

Sustainability is addressed by introducing students to contemporary policy and public health frameworks and emphasizing that it is an important value underpinning current global and national policy. Systems theory is used to critically analyse relationships between environment and policy because environmental issues become a driver for 'inputs' to policy-making and resulting policies have 'outcomes' or consequences that, in turn, affect the environment.

Learning outcome 2: Analysis of health needs using epidemiological data and exploring determinants of health

Sessions on health needs assessment and epidemiology explore the determinants of health and enable students to consider how factors such as traffic pollution are detrimental to health and must be addressed in public health policy. Sustainable transport policy is discussed to address improvements in health and reduced demand on health services, thereby conserving resources for use elsewhere.

Learning outcome 3: Examining health promotion models and applying them to working with individuals, groups and communities

By examining health promotion models and applying them to work with individuals, groups and communities, students are introduced to concepts such as community development, which illustrates that communities can be mobilized to tackle issues such as healthy eating at a collective level. By discouraging use of highly processed fast foods and encouraging communities to consider growing food or learning to cook healthily, sustainability is clearly addressed. Issues such as consumerism and patient involvement in healthcare are also linked to sustainability because by creating expert patients who can support themselves and others, reliance on costly health service staff is reduced. Also, patient involvement should lead to development of more responsive services, thereby avoiding duplication or repetition and helping to eliminate waste.

Box 7.2 continued

Learning outcome 4: Discussing the importance of consumer involvement and empowerment in promoting health

Issues such as consumerism and patient involvement in health care also link to sustainability since by creating expert patients who can support themselves and others, then reliance on costly health service staff is reduced. Also, patient involvement should lead to the development of more responsive services, thereby avoiding duplication or repetition and helping to eliminate waste.

Learning outcome 5: Identifying and addressing ethical issues in health promotion

Finally, in exploring ethical issues such as justice and equity, the module clearly addresses the DH's strategy for delivering SD, emphasizing the need to address diversity, social cohesion and equity as central issues in the government's sustainability agenda.

Prepared by Gerri Clay, lecturer, University of Plymouth; Module Leader, Public Health: Promoting health through policy

---

Box 7.3 Example from a pre-registration nursing module at the University of Plymouth. BSc Nursing

Module title: Management for quality care. Level 5.

Example of learning outcome: Demonstrating the need to set priorities in clinical care through effective decision-making.

This module is aimed at year three students preparing for leadership and management roles. Although sustainability and climate change are not explicit in the module learning outcomes, an online lecture and discussion was developed to highlight to students what priorities for clinical care will be at national and international level. The DH and NHS agendas for sustainability were used as a vehicle to get students to think about the context of clinical care and address responses to climate change as nurses at individual, group, organizational, national and international level.

The generic and common models would pose difficulties for nurse education given the issues of curriculum space and funding. Thus the infusion model seems most appropriate, at least in the first instance.

Boxes 7.1 to 7.3 offer examples of how sustainability is being infused into nursing programmes (e.g. BSc Nursing, BSc Community Specialist Public Health) and come from the University of Plymouth. Box 7.1 is a list of potential ideas to underpin nursing modules, while Boxes 7.2 and 7.3 are developments in modules.

What needs to be done

Nursing along with medicine has a public health core. Both professions are well placed to provide directions to improve public health at both social and individual levels. Given the seriousness of the health threats posed by climate change, we suggest:

- The professional bodies responsible for nursing education should take a lead. For example, the NMC's review of standards of proficiency for pre-registration nursing education should explicitly address the sustainability/climate change/health triad. This would inform universities' development of nursing programmes.

- There should be national nursing statements made and leads taken on sustainability, climate change and health from a chief government adviser (where this post exists) for nursing in each country.

- National nursing organizations could host an activists' forum as one of their communities or networks. For example, the RCN should submit a position statement in line with other national nursing organizations such as the Canadian Nurses Association.

- Nursing academics and nursing departments should get involved in any sustainability projects organized by their HE-wide organizations (for example, the HEA[1] in the UK).

- All interested stakeholders should network, connect and communicate through various interprofessional channels as the Nursing, Midwifery and Health Professions connection on the Climate Connection,[2] the Campaign for Greener Healthcare[3] and the Climate and Health Council[4] and ISHE.[5]

- Universities and the buyers of education (for example, the NHS) should address sustainability and climate change during the pre-purchasing negotiations. Discussions about what is required for the professional development of nurses should highlight sustainability and climate change. HEIs should not only respond to workforce development requests but, in partnership with education buyers, outline what the professional nurse of the future should be in terms of the context of sustainability and climate change.

- Universities and other education/training providers need to be creative in developing research-based learning resources on this subject as well as in modes of delivery, and the development of modules and programmes.

- National and international nursing organizations should be urging universities, professional bodies and their national departments of health to place climate change and sustainability explicitly on the nursing curricula.

- Nurses at national level must be involved in developing national action plans and policies and be part of disaster-preparedness teams to mitigate the impact of climate change on health (Hunt, 2006).

- Curriculum planners could review current programmes and modules and reinterpret learning outcomes so sustainability concepts could be introduced to students. New modules need to be developed that address sustainability and health explicitly.

- Nursing students need to be supported and encouraged to actively engage in issues of sustainability and climate change at various levels.
- Nursing journals should actively commission articles examining the topics, especially those offering action and solutions.

Conclusion

The current state of play is that both the nursing profession and nurse education in the UK are grasping the seriousness of the issues of climate change and unsustainable social, economic and environmental trends, but they need to more highly prioritize an awareness and response. Nursing organizations elsewhere, for instance, in Canada (Canadian Nurses Association, 2008 and 2009) are explicitly addressing nursing roles for climate change.

Leadership in nursing professional and educational bodies is needed to further support this important agenda. Leadership should go beyond accepting the need for carbon reduction on NHS estates and practices to establish educational approaches that prepare nurses of the future with Orr's 'intelligence' rather than technical 'cleverness'. Workforce planning is based on current assumptions (which may not address sustainability) about what skills and competencies are needed for nurses. If this is inward-looking (i.e. it focuses only on national and regional concerns) and short-term, it will miss, for example, preparing nurses for meeting the new disease patterns, conflict management and disaster planning that will arise as a result of climate change and are global in nature and impact.

Learning and teaching methods in nurse education could support further development of knowledge and skills beyond an individually biomedically focused basis for healthcare. Students could be enabled to take responsibility for drawing on as wide an intellectual base as possible to challenge current thinking and practice. This would include challenging the perceived wisdom of nurse educators and clinical nurses. Nursing academics could revisit concepts such as ecocentrism and holism to explore their relevance to curricula.

Alongside medicine, nursing is an important professional body in terms of actual numbers of practitioners and the role they undertake in health education and promotion. Therefore, they should be at the vanguard of addressing the health consequences of climate change and unsustainable living. These consequences will involve shifting patterns of disease from southerly regions to the north, potentially increases in skin cancer, increases in tick-borne disease, the mass displacement of populations and the loss of clean water supplies and land for food production further adding to the disease burden on populations. Nurse education is well placed to address the issues: although it is constrained by its vocational nature, there are nonetheless opportunities through education processes to legitimately focus on climate change, sustainability and health.

References

Abdallah, S., Thompson, S., Michaelson, J., Marks, N. and Steuer, N. (2009) *The Happy Planet Index 2.0: Why Good Lives Don't Have to Cost the Earth*, New Economics Foundation, London www.happyplanetindex.org Accessed 3 September 2009

ANA (2008) *Global Climate Change* www.nursingworld.org/MemberCenterCategories/ ANAGovernance/HODArchives/2008HOD/ActionsAdopted/GlobalClimateChange andHumanHealth.aspx Accessed 25 March 2009

Bali Communiqué (2007) 'The corporate leaders group on climate change', www.cpsl.cam.ac.uk/pdf/Bali%20Communique%20&%20Signatories%201.pdf, accessed 1 March 2010

Basford, L. and Kershaw, B. (2008) *A Key Issues Paper: Underpinning the Future of Health Professional Education in the UK*, University and College Union, London

BMA (2008) 'Health professionals taking action on climate change', available at www.bma.org.uk/health_promotion_ethics/climate_change/, accessed 1 March 2010

Cameron, S. and Christie, G. (2007) 'Exploring health visitors' perceptions of the public health nursing role', *Primary Health Care Research and Development*, vol 1, no 8, pp80–90

Canadian Nurses Association (2008) *The Role of Nurses in Addressing Climate Change*, available at www.cna-aiic.ca/CNA/documents/pdf/publications/Climate_Change_ 2008_e.pdf, accessed 28 January 2010

Canadian Nurses Association (2009) *Nursing and Environmental Health*, www.cna-aiic.ca/ CNA/issues/environment/websites/default_e.aspx Accessed 29 January 2010

Castledine, G. (2005) 'What medical roles should nursing be incorporating?' *British Journal of Nursing*, vol 14, no 7, p419

CSF (2007) www.csf.plymouth.ac.uk, accessed 25 March 2009

CSF (2009) http://erdt.plymouth.ac.uk/csfwiki/index.php/SNACS_Curricula Accessed 30 July 2009

Costello, A., Abbas, M., Allen, A., Ball, S., Bell, S., Bellamy, R., Friel, S., Groce, N., Johnson, A., Kett, M., Lee, M., Levy, C., Maslin, M., McCoy, D., McGuire, B., Montgomery, H., Napier, D., Pagel, C., Patel, J., Patterson, C., Puppim de Oliveira, J.A., Redclift, N., Rees, H., Rogger, D., Scott, J., Stephenson, J., Twigg, J. and Wolff, J. (2009) 'Managing the health effects of climate change', *The Lancet*, vol 373, no 16, pp1693–1733

Danvers, J. (2009), cited in Stibbe, A. (ed)

Dawe, G., Jucker, R. and Martin, S. (2005) *Sustainable Development in Higher Education: Current Practice and Future Developments*, HEA, York, available at www.heacademy.ac.uk/assets/York/documents/ourwork/tla/sustainability/ sustdevinHEfinalreport.pdf, accessed 23 January 2010

DEFRA (2008) *Climate Change Act 2008*, available at www.defra.gov.uk/ ENVIRONMENT/climatechange/uk/legislation, accessed 25 March 2009

DH (2001) *Working Together, Learning Together: A Framework for Lifelong Learning for the NHS*, available at www.dh.gov.uk/en/Publicationsandstatistics/Publications/ PublicationsPolicyAndGuidance/DH_4009558, accessed 6 October 2009

DH (2002) *Skilled for Health*, available at www.dh.gov.uk/en/Publichealth/ Healthimprovement/SkilledforHealth/index.htm, accessed 6 October 2009

DH (2004a) *The NHS Knowledge and Skills Framework and the Development Review Process*, available at www.dh.gov.uk/en/Publicationsandstatistics/Publications/ PublicationsPolicyAndGuidance/DH_4088347, accessed 6 October 2009

DH (2004b) *Securing Good Health for the Whole Population* ['The Wanless Report'], available at www.dh.gov.uk/en/Publicationsandstatistics/Publications/PublicationsPolicyAndGuidance/DH_4074426, accessed 7 October 2009

DH (2006a) *Modernising Nursing Careers – Setting the Direction*, available at www.dh.gov.uk/en/Publicationsandstatistics/Publications/PublicationsPolicyAndGuidance/DH_4138756, accessed 6 October 2009

DH (2006b) *Sustainable Development Action Plan 2006*, available at www.dh.gov.uk/en/Publicationsandstatistics/Publications/PublicationsPolicyAndGuidance/DH_4132222, accessed 6 October 2009

DH (2008a) *Health Effects of Climate Change in the UK: An Update of the Department of Health Report 2001/2002*, available at www.dh.gov.uk/en/Publicationsandstatistics/Publications/PublicationsPolicyAndGuidance/DH_4007935, accessed 6 October 2009

DH (2008b) *The Health Impact of Climate Change: Promoting Sustainable Communities – Guidance Document*, available at www.dh.gov.uk/en/Publicationsandstatistics/Publications/PublicationsPolicyAndGuidance/DH_082690, accessed 6 October 2009

DH (2008c) *Framing the Nursing and Midwifery Contribution: Driving up the Quality of Care*, available at www.dh.gov.uk/en/Publicationsandstatistics/Publications/PublicationsPolicyAndGuidance/DH_089049, accessed 6 October 2009

DH (2008d) *Taking the Long-term View: The Department of Health's Strategy for Delivering Sustainable Development 2008–2011*, available at www.dh.gov.uk/en/Publicationsandstatistics/Publications/PublicationsPolicyAndGuidance/DH_086471, accessed 6 October 2009

Dhara, V. and Dhara, R. (2002) 'The Union Carbide disaster in Bhopal: A review of health effects', *Archives of Environmental Health*, vol 57, no 5, pp391–404

Gill, M., Goodlee, F., Horton, R. and Stott, R. (2007) 'Doctors and climate change', *British Medical Journal*, vol 335, no 7630, pp1104–1105

Greaves, D. and Evans, M. (2000) 'Conceptions of medical humanities', *Medical Humanities*, vol 26, no 65, pp1–2

Griffiths, P. (1998) 'An investigation into the description of patients' problems by nurses using two different needs-based nursing models', *Journal of Advanced Nursing*, vol 289, no 5, pp969–977

Ham-Yin, S. (1993) 'Analysis of the concept of holism within the context of nursing', *British Journal of Nursing*, vol 2, no 15, pp771–775

Hansen, J., Sato, M., Kharecha, P., Russell, G., Lea, D.W. and Siddall, M. (2007) 'Climate change and trace gases', *Philosophical Transactions of the Royal Society A*, vol 365, pp1925–1954, available at http://pubs.giss.nasa.gov/docs/2007/2007_Hansen_etal_2.pdf, accessed 25 March 2009

HEA (2009) *Sustainability* www.heacademy.ac.uk/ourwork/learning/sustainability, accessed 25 March 2009

Hunt, G. (2006) 'Climate change & nursing', *Nursing Ethics*, vol 13, no 6, pp571–72

ICN (2008) *Nurses, Climate Change and Health: Position Statement*, available at www.icn.ch/PS_E08_Nurses%20Climate%20Change.pdf, accessed 25 March 2008

IPCC (2007) *Climate Change (2007) – The Physical Science Basis: Summary for Policymakers*, IPCC Secretariat, Geneva

Jackson, T. (2009) *Prosperity without Growth. Economics for a Finite Planet*, Earthscan, London

Kagawa, F. (2007) 'Dissonance in students' perceptions of sustainable development and sustainability', *IJSHE*, vol 8, no 3, pp317–338

Kirk, M. (2002) 'The impact of globalization and environmental change on health: Challenges for nurse education', *Nurse Education Today*, vol 22, no 1, pp60–71

Kitson, A. (2004) 'The whole person', *Nursing Standard*, vol 19, no 12, pp14–15

Kleffel, D. (1996) 'Environmental paradigms: Moving toward an ecocentric perspective', *Advances in Nursing Science*, vol 18, no 4, pp1–10

Kleffel, D. (2004) 'Advocating the ecocentric paradigm in nursing', *Journal of Holistic Nursing*, vol 22, no 1, pp6–10

Knowles, M.S. (1984) *The Adult Learner: A Neglected Species* (4th ed), Gulf Publishing, Houston TX

Limoges, L. (2007) 'The Hospital Work Experiences of New Nurses: Power Relations and Resistance Within the Professional Project of Caring', PhD thesis University of Toronto

Longley, M., Shaw, C. and Dolan, G. (2007) 'Nursing: Towards 2015 – Alternative Scenarios for Healthcare, Nursing and Nurse Education in the UK in 2015', *NMC*, available at www.nmc-uk.org/aDisplayDocument.aspx?DocumentID=3550, accessed 28 January 2010

McEvoy, L. and Duffy, A. (2008) 'Holistic practice – A concept analysis', *Education in Practice*, vol 8, no 6, pp412–419

Maryon-Davis, A., Gilmore, I. and Hamilton, P. (2007) 'Climate change and health. We must all act now', *British Medical Journal*, vol 335, no 7630, p1110

Mayor, S. (2008) 'NHS should bring in measures to reduce its carbon footprint, BMA says', *British Medical Journal*, vol 336, no 7647, p740

McMichael, A.J. and Powels, J.W. (1999) 'Human numbers, environment, sustainability and health', *British Medical Journal*, vol 319, pp977–980, available at www.bmj.com/cgi/content/full/319/7215/977, accessed 25 March 2009

Meadows, D., Randers, J., and Meadows, D. (2005) *Limits to Growth*, Earthscan, London

Newell, C. (2000) 'Biomedicine, genetics and disability: Reflections on nursing and a philosophy of holism', *Nursing Ethics*, vol 7, no 3, pp227–236

NHSSDU (2008) *Saving Carbon, Improving Health: A Draft Carbon Reduction Strategy for the NHS in England*, available at www.sdu.nhs.uk/downloads/draft_nhs_carbon_reduction_strategy.pdf, accessed 28 January 2010

Naess, P. (2006) 'Unsustainable growth, unsustainable capitalism', *Journal of Critical Realism*, vol 5, no 2, pp197–227

New Internationalist. (2009) 'Four principles for climate justice', *New Internationalist*, no 419, January, available at www.newint.org/features/2009/01/01/principles-climate-justice, accessed 5 October 2009

Newman, R. (2006) 'It's capitalism or a habitable planet – you can't have both', *The Guardian*, 2 February, available at www.guardian.co.uk/environment/2006/feb/02/energy.comment, accessed 30 July 2009

Nichols, A., Maynard, V., Goodman, B. and Richardson, J. (2009) 'Health, climate change and sustainability: A systematic review and thematic analysis of the literature', *Environmental Health Insights*, vol 3, pp63–88, available at www.la-press.com/article.php?article_id=1603, accessed 5 October 2009

Nilekani, R. (2007) 'Is water the next oil?', *YaleGlobal Online*, available at www.globalpolicy.org/component/content/article/215/46071.html, accessed 1 March 2010

Norrie, P. and Dalby, D. (2007) 'How adult are our learners?', *Journal of Research in Nursing*, vol 12, no 4, pp319–328

NMC (2004) *Standards of proficiency for pre-registration nursing education*, available at www.nmc-uk.org/aDisplayDocument.aspx?documentID=328, accessed 6 October 2009

O'Dowd, A. (2007) 'NHS is told it must play its part in tackling climate change', *British Medical Journal (Clinical Research Ed.)*, vol 334, no 7608, pp1343–1343

Orr, D. (1991) *Ecological Literacy: Education and the Transition to a Postmodern World*, SUNY Press, New York NY

Orr, D. (2004) *Earth in Mind: On Education, Environment, and the Human Prospect*, Island Press, Washington DC

Poulton, B., Mason, C., McKenna, H., Lynch, C. and Keenay, S. (2000) *The Contribution of Nurses, Midwives and Health Visitors to the Public Health Agenda*, HMSO, Belfast

Quinn, F. and Hughes, S. (2007) *Principles and Practice of Nurse Education*, Nelson Thornes, London

Ramesh, R. (2008) 'Paradise almost lost: Maldives seek to buy a new homeland' *The Guardian*, 10 November, available at www.guardian.co.uk/environment/2008/nov/10/maldives-climate-change, accessed 6 October 2009

Richardson, J., Kagawa, F and Nichols, A. (2009) 'Health, climate change and energy vulnerability: A retrospective assessment of Primary Care Trust policies and practice', *Public Health*, vol 123, no 12, pp765–70

Roberts, I. and Godlee, F. (2007). 'Reducing the carbon footprint of medical conferences', *British Medical Journal*, vol 334, no 7306, pp 324–325

Roper, N., Logan, W.W. and Tierney, A.J. (1985) *The Elements of Nursing*, Churchill Livingstone, Edinburgh

Rowe, J. (1987) *Ecosphere Thinking*, available at www.ecospherics.net/pages/RoEcoTh.html, accessed 25 March 2009

Royal College of Nursing, Australia (1998) *Position Statement: Nurses, Health and the Environment*, available at www.rcna.org.au/policy/position_statements, accessed 25 March 2009

Ryder, R. (1983, 2nd edition) *Victims of Science: The Use of Animals in Research*, National Vivisection Society, London

Sarkis, J.M. and Skoner, M.M. (1987) 'An analysis of the concept of holism in nursing literature', *Holistic Nursing Practice*, vol 2, no 1, pp61–69

Scrimshaw, P. (1983) *Educational Ideologies, Unit 2, E204, Purpose and Planning in Curriculum*, Open University Press, Milton Keynes

Sinclair, F. (2009) 'What is sustainability?', available at http://ecohearth.com/eco-op-ed/300-what-is-sustainability-.html, accessed 1 March 2010

Singer, P. (1975) *Animal Liberation: A New Ethics for Our Treatment of Animals*, New York Review/Random House, New York NY

Sterling, S. (2001) *Sustainable Education – Revisioning Learning and Change*, Schumacher Briefings 6, Green Books, Dartington

Stott, R. and Godlee, F. (2006) 'What should we do about climate change?' *British Medical Journal*, vol 333, no 7576, pp983–984

Stibbe, A. (ed) (2009) *The Handbook of Sustainable Literacy*, Green Books, Dartington

Strachan, G. (2009), cited in Stibbe, A. (ed)

UK Faculty of Public Health (2008) *Sustaining a Healthy Future: Taking Action on Climate Change*, available at www.fph.org.uk/resources/sustainable_development/

sustaining_a_healthy_future.asp, accessed 25 March 2009

UK Public Health Association. (2007) *Climates and Change. The Urgent Need to Connect Health and Sustainable Development*, available at http://theclimateconnection.org/climates-and-change-urgent-need-connect-health-and-sustainable-development, accessed 1 March 2010

Wells, K. (2004) 'Advocating the ecocentric paradigm in nursing', *Journal of Holistic Nursing*, vol 22, no 1, pp6–8

WCED (1987) *Our Common Future: The Report of the World Commission on Environment and Development* ['The Brundtland Report'], Oxford University Press, Oxford, available at www.un-documents.net/wced-ocf.htm, accessed 26 March 2009

Woods, S. (1998) 'A theory of holism for nursing', *Medicine, Health Care and Philosophy*, vol 1, no 3, pp255–261

WHO (2009) 'Climate change and human health – Risks and responses', available at www.preventionweb.net/files/544_1980VL206501.pdf, accessed 1 March 2010

Wright, S. (2008) 'Resist the urge to dumb down holism', *Nursing Standard*, vol 22, no 52, pp26–27

Notes

1   The HEA is both a registered company and a charity. Its role is to serve as a nation-wide focus for enhancing teaching, learning and student experiences in HE. It works with institutions, discipline groups and individual staff in the four UK nations.

2   The Climate Connection www.theclimateconnection.org

3   The Campaign for Greener Healthcare www.greenerhealthcare.org

4   The Climate and Health Council www.climateandhealth.org

5   ISHE www.uwe.ac.uk/ishe/index.shtml

Sustainability – Is it Legal? The Benefits and Challenges of Introducing Sustainability into the Law Curriculum

Tracey Varnava, Jason Lowther and Simon Payne

What has law to do with sustainability?

The pursuit of SD as policy has been promoted both nationally and internationally using a wide range of tools and methods. These are clearly set out in the Agenda 21 approach and in particular in Section IV on Means of Implementation (UN Division for Sustainable Development [DSD], 1992). They include financial mechanisms, capacity building, institutional changes, education and awareness raising and – most importantly for this chapter – the use of law. Law has been central to the progression, definition and implementation of SD. This chapter considers the role that law has played in relation to SD and then looks at the consequences of this for legal education and legal educators in HE.

SD as a legal concept – international law origins

The translation of the widely accepted Brundtland definition of SD (WCED, 1987) into law was led by a series of international law initiatives – treaties or conventions that have embodied SD and related concepts in one form or another (the origins of SD and its relationship to law are traced in Lang, 1995). This process reached a critical stage in 1992 with the creation of the non-legally binding *Rio Declaration on Environment and Development* (UN General Assembly, 1992) and the series of legally binding treaties (UN, 1992a; 1992b and 1992c) relating to climate change (*UN Framework Convention on Climate Change* [UN FCCC]), from which sprang the Kyoto Protocol), biodiversity (*UN Convention on Biological Diversity*) and desertification (*UN Convention to Combat Desertification*). The *Rio Declaration* sets out a number of broad principles. For example, Principle 1 states that 'Human beings are at the centre of concerns' for SD and Principle 3 that the 'right to development must be fulfilled so as to equitably meet developmental and environmental needs of present and future generations' (UN General Assembly, 1992), capturing a key aspect of the Brundtland approach. The *Declaration* then sets out a number of issues related to the achievement of SD – for example, the promotion of the 'polluter pays' principle, the precautionary principle, the need for effective environmental protection and so on.

The three Rio *Conventions* then apply the SD principles in the particular context of the issues considered. So, for example, Article 3 of the FCCC declares 'The Parties have a right to, and should, promote sustainable development. Policies and measures to protect the climate system against human-induced change should be appropriate for the specific conditions of each Party and should be integrated with national development programmes, taking into account that economic development is essential for adopting measures to address climate change.' Article 4 meanwhile lays down that there should be sustainable management of sinks and reservoirs (the natural means of soaking up greenhouse gases). Even then, these obligations in conventions remain broad in nature and therefore difficult to see as law. This is a recurring issue that has caused significant challenges for the development of sustainable practices through law and presents an interesting scholarly challenge for legal education. Between 1987 and 2005, some 53 international legal instruments (treaties, conventions, protocols and agreements) were adopted relating to SD (Payne et al, 2007). The legal profession has, however, always faced the problem that SD in itself is broad and uncertain as a concept – it feels more like a set of values or aspirations than enforceable law. Inevitably, in the process of negotiation the degree of specific commitment will tend to become diluted to try to encourage as many states as possible to sign and ratify the treaty, so the treaty commitments will often tend to become more general and open to differing interpretations. Indeed, continuing with the example of the FCCC, once the obligations became much clearer and specific in its famous Kyoto Protocol, getting states to sign up and ratify became increasingly difficult. While 166 states signed and ratified the *Framework Convention*, only 84 signed up to Kyoto (and the USA has never ratified it) and, as a result, it took over eight years to come into legal force at all (UN FCCC, 1992a and 1992b).

This leaves an important role for legislation at regional, national or local level in providing more detailed obligations and commitments – translating broad policy aspiration into enforceable legal commitment. In addition, it can be argued that the challenges posed by the generality of statements of international law can be met by legally binding interpretations of the treaty wording – in international law, this may be by the judiciary in judicial decisions or by the work or writings of international legal scholars (Article 38 of the International Court of Justice

Statute; International Court of Justice). All of these have played their part in making SD law.

What does sustainability mean in law?

In order to make SD an enforceable legal commitment, work needed to be done by jurists – whether recognized scholars or the judges charged with its interpretation – to develop its specific meaning. As Justice Singh said in the Supreme Court of India in *Vellore Citizens Welfare Forum v Union of India* [1996], the 'salient features [of SD law] have yet to be finalized'. The International Court of Justice has considered SD in a number of cases, but perhaps of most significance is the Case Concerning the *Gabčíkovo–Nagymaros Project* (Hungary/Slovakia) [1997]. The Court acknowledged the importance of SD but did not use it as part of its critical reasoning and in particular does not identify its legal status or precise definition. Judge Christopher Weeramantry delivered a fascinating separate opinion in this case focusing on the meaning and legal status of SD and stated that SD was a principle of customary international law. The judgment draws on practices from a range of ancient civilizations. Judge Weeramantry concludes that:

It is clear that a principle must be followed which pays due regard to both considerations [development and environmental protection]. Is there such a principle, and does it command recognition in international law? I believe the answer to both questions is in the affirmative. The principle is the principle of sustainable development and, in my view, it is an integral part of modern international law. It is clearly of the utmost importance, both in this case and more generally ... The principle of sustainable development is thus a part of modern international law by reason not only of its inescapable logical necessity, but also by reason of its wide and general acceptance by the global community (p86).

He addresses the issues of certainty (and therefore capability of conferring rights and obligations) by identifying a range of principles contained in the broader concept of SD, such as the principle of trusteeship of the Earth's resources, the principle of intergenerational rights and the principle that development and environmental conservation must go hand in hand. In specific terms in the case, he identifies a principle that environmental impact assessment should be regarded as and required to be a continuous process and that there should be *'Contemporaneity in the Application of Environmental Norms'* (p113; our italics). The judgment of the Court does not go so far as accepting SD as a principle of law at all and certainly does not define it as Judge Weeramantry does in his separate opinion. So his judgment does not provide an accepted version of the law but it is an interesting exposition and an indication of how specific meaning can be given to the broad nature of SD. Interestingly, there is not a specific environmental 'court' as such for the international community, although there has been a recent call for such a forum.[1] It is argued that greater international attention should be focused on the greater environmental challenges that are inextricably tied in to SD (Hey, 2000; Hockman, 2008; Lowther, 2009).

The well-known scholar of international law Phillippe Sands identifies four key principles that make up the legal aspects of SD:

- *'Intergenerational equity'* – Preservation of natural resources for future generations.

- *'Sustainable use'* – The aim of exploiting natural resources in a prudent fashion.

- *'Equitable use or intragenerational equity'* – Equitable use for natural resources between states.

- *'The integration principle'* – The integration of environmental concerns into development decisions and vice versa (Sands, 2003, pp252–266).

All we can conclude from this is that in international law the status and meaning of SD remains uncertain and controversial but there are signs both of its emergence as part of customary international law and some indications of how it may be defined to give it legal meaning (Rieu-Clarke, 2005). Interestingly, one of the leading works on international environmental law concludes that there is 'as yet no international legal obligation that development must be sustainable' and therefore 'decisions on what constitutes sustainability rest primarily with individual governments' (Birnie et al, 2009, p85) This chapter therefore now turns to national laws.

National and sub-national laws

International law has played an important role in leading policy around sustainable development and in some jurisdictions in influencing the decisions of the courts; for example, the Supreme Court of India in *Vellore Citizens Welfare Forum v Union of India* (1996) (7) SC 375-95 where the court had 'no hesitation in holding that sustainable development as a balancing concept between ecology and development has been accepted as part of the customary international law' (p385). The court went on to find that although its 'salient features' had yet to be finalized, they included the 'polluter pays' principle and precautionary principle. However, it is in national law that SD has played its most significant role in terms of implementing the policy in specific and enforceable ways.

National laws relating to SD have in the UK and EU tended to focus on environmental protection. The laws have been made up of a mix of broad aspirational duties to, for example, make a contribution towards achieving SD (see, for example, the UK's Environment Act 1995 section 4 or Natural Environment and Rural Communities Act 2006 section 18) and more specific measures designed to ensure that sustainability is promoted.

The broader legal duties are generally imposed on public bodies (local or central government and government agencies) and present challenges for lawyers.

For instance, how is it possible to enforce a duty to make a contribution to SD (what contribution and when?) or to take SD into account (what if it is considered but cast aside because of a more compelling consideration – for example, development?)? These issues have been considered in the English courts in relation to a duty to have regard to biodiversity in *R (Buglife) v Thurrock Thames Gateway Development Corporation* [2008] EWHC Civ 1209, which concluded that such a duty was weak in law.[2]

Nevertheless, the existence of such duties, although presenting considerable problems with enforcement in specific cases, may be broadly influential in the policy and approach taken by public bodies when dealing with sustainability issues. National laws relating to SD have also focused on developing principles and approaches that support sustainability. So legislation has promoted the 'polluter pays' principle (e.g. European Environmental Liability Directive 2004/35/EC), the precautionary principle (e.g. legislation in New South Wales, Australia, that incorporates the precautionary principle in a broader concept of ecologically sustainable development, namely the Protection of the Environment Administration Act 1991 (NSW) section 6(1), considered in *Conservation Council of SA Inc. v The Development Assessment Commission & Tuna Boat Owners Association* [1999] SAERDC 86)[3], and the use of cost–benefit analysis in decision making (see UK Environment Act 1995 section 39). An interesting example of an integrated approach to sustainability in law incorporating environmental and social aspects is the Québec Sustainable Development Act (2006). This includes a wide range of social concerns (for example, health and well-being, social solidarity, social ethics and equity, cultural heritage preservation, as well as environmental considerations (Québe Government, 2006).

Is it all green?

One of the issues that arises in examining sustainability in a legal context is the dominance of law as relating to environmental protection in one form or another – from spatial planning, development decisions, biodiversity protection and pollution control to liability for environmental harm or the impacts of pollution on health or life. Does law relating to sustainability exist beyond the realms of the environment?

International treaties that deal with SD are dominated by those concerning environment (including marine, fisheries and energy), but also include treaties dealing with security, development, trade, health and human rights (see Payne et al, 2007). In national laws and the decisions of the courts, the environment continues to dominate, but with some examples emerging of sustainability principles being applied in laws relating to communities – see, for example, the Scottish Crofting Reform Act 2007 section 3 (requiring the Crofting Commission to seek to promote the sustainable development of the crofting community), the duties of the Homes and Communities Agency under section 2 of the UK Housing and Regeneration Act 2008 (this Act has as one of its objectives the achievement of sustainable development and good design in England) and international development (see the UK International Development Act 2002 section 1, which has the furtherance of sustainable development as one of two legal objectives for international development assistance and aid).

Legal education curriculum challenges

This brief overview of the relationship between SD and law exposes some important educational themes:

* The relationship between values, policy and law.
* The ways in which lawyers give specific meaning to the broad aspirational concept of sustainability.
* The development of international law and some of the shortcomings of the international legal system.
* The relationship between international law and national law.
* The variety of ways in which national and sub-national law has sought to promote SD.
* The focus of SD law being around environmental issues and particularly environmental protection, with some signs of sustainability influencing other areas of law.

Translating this legal recognition and engagement into HE curriculum design and development is a challenge – but one that needs to be met, not least because the UK Government and the devolved administrations require all education sectors to address the issue of SD and to promote the concept of sustainability literacy through the curriculum (DEFRA, 2005a; Department for Innovation, Universities and Skills [DIUS], 2008). It was in this context of increased policy interest and sector debate that the UK HEA began engaging in ESD, initially with a series of reports for different key stakeholders on the extent to which ESD and sustainability literacy development already took place across different academic disciplines in HE in 2005 and 2006 (Dawe et al, 2005; HEA, 2006a and 2006b). On the basis of this work, the Academy was then able to take forward activity at a Subject Centre level to build on existing practice and support its wider application and development through the disciplines. There are 24 Subject Centres associated with the HEA, each hosted by HEIs across the UK. The next section considers the work done to embed ESD perspectives and promote pedagogic innovation in law.

ESD in Law

The HEA Subject Centre for Law,[4] the UK Centre for Legal Education (UKCLE), was an early member of the Planning Group of the HEA's ESD

Project[5] and in 2006 was funded through this group to run a project on Developing Global Citizens through Legal Education. This ran until 2008 and aimed to:

- assess the extent to which the law curriculum is already making a contribution to sustainability literacy;
- identify opportunities for, and barriers to, the development of sustainability literacy in legal education;
- raise awareness, encourage debate and generate the development of a shared understanding in the academy and the profession of the ways in which legal education can prepare students to be 'global citizens' (UKCLE, 2008).

The experience of being involved in developing activity and support around sustainability literacy in law has raised a number of issues, of principle, pedagogy and practicality, that others elsewhere may also encounter. Below, we set out some of the key issues and offer practical responses for successfully integrating sustainability literacy into the law curriculum.

Defining terms

An initial challenge for the project was agreeing what 'sustainability literacy' actually means, or indeed its relevance, in the context of legal education. Worn down by years of initiatives and new agendas for HE, many staff have become cynical about what they see as policy 'fads'. While courses on environmental law have been a standard offering on many programmes for years, the significance of sustainability to the rest of the law curriculum was not always easy for non-environmental lawyers to grasp, let alone accept.

The approach of UKCLE in encouraging engagement has been to avoid jargon where possible and to focus on the pedagogical value of an approach that can, for example, locate law in real-world scenarios, dealing with issues such as equitable distribution of scarce resources. The potential for inter- and cross-disciplinary learning and the appeal of developing 'global citizenship' through legal education has helped to make Subject Centre work in this area more attractive to colleagues. From a survey carried out by StudentForce for Sustainability, it is evident that 40 per cent of law students strongly agreed that the social and environmental ethics of an employer were important when selecting a job, and 35 per cent thought it was very important that the competency to act as a globally responsible citizen was developed through university education (Cade, 2008a and 2008b). This sort of evidence helped to convince lecturers that students may well engage enthusiastically with attempts to make the law curriculum relevant to global concerns.

As part of UKCLE's efforts to understand sustainability literacy in the context of legal education, the issues were explored with a group of enthusiastic law lecturers who contacted the Subject Centre following publicity about the work being carried out in this area. These discussions were followed up with a session on ESD at the UKCLE annual conference in January 2007. Participants were asked to discuss the definition of 'sustainable development' that made the most sense to them in a legal education context. After much debate it was agreed that for the purposes of UKCLE work, someone who is sustainability literate is able to take account of social, economic and environment considerations when making decisions, taking action and informing and influencing others accordingly.

However, concerns about meaning centred not only on definitional issues but also on the implications of melding a sustainability approach with the underlying values, purpose and content of legal education.

Implications for the nature and values of law

There are immediate and real obstacles facing those who claim that sustainability should be embedded into legal education. The first obstacle is faced in all subjects – the profound objection of academics to any attempt to indoctrinate their students with one preferred or 'correct' understanding of the world. Key questions are therefore raised about the nature and values of law, and, in particular, the extent to which lawyers are to be trained to be impartial and disinterested. Is it appropriate that law graduates should be activists, passionate about improving the world? If not, can we do more than pay lip service to the ideals of sustainability literacy?

UKCLE ultimately took the view that sustainability literacy is so important that law's traditional impartiality and balance should not automatically outweigh a call for engagement and commitment. While evangelism for a cause can be off-putting and, worse, lead to a loss of objectivity, maintaining total disinterest would imply that academics should not try to make the world a better place. This would, for lawyers, throw into question work on promoting human rights, fair trials, access to justice, maintenance of the rule of law, legislative improvements, pro bono activities and so on.

Law is underpinned by values – what they are may be endlessly debatable, but it is certainly not a value-free topic. The practice of law has traditionally been associated with the values of service, compassion and professional obligation to society. However, ESD itself is not value-free, and there was a strong feeling among those participating in the UKCLE project that it was not desirable for law teachers to present SD as a taken-for-granted 'good' to their students. Bearing this in mind, colleagues may nevertheless legitimately consider issues such as:

- the extent to which they are developing critical and ethically aware thinkers;
- the fundamental role of higher education itself;
- the extent to which law is a discourse of top-down power;
- the relationship between law, politics, society and morality;
- the extent to which law sits uneasily with an unregulated capitalist economy;
- the nature of law in the context of complex social interactions;
- problems raised by a Western/Eurocentric perspective on the issue of SD.

However, even if colleagues welcome the opportunity to re-address their underlying approach to legal education, the process of integrating sustainability into the curriculum remains problematic.

What are the other main obstacles to integrating sustainability?

Research indicates many perceived obstacles, including an already full curriculum, irrelevance of ESD to the subject, student hostility, lack of expertise and contradictions between espoused values and personal or institutional behaviour (see, for example, HEA, 2006a, p11). The following observation in a guide written for HEIs by Forum for the Future may also ring bells:

> *We are not in the habit of thinking about the economy, the sort of society we would like, or the sort of environment we would like to live in at the same time. In higher education institutions, each is taught as different subjects, in different departments* (Forum for the Future, 2005, p5).

Those participating in the UKCLE project were also asked to identify what they regarded as the main obstacles to addressing sustainable development in the law curriculum. Answers included:

- Staff and students who define the curriculum too narrowly.
- A perception that it isn't really about law, but more akin to teaching citizenship.
- Inherent bias towards a narrowly conceived vocationalism and the dominance of the legal professions.
- Inherent conservatism of university legal education.
- Lack of imagination.

Responses to a question on how these obstacles might be overcome included:

- Recapturing a sense of law as a 'great anthropological document'.
- Encouraging academics and involving students.
- Providing examples of creative practice.
- Emphasizing the importance of a broad-based critical education and reflection on the nature of law in its multiple contexts.

Integrating sustainability literacy into the curriculum

Existing literature on learning and teaching in HE would tend to suggest that ESD will work best if it follows long-established principles of what works in education (and legal education) generally (see, for example, Biggs and Moore, 1993; Prosser and Trigwell, 1999; Fry et al, 2009). A few pointers include:

- A lot of learning is informal – learning from the teacher as role model is often more powerful than learning from the formal curriculum.
- Students learn from the values and procedures of the institution.
- Students should have maximum control of their learning, including where possible the design of the curriculum.
- Involvement in the community is desirable.
- Students should learn from each other, including working with students from other disciplines.
- Students should not focus simply on their own discipline or society.
- Students should be personally aware of the impact of their own actions on others and on the environment.
- Students should critically examine all the evidence for assertions made and values stated.

In law, the place of sustainability is not immediately apparent; but law is at the heart of the way our society runs and therefore if change is needed for sustainability, it must play a role, and those who use it (including law graduates) must be educated for that role. Below are some ideas for developing opportunities to address SD issues, ranging from wholesale changes to minor adjustments to what is currently provided.

Ideas for curriculum changes

- Develop courses in environmental law, energy law, transport law and planning law.
- Introduce elements into areas such as company law (present or desired responsibilities of companies to non-shareholders or to the environment, for example) or commercial law (encouraging sustainable behaviours through contractual terms or arguing for new implied contractual terms), intellectual property and patenting rights (the right to ownership of seeds or pharmaceuticals developed from biological resources, access to existing drug patents).
- Include the impact that legal decisions or doctrines have on communities and individuals when studying topics such as tort or crime.
- Introduce interdisciplinary contexts into law topics; for example, economics in commercial law or tort, ecology in land law, the impact of crime and punishment on communities.
- Introduce a comparative or international element into courses; for example, comparing labour or health and safety law in the UK with that of trading partners.

Ideas for new teaching approaches

- Clinical legal educational methods could be used to help empower community groups to improve their lives, whether through test cases and conventional advice, better understanding of power and decision-making processes or engagement in community issues regardless of legal content. In its broadest sense, 'clinical legal education' has been used to encompass learning that:

1 is experiential in design;
2 focuses on enabling students to understand how the law works in action;
3 involves real, or realistically simulated, casework (Webb, 2004).

- Develop projects involving multidisciplinary inputs; for example, working with engineering or ecology students on projects involving contractual rights, land-use issues or intellectual property disputes.

Discussion topics for existing courses or modules

- Examine law as a neutral or partisan phenomenon.
- Assess the role of present or past law in permitting or encouraging unsustainable development in identified areas.
- Examine the rights of and obligations to members of other societies, future generations, other species and the planet.
- Look at law as a passive phenomenon or agent for change and justice.

Exercises for existing courses or modules

- Examine draft legislation for its impact and proposed improvement.
- Examine UN and other declarations and writings on economic, social and cultural rights.
- Identify the explicit and assumed values that underpin legal doctrine and identify the extent to which these values match the values of students and teachers or the values contained in other documents or statements (e.g. political speeches, UN treaties).
- Engage students in supplementary research away from black letter law – for example, in contract law, ask them to research a tribal form of bargaining.

ESD in law at the University of Plymouth: A case study

Translating the sustainability drivers into deliverable module content at the University of Plymouth has proved to be a challenging and interesting exercise. As noted, law has a 'special relationship' with SD, as it is through the process of law that the broad concept finds its practical definition, application and ability to create predictable obligations. The context in which laws are made and the wider implications of those laws represents familiar territory for the academic study of law, and as discussed above there are opportunities to build sustainability literacy in existing frameworks and curriculum areas. Law graduates are, obviously, represented in the legal profession and also prominent in the business world and all levels of government. They are involved with determining rights and responsibilities, what is enforceable and what is 'just'. In that connection, particularly if they are sustainability literate, they might be pivotal influences in shaping the development of all aspects of society by bringing that knowledge to bear on global concerns.

Beyond the 'legal' case for the inclusion of sustainability considerations, as well as educational policy and institutional drivers, the desire to help our undergraduates to become sustainability literate adds a further dimension to their skills development (Forum for the Future, 2005). In line with the university's vision in its Sustainability Policy and Strategic Action Plan (University of Plymouth, 2008), the aim is for sustainability to become pervasive throughout law programmes. The current formulation of validated law programmes provides for all students to have exposure to SD principles in their first year of study through taking a core module. The approach is probably more accurately described as teaching *about* SD, a content-oriented approach, as opposed to *for* SD (i.e. ESD), with a focus on values and competency (Sterling, 2001). Details of the modules outlined below are located on the UKCLE's ESD resources pages (UKCLE, 2008).

Staff at Plymouth were fortunate to have been offered the opportunity to become seconded fellows at the University's CSF, a centre for excellence in teaching and learning in ESD awarded to the University by the HEFCE (Dyer, Selby and Chalkley, 2009). From 2006 to 2008 two of this chapter's authors, Simon Payne and Jason Lowther, were CSF fellows. Both are environmental lawyers and are therefore familiar with the legal formulation of SD as already featuring in Plymouth environmental law courses for students specializing in law and in environmental law sessions for students of other disciplines, such as environmental science (details of cross-disciplinary teaching are elaborated below). Having brought the sustainability 'message' back to academic colleagues, discussion took place amongst the full law teaching team at the end of the 2006–2007 academic year about how they might include ESD in the curriculum beyond its 'obvious' placement in environmental law.

A range of opinion was reflected across the group, but a general consensus was reached that there should be the opportunity for students to be exposed to SD in the law curriculum and that it was appropriate for this opportunity to be expressed in course documentation. Our experience has taught us that encouraging a full debate among colleagues – we, for example, tabled a paper at a staff away day – is imperative, so as to both gauge opinion and ensure that there is a clear sense of what the purposes of any changes to the status quo might be. Starting in the academic year 2007–2008, SD became a constituent of a first-year core module, meaning that all law students are required to take it. Its place in environmental law was further cemented and SD was also brought into the company law syllabus. The momentum has not stopped. In the academic year 2009–2010, a second-year core module, European Community Law, has been infused with opportunities to consider SD. Following the 'workbook' pattern described below for the Legal Skills and Systems module, EC environmental law and sustainability concepts will be used as a means to provide case study examples of legal enforcement actions available to respond to breaches of community laws.

Legal skills and systems

The Legal Skills and Systems (LSS) module, a core module at stage 1 of the law programme, was adapted in the 2007–2008 academic year to incorporate an introduction to EC and international legal systems. The module, in common with those taught on the majority of UK law programmes, seeks to provide students with foundational knowledge of the structures and personnel of the law. The changes made to the module aim to reflect the increasingly global nature of legal obligations; and to enable a broader view of the impact of law in a more global context than would be possible with a narrow focus on just the UK legal system. As outlined earlier, SD/sustainability has considerable legal impetus in international law and has found significant expression in EC law, particularly as sustainability (according to Article 2 of the EC Treaty, Europa, 2002) is included among the tasks the EC has set for itself. Contemporary legal literature (Ross, 2008 and 2009) has observed that the concept has developed in UK policy and law to include wider considerations comprised in broader notions of justice and good governance, considerations that are extremely relevant in understanding contemporary legal systems. Against this backdrop it was felt that the module was an appropriate vehicle for introducing concepts of sustainability, in the context of international and EC obligations, which are later developed in subsequent parts of the law programme. It is not envisaged that students will gain a deep knowledge of sustainability principles; rather, that they are exposed to them, their component concepts and the role of law in their development and delivery.

The module is also concerned to develop the students' research skills and assist them in becoming autonomous learners. In that regard, the mode of delivery of the EC and international law content is by way of a workbook. This is distributed via the university's virtual learning environment, containing both text and a series of directed exercises, with the content assessed at the end of the module. There is no textbook as such that adequately deals with this aspect of the module content, which has required significant staff input to make the approach workable. The exercises require the location and use of certain information, examples of which are outlined in the following section. The materials also contain a series of self-assessment exercises to build knowledge as the learners progress.

Examples of the tasks

The text of the workbook introduces the areas of interest. For example, the section on internationalization notes that 'Challenges facing the international community … and consequently international law and its institutions … include fears that the globalization process will bring an increase in economic inequality, thereby disadvantaging the poorest and that the effects of climate change pose an enormous threat to the very existence of humanity' (Sellick, 2007, p5). Tasks then attempt to acquaint the student with the place of law in addressing these challenges:

- Introduction to the concept of globalization through explanation of, for example, the World Trade Organization and human rights protection.
- Students are then required to identify the UN Millennium Development Goals from the UN's website and reflect on their environment and sustainability targets.
- Students are next required to access UN Environment Programme (UNEP), find the 'governance and law' section, discover UNCED 1992, and to note what are the defined rights and responsibilities of states regarding SD.
- Finally, students are required to locate the European Commission's home page and locate the EU's policies, then via that link to the 'SD resources' to note the seven key themes of the EU's revised sustainability strategy.

Feedback from students has been positive to date, reflecting on the method of delivery as well as the content. Being able to demonstrate SD through different legal structures in tandem with an explanation of foundational principles appears to have helped to contextualize its place within international and EC law. It has also, according to feedback, been perceived as being 'interesting, relevant and challenging'. At this stage, the fact-finding aspect of the requirements has prevented any students feeling that sustainability is delivered with a missionary zeal, while at the same time promoting opportunities for discussion. In order to keep the material fresh and relevant there is always the need to continually reflect on the content and emphasis.

Environmental and company law

At stages 2 and 3, elective modules in environmental law and company law provide an opportunity to consider sustainability in a more structured and applied way. The environmental sustainability strand has obvious links with the teaching of environmental law, and, as discussed above, is often seen as the traditional home for the teaching of sustainability concepts in law. Sustainability is a pervasive theme in the module, against which substantive environmental laws can be tested. Incorporating sustainability into the company law syllabus, specifically in relation to corporate governance, enables greater consideration of the social and economic facets of sustainability. Both modules are open to stage 2 and 3 students, lectures being taken in common, although tutorials and assessment differ between the stages. In both areas, a key learning outcome for the students is that they are able to demonstrate research skills as well as critical reflection and analysis of the law. Sustainability provides a further context in which to promote these outcomes.

Environmental law

SD has become a key plank of environmental law thinking and practice. As has been noted, the environmental strand of sustainability has been where the greatest overt progress has been made in international, regional and domestic legal systems. UK environmental policy since 1990 makes explicit reference to the concept and specific laws have been enacted that draw on the concept for their legitimacy. All current general and specialist environmental law texts provide reasonably detailed and clear explanation and analysis of SD and constituent principles of precaution and polluter liability. In explaining the law to students, a deeper understanding is offered through provision of a pervasive, contextual means by which the development of laws can be measured against the objectives of an SD imperative. Regulatory developments in relation to issues such as climate change and environmental assessment through to land contamination and the conservation of biodiversity, nature and habitat of necessity involve consideration of resource allocation and use. Depending on the state of the law at a given time, emphasis has been placed on aspects of these laws to test their sustainability credentials. Specific environmental law examples include:

- Tutorial discussion in relation to sustainability and environmental impacts and patterns of consumption (The Power of Community, 2009).
- Location and discussion of human rights as they interface with environmental protection.
- Consideration of the contaminated land remediation system against a backdrop of brownfield site reuse and general land-use planning.
- Discussion of 'Earth Jurisprudence' (Cullinan, 2004; Boyle and Elcoate, 2006; Warren et al, 2009) as an alternative philosophy of law.

A fruitful area of focus popular with the students has concerned the regulation of ship-breaking in the UK and the developing world, notably India and Bangladesh. Visually dramatic and very accessible, the subject matter provides a *real* context on which to examine sustainable waste management and recycling ideas – as well as the impact of law on international waste movements and issues concerning different environmental standards. The huge contrast between the socio-environmental impacts of the trade presents an opportunity to assess the means by which key legal stakeholders have sought to accept responsibility for ship recycling. As well as having a clear ecological sustainability component, the topic brings issues of environmental justice to the fore. There is legal and policy provision at international, EC and domestic levels via UNEP, the International Maritime Organization, the EU, the UK Government and a plethora of material from concerned NGOs such as the Basel Action Network (BAN, undated) and Friends of the Earth, and international human rights organizations (International Federation for Human Rights [FIDH], undated).

Company law

The teaching of company law at undergraduate level is traditionally concerned with company formation, legal 'personality', accountability and corporate liabilities. It has been perceived as a somewhat 'dry' subject, with heavy emphasis on statute law, and with a prevailing market ethos. Contemporary regulation has resulted in changes in the nature of company types, such as community interest companies[6] and also in relation to company reporting requirements, combined with the growth of concepts such as CSR. Duties towards shareholders have been more overtly defined, and environmental reporting in the UK has become a requirement for companies since the UK Companies Act 2006. Incorporating a study of sustainability has been a challenge, as most textbooks only pay cursory attention to the issue, and only one (Dine, 2005) contains a chapter dedicated to CSR. Specific company law examples include the following:

- Locating and navigating a range of materials, for example, government pages defining CSR, and appreciating the role government policy has on company law.

- Examining what companies are *actually* doing in respect of CSR. This has been enabled through links with local firms and inviting directors to speak to the students about their CSR policies.

- Drafting a company CSR policy in line with regulatory guidance for a tutorial presentation.

- A component of stage 3 assessment requires independent research to critically analyse a published CSR policy, measuring it against legal requirements and in relation to sustainability drivers – here, studies have been undertaken on, for example, the Co-operative Bank, Marks & Spencer and Primark.[7]

Closing thoughts

It should be noted that the approach adopted at Plymouth has not been limited to the law programmes. The School of Law has also had a key role in developing partnerships with other schools and faculties for teaching environmental law and policy, for example, in the context of environmental science or sustainable construction. This is underpinned by a commitment to interdisciplinarity in teaching and research and a strong belief that teaching environmental law in the context of other disciplines brings real insights and benefits to the law staff. It has also led to research projects and partnerships as well as new approaches to teaching and learning; for example, a postgraduate module bringing together law, policy principles and ethics in the broad context of sustainability. At Plymouth the approach has been to actively seek collaborations with other parts of the university and not to regard these teaching partnerships as secondary to Law School service teaching.

It appears that the foundations exist for deep and continuing symbiosis between law and sustainability. Law in practice attempts to define sustainability and shape it into deliverable and enforceable obligations, whether imposed on governments, corporations or individuals. To the extent it has managed to do so, it is undoubtedly worthy of informing the teaching of law – after all as a society and global community, we would want the policy-makers, opinion-leaders and rule-drafters to be 'on the same page'. To do so necessitates our law graduates developing sustainability literacy and comprehension of the place of law in a broader ethic (Philippopoulos-Mihalopoulos, 2008). To enable that, the HEA has taken a crucial lead and demonstrated that sustainability represents a bundle of concepts, the understanding and practice of which is something to benefit our graduates' skill sets and thus eventually positively enhance all our futures. The discipline is changing, and there is new jurisprudence to consider (Boyle and Elcoate, 2006; Warren et al, 2009). In this chapter, we have attempted to show the link between the law as it is and the law that could be taught in HE. Increasingly, as a result of the work undertaken by UKCLE in particular, there is evidence that ESD is being considered and adopted by other law programmes, although to date we are unaware of any that are quite so systematic as those at the University of Plymouth. Symposia have been held, for example, at University College London (UCL, 2008) and staff have presented their approach to other colleagues in the discipline (Sellick and Lowther, 2009a) and to a wider humanities base (Sellick and Lowther, 2009b) at relevant conferences. We, naturally, hope that this might be the beginning of a trend that can add another dimension to law programmes and give law students the tools they require to become sustainability-minded professionals.

We have highlighted the key debates in legal education and offered a snapshot of practice at the University of Plymouth. This practice, along with the thinking, is sure to continue to evolve in the future. This chapter is offered as an account of progress to date.

Acknowledgements

We would like to acknowledge the contributions of Hugh Brayne, a former Associate of UKCLE, and Joanne Sellick, the Undergraduate Law Programme Manager at the University of Plymouth and creator of the stage one workbook in LSS. Both have contributed significantly to the work that is reported in this chapter and, accordingly, the authors would like to record their gratitude.

References

BAN (undated) homepage www.ban.org, accessed 10 April 2009

Biggs, J. and Moore, P. (1993) *The Process of Learning* (3rd ed), Prentice Hall, New York NY

Birnie, P, Boyle, A. and Redgwell, C. (2009) *International Law and the Environment* (3rd ed), Oxford University Press, Oxford

Boyle, S. and Elcoate, V. (2006) 'Could 'wild laws' protecting all the Earth's community – including animals, plants, rivers and ecosystems – save our natural world?', *The Guardian*, 8 November, available at www.guardian.co.uk/environment/2006/nov/08/ethicalliving.society, accessed 31 January 2010

Cade, A. (2008a) *Employable Graduates for Responsible Employers: Appendix*, available at www.heacademy.ac.uk/assets/York/documents/ourwork/sustainability/employable_briefing2008.pdf, accessed 30 June 2009

Cade, A. (2008b) *Employable Graduates for Responsible Employers*, available at www.heacademy.ac.uk/assets/York/documents/ourwork/tla/sustainability/EmployableGraduates2008.pdf, accessed 23 April 2009

Conservation Council of SA Inc. v. The Development Assessment Commission & Tuna Boat Owners Association. (1999) SAERDC 86

Cullinan, C. (2004) *Wild Law – A Manifesto for Earth Justice*, Green Books, Dartington

Dawe, G., Jucker, R. and Martin, S. (2005) *Sustainable Development in Higher Education: Current Practice and Future Developments*, HEA, York, available at www.heacademy.ac.uk/assets/York/documents/ourwork/tla/sustainability/ sustdevinHEfinalreport.pdf, accessed 6 July 2009

DEFRA (2005a) *One Future – Different Paths: The UK's Shared Framework for Sustainable Development*, available at www.defra.gov.uk/sustainable/government/documents/ SDFramework.pdf, accessed 23 April 2009

DEFRA (2005b) *Securing the Future: The UK Government Sustainable Development Strategy*, The Stationery Office, London, available at www.defra.gov.uk/sustainable/ government/publications/uk-strategy/documents/SecFut_complete.pdf, accessed 31 January 2010

Dine, J. (2005) *Company Law*, Palgrave MacMillan, Basingstoke

DIUS (2008) *Investing in Our Future: Sustainable Development Action Plan 2008–09*, available at www.dius.gov.uk/about_us/~/media/publications/7/76-08-C_on, accessed 12 August 2009

Dyer, A., Selby, D. and Chalkley, B. (2009) 'A centre for excellence in education for sustainable development', In Chalkley, B., Haigh, M. and Higgitt, D (eds), *Education for Sustainable Development: Papers in Honour of the United Nations Decade of Education for Sustainable Development (2005–2014)*, Routledge, London, pp155–60

Europa (2002) *Consolidated Version of the Treaty Establishing the European Community*, available at http://eurlex.europa.eu/en/treaties/dat/12002E/pdf/12002E_EN.pdf, accessed 6 July 2009

Europa (2004) *Directive 2004/35/CE of the European Parliament and of the Council*, available at http://eur-lex.europa.eu/LexUriServ/LexUriServ.do?uri=CELEX: 32004L0035:EN:NOT, accessed 31 January 2010

FIDH (undated) homepage www.fidh.org, accessed 10 April 2009

Forum for the Future (2005) *Learning and Skills for Sustainable Development: Developing a Sustainability Literate Society*, available at www.forumforthefuture.org/files/ learningandskills.pdf, accessed 24 April 2009

Fry, H., Ketteridge, S. and Marshall, S. (2009) 'Understanding student learning', In Fry, H., Ketteridge, S. and Marshall, S. (eds), *A Handbook for Teaching and Learning in Higher Education* (3rd ed), Routledge, London

Gabčíkovo–Nagymaros Project (Hungary/Slovakia) (1997) 37 ILM 162, available at www.icj-cij.org/docket/files/92/7375.pdf, accessed 30 January 2010

HEA (2006a) *Sustainable Development in Higher Education: Current Practice and Future Developments – A Progress Report for Senior Managers in Higher Education*, available at www.heacademy.ac.uk/assets/York/documents/resources/resourcedatabase/ id587_sustainable_development_managers_report.pdf, accessed 23 April 2009

HEA (2006b) *Sustainable Development in Higher Education: Current Practice and Future Developments – A Progress Report for Employers, Unions and the Professions*, available at www.heacademy.ac.uk/assets/York/documents/resources/resourcedatabase/ id586_sustainable%20development_employers_report.pdf, accessed 6 July 2009

Hey, E. (2000) *Reflections on an International Environment Court*, Kluwer Law International, The Hague

Hockman, D. (2008) 'Climate change and the new world order', British Library, London, November, available at www.environmentcourt.org, accessed 30 January 2010

International Court of Justice (1945) *Statute of the International Court of Justice*, available at www.icj-cij.org/documents/index.php?p1=4&p2=2&p3=0&PHPSESSID=d11e74f95a8b70d35ab11f52d29b0d33, accessed 30 January 2010

Lang, W. (ed) (1995) *Sustainable Development and International Law*, Martinus Nijhoff Publishers, Dordrecht

Lowther,J. (2009) 'An international court for the environment?' *Student Law Review*, vol 57, pp30–34

New South Wales Government (1991) Protection of the Environment Administration Act, available at, www.legislation.nsw.gov.au/viewtop/inforce/act+60+1991+FIRST+0+N/, accessed 31 January 2010

The Power of Community (2009) *How Cuba Survived Peak Oil*, available at www.powerofcommunity.org/cm/index.php, accessed 31 January 2010

Payne, S., Lowther,J. and Gray-Donald,J. (2007) 'Sustainable development and the role of judges: From international agreements to national laws?', *International Journal of Environmental, Cultural, Economic and Social Sustainability*, vol 3, no 5, pp193–204

Philippopoulos-Mihalopoulos, A. (2008) 'Teaching beyond discipline: The ethical challenge of environmental law', *The Sustainable University: Relating Ecological Thinking, Learning and Research*, University College London, November, available at www.ucl.ac.uk/environment-institute/News/sustainableuni.html, accessed 20 April 2009

Prosser, M. and Trigwell, K. (1999) *Understanding Learning and Teaching. The Experience in Higher Education*, Society for Research into Higher Education/Open University Press, Buckingham

Québec Government (2006) *Québec Sustainable Development Act*, available at www.mddep.gouv.qc.ca/developpement/loi_en.htm#elements, accessed 12 August 2009

R (Buglife) v Thurrock Thames Gateway Development Corporation (2008) EWHC Civ 1209

Rieu-Clarke, A. (2005) *International Law and Sustainable Development: Lessons from the Law of International Watercourses*, IWA Publishing, London

Ross, A. (2008). 'Why legislate for sustainable development? An examination of sustainable development provisions in UK and Scottish statutes', *Journal of Environmental Law*, vol 20, no 5, pp35–68

Ross, A. (2009) 'Modern interpretations of sustainable development', *Journal of Law and Society*, vol 36, no 1, pp32–54

Sands, P. (2003) *Principles of International Environmental Law* (2nd ed), Cambridge University Press, Cambridge

Scottish Government (2007) *Crofting Reform etc Act*, available at http://opsi.gov.uk/legislation/scotland/acts2007/asp_20070007_en_1, accessed 31 January 2010

Sellick,J. (2007) *Public International and European Law Workbook* (for module LAW1050/51 LSS), University of Plymouth

Sellick,J. and Lowther,J. (2009a) *Education for Sustainable Development in Law: The Plymouth Experience*, Association of Law Teachers 44th Annual Conference, Amsterdam, April, available at www.lawteacher.ac.uk/events/?id=15, accessed 31 January 2010

Sellick,J. and Lowther,J. (2009b) *Education for Sustainable Development in Law: The Plymouth Experience*, 7th International Conference on New Directions in the Humanities, Beijing, June, available at http://2009.thehumanities.com, accessed 31 January 2010

Sterling, S. (2001) *Sustainable Education. Re-visioning Learning and Change*, Schumacher Briefing 6, Green Books, Dartington, UKCLE. (2008) 'Case studies on education for sustainable development in law', available at www.ukcle.ac.uk/resources/esd/cases/index.html, accessed 6 July 2009

UK Government (1995) *Environment Act*, available at www.opsi.gov.uk/acts/acts1995/Ukpga_19950025_en_1, accessed 30 January 2010

UK Government (2002) *International Development Act*, available at http://opsi.gov.uk/acts/acts2002/ukpga_20020001_en_1, accessed 31 January 2010

UK Government (2006) *Natural Environment and Rural Communities Act* www.opsi.gov.uk/acts/acts2006/ukpga_20060016_en_1 Accessed 30 January 2010

UK Government (2006) *Companies Act*, available at www.opsi.gov.uk/acts/acts2006/ukpga_20060046_en_1, accessed 31 January 2010

UK Government (2008) *Housing and Regeneration Act*, available at http://opsi.gov.uk/acts/acts2008/ukpga_20080017_en_1

UN (1992a) *UN Framework Convention on Climate Change*, available at http://unfccc.int/resource/docs/convkp/conveng.pdf, accessed 30 January 2010

UN (1992b) *UN Convention on Biological Diversity*, available at http://treaties.un.org/doc/Treaties/1992/06/19920605%2008-44%20PM/Ch_XXVII_08p.pdf, accessed 30 January 2010

UN (1992c) *UN Convention to Combat Desertification*, available at www.uncd.int/convention/text/convention.php, accessed 30 January 2010

UN DSD (1992) 'Section IV – Means of Implementation. Chapter 33: Financial Resources & Mechanisms', *Agenda 21*, available at www.un.org/esa/dsd/agenda21/res_agenda21_33.shtml, accessed 12 August 2009

UN General Assembly (1992) *Report to the United Nations Conference on Environment and Development: Annex 1 Rio Declaration on Environment and Development*, Rio de Janeiro June, available at www.unep.org/Documents.Multilingual/Default.asp?documentID=78&articleID=1163, accessed 30 January 2010

UCL (2008) *The Sustainable University: Relating Ecological Thinking, Learning and Research*, One-day symposium hosted by the Faculty of Laws and the Environment Institute, September, available at www.ucl.ac.uk/environment-institute/News/sustainableuni.html, accessed 31 January 2010

University of Plymouth (2008) *Sustainability Policy and Strategic Action Plan*, available at http://csf.plymouth.ac.uk/?q=policy, accessed 12 August 2009

UN FCCC (1992a) *Kyoto Protocol Status of Ratification*, available at http://unfccc.int/files/kyoto_protocol/status_of_ratification/application/pdf/kp_ratification_20091203.pdf, accessed 30 January 2010

UN FCCC (1992b) available at http://unfccc.int/essential_background/convention/status_of_ratification/items/2631.php, accessed 20 March 2009

Vellore Citizens Welfare Forum v Union of India (1996) AIR SC 149, available at www.ielrc.org/content/e9607.pdf, accessed 30 January 2010

Warren, L., Filgueira, B. and Mason, I. (2009) *Wild Law: Is there Any Evidence of Earth Jurisprudence in Existing Law and Practice*, UK Environmental Law Association and The Gaia Foundation, London, available at www.earthjurisprudence.org/documents/WildLaw_Report.pdf, accessed 31 January 2010

WCED (1987) *Our Common Future: The Report of the World Commission on Environment and Development* ['The Brundtland Report'], Oxford University Press, Oxford, available at www.un-documents.net/wced-ocf.htm, accessed 29 January 2010

Webb, J. (2004) *Designing and Delivering Clinical Legal Education*', available at www.ukcle.ac.uk/resources/trns/clinic/index.html, accessed 30 June 2009

Notes

1   By Stephen Hockman QC www.youtube.com/watch?v=PPu9sfPFcQ4, accessed 30 January 2010.

2   *R (Buglife) v Thurrock Thames Gateway Development Corporation* [2008] EWHC Civ 1209 concerned a legal challenge to the grant of planning permission to the Royal Mail for the development of a distribution depot on the site of a former power station. The relevant legislation requires all local planning authorities 'in exercising their functions, to have regard so far as is consistent with the proper exercise of those functions, to the purpose of conserving biodiversity' – section 40(1) of the Natural Environment and Rural Communities Act 2006. Despite evidence of harm to some highly endangered invertebrate species, the planning permission was upheld in law. Subsequently, however, Royal Mail decided not to proceed with the development; the full story is told at www.buglife.org.uk/conservation/campaigns/westthurrockmarshes.htm (accessed 31 January 2010).

3   'SAERDC' refers to the reports of the South Australia Environment, Resource and Development Court, some of which are online, while others may be accessed via a Law Library with an Australian Collection or via legal databases. See also Parnell, Mark (1999) 'Southern Bluefin Tuna feedloting — ESD, the precautionary principle and burden of proof', *Journal of International Wildlife Law & Policy*, vol 2, no 3, pp334–337, available at www.informaworld.com/smpp/content~content=a90602719 6&db=all, accessed 22 March 2010.

4   The system of Subject Centres and the overall policy of a subject-based approach to enhancing learning, teaching and assessment in HE arose out of the review of the Computers in Teaching Initiative and the Teaching and Learning Technology Support Network (HEFCE 98/47). Established in January 2000 as the Learning and Teaching Support Network, 24 Subject Centres came into operation based in universities around the UK. Since 2004, the Subject Centres have formed part of the HEA.

5   The Academy's ESD Project was established following the publication of *Securing the Future* (DEFRA, 2005b), the UK Government's SD strategy, which identified the need for all education sectors to promote the concept of sustainability literacy. The project has a core team of staff who promote ESD at a national level, supported by Subject Centres working at a disciplinary level to develop curricula and pedagogy that will give students the skills and knowledge to live and work sustainably. Details of the Project's work can be found at: www.heacademy.ac.uk/ourwork/learning/sustainability (accessed 31 January 2010).

6   A community interest company is one not established purely for the benefit of the members but also has distinct community benefit. In order to be a community interest company, the appropriate regulator must approve the company registration and is involved in a continuing monitoring role. More details are available at www.cicregulator.gov.uk (accessed 31 January 2010).

7   All three companies have declared 'ethical' policies: the Co-operative Bank, for example, will only invest in 'ethical' developments and supports broad campaigns seeking to tackle global poverty and the effects of landmines among others. Marks & Spencer is an established high-street retailer, which published 'Plan A' in 2007; this is a five-year plan to '*see us working with our customers and our suppliers to combat climate change, reduce waste, safeguard natural resources, trade ethically and build a healthier nation*'. Primark is a low-end mass fashion chain, which has declared policies on its materials sourcing and majority-world employment practices.

For more details, visit the following respective sites:

www.goodwithmoney.co.uk/your-world (accessed 31 January 2010)

http://plana.marksandspencer.com/about (accessed 31 January 2010)

www.primark.co.uk/Ethical (accessed 31 January 2010).

Chapter 9

Staging Sustainability: Making Sense of Sustainability in HE Dance, Drama and Music

Paul Kleiman

Universities bear profound responsibilities to increase the awareness, knowledge, technologies, and tools to create an environmentally sustainable future. (ULSF, 1990)

What we use on stage is a way to demonstrate that we are accountable to our relationship with the planet (May, 2008).

Introduction

While for some disciplines the sustainability agenda is regarded as 'natural territory', the relationship of the performing arts (dance, drama and music) and the act of performance with that agenda is somewhat indirect and problematic. As a consequence, there are a wide and diverse set of understandings, discourses and practices around the notion of sustainability. These range from basic issues such as the use and recycling of the materials used in performances and productions through to more complex issues such as the role of the arts as a tangible means of articulating and disseminating ideas about sustainability by, for example, exploring narratives of consumption and investigating our relationship with landscape and the environment. There is also the important issue of personal and professional sustainability in the face of an uncertain future. This chapter will explore and illustrate the manner in which some of these discourses and practices around sustainability appear in performing arts HE.

Working with sustainability

In 2008, a job advert appeared for a professorship in performance design and technical theatre at the University of Colorado. Alongside the usual outline of the responsibilities of such a position, the advert asked for: 'an understanding of sustainability issues and willingness to articulate environmentally sensitive designs' (*Inside Higher Ed*, 2008). Such a requirement probably would not have appeared until relatively recently, and its inclusion might be perceived as an indication of the extent to which the sustainability agenda has impacted on the performing arts in HE. Yet in their report *Sustainable Development in Higher Education*, Dawe et al investigated 'how different subject disciplines taught within the higher education system are contributing to creating sustainability literate graduates' and reported that the arts and humanities subject areas generally – and the performing arts in particular – identified the largest number of barriers to embedding sustainability in the curriculum. Those barriers ranged from an 'awkward fit with the subject area to lack of staff expertise, irrelevance, financial restrictions and limited institutional commitment' (Dawe et al, 2005, p4).

When I started out to research material for this chapter, I sent an email in September 2008 with the subject line 'Do we do sustainability in higher education performing arts?' to the online discussion lists of the three main subject associations in HE in the UK: the National Association for Music in Higher Education (NAMHE), the Standing Conference on Dance in Higher Education (SCODHE), and the Standing Conference University Drama Departments (SCUDD). The email asked colleagues to comment on and, if possible, provide examples of how sustainability is understood and how it manifests itself in these subject areas. I received a number of interesting and detailed replies, many of which have informed what follows. But one in particular struck me as exemplifying both the possibilities and problems of addressing the notion of sustainability in the performing arts.

The response in question was from a colleague in music, and he provided several examples of where he thought music is addressing, or could address, sustainability. The first was through the use of open, sustainable technologies to generate and disseminate music as a way of countering the 'throwaway culture of mobile phones, mp3 players etc.' This included teaching 'as much programming as we can afford to so that students can make their own solutions'.

The second was through encouraging and enabling students to be active listeners, who have 'the respect for sound which comes from recording it, shaping it and listening to it in an active and engaging way.' It is through this 'active listening' that one can build 'a sustainable aural understanding and thus a greater relationship with the changing sonic planet. The [use of] mp3 in-ear headphones is isolationist and should be strongly discouraged.'

The third was a recommendation to read Eric Clarke's book, *Ways of Listening: An Ecological Approach to the Perception of Musical Meaning* (2005). This is an explication and application to the field of music of James Gibson's influential ecological perceptual theory – which assumes that structure is inherent in the environment, not a construction of the mind, and that perception and action are tightly interlocked and mutually constraining (Spiegelberg, 2006; Zhang and Patel, 2006).

For the fourth he suggested 'the study (and performance) of Beethoven. While I might think it's time we listened to composers of the 21st century, Beethoven did die in 1827 – how sustained do they want it? (this is yet another reading of sustained, sorry)'.

Finally, he wrote that the biggest challenge for music in the academy is 'the perceived need to adapt to uncharted changes in a mass-media dominated bums-on-seats driven climate'.

Although all the examples provided interesting and potentially valuable avenues to explore further, perhaps the most memorable and relevant of his comments was the final sentence of his message: 'I'm afraid I don't understand the term sustainability at all. My apologies.'

The apparent confusion is, perhaps, unsurprising. While it is very noticeable – and the more one looks, the more noticeable it becomes – how the words 'sustainable', 'sustainable development' and 'sustainability' have become part of the strategic, operational and everyday discourses and practices of both HE and the arts, one of the consequences of their ubiquity has been a multiplicity of definitions, understandings and misunderstandings of what the terms actually mean. The influences and impact of these various and varied currents and streams of discourse around the notion of sustainability manifest themselves in a plethora of ways in HE dance, drama, music and performance.

Sustainability and performance

Performance is increasingly regarded not only as a creative practice and mode of representation but also as a vital means of embodied enquiry and as analytical trope (Arts and Humanities Research Council [AHRC], 2009).

If one looks beyond and behind the word 'sustainability', and understands it – at least in part – as an active concern with the relationship between humans and their environment, and the impact and consequences of the activities of the former on the latter, then it becomes obvious that there is a sustained and rich tradition of that concern manifested in the performing arts. The arts, generally, have long been a powerful source of awareness, understanding and appreciation of our environment, whether it is the 'natural' world or the urban and industrial landscapes that the majority of the world's population now inhabit. There are numerous works of art, literature and music in which natural, urban or industrial environments play a major role, and many of these – for example, the art and literature of the Romantic movement – have left powerful and indelible marks on our individual and collective psyches. As Wasserloos reminds us: 'The deep embedding of natural experience has remained a characteristic of Northern literature, painting and music as a mirror of nature since the 19th century to the present day' (Wasserloos, 2007, pp1–2). Similarly, there are numerous works of art and performance that tell of humankind's often baleful impact on these environments and the communities that inhabit them.

Performance is not only an action and an art form. In the discourses and practices of performing arts higher education, it is also a field of study and a method of enquiry (or a way of knowing):

Arts-informed research ... may trump conventional forms of research when it comes to generating questions or raising awareness of complex subtleties that matter. The deep strength of using arts in research may be closer to the act of problematizing traditional conclusions than it is to providing answers in containers that are watertight. In this sense, the products of this research are closer in function to deep conversation and insightful dialogue than they are to error-free conclusions (Eisner, 2008, p7).

The arts can be seen as ways of doing, knowing and being that often involve multiple paradoxes and the holding-in-mind of many interpretations and positions (Danvers, 2007). The philosopher Alva Noë, who has worked closely with dancers and choreographers, states that 'experience, consciousness, is always necessarily embodied. It is always, necessarily, environmentally situated'. He goes on to say that performance – particularly dance – 'is an enactment or modelling of the fundamental fact of our relationship to the world around us' (Noë, 2008), and that dancers perceive of their dancing not simply as a form of doing or action but primarily as a research tool, a way to explore the world and to generate knowledge and understanding.

There can be no doubt that a concern with sustainability and, particularly, an interest in the relationship between performance and the environment has become an established strand in those discourses and practices. In 2005, the AHRC established its £5.5 million *Landscape & Environment* transdisciplinary research programme. The aim of this four-year programme is to develop 'arts and humanities understandings of landscape and environment in distinctive, innovative and engaging ways' (AHRC, 2005). Following the announcement of the programme, a symposium of academics from a range of disciplines including anthropology, archaeology, architecture, dance, drama and theatre, geography, literature, music and the visual arts, met under the title *Enchantment and Haunting: Creating Landscape Through Performance* to explore how the AHRC's programme might be used to investigate the relationship between performance, landscape and environment.

The AHRC's initiative was welcomed at the symposium 'not least for how it might demonstrate distinctive arts and humanities contributions to our understanding of the bio-physical world, human relations to it, and their current constellation around both various environmentalisms and politics of place' (Clang, 2005, p2). Among the many responses and ideas that the symposium produced, the emergent interest in ecologies of performance was highlighted 'for its concern with relating epistemologies of performance and ecology, and for mobilising notions such as sustainability and recycling in performance studies' (Clang, 2005, p4). There was also an interest in 'investigating site-based or site-inspired "eco-theatre", various environmental and land arts, and the role of performance in environmental education and environmentalism more generally' (Clang, 2005, p4).

The importance of considering performance in relation to sustainability is that it is both a conceptual and practical terrain that has the potential to generate and provoke genuine shifts in attitude and behaviour by engaging the emotions and senses as well as the intellect, by disturbing accepted attitudes and behaviours, and by making the ordinary extraordinary.

Sustainability and drama

Theatre reaches audiences in a very personal and compelling way, touching both the heart and the mind. Because theatre can also impart technical information and encourage action, it addresses one of the most notorious challenges of the sustainability project: moving people from the status quo to sustainability action (Clark, 2008, p5).

In 1882 Henrik Ibsen wrote the play *Enemy of the People*, which is set in a small town that has invested heavily in tourism by developing a spa. The local doctor discovers and points out that pollution from the town's tannery is causing serious illness amongst the tourists visiting the spa. The doctor is denounced by the local authorities, businessmen and press for threatening to ruin the town's reputation and prosperity. Ultimately he is cast out of the town and branded 'an enemy of the people'. Calouste Gulbenkian Foundation Director Siân Ede, in an interview for *The Ashden Directory* (a website dedicated to 'bringing together environmentalism and performing arts') says of the play:

[It is] the most interesting play in the field of environmental issues, and it's one which I draw on all the time… It is a brilliant piece of writing that shows the political dilemmas surrounding environmental issues. It is the most fantastic example of somebody standing up for freedom and not looking at the commercial aspects of it. You see how unpopular the hero has to make himself and the effects on his family as a result of that. It ought to be done over and over again. You can hardly better that play (Ede, 2004).

While productions of *Enemy of the People* are relatively rare nowadays, there is a more recent history of education engaging directly with environmental issues and the performing arts. The Theatre in Education (TIE) movement that thrived in the UK, particularly from the mid-1960s to the 1980s, focused its work in schools. Working and engaging *with* (rather than simply performing *to*) young people and teachers, TIE companies developed, produced and performed drama-based programmes 'around a topic of relevance both to the school curriculum and to the children's own lives' (Jackson, 1993, p4). TIE was an 'issue-based' movement, and many of the companies pursued an agenda that enabled them to combine theatre, politics and education in a unique, potent and sometimes controversial mix.

One of the most influential of the many environmentally focused plays and projects produced by the TIE movement was *Drink the Mercury* by David Holman, who has written a number of plays directly tackling environmental issues. First produced in 1972 by the Belgrade TIE in Coventry, the play is still performed regularly around the world – an example, perhaps, of creating sustainable theatre? The play dramatizes, in an extraordinarily powerful way, the medical and social impact of 36 years of industrial effluent poisoning on the once-prosperous Japanese fishing community of Minamata and tells the story of the struggle of the surviving victims and their families for justice and reparation (the famous 'Minamata' series of photographs by W. Eugene Smith (1996) is an eloquent and terrible testimony of that particular tragedy).

An important feature of both the plays mentioned above[1] is the quality of the work – not only in the original writing but in their production. One of the challenges of the sustainability agenda in regard to the arts and arts education is that, perhaps inevitably, the discourses and practices of sustainability are often framed and influenced by the rationalism of the scientist and the pragmatism of the bureaucrat rather than the passion of the artist. Each, of course, is important in its own way, but when the artistic agenda is set by the scientists and/or the bureaucrats, the art tends to lose out. Siân Ede provides a typical example of this tension:

All our [arts] grants are for early research and development activities. I'm now half-wondering whether to do an arts and environment strand. But I think I probably won't call it that. I'll probably say we're continuing to do R&D but this will include environmental issues. My fear is that very poor applications will come forward. My joke is always – and this is absolutely true – when I was on the Science on Stage and Screen Committee at the Wellcome Trust[2] and we asked for things addressing science we got I can't remember how many plays with the title Hello, hello, hello, Dolly, Dolly, Dolly. They were all really dreadful plays about cloning. Nothing had broken boundaries. Quality is the key issue. When people write to me with an application and say 'We're writing a play to change the world and these are the issues,' I say, 'Well, who's going to disagree with that? But are you any good?' (Ede, 2004).

That 'But are you any good?' describes one of the tensions inherent in tackling sustainability in the performing arts curriculum. As Ede points out, very few if any would disagree with the sustainability agenda, so the 'what' is not in question.

It is the *how best to do it* in a way *that works* which exercises those with responsibility for designing and delivering meaningful learning experiences in HE performing arts.

Such developments in HE performing arts are a response to some of the 'hard questions' identified by Kershaw about the theatre's relationship with and response to the environment and environmental issues, and 'the ambivalence of theatre in the face of a calamity for humanity' (Kershaw, 2007, p10).

One of the hard questions Kershaw asks is 'In what ways has the theatre been unavoidably embroiled in the ecological mess that is climate change?' (Kershaw, 2007, p10), and anyone who has been involved in theatre-making and production will know that the theatre has a complex and difficult relationship with the notion of sustainability. On the one hand, the theatre is intensely frugal in the acquisition and use of resources, and simultaneously wildly profligate in relation to their disposal. In the face of the general lack of financial resources in the arts and the resulting, often severe, limitations on production budgets, designers have to be particularly innovative in their design solutions, and very resourceful in acquiring the materials to realize their designs. The constraints also mean that, when purchasing items, frequently only the cheapest options are or, up until recently, were pursued. Inevitably, questions such as where and how items such as timber were sourced were rarely, if ever, considered.

More troubling, perhaps, from a sustainability perspective was the matter of disposal once a production had finished. The traditional theatre flat of painted canvas stretched over wooden frames was eminently recyclable. It is now rarely if ever seen, and many companies and theatres utilize the latest (affordable) developments in materials and technology.

Building-based theatre companies had scenic stores, props rooms and wardrobes where scenery, properties and costumes could be kept to be used or adapted in other productions. But in many cases, at the end of the last performance, the crew would dismantle everything on stage and much of it would go into a skip to be taken away to some landfill site.

Those practices were frequently replicated in the conservatoires, universities and colleges where the performing arts were studied and performed. With the increasing focus on sustainability and the environment, while the skip may still stand outside at the end of a production period, it now often remains partially filled or even empty, as policies – both explicit and implicit – on the acquisition, use and re-use of materials are taken on board and implemented.

Some HEIs are actively developing and promoting the sustainability agenda as it relates to the performing arts. In 2008, the Centre for Excellence for Theatre Training at the Central School of Speech and Drama in London took part in the Mayor of London's Climate Change Action Plan for London Theatre, with a series of focused discussions and open access forums. The conference, *Theatre Materials/Material Theatres* (Central School of Speech and Drama, 2008), included discussions on 'sustainable theatre architecture' and 'sustainable theatre production'. Central is also involved with the Bartlett School of Architecture at University College London (UCL) on a project to rethink the design, fabrication and purpose of performance spaces and to explore 'issues of sustainability and spatial innovation'.

As an example of the importance of demonstrating an institution's sustainability credentials, a new music and performance centre was recently heralded by West Chester University in the USA for winning a prestigious rating for 'features including use of products made from recycled materials, locally manufactured or harvested wood products from a sustainably managed forest, materials with low or no volatile organic compounds, and energy-efficient mechanical and electrical systems' (Arnold Creek Productions, 2009). While this is, of course, admirable and welcome, in the light of Ede's question 'But is it any good?' there is no clue as to whether the building works as a performance space.

Theatre companies, too, are now proclaiming their sustainability credentials. The 2009 tour of the musical *Cloudcuckooland*, produced by the Onassis Programme at Oxford University, which supports new writing based on classical Greek drama, claimed that it was perhaps 'the first ever environmentally sustainable touring musical' (Eastman, 2009). This claim, perhaps inevitably, set off a series of questioning and sceptical exchanges when it appeared on the SCUDD list, the discussion list of university drama departments (SCUDD, 2009).

As the notion of sustainability has risen up the agenda for HE, its integration into institutional practices has occurred not only at the macro level of strategy and policy, but also at the micro level of course content. Increasingly, performing arts students encounter course curricula and content that requires them to consider and demonstrate an awareness and understanding of sustainability issues in relation to their subjects of study and related activities.

In a typical example, students on a new technical/production degree course at Rose Bruford College (RBC), a specialist higher education performing arts institution in Kent in the UK, have to 'demonstrate an awareness of the environmental issues associated with the live performance industry' (RBC, 2008). This learning outcome is developed at all three levels of the degree course, but is only assessed at level three in a module that has the assessment task outlined in Box 9.1.

Box 9.1 Project specification for RBC level three assessment

Students will develop a specification for a real-world live performance event with

EITHER

a) Full costings, technical specifications, creative overview, profit/loss breakdowns and environmental impact assessment for taking the performance to two commercial venues.

OR

b) Full costings, technical specifications, creative overview, environmental impact assessment and completed grant application (Arts Council, Lottery or others) for taking the performance to two venues. (RBC, 2008)

RBC is now planning to introduce a sustainability element into all its courses (Email correspondence with author, 2008).

At another UK HEI, the University of Chichester, although sustainability per se is not addressed formally in the curriculum there is, as in other institutions, a significant amount of concern among students and staff about environmental issues. A senior lecturer reports that a considerable proportion of final year devised productions devote an element of their considerations 'to the narratives of consumption and sustainability' (Email correspondence with author, 2008):

> *In the past three years we have had a number of ecological disaster zones (exploded suns, waste-filled landscapes, spaces where the 'natural' reclaims a redundant 'technological' space etc.). Following more recent work and collaboration with an architect who designed 'rain water capacitors' blending glass architecture with gardening, I have engaged with two undergraduate devising processes that have engaged with 'sustainability'.* United States Of Austerity (2006) *drew on the imagining of an unsustainable city and worked from Paul Auster's novel* Country Of Last Things *and Donald Barthelme's* They Called For More Structure
> (Email correspondence with author, 2008).

At Edith Cowan University in Australia, one of the project units on its Contemporary Performance course was based entirely on sustainability and the environment. Students created four original performances that were presented as part of the university's annual theatre festival. The festival was staged entirely at an inner city site that, 14 years previously, had been a heavily degraded and polluted industrial area, and which, by the time the Peppercorn Festival took place in 1997, had become a rehabilitated wasteland developed according to permaculture principles. The titles and descriptions of the productions, which were produced to coincide with World Environment Day, demonstrate very different takes on the project theme (Edith Cowan University, 2007).

The examples above demonstrate that there are clearly a number of opportunities and a variety of ways in which sustainability issues can be and are being addressed in performing arts curricula. The first example, namely ensuring that students have properly to consider the environmental impact of their plans and activities, is a more formal approach that is more in line with the legal and regulatory framework that has developed around sustainability. While it is clearly essential that students who are planning careers in the performing arts – particularly in the areas of design, management and technical production – are made aware and have some experience of sustainability considerations in relation to their work, it does not necessarily follow that they themselves are interested in or committed to sustainability. Rather like health and safety regulations, there is a danger that sustainability issues can be perceived merely as something that have to be taken into consideration along with everything else.

In the other examples, students are creating work that has a sustainability theme. This approach may not have the *force majeure* of legal obligation, but it does provide the opportunity, through the process of research, devising, performance and reflection, for students to develop, individually and collectively, an intellectual, emotional and even a political commitment to the idea of sustainability. Students are increasingly creating work, and being increasingly encouraged to create work, that is ecologically themed because it is clear that it is important to society and its survival. This work is then communicated through various arts and performance practices to the wider culture, where it contributes to the 'warming effect' around sustainability. One of the academics who responded to the question 'Do we do sustainability in the performing arts?' described this process as follows:

> *While it may be considered that the performing arts subject areas do not share the immediacy of subjects such as architecture or engineering sciences, they are valued by colleagues in these areas who welcome the opportunity to either use the performing arts as a means of communicating ecological sustainability issues and practices, or draw on the knowledges (e.g. of space, narrative and decision-making processes) of the subject area* (Email correspondence with author, 2008).

One curriculum area in drama/theatre that does lend itself to the integration and promotion of sustainability is that of applied drama or applied theatre (Nicholson, 2005). Both terms are used to describe an expanding set of practices and accompanying discourses in which theatre and drama skills and a range of other skills are applied in specific contexts such as communities, prisons, schools or hospitals. The teaching of applied theatre and drama necessarily involves equipping students with the pedagogic experiences and tools that enable them to conceptualize and develop into their roles as emerging applied theatre practitioners who will, as graduates, go out into the community and find work in such roles, thus continuing and expanding the field and themselves.

Courses in applied theatre have embedded in them many opportunities for students to engage with sustainability issues through placements and the development of applied theatre projects for and with a range of arts and non-arts organizations and communities. At the Central School of Speech and Drama and at Royal Holloway, University of London, part of this provision enables students to set up and run projects in developing countries. Providing these curriculum opportunities creates the first layers of potential sustainability, that is, the students develop links (and future jobs) while on their course, and through undertaking projects in the community develop their skills as practitioners.

Sustainability and music

Imagine if all sound-related disciplines added soundscape listening, analysis and topics of acoustic ecology to their course curriculum (Westerkamp, 2001, pp3–4).

The ethnomusicologist Jeff Titon describes music as 'a human bio-cultural resource', and writes about 'worlds of music' as ecological systems (Titon, 1984, p9). The subject area of music – which in HE includes related areas such as sound technology and sonic arts – offers a range of approaches and activities that provide opportunities for students to enhance their thinking and practice on the environment and sustainability.

The importance of, and threats to, the physical environment – both locally and globally – has been paralleled, but in a much smaller way, by a recognition of the importance of the acoustic environment. In this respect, the development of the discipline of acoustic ecology has been very significant. The underpinning philosophic principles of acoustic ecology were developed 30 years ago by R. Murray Schafer in his seminal book *The Tuning of the World* (Schafer, 1977). A sophisticated and complex discipline, it focuses on the relationship, mediated through sound, between living beings and their environment. It considers the acoustic environment as a 'soundscape' in much the same way one might consider the physical environment as a landscape. For example, there are 'soundmarks' that are analogous with landmarks, and which are sounds of particular significance (e.g. waterfalls, church bells, trains) in a particular community or environment (Wrightson, 2000).

Schafer's terminology helps to express the idea that the sound of a particular locality (its keynotes, sound signals and soundmarks) can – like local architecture, customs and dress – express a community's identity to the extent that settlements can be recognised and characterised by their soundscapes. Unfortunately, since the industrial revolution, an ever increasing number of unique soundscapes have disappeared completely or submerged into the cloud of homogenised, anonymous noise that is the contemporary city soundscape, with its ubiquitous keynote – traffic (Wrightson, 2000, p10).

The influence of Schafer's ideas can be seen, for example, in a 2008 project for music students at Bristol University called *Urban Soundscapes: Music in the English Town 1800–1900*. The project entailed second- and third-year music students exploring the 19th century soundscape of a particular city. According to the course documentation, they had to do this in 'as specific and unique detail as you can muster, relating it to whatever concept of overall coherence seems to you most fruitful... Give attention, where appropriate, to geography, architecture, institutions, communities and significant individuals' (Banfield, 2008).

At Tufts University in Massachusetts, 100 students from across a range of disciplines worked with a composer to create a 'cross-disciplinary audio exhibition', using the university campus as a psycho-acoustic map. One of the aims of the project was to make people become far more aware of their audio environment, to think about and question the elements that go into making it. The instigators of the project also recognized that it had a political purpose in enabling people – through enhancing their understanding – to take or at least have some control over their acoustic environments.

Although neither of the projects above has nor makes explicit links to sustainability, they fall clearly into the category of work that raises an awareness of and concern for the environment that is one of the essential first steps in changing not only peoples' attitudes but also their practices:

Soundscape and acoustic ecology approaches are important to us pedagogically... In these projects we explored a range of technologies that allow environments to be 'brought inside' the classroom, to be considered and reflected on and used as a source of musical expression. Whether this is a geographical or social environment, individual or collaborative reflections can lead to an increasing sense of environmental awareness (Savage and Challis, 2001, p38).

One of the problems that music has in relation to sustainability (or any other non-musical topic) is that music, for many, essentially concerns itself with composition, performance and analysis – that is, it is all about the music, musicianship and musicology. However, reporting on a cross-disciplinary initiative that involved academics reflecting on how sustainability might be made relevant to their subjects and demonstrating how environmental sustainability could be integrated into at least one course, Wachholz describes an approach to a music curriculum that explicitly links music to sustainability. It takes the form of asking music students to explore a number of sustainability-related topics and questions (Wachholz, 2007, pp5–6). These include:

- What might be the consequences of global warming on the music and music traditions of African peoples and communities who have to leave their homelands due to drought and famine?

- How might an unclean or polluted environment affect musicians? (Example: an increase in asthma and other respiratory conditions.)

- How might music have contributed to the problem? (Example: the glorification of the automobile in popular music.)

- Exploring sustainability in music instrument production. (Example: Investigating what and how many different types of wood and other materials are involved in making string instruments, pianos and so on.)

- Exploring sustainability in music consumption. (Example: What is required of the environment for the production or dissemination of music – the energy consumption in mounting a huge venue concert, the energy needed and waste produced in the glass mastering, electroplating, stamping, moulding, metallization, lacquering, printing and packaging of CDs or DVDs, the necessity of battery disposal for iPods and other such gadgets, and so on) (based on Wachholz, 2007, pp5–6).

If one accepts Titon's description of music as a 'bio-cultural resource' (Titon, 1984, p9) then one could add to those questions and topics an exploration of what it is to be a musician in a rapidly changing cultural environment (Bennett, 2008, preface). It is perhaps no accident that Helen Stowasser, in her foreword to Bennett's work, uses an environmental analogy:

It is widely recognised that the survival of all living things on this planet depends largely on their ability to adapt to environmental changes. It is also acknowledged that plants nurtured in a hothouse (also known as a conservatory!) do not always survive when transplanted into the open air. Classical musicians are no different, and if they are to avoid extinction they need to develop the diverse skills required to survive in our present day multicultural, economic rationalist and computer-dependent society (Stowasser in Bennett, 2008, foreword).

Although music is not immediately a candidate for the integration of sustainability into its curriculum, the examples in this section demonstrate that – as a discipline – it provides a number of fascinating and excellent opportunities to explore sustainability: from the personal to the practical and political.

Sustainability and dance

Dance, as with drama and music, has had a long-standing relationship with the environment and, particularly, landscape. This relationship has become ever more explicit with the development of organizations and companies such as Interdisciplinary Laboratory for Art, Nature and Dance (iLand) and Human Landscape Dance. iLand describes itself as 'a dance research organization with a fundamental commitment to environmental sustainability as it relates to art and the urban context, cultivates cross-disciplinary research among artists, environmentalists, scientists, urban designers and other fields' (iLand, 2009). Matthew Shute, the Artistic Director of Human Landscape Dance, writes:

By plying the counter-tension between person and space, this group reveals humanity's interdependence with our world... The group treats the interconnectedness of man and nature through modern dance in public spaces (Shute, 2009).

The concerns about the environment, and questions about sustainability and sustainable practices, have become increasingly the concerns of the discipline, and because many dance practitioners are also dance teachers in HE, there is a constant flow of ideas, practices and people between the dance world and that of HE dance. It is important to remember that dance is not just an art form but also a form of enquiry and research (Noë, 2008; Eisner, 2008), and the HE dance curriculum reflects these concerns. Dance courses and dance institutions have begun to explore questions that range from 'How can we better understand the environment through movement practice?' to 'What are sustainable dance practices?' and 'What constitutes a healthy dance ecology?'

Also as with drama and music, one of the recurring themes in dance is that of personal sustainability, that is developing the knowledge, the skills and, importantly, the attitudes that might enable an individual to sustain a career in what is a particularly demanding and difficult field of work (Bennett, 2008, p1). Professional dancers, in particular, tend to have relatively short careers as 'working dancers', and teachers, researchers and practitioners in dance have grappled increasingly with the notion of sustainability, not only for what it means for individual dancers but also for what it means generally for dance. These and similar questions formed the agenda for a student-focused symposium on *Sustainability, Ecology and the Moving Body* (University of Northumbria, 2009) that explored ways that the discourses and practices surrounding sustainability might become core discourses and practices in the discipline of dance.

Endnote

Finally, it is worth mentioning an alternative approach to encouraging students to engage with sustainability. Some US HEIs, as part of their strategic and operational commitment to sustainability, have recently begun to require that all students, regardless of their main subject of study, undertake a sustainability-related course. At Goucher College in Baltimore, for example, all first-year students are 'required to explore the ecological and/or policy dimensions of environmental sustainability', and they are offered a choice of 17 courses that range from the scientific to the philosophical and ethical (Goucher, 2009). One of the courses, *Consumerism, the Media, Popular Culture and the Environment*, is one that might well attract dance, drama and music students. The course description is, perhaps, a useful way to end this chapter on sustainability and the performing arts curriculum because it encapsulates many of the themes that have been discussed, as well as some of its aspirations for a more sustainable world:

> *This course will examine the relationship between culture and environment. We will focus on how the mass media and popular culture create and perpetuate the mythology of the American Dream and the 'good life' – with all its material abundance and consequent wastefulness. How does our culture talk about various forms of consumption? What is the relationship between the media, cultural and political elites, corporate entities, and the consumer? How do we, as an audience, receive, internalize, and operationalize these messages? And how can we escape the mantra of 'more is better'? The course will include a strong experiential component meant to encourage students to live in more sustainable ways* (Goucher College, 2009, p93).

This chapter has demonstrated that while dance, drama and music in HE may well appear to have an 'awkward fit' with the sustainability agenda (Dawe et al, 2005), appearances can be deceptive. It is perhaps the nature of that agenda and, particularly, assumptions about how best it should be implemented that provide the awkwardness. It is clear that the performing arts not only have a long and significant history of creative engagement with environmental issues, but also that they continue to play an important and influential role in the development and transmission of ideas, attitudes and calls to action in relation to sustainability.

Acknowledgements

I am indebted to the following dance, drama and music colleagues across the UK and further afield for their invaluable help, advice and comments:

Stephen Banfield, Janette Barrington, Gill Clarke, Dave Coslett, Nick Fells, Ashley Hanson, Nick Hunt, Adrian Moore, Misha Myers, Kate Newey, Mary Oliver, Claire Parfitt, Sheila Preston, Tina Ramnarine, Julie Robson (Australia), Matthew Sansom, Mark Seton (Australia), Trevor Wiggins and Andrew Wilford.

References

AHRC (2005) *Landscape & Environment* www.landscape.ac.uk/index.html Accessed 30 March 2009

AHRC (2009) *Living Landscapes*, Landscape and Environment Programme Conference, Aberystwyth University, June www.landscape.ac.uk/2009conference.html Accessed 30 March 2009

Arnold Creek Productions (2008) *A New Course for Higher Education: Integrating Sustainability Across the Campus*, available at www.arnoldcreekproductions.com/ SustainabilityHigherEducation.htm Accessed 2 July 2009, accessed 30 March 2009

Banfield, S. (2008) Unit booklet for course MUS120134/MUS130134 , Music Department, University of Bristol

Bennett, D.E. (2008) *Understanding the Classical Music Profession: The Past, the Present and Strategies for the Future*, Ashgate Publishing, Aldershot

Central School of Speech and Drama (2008) *Theatre Materials/Material Theatres*, available at www.theatrematerials.org.uk, accessed 2 July 2009

Clang, P. (2005) *Enchantment and Haunting: Creating Landscape Through Performance*, Report on the AHRC Landscape and Environment Framework Seminar, Royal Holloway, University of London, June

Clark, G.E. (2008) 'Bytes of Note: Sustainability Theater', *Environment Magazine* Sept–Oct, available at www.environmentmagazine.org/Bytes%20of%20Note/ Bytes-so08.html, accessed 3 July 2009

Clarke, E.F. (2005) *Ways of Listening: An Ecological Approach to the Perception of Musical Meaning*, Oxford University Press, New York NY

Danvers, J. (2007) 'A coincidence of opposites: notes on inbetweeness in art-as-enquiry', *Discourse Power Resistance: Research as a Subversive Activity* conference, Manchester Metropolitan University, April, available at www.johndanversart.co.uk/research/ coincidence.htm, accessed 2 July 2009

Dawe, G., Jucker, R. and Martin, S. (2005) *Sustainable Development in Higher Education: Current Practice and Future Developments*, HEA, York, available at www.heacademy.ac.uk/

assets/York/documents/ourwork/tla/sustainability/sustdevinHEIfinalreport.pdf, accessed 23 January 2010

Eastman, H. (2009) 'Theatre and the Environment', Email to the SCUDD discussion list, 23 March, available at www.jiscmail.ac.uk/cgi-bin/webadmin?A2=ind0903&L= SCUDD&P=R42034, accessed 3 July 2009

Ede, S. (2004) 'But is it any good?', Interview with *The Ashden Directory*, available at www.ashdendirectory.org.uk/featuresView.asp?pageIdentifier=2004824_19169253, accessed 30 March 2009

Edith Cowan University (2007) *The Peppercorn Festival: Growing Contemporary Performance*, available at www.sca.ecu.edu.au/data/tmp/the_peppercorn_festival_web2.pdf, accessed 2 July 2009

Eisner, M. (2008) 'Art and knowledge', In Knowles, J.G. and Cole, A.L. (eds), *Handbook of the Arts in Qualitative Research: Perspective, Methodologies, Example and Issues*, Sage Publications, Thousand Oaks CA

Goucher College (2009) Academic Catalog, available at www.goucher.edu/documents/ Records/Goucher_Academic_Catalogue_2009-10.pdf, accessed 21 Feb 2010

Holman, D. (1972) *Drink the Mercury*, The Belgrade TIE, Amber Lane Press

Ibsen, H. (1882/1997) *Enemy of the People*, Faber & Faber, London

iLand (2009) *Mission*, available at www.ilandart.org/about.cfm, accessed 3 July 2009

Jackson, A. (1993) *Learning Through Theatre: New Perspectives on Theatre-in-Education* (2nd ed), Routledge, London

Kershaw, B. (2007) *Theatre Ecology: Environments and Performance Events*, Cambridge University Press, Cambridge

May, T. and Fried, L. (2009) 'The urban animal: a conversation with Theresa May & Larry Fried (part i)', Interview with *eco Theater*, available at http://ecotheater.wordpress.com/2007/08/24/the-urban-animal-a-conversation-with-theresa-may-larry-fried-part-i, accessed 14 July 2009

Nicholson, H. (2005) *Applied Drama (Theatre and Performance Practices)*, Palgrave Macmillan, Basingstoke

Noë, A. (2008) *Dance as a Form of Knowing*, available at www.blip.tv/file/996998, accessed 19 Feb 2010

RBC (2008a) Course documentation, BA (Hons) Digital Live Arts Programme, RBC, Sidcup

Savage, J. and Challis, M. (2001) 'Sound reflections', *Soundscape: The Journal of Acoustic Ecology*, vol 2, no 2, pp35–38

Schafer, R.M. (1977) *The Tuning of the World (The Soundscape)*, Random House, New York NY

SCUDD (2009) Discussion thread on Theatre and the Environment, available at www.jiscmail.ac.uk/cgi-bin/webadmin?A2=ind0903&L=SCUDD&P=R42443, accessed 14 July 2009

Shute, M. (2009) *Artistic director's note*, available at http://forum.article19.co.uk/topic.php?id=229, accessed 19 February 2010

Smith, W.E. (1996) *Minamata*, available at http://aileenarchive.or.jp/aileenarchive_en/slides/index.html, accessed 2 July 2009

Spiegelberg, S. (2006) 'Review of Eric Clarke's *Ways of Listening*', *Empirical Musicology Review*, vol 1, no 2

Stowasser, H. (2008) 'Foreword', In Bennett (2008)

Titon, J. (1984) *Worlds of Music*, Schirmer Books, New York NY

ULSF (1990) *The Talloires Declaration*, available at www.ulsf.org/programs_talloires.html, accessed 27 June 2009

University of Northumbria (2009) *Sustainability, Ecology and the Moving Body* January, available at http://dissolvingborders.wordpress.com/sustainability-ecology-and-the-moving-body, accessed 2 July 2009

Wachholz, S. (2007) 'Engaging faculty and greening the curriculum: Teaching for sustainability', Northeast Campus Sustainability Consortium Sustainability Conference, Bowdoin College, Brunswick ME, October

Wasserloos, Y. (2007) 'Beyond Grieg – Edvard Grieg and his diverse influences on music of the 20th and 21st centuries', The International Grieg Society Conference, Bergen May, available at www.griegsociety.org/filer/1139.pdf, accessed 31 January 2010

Westerkamp, H. (2001) Editorial, *Soundscape: The Journal of Acoustic Ecology*, vol 1, no 2, pp3–4

Wrightson, K. (2000) 'An introduction to acoustic ecology', *Soundscape: Journal of Acoustic Ecology*, vol 1, no 1, p10

Zhang, J. and Patel, V. L. (2006) 'Distributed cognition, representation, and affordance', *Cognition & Pragmatics*, vol 14, no 2, pp333–341

Notes

1   In a remarkable but potentially tragic example of life imitating art, on 21 February 2008 the *New York Times* reported a story under the headline 'Mercury Taint Divides a Japanese Whaling Town' (www.nytimes.com/2008/02/21/world/asia/21dolphin.html?scp=1&sq=Mercury%20Taint&st=cse accessed 1 February 2010). The story combines elements of *Enemy of the People* and *Drink the Mercury*. Taiji, a seafaring town in Japan, is (in)famous for its annual dolphin drive, involving the slaughter of hundreds of dolphins. The *New York Times* reported that high levels of mercury had been found in the mammals, and that a member of the town's council, backed by scientific evidence, was fighting a lone battle against the authorities and the local fishing community who insisted that the danger was overblown.

2   The Wellcome Trust is an independent charity funding research to improve human and animal health. Established in 1936 and with an endowment of around £13 billion, it is the UK's largest non-governmental source of funds for biomedical research.

Chapter 10

Engineering Our World Towards a Sustainable Future

Edited by Simon Steiner,
with acknowledged contributions

Introduction

Engineers have the distinct advantage that, by virtue of their education and training, they are able to apply ingenuity and imagination to the rhetoric of others to create solutions for otherwise insoluble problems. It is this ability to take the ethos and words of others and to evolve realistic and working solutions that defines an engineer.

The Engineering Council (EC), through its *UK Standard for Professional Engineering Competence* for the accreditation of higher education (HE) degree programmes, recognizes this expectation of graduate engineers towards achieving either their chartered or incorporated engineer status. The standard states that accredited programmes must demonstrate both general and specific learning outcomes, where the latter includes the economic, social and environmental context – in particular, 'understanding of the requirement for engineering activities to promote sustainable development' (EC, 2008, p13).

In the past, there was little requirement for engineering graduates to consider social, economic and environmental issues. The embedding of sustainable development (SD) into the curriculum, however, now requires engineers to both understand and be able to work with knowledge of these contexts towards the solution of complex problems, particularly the kind of problems that they can expect to experience in their working lives as a professional engineer. This has been most recently recognized by the Engineering Council in promotion of its publication, *Guidance on Sustainability* (EC, 2009) to all professional engineers.

This chapter draws together contributed case studies and discussion with the differing approaches that have been adopted by a number of UK university engineering faculties to embed SD into their taught curricula. It is organized into a number of sub-sections looking at learning approaches that engage engineering students with sustainability. Consideration is given to reaching out from engineering in to design, to the environment and to international linkages between research and teaching. The overall aim is therefore for the transformation of student engineers into employable graduates who are articulate in their understanding of the issues and effective in their resolution of cross-disciplinary problems on the way to a world with a sustainable future.

Learning approaches that engage with students

The Royal Academy of Engineering's Visiting Professor Scheme

Richard Dodds, Visiting Professor, Department of Engineering, University of Liverpool

Since the introduction in 1989 of the first Visiting Professor (VP) scheme, The Principles of Engineering Design, the UK Royal Academy of Engineering (RAEng) has appointed over 200 VPs across 49 higher education institutions (HEIs), thus reaching around half of such institutions in the UK that offer accredited engineering degrees.

Three other schemes have since been introduced. The general objective of all the schemes is to enrich the curriculum of engineering courses by placing senior practising engineers into universities who can inject up-to-date engineering practices and case studies into the teaching of undergraduates.

Typically, each VP is supported by the RAEng for part-time involvement over a period of three years, with an extension of two years normally being granted. After five years of support, the teaching material, and often new teaching approaches, should have been implanted into the curriculum. In many cases, the university finds alternative sources of funding to continue the appointment.

The early success of the model and the acceptance of its guiding philosophy led the RAEng to introduce its second VP scheme in 1998, Engineering Design for Sustainable Development. In retrospect, this was a much-needed visionary initiative by the Academy. At that time, SD was poorly understood and did not occupy the prominent public position it does today. The challenge of creating space in an increasingly overcrowded undergraduate teaching timetable was recognized and was exacerbated by the absence of relevant teaching materials and the frequent lack of relevant experience among teaching staff. The introduction of VPs with relevant industrial experience was identified as the appropriate solution. This scheme has, at the time of writing, appointed 26 VPs across 26 HEIs. The impact of the VPs continues to be felt, either through their own continued activity, the continued use of their teaching materials or the new ways in which SD has been included in the curriculum.

The experience of these VPs has been captured in a RAEng publication entitled *Engineering for Sustainable Development: Guiding Principles* (RAEng, 2005), which provides a framework of 12 'guiding principles'[1] linked to several selected VP case studies to illustrate their relevance.

Four case examples to demonstrate the range of activities of the VPs in Engineering Design for Sustainable Development are given below (RAEng, 2005; Crawley et al, 2007; Gough and Scott, 2007).

Case study 1: Bradford University Whitby Field Course
Mark Fletcher, Arup; Visiting Professor, Bradford University

The (UN DESD) runs from 2005 to 2014, and the global firm Arup has been actively supporting the decade through the RAEng VP Scheme. This has provided an opportunity to raise awareness of SD issues from 2002 to date. Arup is a firm of designers, engineers, planners and business consultants, with over 10,000 staff in over 50 countries.[2] Mark Fletcher was appointed to the role of VP in the School of Engineering, Design and Technology at Bradford University in the north of England in 2002. Over 1500 students and staff have since been engaged through the activities of the VP, whose role in support of SD education initiatives ranges from pre-university and undergraduate students to postgraduates and teaching personnel, through the use of seminars, workshops, lectures, coursework, field-work and site visits.

During a week-long residential field course at the coastal resort of Whitby in North Yorkshire, students are sub-divided into project teams. Their projects are focused around their own ideas for the sustainable regeneration of Whitby's coast-line. They meet local authority representatives, visit local archive sources and are provided with geotechnical and other related information to develop their frame-work of understanding. This is supplemented by online research and information-gathering under their own initiative (e.g. at libraries and through surveys and personal interviews with local people).

The sustainability teaching element comprises an initial introduction to SD by the VP and is followed by a question-and-answer session then a site visit around the specific study area. The VP is in attendance to point out specific issues, stimulate debate and share questions and answers across the group. During the rest of the week, the students receive further presentations covering ground conditions, transport issues, structural condition assessment and wider social and environmental issues. They are encouraged to develop their own sustainability assessment framework to help demonstrate how they have taken sustainability into account through their thinking, design process and ultimately in their proposed development ideas.

The project teams are maintained for the duration of the field course and subsequently during term-time back at the university. The field course and term study together culminate in the presentation of draft ideas to a panel that includes the VP, a representative of the local authority and their course tutor. The teams are questioned and marked on this draft by the judges and given feedback from this process. They then have a period of term-time to complete their project report and submit it for marking by their tutor. The team judged best is then supported by Arup in preparing a poster for submission to the RAEng's national poster competition (RAEng, 2007).

Case study 2: Working at socially responsible water use

Alan Emery, Visiting Professor, Department of Chemical Engineering, University of Bath

A chemical engineering undergraduate is typically exposed to the environmental and economic aspects of the profession in their curriculum but little exposed to the social considerations. The VP's task is to ensure that all three of these pillars of SD are covered in an integrated way.

The UN's seventh millennium goal on ensuring environmental sustainability includes the basic target to halve the proportion of the population without sustainable access to safe drinking water and basic sanitation by 2015 (UN, 2008). This has given rise in some countries to regulations requiring businesses to reduce their water consumption so communities and the environment might receive their share of available resources.

In their first year, chemical engineering undergraduates perform mass and energy balance calculations and are required to construct a water balance. Real data are used and applied to a mining operation set in an arid region of southern Africa. This mine is the major user of the region's available water resource to the extent that it is likely to inhibit the future well-being and development of local communities. The balance identifies the situations where water is lost and from this the student is expected to derive freshwater use reduction strategies (thus making more water available to others in the community) and to comment on the effects that such changes may have on the overall processes used on the site.

Students are introduced to SD through a lecture that explains its origins, the challenge it presents to governments, business and individuals and what it might mean for them in their future role as professional engineers. They are also given a simple introduction to mining to help them understand the context of the balance they are asked to construct.

The students are asked to investigate the world water situation through the literature and to comment on this in terms of classifications of water and the availability of each kind of water resource, the uses to which fresh water is put, amounts used by different economic sectors and factors affecting its availability.

Students work on their own and in teams as part of this marked assignment. This exemplar is now being expanded in a web-based form: first, to introduce the concept of eco-efficiency and its role in assisting progress in the context of SD, and second for the students working as groups to examine the communities' relationship with the mine as the issues concerning water are addressed.

Case study 3: Embedding sustainability in the civil engineering curriculum at Queen's University Belfast

Roger Venables, Visiting Professor in Engineering for Sustainable Development, Queen's University Belfast

Students in civil engineering and related disciplines need to graduate with a real understanding both of the concepts and the principles of sustainability (and sustainable development), and of their implications for the practice of civil engineering in helping society to move to a more sustainable future. This premise is additionally motivated by the increasing level of interest shown by the Joint Board of Moderators of the Institution of Civil Engineers (ICE) and their establishment of an Environment and Sustainability Board (ICE, 2009).

The VP has developed a series of interlinked activities over the past six years with a combination of lectures that connect existing teaching modules to the sustainability agenda. For example:

- An introductory lecture on sustainability, SD and the connection to civil engineering, architecture and planning is given in registration week to all freshers in the school.

- The level 1 communications module focuses on a range of sustainability issues. The VP gives a second lecture focusing on a particular facet of the sustainability agenda, on which the students then write an essay.

- The VP (aided increasingly by full-time staff) delivers lectures to each of the design modules at levels 1, 2, 3 and 4 (MEng). These extend the themes covered in the introductory lecture to the application of particular aspects of the sustainability agenda, covering, for example, resource efficiency, waste minimization, the durability–flexibility balance to be struck when determining design lives and buildability/disassemblability objectives, the sourcing of materials and the importance of energy efficiency in water and wastewater treatment. At levels 3 and 4, the sustainability of the design proposed by student groups must be explicitly studied and reported on.

- A biennial mock planning inquiry exercise undertaken jointly by level 1 and 2 students has also been modified, with the sustainability of the projects put before the inquiry being one of the strands on which student groups have to study and report.

- Changes to the water and wastewater module provide an example of the influence brought by the VP. The module description now makes explicit mention of human well-being as the driver for why we treat water for drinking and wastewater before passing as effluent to a water body. Similarly, the increasing importance of matters such as energy efficiency and recovery and the use of resources such as methane from digestion are covered.

Finally, case studies are being used both at level 3 and at MEng and MSc levels. For example, the Jubilee River case study, as presented in the RAEng's *Guiding Principles* (RAEng, 2005, p11), comes complete with slides and videos to demonstrate a failed weir and failed channel banks (RAEng, 2005; Joint Board of Moderators, 2009; Queen's University Belfast, 2009).

Case study 4: Chemical and manufacturing engineering – laundry cleaning products

Richard Dodds, Visiting Professor, Department of Engineering, University of Liverpool

The particular aspect of the industry selected for the case study was the introduction of unit-dosed laundry cleaning products – the use of laundry tablets and capsules is of course now well-established in the Northern Hemisphere. The attractiveness of laundry cleaning for a case study is that all students can identify directly with this household chore, especially as most are now living independently. Students are also surprised to learn how large the consumer goods industry is, the intense level of competition between the major players and the scientific and technological sophistication of the product and pack design and its manufacture. This product area is, of course, rich in marketing and advertising material; thus as a subject it is suitable to engage students both in small groups or large lecture theatres.

The teaching material was originally developed and tested as part of a new SD component on a masters course in product design management. It was possible to emphasize the various aspects of technology related to the stages of design, manufacture and distribution and also the importance of the changing attitudes of the consumer towards sustainability. Key factors in this are a reduction in use of raw materials and packaging, lowering of wash temperatures and consideration of environmental impacts at all stages, including the consumer use stage. It is also possible to bring out the vulnerability of global brands to adverse publicity and the importance of corporate responsibility. This awareness prepares the students to carry out a team exercise on other consumer products. Typically four teams of four or five students of various nationalities consider a product type, choosing from white goods (such as domestic appliances), automobiles, hand-held electronic devices and bottled and canned drinks, and carry out a general life-cycle assessment, then each member will take a region of the globe and identify the current and potential SD issues and potential design solutions. These solutions can be infrastructural and regulatory as well as improvements in product design. This approach continues and the products chosen for analysis have been expanded at the request of students to include the nuclear industry. It is now the intention to use the team approach to test and develop ideas for more sustainable products with the direct involvement of industry.

The same material has been adapted with less detailed content for use in large lecture sessions for the entire first year across the Faculty of Engineering, involving over 200 students each year and lecture-class sizes of around 80 to 150. Students have to complete a templated analysis of a product of their choice from an SD perspective with the help of a simple life-cycle assessment; they then identify three design improvements, selecting one for a more detailed proposal for implementation. Again, the laundry product analysis enables them to appreciate the importance of considering all the life-cycle stages and consumer and regulatory aspects as well as the more conventional technology and economic factors (RAEng, 2005, p14).

Experience at the University of Manchester

Bland Tomkinson, University of Manchester

Reduce, reuse, recycle: The 'three Rs' can be useful precepts in ESD, but sometimes things have to be re-engineered from the ground up to have long-term sustainability. Economic forces in education sometimes lead to reusing and recycling old curricula, but Manchester has undertaken two projects that look afresh at educating engineers for SD.

The first was an interdisciplinary module for engineers and scientists (University of Manchester, Faculty of Engineering and Physical Sciences, 2009), supported by the RAEng through its VP Scheme; a report on this project (University of Manchester, Faculty of Engineering and Physical Sciences, 2008) was produced for the RAEng. The second was to garner expert opinion on appropriate ways to build SD into engineering education. This was supported by funding from the Higher Education Academy's Engineering Subject Centre (EngSC, 2008a), and a report was produced for them (EngSC, 2008a).

The interdisciplinary course is built on the ideas of VP Charles Engel (Engel et al, 2007) and was promoted through four advisory groups that advised on:

- setting out a working definition of SD;
- identifying abilities and skills needed to be developed in the pilot module in the context of realistic case studies;
- recommending how learning outcomes of this module might be assessed and successful participation by students recognized;
- evaluating and monitoring the implementation of the pilot module.

Teams of eight students from several engineering disciplines and also from environmental sciences tackled complex issues with no clear answers. The process was supervised by specially trained postdoctoral researchers, a few of whom had knowledge or experience of the issues under consideration. Each of the five exercises, covering a two-week period, aimed to develop not merely knowledge acquisition but also abilities and skills for participation in managing change. This required that:

- problems be complex or *wicked* (Rittel and Webber, 1973);
- scenarios be appropriate to a recent graduate;
- exercises develop skills in managing change;
- problems help students to identify core principles of SD;
- exercises develop professional skills;
- exercises build cumulatively on previous ones;
- issues be current;
- exercises encourage thinking across disciplinary boundaries;
- students' own questions lead to integrated learning;
- formative assessments help students to plan their learning.

Each *wicked* scenario was designed and marked, formatively, by a different member of academic staff and prompt feedback given.

Monitoring through the nominal group process (Delbecq et al, 1975) enabled fine-tuning and provided data for evaluation. At the year's end, the approach's efficacy was assayed through acceptability to staff and students, effectiveness of the learning process and efficiency of the educational approach. Scores on the university's student satisfaction questionnaire were exceedingly high. The chief positives in nominal groups in both years were the interdisciplinary nature, development of teamwork skills, the nature of the facilitation, the realistic content of the module and methods of assessment. Negatives included 9am starts and the fact that some exercises did not count towards overall marks. A learning styles questionnaire, completed at the beginning and end of the first year, showed that students had made a significant shift towards a deep rather than a surface approach (Enhancing Teaching–Learning Environments in Undergraduate Courses, 2008).

The project was highly commended in the 2008 UK Green Gown Awards (Higher Education – Environmental Performance Improvement, 2009).

The second project paralleled the RAEng-sponsored course unit, which helped to prime some of the questions. The Delphi technique (Dalkey, 1969) sought to bring a convergence of views of experts from a range of engineering disciplines, focusing on a small number of related questions about approaches to SD education for engineers. The approach solicited open-ended answers to questions to enhance the richness of the response. The consultation was in four phases:

1   A suggested list of questions, primed by work on the RAEng project, was circulated and participants invited to comment on the questions and to suggest others.
2   Open-ended suggestions were invited in relation to an overarching question and a wider list of considerations.
3   Participants were invited to review the summary of suggestions from Round 2, ranking them and adding further suggestions.
4   There was a report back to the participants on the outcomes.

Gratifyingly, the conclusions reached echoed ideas incorporated into the RAEng project. In this context, the Delphi results suggested that:

*   the main SD challenges for engineers are social and political rather than technical;
*   awareness-raising and communication are key responsibilities for newly graduated professional engineers, with technical skills in second place;
*   prime concerns in SD tasks for engineers are in evaluating complex problems and in systems modelling to cope with this complexity;
*   the dominant transferable skill for graduate engineers is dealing with complexity and being able to think 'outside the box';
*   SD should be embedded throughout the curriculum – student-centred learning methods, in particular role-play and case studies, are most appropriate;
*   final-year projects can demonstrate that the lessons of sustainability literacy have been learned, but with wider perspectives not just narrow technical ones;
*   engineering bodies should support the idea of SD.

The study also verified the Delphi technique as an approach to consensus-seeking on good curriculum design practice.

Emerging from both studies was the understanding that ESD aims to enable the professional engineer to participate (with a leading contribution) in decisions about the way we do things individually and collectively, both locally and globally, to meet the needs and aspirations of the present generation without compromising the ability of future generations to meet their own needs and aspirations, Brundtland's definition of SD (WCED, 1987).

Tool box for sustainable design education

Tracy Bhamra and Vicky Lofthouse, Department of Design and Technology, Loughborough University

In 2000, Forum for the Future published the report *The Engineer of the 21st Century*, recommending a number of ways in which engineering and the education of engineers had to change to meet the challenge of sustainability. One of the key recommendations was that by 2005, all engineering courses 'should have integrated a "sustainability syllabus" into the first and second year and be assessed to ensure they reflect this learning in their final year design project' (Forum for the Future, 2000). In the follow-up report (Forum for the Future, 2005), the Forum found few examples of this happening. One of the key issues it identified was the lack of competence and skills among academic staff in the area of SD.

In 2004, the Department of Design and Technology at Loughborough University secured mini-project funding from the EngSC with the aim of overcoming this obstacle by providing a key resource for academic staff in the understanding of the issues behind SD and applying this in the area of design.

Before the start of the mini-project, many initiatives and actions in HE focused on end-of-pipe and end-of-life issues. While these were beneficial in addressing issues of pollution and waste, their overall contribution towards sustainability was limited. There was also a growing body of research in the field of sustainable design; however, at the start of the project, there were few examples of this being taught as an integrated part of engineering and design education at postgraduate and undergraduate levels. By developing and making generic the existing expertise of the project team, the project aimed to develop a pedagogic tool box to support the teaching of sustainable design to students in engineering and design departments.

The toolbox contains a number of key features to assist in the design and delivery of modules in sustainable design. A guide is given to help identify which part of the toolbox should be taught depending on the time available and specific learning objectives. A set of key learning objectives for sustainable design are outlined and these are linked to different learning blocks, enabling the user to quickly identify the relevant resources. These learning blocks identify key sustainability concepts and outline activities and resource material to facilitate their understanding. The focus and content for a range of suggested lectures, tutorials and seminars is linked to each block, with example PowerPoint presentations, activity sheets and supporting documents to aid lecture preparation. Finally, a comprehensive list of additional resources and links to online material is given.

This tool box enables UK HEIs to begin integrating sustainable design into undergraduate and postgraduate courses in a way that helps meet the targets set out by Forum for the Future. The tool box helps to bolster the capacity of staff in HEIs to design and deliver sustainability learning opportunities. It is available both on CD-ROM and as a download (EngSC, 2004).

Sustainability appraisal tool for structures

Chanakya Arya, Perry Vassie and Ali Amiri, University College, London (UCL)

The UCL Department of Civil, Environmental and Geomatic Engineering (CEGE) received funding from the EngSC in 2008 to undertake a mini-project called 'Embedding Sustainable Development into structural design teaching using sustainability appraisal tools' (EngSC, 2009).

Structural design teaching at universities currently focuses on technical and economic issues, whereas environmental factors such as global warming and social factors such as noise are largely ignored. The choice of construction materials and methods has a significant effect on environmental and social factors. This omission in the teaching syllabus arises because it is not clear how the impact associated with each of these factors should be evaluated and accounted for. Knowledge of sustainability appraisal tools would offer a solution to this problem while also developing some expertise in the kinds of sustainability appraisal that are now routinely carried out.

The aims of the project are to develop teaching materials and student exercises that will:

1 develop expertise in sustainability appraisal tools;
2 help civil engineering students develop a deeper understanding of SD and its relevance to structural design;
3 introduce students to a new method of sustainability appraisal, the System for Appraising the Sustainability of Structures (SASS), which has been developed for civil engineering structures such as bridges.

There are a number of tools that can evaluate or appraise construction projects on a sustainable whole-life basis. These include:

- The Building Research Establishment Environmental Assessment Method (BREEAM)
- The Civil Engineering Environmental Quality Assessment and Award Scheme (CEEQUAL)
- The Gifford Sustainability Appraisal Process (GSAP)
- The Sustainable Project Appraisal Routine (SPeAR), and
- Sustainability Accounting.[3]

The teaching material will provide an overview of each of these tools, explain how they are used and discuss their merits.

The Department has adopted sustainability as one of its main teaching and research themes. SASS has been developed as part of this effort, enabling a quantitative assessment of sustainability and the effect of changes in the relative priority given to the environment, economy and society to be made. This approach should appeal to engineering students, who are used to precision, and also allow them to explore the effect of design decisions on sustainability. The methodology will be explained via a series of worked examples based on a particular bridge project. Related exercises will be provided to test understanding. In the exercises and worked examples, two phases of bridge provision are considered, namely the construction and in-service phases, so as to look at lifetime sustainability.

Students enrolling on civil and structural engineering courses are all too aware of issues such as global warming, resource depletion, pollution and waste. It is hoped that the teaching material, examples and student exercises from this project will focus on the topics that graduating students will find important, particularly when set in the context of their chosen field.

Reaching out from engineering

Postgraduate distance learning

Richard Blanchard, Loughborough University

The Department of Electronic and Electrical Engineering at Loughborough University hosts the MSc in Renewable Energy Systems Technology by distance learning (RESTDL). Typically, students are graduate engineers or physical scientists from around the world. Students take about three years to complete the taught and research components of the course by distance learning. There were around 300 distance learning students registered on the course in August 2009.

The course aims to provide an advanced understanding of renewable energy technologies to enable the implementation of sustainable energy projects around the world. Students make in-depth studies on a range of renewable energy resources including wind, water, solar and biomass. They examine the availability of these resources as well as technology, system designs and integration of renewables into energy supply systems. The main topics draw on the need to understand concepts in a broad range of engineering fields including electrical, mechanical, fluid mechanics, thermal and biochemical, as well as the environment in which they will operate. The latter includes the physical as well as the socio-economic environments.

RESTDL students are able to make use of learning resources through Loughborough University's virtual learning environment, Learn (Loughborough University, 2009). The resources include stimulus materials and communication tools such as discussion boards and blogs, which enable students to interact with each other, and live web conference tutorials give students access to tutors to ask direct questions. These online tools are essential for a group distance learning project where students are set the challenge of contextualizing their understanding of renewable energy within the three pillars of SD – the social, economic and environmental issues.

The group assignment takes a problem-based learning approach so students have to develop their understanding of the issues. Examples of past RESTDL assignments include developing a sustainable energy policy for the EU and developing strategies for deploying micro-generation in the UK. Stimulus material is provided on SD and sustainability indicator techniques with an annual in-course workshop led by Jonathon Porritt, co-founder of Forum for the Future and former Chairman of the UK's Sustainable Development Commission (UK-SDC)[4] to give students a clear understanding of the challenges of sustainability. Each group of five RESTDL students develop a technical report between them and these are graded on the process and final document.

One of the advantages of the RESTDL course is that it lets students continue living and working in their own country; another is that it allows them to work with colleagues from different countries around the world. In particular, graduates develop the knowledge and skills to make informed decisions about developing sustainable energy systems for the 21st century.

The RESTDL MSc course is also accredited by several professional bodies, including the Institution of Engineering and Technology (IET), the Institution of Mechanical Engineers (IMechE) and the Energy Institute[5] under the UK Standard for Professional Engineering Competence (UKSPEC) for Chartered Engineer status.

Design for behavioural change

Vicky Lofthouse and Debra Lilley, Department of Design and Technology, Loughborough University

In 2007, the EngSC funded a mini-project (EngSC, 2008b) to establish a resource that would support the teaching and learning of design for behavioural change, a new field of interest for designers and engineers. Design for behavioural change explores how design (in its broadest sense) can influence user behaviour so as to reduce the social and environmental impacts of products during their use. The output of the project was the design and development of the 'Design-Behaviour' website[6].

The greatest environmental impact of electrical and electronic products often occurs during their use; for example, the energy use of a cooker has a greater environmental impact than other life-cycle stages such as manufacture or disposal (Boardman et al, 1995). This impact can be heavily influenced by consumer behaviour, for example, whether the user opens the door to view cooking food, uses lids on pans, leaves the cooker to warm up for a long period of time and so on. Influencing user behaviour, therefore, is key. Before 2007, design-led research into behavioural change was limited, with knowledge residing across several disciplinary areas (McCalley, 2006; Jelsma and Knot, 2002; Akrich, 1992; Fogg, 2003), making it difficult to access. Few publications effectively captured all existing approaches within one central framework (Wever et al, 2008). The doctoral findings of Debra Lilley aimed to move beyond this and reframe design for behavioural change from the perspective of the designer (Lilley, 2007). The 'Design-Behaviour' website builds on these findings.

'Design-Behaviour' is not a 'how to' guide, but rather a starting point intended to spark new ideas and promote discussion. It provides information about:

- user-centred research methods used to uncover user behaviour;
- design-led strategies for instigating behavioural change;
- insights into how others have applied these strategies in practice.

User-centred research methods in the resource include 'Scenario-of-use' – this is a technique that aims to uncover previously unvoiced needs using role-play as a cue for recall (Evans et al, 2002) and the 'Consumer Vision System' – this is a visor fitted with mini video cameras linked to a recording device, which enables designers to see the product through consumers' eyes (Wasserman, 2005). These examples and the many other techniques have proven to be a useful support mechanism for teaching undergraduate and postgraduate designers about techniques through which they can better understand user behaviour – a key skill for industrial designers.

Many case studies are also included in the resource, two illustrative examples being the 'FlowerPod', a 'semi-transparent screen with an electronic flower display that grows, blooms or wilts according to how smartly the inhabitants of a house or apartment are using heating, cooling, water and electricity' (Streeter, 2008), and the AWARE 'Puzzle Switch'[7], an on/off button designed to encourage occupants to switch off their lights by playing with their built-in desire for order (Interactive Institute, 2006). The case studies help to illustrate how others have utilized design for behavioural change, helping to demystify the process for designers and building their confidence that they too can engage with this field of study (Lofthouse, 2001).

Providing this type of resource to support studio-based learning builds on a tradition of independent study that is encouraged throughout the BA and BSc Industrial and Product Design courses at Loughborough University. Through the functionality afforded by a website, this approach allows students to identify and explore links that are particularly relevant to their studies and makes the case studies accessible outside taught classes.

The free availability of the resource over the web also allows the material to be accessed by anyone with an interest in this area. This facility has helped to inspire the development of a new Google group – 'Design and Behaviour' – which provides a forum for bringing together academics interested in the subject to discuss issues further.

The resource addresses the needs of the user who seeks understanding having developed their own questions as well as the user who is looking for quick solutions rather than meaning, meeting both surface and deeper learning requirements.

Feedback on the resource at every stage has indicated a real need for this type of mechanism, with comments on the latter stages also indicating that the approach being taken is not only relevant and interesting but also highly appropriate to the intended audience (Lilley and Lofthouse, 2009). The 'design–behaviour' resource continues to evolve and is updated on a regular basis with new case studies, techniques and resources.

Sustainable Design Network

Vicky Lofthouse, Department of Design and Technology, Loughborough University

The Sustainable Design Network (SDN) is *the* inter-industry, inter-university, multidisciplinary research network based in the UK that brings together like-minded people interested in discussing and debating issues around the broad area of sustainable design with the intention of creating change (SDN, 2009).[8] The SDN offers free membership and welcomes members from a wide range of disciplines such as engineering design, industrial design, manufacturing management, environmental management and built environment. This helps to encourage cross-disciplinary discussion and provides the opportunity for ideas (including pedagogic ideas) to be cross-fertilized.

At the time of writing, the SDN has a membership of around 200 people from academia, industry, the public sector and NGOs. Through its mailing list, it informs members about upcoming events, conferences and funding opportunities in the wide field of sustainable design. A social networking facility[9] allows members to set up virtual conversations with one another to discuss topics that arise out of meetings or that are of general interest to members. It organizes up to four one-day seminars per year at different locations around the UK, covering a wide range of subjects related to sustainable design, including sustainability and design, sustainable design education, visioning, product and packaging, design and behaviour, and construction and engineering. Whether specifically pedagogic in nature, much of the material that is shared at these events can be and is often fed into members' teaching material.

Members can drive the focus of these events and often offer facilities for hosting them. All members benefit from the opportunity to run or attend sustainability-focused workshops and to test out approaches and ideas in a supportive environment. The events attract a diverse delegation of academics, industrialists, NGOs and those from the public sector and provide the opportunity for lively and interesting debate. Generally consisting of a number of 20-minute presentations and workshop events, they tend to have an informal air so as to encourage discussion and networking so members can establish areas of common interest – a key aim of the SDN. The PowerPoint presentations from invited speakers are published and freely available online[10] after the event.

The network develops and sustains working partnerships that explore sustainable design to provide a mechanism for exchanging knowledge and experience between academia, industry and the public sectors.

By bringing together like-minded academics and industrialists, the links between the two are strengthened and it helps to form lasting relationships that benefit both the university and the company. Meeting and working with businesses in this way has been seen to inform the curriculum (e.g. with respect to understanding how sustainable design issues are viewed in industry) and has led to certain firms setting student projects (for example, the UK pharmaceuticals company Boots has set projects for second-year undergraduates at Loughborough for the last six years, at the time of writing).

In addition to this, industry and the public sector can benefit from gaining increased knowledge on sustainable design issues and shared experiences and meet others who may be having similar experiences in trying to implement sustainability within a company structure or can offer advice and support. Working with student designers helps members to gather insights into the level of sustainable design currently being taught at university and enables companies to draw on novel ecodesign tools. In addition to this, the companies benefit from seeing the wide range of creative solutions that students generate in response to external briefs. Finally, companies in the SDN also benefit from early access to the fruits of academic research, often in the form of practical tools and techniques for sustainable design, which yet again strengthens the links between the different parties.

Sociocentric sustainability

Tania Humphries-Smith, Bournemouth University

A number of studies indicate that the embedding of sustainability in the design and engineering curriculum is far from complete (Ramirez, 2006 and 2007; Humphries-Smith, 2007), particularly when working with an holistic interpretation of sustainability that spans technical, social and economic pillars or dimensions as defined by the Royal Academy of Engineering (RAEng, 2005).

Taking these three pillars of sustainability, it is generally considered that the eco- and technocentric dimensions are considered, at least in part, in many design and engineering curricula in the UK and around the globe. However, the sociocentric dimension is rarely considered, yet research (Brezet and Van Hemel, 1997; Chapman, 2005; McDonough and Braungart, 2002) indicates that it is only by taking an holistic approach to sustainable design – which entails considering the sustainable aspects at the very outset of devising a solution to a design or engineering problem – that we will be able to produce products that are truly sustainable. Manzini and Jegou (2003) conclude that there needs to be a focus on strategies for living rather than applying more technology to the traditional functions of living. They take the approach of investigating the user's social behaviour and then considering the role of the technical system, leading to solutions that are less product-focused and more system-focused (Manzini and Jegou, 2003).

The EngSC funded a mini-project (EngSC, 2008c) at the Sustainable Design Research Centre at Bournemouth University focusing on the sociocentric dimension. The aim of the project is to produce an online resource for undergraduate engineering and design students specifically addressing the sociocentric aspects of sustainable design. There are a number of existing online resources, but these mainly focus on the eco- and technocentric dimensions. It is the intention that the resource produced as an outcome of this project will complement those resources already available, in particular the InformationInspiration[11] and 'Design-Behaviour'[6] web resources as developed at Loughborough University.

Of course, the immediate challenge is that the engineering and design curricula are already packed full with material; undergraduates frequently have more contact hours than in many other disciplines. So how can anything else be fitted in? Ongoing research at Bournemouth is suggesting that, from the outset, what is most critical in encouraging student engagement with sustainability is exposure to the breadth of issues it involves and then giving students space to discuss these. At Bournemouth, the use of virtual discussion forums based around exploring online resources has proved very useful in engaging students with sustainable issues from the beginning of a project (Humphries-Smith, 2008).

Using the Bournemouth University virtual learning environment, a structured and tutor-managed discussion forum based around InformationInspiration has been used with second-year product design students. The purpose is to engage learners in debate about a wider range of sustainable design issues than they have previously been exposed to. This has provided an opportunity for students to form their own initial thoughts by discussing and defending their ideas with their peers about the material presented online. The process has been shown to provide a deeper learning experience than more traditional methods, as reported in Humphries-Smith (2008).

Engineers Without Borders UK

Andrew Lamb

Engineers Without Borders UK (EWB-UK, 2009a) is an organization that was established by student engineers as a way for them to make a contribution to sustainable human development. It has six programme areas, ranging from Placements, Training and Research, to Bursaries, Outreach and Education (EWB-UK, 2009b). It focuses its concerns on places where, used properly, technology can make a profound difference. Projects include work in Ecuador, Nepal, Tanzania, Nigeria, the Philippines and other countries where people live in severe poverty.

In doing so, EWB-UK has inspired and re-energized young people about engineering, showing them that engineering doesn't just have to be about making big bridges bigger, fast computers faster and cheap production cheaper. It highlights the true role of engineering as helping people use technology to improve their lives. As an organization, it is playing an increasingly important role in the international development sector, in the engineering industry and in engineering education.

Its vision is of a world where access to technology and infrastructure is not a barrier to human development. It takes a complete view of engineering practice and promotes transferable and interdisciplinary skills. Indeed, in an attempt to make engineering more relevant to people, EWB-UK organizes its work around the areas of water, habitat, transport, information and communication technology, industry and energy rather than the traditional divisions of civil, mechanical and electrical. Its international agenda reflects the global nature of the problems that the next generation of engineers are inheriting and it is working to train and educate them to help solve those problems. The organization looks to the long term, emphasizing that sustainability can only be achieved if young people get involved.

Examples of the work of some student members of EWB-UK include the introduction of sustainable stoves in Nepal (EWB-UK, 2009c), sustainable income generation for the Pamirs in Tajikistan and the fight against HIV transmission (International Development Design Summit, 2009; JustMilk, 2009).

Organizations exist under the name of EWB in many countries (EWB International, 2009) and attest to a growing movement of young people who have realized that the issues of the future mean they need to challenge business as usual, whether in their education, in their jobs or in their lives in general. They know they need to prepare to solve global problems of poverty, climate change and sustainability, and to work across disciplinary and international borders. Their grassroots activities are finding high-level support, but there remains a great deal of work to be done.

Linking research into teaching

Embedding sustainable development into the curriculum

Mike Clifford, University of Nottingham

In the School of Mechanical, Materials and Manufacturing Engineering at the University of Nottingham, second-year design coursework, third-year individual projects and fourth-year group projects have been based around problems faced by communities in the developing world.

The inspiration for the projects came from EWB, Tearfund,[12] a UK-based relief and development charity (Tearfund, 2009) and from individual requests received as a result of a 'problems wanted' advertisement placed in *Footsteps*, a magazine produced by Tearfund. As a result, suggestions for engineering projects have come from Cambodia, India, Uganda, Mongolia, Bolivia, Kenya, Afghanistan and Nepal. Student projects based on these suggestions have solved practical problems and have provided sources of income generation for deprived communities.

Students who have worked on these projects learnt, for example, how to design with a new set of rules and priorities, and have also been inspired to investigate the relationship between technology and development. Perhaps the most obvious impact that the teaching has had is that ten students have subsequently taken up summer placements overseas with EWB to experience the challenges of working with developing communities at first hand.

As a result of these activities, the profile of the university and the UK has been enhanced and media interest has raised the awareness of the role engineering can play in changing communities for the better.

Research project work actually crosses the boundary between research and teaching (Parker, 1997). Although appropriate technology projects are assessed to a large extent on the quality of research carried out by students, there must also be evidence of a wider appreciation of the subject, both relating directly to the topic of the candidate's thesis and to engineering in a broader sense. Elton notes that the way forward is to make sure that scholarship supports both research and teaching (Elton, 1987). In science-based subjects, including engineering, there is a tendency to rely on a technical, rational approach, concentrating on knowledge, skills and strategies, which may be less effective in preparing students for careers in industry than a more reflective approach where professional judgement is more important than absolute truths (Cann, 1997). A complete understanding of a very specific academic problem is less likely to be of interest to an employer than the methodologies developed in the course of solving appropriate technology problems such as implementing small-scale recycling in developing countries, improving water transport, designing energy-efficient wood stoves and off-grid power generation for remote communities.

By undertaking projects based around difficulties encountered in the developing world, students are encouraged to reflect on the technological challenges involved as well as the availability of materials, workshop resources and so forth. This holistic approach encourages reflective learning (Brockbank and McGill, 1998) in a cyclic methodology of conceptualization, design, realization, evaluation and redesign. Feedback from students engaged in these projects has been very positive, particularly where the projects have been successful. Designing with appropriate technology in mind has challenged student preconceptions about the suitability of materials and manufacturing methods for a task. For instance, designing a bread oven for manufacture in Uganda introduced a series of limitations on manufacturing processes and changed the economics, such that it was necessary to use bolted joints rather than welded sections. Students working with remote communities have had to work cooperatively rather than impose solutions, taking into account local customs, working practices and lifestyles.

Centre for Sustainable Development

Heather Cruickshank, Cambridge University

Cambridge University Engineering Department has had a serious commitment towards including SD in its undergraduate curriculum since 1999, when Peter Guthrie was appointed an RAEng VP. This gave the opportunity to take a critical look at the current teaching provision and at ways of incorporating principal concepts of sustainable development.

Initially, contact with the students was through an elective module offered as part of the fourth (MEng) year. The initial class received a good response from the students but it soon became apparent that there was a wider need to address the mismatch between students' growing interests and expectations and the wider contextual issues that were part of the engineering degree. There was mounting evidence of students coming through the school system with increasing levels of understanding across a range of associated environmental and social topics and expecting, and then demanding, that those issues be addressed in their HE courses and on into their professional careers.

Cambridge took the opportunity to better cater for the requirements of these students when Charles Ainger took over as both VP and Director of the Centre for Sustainable Development. The Centre was originally established in 2000 to facilitate undergraduate teaching and lobby the Department on behalf of the students on SD issues. Ainger was able to expand the Centre's remit into research work with an industry focus (by partnering with practitioners such as property developer Land Securities,[13] which has interests in the Thames Gateway development,[14] and in delivering sustainable communities), into PhD work and also through the development of a new postgraduate course, the MPhil in Engineering for Sustainable Development (Fenner et al, 2005).

Through these new ventures, routes were opened for students to more fully explore their SD interests. The philosophy of the teaching has been to explore wider SD issues and equip students with an ability to enquire more deeply, to interpret information from a range of sources in the context of a specific situation and to look at a widened framework with greater geographical and temporal scales. Essentially, the aim is to enable engineers to ask better questions (Fenner et al, 2006).

In terms of research interests, whether through student projects and dissertations or conducted by contract research staff, the emphasis has been on the application of research findings and has remained user-focused as far as possible. This work has been continuously fed back into the teaching at all levels. A range of research has been carried out, but what perhaps makes it rather different from more traditional engineering investigations has been its transdisciplinary nature – it reaches beyond technical engineering into other professional fields, notably the social sciences. The Centre continues with its efforts to more fully embed the concepts of SD in teaching and practice (Cruickshank et al, 2006).

Ecoversity: A case study

Dave Hughes, University of Bradford

In 2005, the University of Bradford launched Ecoversity, an initiative to embed SD in and across the institution. A key part of Ecoversity is to promote embedding ESD into the curriculum.

The School of Engineering, Design and Technology, comprising civil, electrical and mechanical engineering, reviewed its curriculum throughout 2007 to examine the extent of current ESD-related teaching as a basis for developing an ESD action plan. The UNESCO framework for ESD (UNESCO, 2003) was used as a starting point for the review, providing a broad-based resource to interpret ESD at a subject level. The specific interpretation and subsequent analysis, however, was determined by the academic groupings in the School rather than trying to impose or force a particular definition, approach or outcome.

A total of 211 module descriptors and 43 undergraduate and postgraduate programme specifications[15] were identified for review. Meetings were held with the majority of School staff (36 out of 51) and written communications exchanged with the remainder. Across the entire School, only 32 modules were found to have explicit reference to SD, bearing in mind that just 1 programme (mathematics and computing) is not modular in its structure. A further 29 modules were found to have implicit reference to SD, meaning coverage or assessment of social, environmental, ethical or economic issues consistent with SD but not using that term.

The results of the review and analysis were internally reported in April 2008. These findings were then taken back to the subject and programme leaders for discussion and further comment, with the aim of increasing staff understanding and their buy-in to the process of embedding sustainability into their curricula – and also to check on responses to the findings. The ESD report was then taken to the School board for discussion. From the review, the School has produced an action plan with the vision to embed SD into curriculum activities over the next three years. In this vision, the School seeks to prepare students who are able to contribute to achieving a better balance between social, economic and environmental progress by embedding the principles of SD into professional activities and decision making. From this, the vision is to prepare graduates who will be able to play their full role in the creation and maintenance of sustainable communities in harmony with their natural environment.

One principle arising from the School's action plan is to consider its approach to sustainability as being embedded in professional activity rather than a consideration to be bolted on at the end of the process. In particular it seeks to make its students:

- agents for change, promoting strong leadership for establishing the culture of SD within organizations;
- aware of the underpinning principles and current issues affecting SD pertaining to their field of study;
- able to recognize cultural differences influencing the application of the principles of SD throughout the world;
- able to be innovative and creative in seeking a solution to the problem that balances principles and issues.

Students as employable graduates

Student perceptions of sustainability at the University of Northumbria

Roger Penlington

In the UK, a significant proportion of undergraduate engineering education is conducted to meet the competencies required for professional registration.

Graduates are required to 'undertake engineering activities in a way that contributes to sustainable development' (EC, 2008).

The EngSC funded a mini-project to investigate student perceptions of sustainability (EngSC, 2007). The study set out to obtain data on student perceptions by both questionnaire and focus group. The questionnaire sought first to obtain a measure of the students' concern for the environment and their views of their university's demonstration of a commitment to operate in a sustainable way. Second, it set out to establish the students' perceived level of knowledge of SD topics; this was by both questionnaire and focus groups.

Participants said they were very concerned about sustainability and the majority also thought that huge problems are being created for future generations as a result of resource use. In expressing this, it was very clear that universities were not seen as providing leadership or clear demonstrations of sustainable behaviour.

The focus group discussions regularly contrasted specific issues with the wider social context, whereas the questionnaire outcomes clearly demonstrated a student preference for technology rather than social or management aspects. A strong preference for learning more about design for energy efficiency, one of the topics with which students were already familiar, was contrasted with less desire to learn about environmental regulation, of which they knew little.

In considering whether sustainability should be taught as a discrete module or incorporated across a course, feelings were mixed, but more examples of inspiration were derived from integrated teaching. Student responses included one suggestion that it should be:

'Integrated most certainly, it will make more sense to people that way', another one saying: 'It would never occur to me to have it any other way than integrated across the whole course.' (EngSC, 2007).

The responsibility for sustainable practice was therefore seen to go beyond course content and into professional practice.

Sustainability was characterized as being a broad and ill-defined subject when considered alongside many aspects of the engineering curriculum:

'It's more than that, it's a very broad area. It's difficult to pinpoint what it is exactly' (EngSC, 2007).

Sustainability has been given some boundaries, for example, by the 12 guiding principles defined by the RAEng (2005), but it still means different things to different people. In this it is an ideal and challenging subject in providing an engaging context for demonstration of a wide range of engineering practice and technical competencies. Additional value may be obtained in a context that grounds and melds technological and social aspects by employing interdisciplinary teaching: 'It's a moral issue and a cultural one.' (EngSC, 2007).

Does the task of exploring a definition and boundaries for SD become a suitable learning exercise for students? When it becomes an enquiry-based activity, the student may be faced with potentially complex views of self and profession that lead to uncertainty, conflict and educational challenge. Many students identified generational issues and the need for staff development as barriers to satisfying the recognized student interest in sustainability.

The key conclusion to be drawn from this project is that there is a demand for a deeper understanding of sustainability (sociological, environmental and techno-logical) in the undergraduate body:

'Yes, I do care as I want my children (when I have children) to have a good life'. (EngSC, 2007)

This offers many educational opportunities while having a bias towards the technological and design aspects rather than the regulation and management of SD.

Deepening understanding – the next step

Paul Murray, University of Plymouth

The RAEng and Forum for the Future (RAEng, 2005; Forum for the Future, 2005) recognize the role of engineering in taking SD forward. The discipline has an impressive record in ESD innovation at a number of universities. However, despite being a key curriculum requirement for accredited degrees (EC, 2008; Joint Board of Moderators, 2009), there is little published evidence, as yet, of the extent to which sustainability has been embedded at the heart of the engineering curriculum.

When Forum for the Future first defined 'sustainability literacy' (2005), the main focus was on developing sustainability knowledge and skills, where a sustainability literate person:

1   understands the need for change to a sustainable way of doing things, individually and collectively;
2   has sufficient knowledge and skills to decide to act in a way that favours SD;
3   is able to recognize and reward other people's decisions and actions that favour SD.

This framework is helpful in equipping engineers with the basics to develop sustainable solutions and sustainable working practices, although little progress will be made in the real world unless they also possess the deep personal motivation to act positively, not only in their professional work but in their life generally.

Mobilizing this level of personal motivation means individuals must pay attention to how their values and beliefs align with the ideal of sustainability. Anecdotal evidence at the University of Plymouth, whose School of Engineering has run sustainability-themed construction degrees since 1996, is that engaging staff and students personally and professionally with sustainability brings an increased sense of meaning and passion to their courses. A key aspect of the educational programme at Plymouth is one-day, values-led sustainability training workshops for both staff and students. The workshops comprise a suite of face-to-face enquiry based learning activities designed to provoke thought, to deepen understanding of sustainability as a real-world issue and to enable participants to elicit their core values and beliefs and reflect on these in the context of sustainability.

At the time of writing, the sessions have been held for over 400 individuals, including practising professionals and staff at the Higher Education Funding Council for England (HEFCE). The workshops, being highly learner focused and open-ended, have proved very successful, achieving a 95 per cent approval rating from all categories of participant. Most importantly, the activities involved are readily transferable across discipline and institutional boundaries, constituting a potentially useful way forward for academic teams to consider adopting in their endeavours to embed ESD meaningfully in their curricula.

Conclusion

The aim of this chapter has been to explore alternative approaches that have been adopted by staff in engineering faculties at UK universities as they seek to embed SD into their taught curricula. The chapter has looked at learning approaches that engage engineering students with sustainability, reaching out from engineering to design, to the environment and to international linkages between research and teaching. This has been illustrated by the use of contributed case studies and discussions of practice.

Readers of this chapter who teach students in engineering on HE programmes are invited to reflect on their own teaching practices in ESD, and to consider how they might choose to adopt, adapt and blend from the examples given here. The aspiration is that this will lead to the development of an approach that is most appropriate to their own institutional environment and culture, with the ultimate purpose of enhancing the transformation of their engineering students into employable graduates who are articulate in the understanding of the issues and the resolution of cross-disciplinary problems towards a world with a sustainable future.

References

Akrich, M. (1992) 'The de-scription of technical objects', In Bijker, W.E. and Law, J. (eds), *Shaping Technology/Building Society: Studies in Sociotechnical Change*, Massachusetts Institute of Technology, Cambridge MA pp205–224

Boardman, B., Favis-Mortlock, D., Hinnells, M., Lane, K., Milne, G., Palmer, J., Small, E., Strang, V. and Wade, J. (1995) *DECADE – Domestic Equipment and Carbon Dioxide Emissions, Second Year Report*, Energy and Environment Programme, Environmental Change Unit, University of Oxford, www.eci.ox.ac.uk/research/energy/downloads/decade2.pdf, accessed 2 February 2010

Brezet, H. and Van Hemel, C. (1997) *Ecodesign: A Promising Approach to Sustainable Production and Consumption*, UNEP, Paris

Brockbank, A. and McGill, A. (1998) *Facilitating Reflective Learning in Higher Education*, Open University Press, Buckingham

Cann, A.J. (1997) 'Working with the web: A case study at the University of Leicester', *Life Sciences Educational Computing*, vol 8 no 2, pp20–22

Chapman, J. (2005) *Emotionally Durable Design – Objects, Experience and Empathy*, Earthscan, London

Crawley, E., Malmqvist, J., Ostlund, S. and Brodeur, D. (2007) *Rethinking Engineering Education: The CDIO Approach*, Springer-Verlag, New York NY

Cruickshank, H. J., Bertényi, T., Cardwell, D. and Jackson, S. (2006) 'Sustainable development for engineers: Developing resources to deliver transferable skills', in Doyle, S. and Mannis, A. (eds), *Proceedings of the International Conference on Innovation, Good Practice and Research in Engineering Education*, HEA, Liverpool, July

Dalkey, N.C. (1969) *The Delphi Method: An Experimental Study of Group Opinion*, available at www.rand.org/pubs/research_memoranda/2005/RM5888.pdf, accessed 4 February 2008

Delbecq, A.L., Van de Ven, A.H. and Gustafson, D.H. (1975) *Group Techniques for Program Planning: A Guide to Nominal Group and Delphi Processes*, Scott, Foresman and Company, Glenview, available at www.design-behaviour.co.uk/

EC (2008) *The Accreditation of Higher Education Degrees – UK Standard for Professional Engineering Competence*, EC, London

EC (2009) *Guidance on Sustainability for the Engineering Profession*, available at www.engc.org.uk/sustainability, accessed 14 July 2009

Elton, L. (1987) *Teaching in Higher Education: Appraisal and Training*, Kogan Page, London

Engel, C.E., Dangerfield, P., Dornan, T., Maudsley, G., Naqvi, J., Powis, D. and Sefton, A. (2007) *A Whole System Approach to Problem-Based Learning in Dental, Medical and Veterinary Sciences – A Guide to Important Variables*, available at www.campus.manchester.ac.uk/ceebl/resources/guides/pblsystemapproach_v1.pdf, accessed 19 January 2009

EngSC (2004) *Tool box for Sustainable Design Education*, available at www.lboro.ac.uk/research/susdesign/LTSN/Index.htm, accessed 1 April 2009

EngSC (2007) *The Wider Teaching of Sustainability Based Upon Student Perceptions and the Expectations of Professional Bodies*, EngSC, Loughborough University, available at www.engsc.ac.uk/downloads/scholarart/penlington-sustainability-report.pdf, accessed 1 April 2009

EngSC (2008a) *Education for Sustainable Development in Engineering: Report of a Delphi Consultation*, EngSC, Loughborough University, available at www.engsc.ac.uk/downloads/scholarart/delphi-consultation.pdf, accessed 1 April 2009

EngSC (2008b) *Design for Behavioural Change*, EngSC, Loughborough University, available at www.engsc.ac.uk/downloads/scholarart/design-for-behavioural-change.pdf, accessed 1 April 2009

EngSC (2008c) 'Socio-centric sustainability for engineers and product designers', *Engineering Subject Centre Mini-Projects*, available at www.engsc.ac.uk/an/mini_projects/index.asp#socio, accessed 1 April 2009

EngSC (2009) 'Embedding sustainable development into structural design teaching using sustainability assessment tools', *Engineering Subject Centre Mini-Projects*, available at www.engsc.ac.uk/an/mini_projects/index.asp#susasstools, accessed 1 April 2009

Enhancing Teaching–Learning Environments in Undergraduate Courses (2008) *Shortened Experiences of Teaching and Learning Questionnaire*, available at www.etl.tla.ed.ac.uk/docs/SETLQ.pdf, accessed 8 August 2008

Evans, S., Burns, A. and Barrett, R. (2002) *Empathic Design Tutor*, International Ecotechnology Research Centre, Cranfield University

EWB-UK (2009a) *Engineers Without Borders UK*, available at www.ewb-uk.org, accessed 14 July 2009

EWB-UK (2009b) *Engineers Without Borders UK – Bursaries*, available at www.ewb-uk.org/programmes/bursaries, accessed 14 July 2009

EWB-UK (2009c) *Engineers Without Borders UK – Completed Research Projects*, www.ewb-uk.org/node/3528, accessed 14 July 2009

EWB International (2009) *Engineers Without Borders International – Membership*, www.ewb-international.org/members.htm, accessed 2 February 2010

Fenner, R.A., Ainger, C.M., Cruickshank, H.J. and Guthrie, P.M. (2005) 'Embedding sustainable development into Cambridge University Engineering Department', *IJSHE*, vol 6, no 3, pp229–241

Fenner, R.A., Ainger, C.M., Cruickshank, H.J. and Guthrie, P.M. (2006) 'Widening engineering horizons: Addressing the complexity of sustainable development', *Proceedings of the Institution of Civil Engineers, Engineering Sustainability Journal*, vol 159, pp145–154

Fogg, B.J. (2003) *Persuasive Technology: Using Computers to Change What We Think and Do*, Morgan Kaufmann, San Francisco CA

Forum for the Future (2000) *The Engineer of the 21st Century Inquiry – Engineers for Sustainability*, available at www.forumforthefuture.org/greenfutures/articles/60294, accessed 9 July 2009

Forum for the Future (2005) *Learning and Skills for Sustainable Development: Developing a Sustainability Literate Society*, available at www.forumforthefuture.org/files/learningandskills.pdf, accessed 2 February 2010

Gough, S. and Scott, W. (2007) *Higher Education and Sustainable Development – Paradox and Possibility*, Routledge, London

Higher Education – Environmental Performance Improvement (2009) *The Green Gown Awards 2007–8*, available at www.heepi.org.uk, accessed 1 February 2010

Humphries-Smith, T. (2007) 'To embed or not to embed (sustainability in the curriculum) that is the question – and do we have a choice?', in Bohemia, E. Hilton, K. McMahon, C. and Clarke, A. (eds), *Shaping the Future? 9th International Conference on Engineering and Product Design Education*, Northumbria University, Newcastle, September, pp27–32

Humphries-Smith, T. (2008) 'An evaluation of existing on-line learning & teaching resources for the socio-centric aspects of sustainable design', in Clarke, A., Evatt, M., Hogarth, P., Lloveras, J. and Pons, L. (eds), *New Perspectives in Design Education – Proceedings of the 10th International Conference on Engineering and Product Design Education*, Universitat Politecnica de Catalunya, Barcelona, Spain, September, pp 485–490

ICE (2009) *Environment and Sustainability*, available at www.ice.org.uk/knowledge/specialist_environment.asp, accessed 14 July 2009

International Development Design Summit (2009) *International Development Design Summit – Staff*, http://idsummit.org/staff, accessed 2 February 2010

Interactive Institute (2006) AWARE Puzzle Switch, www.tii.se/awaredesignconcept.html, accessed 20 August 2009

Jelsma, J. and Knot, M. (2002) 'Designing environmentally efficient services: A "script" approach', *The Journal of Sustainable Product Design*, vol 2, nos 3–4, pp119–130

Joint Board of Moderators (2009) *Annex C – Sustainability in Degree Programmes*, available at www.jbm.org.uk/uploads/JBM123AnnexCSustainability.doc, accessed 1 February 2010

JustMilk (2009) *JustMilk team*, available at http://justmilk.org/team.html, accessed 2 February 2010

Lilley, D (2007) *Towards Sustainable Use: An Exploration of Design for Behavioural Change*, Loughborough University

Lilley, D. and Lofthouse, V. (2009) 'Sustainable design education – Considering design for behavioural change', *Engineering Education: Journal of the Higher Education Academy Engineering Subject Centre*, vol 4, no 1, pp29–41

Lofthouse, V.A. (2001) *Facilitating Ecodesign in an Industrial Design Context: An Exploratory Study In Enterprise Integration*, PhD thesis, Cranfield University

Loughborough University (2009) *Learn* Virtual Learning Environment, available at www.learn.lboro.ac.uk, accessed 14 July 2009

Manzini, E. and Jegou, F. (2003) *Sustainable Everyday: Scenarios of Urban Life*, Edizione Ambiente, Milan

McCalley, L.T. (2006) 'From motivation and cognition theories to everyday applications and back again: The case of product-integrated information and feedback', *Energy Policy*, vol 34, no 2, pp129–137

McDonough, W. and Braungart, M. (2002) *Cradle to Cradle – Remaking the Way We Make Things*, North Point Press, New York NY

Parker, S. (1997) *Reflective Teaching in the Postmodern World: A Manifesto for Education in Postmodernity*, Open University Press, Buckingham

Queen's University Belfast (2009) *Welcome to Sustainable Development at Queen's*, available at www.qub.ac.uk/research-centres/WelcometoSustainableDevelopmentatQueens, accessed 1 April 2009

RAEng (2005) *Engineering for Sustainable Development: Guiding Principles*, RAEng, London, available at www.raeng.org.uk/events/pdf/Engineering_for_Sustainable_Development.pdf, accessed 1 February 2010

RAEng (2007) *Student Design Poster Competition*, available at www.raeng.org.uk/education/vps/postercomp/2007.htm, accessed 14 July 2009

Ramirez, M. (2006) 'Sustainability in the education of industrial designers: The case for Australia', *IJSHE*, vol 7, no 2, pp189–202

Ramirez, M. (2007) 'Sustainability integration in industrial design education: A worldwide survey', *ConnectED 2007: International Conference on Design Education*, University of New South Wales, Sydney, July

Rittel, H. and Webber, M. (1973) 'Dilemmas in a general theory of planning', *Policy Sciences*, vol 4, pp155–169

SDN (2009) 'Sustainable development network', www.sustainabledesignnet.org.uk, accessed 1 April 2009

Streeter, A. (2008) 'FlowerPod Makes Energy Efficiency A Growing Concern', *Treehugger*, available at www.treehugger.com/files/2008/02/flowerpod_makes.php, accessed 20 August 2009

UNESCO (2003) *Framework for a Draft Implementation Scheme*, UNESCO, New York NY

UN (2008) 'Goal 7: Ensure environmental sustainability', *Millennium Development Goals*, available at www.un.org/millenniumgoals/environ.shtml, accessed 21 September 2009

University of Manchester, Faculty of Engineering and Physical Sciences (2008) *Educating Engineers for Sustainable Development – Report of a Royal Academy of Engineering Sponsored Pilot Study*, www.eps.manchester.ac.uk/tlc/sd/raeng/RAEng%20Report.pdf, accessed 1 April 2009

University of Manchester, Faculty of Engineering and Physical Sciences (2009) *Interdisciplinary sustainable development (MSEC 30052/31151)*, www.eps.manchester.ac.uk/tlc/sd, accessed 1 April 2009

Wasserman, T. (2005) 'Kimberly-Clark Tries Seeing Things From Consumer's POV', *Brandweek*, 5 September, available at www.brandweek.com/bw/esearch/article_display.jsp?vnu_content_id=1001054402, accessed 22 September 2009

WCED (1987) *Our Common Future: The Report of the World Commission on Environment and Development* ['The Brundtland Report'], Oxford University Press, Oxford, available at www.un-documents.net/wced-ocf.htm, accessed 29 January 2010

Wever, R., van Kuijk, J. and Boks, C. (2008) 'User-centred design for sustainable behaviour', *International Journal of Sustainable Engineering*, vol 1 no 1, pp9–20

Notes

1   The 12 Principles of Engineering for Sustainable Development are:
    1   Look beyond your own locality and the immediate future.
    2   Innovate and be creative.
    3   Seek a balanced solution.
    4   Seek engagement from all stakeholders.
    5   Make sure you know their needs and wants.
    6   Plan and manage effectively.
    7   Give sustainability the benefit of any doubt.
    8   If polluters must pollute … then they must pay as well.
    9   Adopt an holistic, 'cradle-to-grave' approach.
    10 Do things right, having decided on the right thing to do.
    11 Beware cost reductions that masquerade as value engineering.
    12 Practice what you preach (RAEng, 2005, p25).

2   For more details of the firm, visit www.arup.com (accessed 1 February 2010).

3   More details of these appraisal tools are available at the following websites, respectively: www.breeam.org, www.ceequal.com, www.gifford.uk.com/services/sustainability/project/project/gifford-sustainability-appraisal-process, www.petus.eu.com/left.php?sct=6&sbsct=2&pageid=41&pagesect=0&pagelang=en, www.constructingexcellence.org.uk/pdf/fact_sheet/sus_accounting.pdf (all accessed 2 February 2010).

4   For more about the Commission, please visit www.sd-commission.org.uk.

5   More on these bodies can be found at the following websites respectively: www.theiet.org/, www.imeche.org, www.energyinst.org.uk (all accessed 2 February 2010).

6   The resource is available at www-staff.lboro.ac.uk/~cddl/ (accessed 2 February 2010).

7   Details of the product can be found at www.tii.se/aware/designConcept.html (accessed 20 August 2009).

8   See the Network's website, www.sustainabledesignet.org.uk (accessed 1 April 2009).

9   This resource, the SDN ning, is online at http://sustainabledesignnet.ning.com/ (accessed 2 February 2010).

10 Seminar presentations are available at www.lboro.ac.uk/research/susdesign/SDN/seminar-archive/seminar_archive-all.htm (accessed 2 February 2010).

11 The InformationInspiration ecodesign resource can be found at www.informationinspiration.org.uk (accessed 1 April 2009).

12 More details about Tearfund, a Christian relief and development agency, can be found at www.tearfund.org (accessed 14 July 2009).

13 For more on Land Securities, visit www.landsecurities.com/home (accessed 2 February 2010).

14 The London Thames Gateway Development Corporation www.ltgdc.org.uk has a statutory remit to regenerate its area; see www.ltgdc.org.uk (accessed 2 February 2010) for more information.

15 Programme specifications are documents that outline the rationale, learning outcomes, modules and teaching strategies for courses.

Chapter 11

Developing Critical Faculties: Environmental Sustainability in Media, Communications and Cultural Studies in Higher Education

Debbie Flint

Introduction

Media, communications and cultural studies graduates enter a very wide range of professions. Many will develop careers directly related to their HE programmes of study; as graphic designers, film and television producers, journalists, advertisers and games designers. Many will also move into 'areas such as teaching, archiving, social and community work, management, or the civil service' (Media, Communication and Cultural Studies Association [MeCCSA], undated). Those who consider establishing careers in the media industries are warned of the rapidly changing technological context, that 'specific skills taught today may well be redundant in a very few years' (MeCCSA, undated). They are told that they will need 'an understanding of this fast-changing context and a proven capacity to learn and use … initiative.' (MeCCSA, undated). However, the shifting environmental context of students' futures is not always considered alongside or as part of this employment context even though the knowledge, skills and values developed (or not) in media, communications and cultural studies in HE have a key role in the environmental effect of these industries and, consequently, the 'employability' of students. Addressing this problem is urgent: 'we inhabit an ecological crisis that demands rethinking of first principles, research frameworks, methods, activism, and policy work' (Maxwell and Miller, 2008, p331), and also reconsideration of HE teaching and learning.

The term 'sustainable development' is described by the UK Government sustainability strategy as a goal to enable 'all people throughout the world to satisfy their basic needs and enjoy a better quality of life without compromising the quality of life of future generations' (DEFRA, 2005, p6). This strategy articulates five 'guiding principles for sustainable development' including the principle of 'Living Within Environmental Limits – Respecting the limits of the planet's environment, resources and biodiversity – to improve our environment and ensure that the natural resources needed for life are unimpaired and remain so for future generations' (DEFRA, 2005, p16). This and other more recent reports have stressed the fast-changing environmental conditions that will demand of graduates a different set of skills and knowledge; climate change, for example, 'will present new challenges to all sectors of the economy; workforces in all sectors and industries will need new and/or different sets of skills, capabilities and knowledge to deal effectively with them' (DIUS, 2008, p14).

As an example, the following account from George Monbiot's *Heat: How We Can Stop the Planet Burning* (2007) highlights the kind of challenges facing journalism as a profession. In *Heat*, Monbiot – a journalist himself – methodically traces the sources of evidence underpinning a series of articles relating to climate change featured in the British press. He traces a line from the *Daily Mail* to the American oil and gas corporation ExxonMobil via botanist and broadcaster, David Bellamy.[1] The story recounted by Monbiot is as follows. In 2004, the Mail published an article by Bellamy entitled 'Global Warming? What a load of Poppycock' (Bellamy, 2004; Monbiot, 2007, p24). Monbiot traces Bellamy's sources to a website produced by the 'Science and Environmental Policy Project' (funded by ExxonMobil), which in turn sources 'a paper published in *Science* in 1989' (Monbiot, 2007, p25). This paper, Monbiot discovers, turned out to be non-existent. Nevertheless, the data presented on the Science and Environmental Policy project website had informed a number of articles in the British press maintaining that 'climate change was not happening' (Monbiot, 2007, p24).

This example foregrounds the powerful roles of media creation as well as its critique and the importance of a critical approach to practice in debates about, and actions towards achieving, environmental sustainability. What kinds of knowledge, skills and values led these two media professionals to two different conclusions and outcomes? How might HE contribute to equipping students with the knowledge, skills and values to question received wisdom and practice and pursue change towards environmental sustainability in their chosen professions?

This chapter explores the opportunities for, challenges to, and current positioning of curriculum, teaching and learning for environmental sustainability in media, communications and cultural studies in HE. The chapter has been informed by documents that articulate perceptions of HE's role and purposes in this cluster of disciplines, for example, the subject benchmark statement *Communication, media, film and cultural studies* (QAA, 2008).[2] The chapter has also been informed by papers produced by those exploring aspects of environmental sustainability in the media, communications and cultural studies fields. Further, feedback was sought from lecturers subscribing to the MeCCSA

JISCmail list 'developing relationships between environmental sustainability and media / communications / cultural studies curriculum, teaching and learning' (Flint, 2008).[3] Information provided by those that responded is also considered here.

Media, communications and cultural studies

HE in media, communications and cultural studies encompasses a broad and diverse range of subjects taught in a variety of HE contexts including art and design, social science and humanities departments. In this chapter, 'media, communications and cultural studies' is used to indicate courses that involve both media creation and critique. The former category includes programmes that teach creative cultural production practices such as animation, games and graphic design and that are often geared towards a particular area of employment. The latter programmes embrace methodologies from the political and social sciences to study aspects of media production, distribution and consumption. These courses emphasize research into media content and how it 'affects the way people think about themselves and other social groups, [and] cultural changes such as globalisation and consumerism' (MeCCSA, undated). Further, they are concerned with the development of new media technologies and 'the impact they have on everyday life' (MeCCSA, undated).

For ease of communication, as in the MeCCSA leaflet produced to guide student applicants, the two types of programme described above are sometimes characterized as 'practical' or 'analytical' respectively (MeCCSA, undated). In reality, however, most courses shift between these two provisions and, in the words of the UK benchmark statements, 'share the aim of producing graduates who have an informed, critical and creative approach both to understanding media, culture and communications in contemporary society, and to their own forms of media, communicative and expressive practice' (QAA, 2008, p7).

Back in 2005, the UK HEA's[4] investigation into how different subject disciplines are 'contributing to creating sustainability-literate graduates' (Dawe et al, 2005, p4) identified a wide range of connections between HE curricula and the 'sustainability agenda' but pointed to 'major gaps in areas such as sustainable production and consumption' (Dawe et al, 2005, p5). Further, it suggested that many subject areas, including art, design and media, found it difficult to make easy connections between sustainability and the subject curriculum (Dawe et al, 2005, p25). A discussion about sustainability literacy and how it might relate to a media, communications and cultural studies curriculum as well as opportunities for embedding skills, knowledge and values for environmental sustainability follows.

Opportunities – systems, critical and reflective thinking

In their study, Dawe et al defined 'sustainability literacy' as 'learning about how human actions affect the immediate and long-term future of the economy and ecology of our communities' (Dawe et al, 2008, p4). According to Wayman:

Sustainability literacy involves both social and environmental aspects, taking account of the economic, social, and environmental power our actions exert through space and time, the historically, socially and cultur- ally diverse ways in which we construct ourselves in relation to natural systems, and how we might learn to live in greater harmony within these systems (Wayman, 2009, p94).

These two definitions make it clear that, in order to develop sustainability literate media, communication and cultural studies graduates in HE, the aims expressed by the QAA benchmark statements and the learning opportunities available will need to be extended. The statements articulate a defining principle of the subject area as a 'focus on cultural and communicative activities as central forces in shaping everyday social and psychological life' (QAA, 2008, p7). However, as Arran Stibbe and other commentators point out, the realm of study will need to be expanded to consider the ways in which cultural and communicative activities impact on the ecological context. Stibbe (2009, p15) writes:

it is becoming increasingly important to go beyond the interactions of human systems with each other (e.g. media, society and economy), to a broader focus on the complex dialectical relationship between human systems and the larger systems which support life on earth.

The appeal for an expanded media studies is shared by Maxwell and Miller (2008, p331) who advocate an 'eco-ethical' approach to the discipline. By 'eco- ethics', they refer to a 'subset of ethics' concerned with 'how human beings ought to behave in relation to non-human nature' (Curry, 2006, p47). An eco-ethical approach to media and communications studies would turn its attention to the ecological context of 'the technologies the field has expertly studied during its half-century existence' (Maxwell and Miller, 2008, p331).

The 'ability to recognise and analyse the interconnections within and between systems' is known as 'systems thinking' (Strachan, 2009, p84. For Flood, 'systems thinking' is based on the idea that 'valid knowledge and meaningful understanding comes from building up whole pictures of phenomena, not by breaking them into parts' (Flood, 2001, p133).While 'sustainability literacy' may not be a familiar term for HE teachers, 'systems thinking' is fundamental, and provides a very useful way of thinking about media, communications and cultural studies in HE. In these disciplines, learning activities are concerned with developing under-standings of ways in which cultural production practices intersect with their social, economic and political context. This is illustrated in a leaflet aimed at potential students of media, communications and cultural studies; 'analytical' courses are described as exploring 'how media content affects the way people think about themselves and other social groups,' [and] cultural changes such as globalisation and consumerism' (MeCCSA, undated). Further, they explore 'technological developments and the impact they have on everyday life' (MeCCSA, undated). Other more 'practical' courses 'offer opportunities to 'gain a broad understanding of the media in relation to the changing contexts of the modern world whilst simultaneously developing practical skills, using digital technolo-gies to construct media texts' (MeCCSA, undated).

The 'interconnectedness' of the learning experience in this cluster of disciplines is illustrated by a student respondent in research into UK media and communica-tions HE:

I can't do anything now without analysing it … television, reading – I have to bring in the theory. It's the connections, links through to every-thing that make it interesting. I'm not just studying media, it's everything, how it all links (Mallinder and Kent, 2008, p15).

Stibbe and Maxwell and Miller propose a number of 'objects of study' for a cluster of disciplines now concerned with the intersections between cultural practices and their social, economic *and* environmental contexts. Stibbe focuses on aspects of HE communication and media studies curricula; advertising, economic and environmental discourses, that could have important implications for graduating media practitioners. In the case of advertising discourses, he argues, an expanded media studies thinking might lead to valuable understandings about 'connections between the media, the construction of consumerist identities, the larger economic systems that consumerism arises from, and … the social and ecological impact of consuming' (Stibbe, 2009, p16).

Maxwell and Miller's expanded media studies would engage scholars in a number of eco-ethical challenges and, in particular, involve paying attention to the material impact of media technologies: 'the sheer materiality of the technology begs the question about the neglect of its environmental impact in the key writings of our discipline' (Maxwell and Miller, 2008, p333). Examples of issues they believe that the field of media studies could (and should) confront include inequitable distribution of polluting technology and carbon dioxide emissions produced by the communications industry. They argue that media studies could draw on the varying schools of 'ecological ethics' positioned on a spectrum from ecocentric to anthropocentric with many shades of green in between, 'to develop an ethical orientation to the study of media technology' (Maxwell and Miller, 2008, p335).

Alongside systemic thinking skills, commentators have underlined the strong links between the critical and reflective thinking skills development that already form a key part of the media, communications and cultural studies HE curricula, as reflected in the UK *Communications, Media, Film and Cultural Studies* bench-mark statement (QAA, 2008) and those required to deal with 'some of the global challenges that students are likely to face as they lead their lives in the 21st century' (Stibbe, 2009, p14). For Stibbe, this means the ability to 'deeply question the society and culture they live in and influence the direction of change' (Stibbe, 2009, p15). A 'reflective education' enables students to 'develop the ability to constantly question whether the social practices that make them who they are, are aligned with the direction of social change that they would like to see' (Stibbe, 2009, p15).

Turning learning into action

As previously indicated, 'sustainability literacy' concerns critical engagement with 'the economic, social, and environmental power human actions exert through space and time, the historically, socially and culturally diverse ways in which we construct ourselves in relation to natural systems' (Wayman, 2009, p94). The second part of this involves working out 'how we might learn to live in greater harmony within these systems' (Wayman, 2009, p94). The emphasis shifts from 'knowing' to 'doing'; sustainability literacy skills enable people to 'engage with those social structures and contribute to the re-writing of self and society along more sustainable lines' (Luna and Stibbe, 2009, p11).

Myshele Goldberg explains how 'social conscience' compels individuals 'to insist on moral action from the wider institutions of society and seek the transfor-mation of social structures that cause suffering' (Goldberg, 2009, p105). Her model for understanding social conscience comprises three elements: 'conscious-ness', 'structure' and 'agency' (Goldberg, 2009, p106). These enable people to bridge the 'gap between the kind of world they see and the kind they want' (Goldberg, 2009, p105). 'Consciousness' describes a person's knowledge and awareness of this gap; 'structure' relates to an understanding of the social struc-tures that contribute to the gap and 'agency' is described as 'a sense of personal power, as well as personal responsibility' (Goldberg, 2009, pp106–107). 'All three elements – consciousness, structure and agency – must be in place for a strong sense of social conscience' (Goldberg, 2009, p108), that is the compulsion and determination to seek social change.

This model is useful for revealing relationships between the foci of media, communications and cultural studies learning and teaching and sustainability literacy. Again, these parallels can be seen from the *Communication, Media, Film and Cultural Studies* benchmark statement (QAA, 2008). For example, the courses share the proposition that 'communicative, cultural and media industries play key roles in generating symbolic resources through which people individually and collectively imagine the past, define the present and develop projects for the future' (QAA, 2008, p8). This is underpinned by the principle that graduates are expected to maintain 'a critical grasp of their responsibilities as practitioners, and awareness of the dynamics, whether cultural, economic, ethical, legal, political, social or affective, which shape working environments' (QAA, 2008, p9). Returning to Goldberg's model, 'consciousness' can be related, for example, to students' knowledge of the way that the media reports climate change; 'structure' can be related to understanding of the structural (economic, political, etc.) forces that result from this; and 'agency' can align with graduates' 'critical grasp of their responsibilities as practitioners' (QAA, 2008, p9).

Media, communications and cultural studies have, then, a firm basis on which to build sustainability literacies that can enable students to deal with some of the ethical dilemmas they are likely to face in their working lives. In the media industries, opportunities for professional gain and ecological ethics often conflict, particularly 'since the media both inform people about the state of the natural systems they depend on for life, as well as being heavily reliant on the advertising revenue of energy-intensive industries which are undermining those systems' (Stibbe, 2009, p14). As Miller and Maxwell point out, the study of media will require interrogation of 'our own investments' and the deployment of 'our critical skills to reassess the role of the media in shaping the environment' (Maxwell and Miller, 2008, p347).

These commentators have highlighted opportunities to build on pre-existing skills, practices and defining principles of the disciplinary cluster, as well as to expand the disciplinary field to incorporate an eco-ethical dimension.

Curriculum opportunities

An email to MeCCSA's JISCmail list invited contact from lecturers 'developing relationships between environmental sustainability and media/communications/cultural studies curriculum teaching and learning' (Flint, 2008). The list has 1,403 subscribers among those who teach and research in media, communication, film, television and cultural studies. Sixteen subscribers, working in a broad set of disciplines including media studies, graphic design, politics and communication studies, digital media, new media, magazine journalism, film studies, cinema studies, contemporary media theory, creative media and advertising, made contact outlining their interests. Six of these gave detailed answers to four questions about their perceptions of the opportunities, benefits and obstacles to embedding issues and concepts of environmental sustainability in the curriculum and teaching and learning practices. While this feedback provides nothing like a full picture, it does give some indication of perceived potential for, and challenges to, the development of environmental sustainability-related activity in the cluster of disciplines, as well as some examples of current practices.

Respondents provided a number of examples of opportunities for embedding 'issues and concepts' relating to 'environmental sustainability' in media, communications and cultural studies HE curricula, teaching and learning. Some of the connections made reflect disciplinary connections articulated by Maxwell and Miller. For example, one lecturer proposes:

> *Questions of sustainability could, in theory, be posed of media industries and technologies and the assumptions and imagery around and within them, as well as the ways their products represent the area of debate, etc.*

Another respondent suggests:

> *Media and cultural studies have a lot to offer—however, feminist analysis has a lot to offer too (such as the domestication of the sustainability problem, etc.) and the combination of the three foci of analysis would be beneficial in revealing the cultural politics of sustainability.*

However, other respondents refer not to disciplinary connections but rather to opportunities for curriculum development facilitated or enabled (or prevented – see 'Challenges', below) by institutional structures and the benefits this might bring. For example, some tutors report a level of autonomy that enabled the shaping of curriculum content at modular level ('I am in the fortunate position of being able to determine to a large extent the content of our programme') and also for making 'changes that need to go to official module or quality boards'. Several tutors find themselves able to make changes themselves and for those which required 'validation', the relevant official structures often proved to be 'receptive and generally much quicker to get things done than I had expected'. These changes appear in some cases to be supported by heads of department; 'encouragingly our head of school is keen we explore sustainability with the students.'

Further, respondents articulate a number of benefits that the fulfilment of these opportunities would bring to the disciplinary field. In two cases, it was felt that environmental sustainability has potential to generate further interest in the media, communications and cultural studies curricula and the disciplinary area as a whole. In one case, this is perceived to be related to a keenly felt interest from students in sustainability issues:

> *Students show more sensitivity to and interest in environmental issues generally, so insofar as it generates interest in the curriculum it's embedded in, it's a good thing.*

Two respondents also suspect that the fields of media and cultural studies would benefit from the direct connections that a focus on environmental sustainability would make to media industries: 'Education benefits because it is playing a connected, integrated role in developing the industry which it is linked to.' This focus also has potential to render media and cultural studies 'more visibly relevant to the real world and in the students' eyes.'

Challenges

While disciplinary and institutional opportunities for embedding aspects of environmental sustainability into disciplinary research, curriculum, teaching and learning evidently exist, there are also a number of challenges. Maxwell and Miller characterize the greatest challenge for media and communications scholars and students as 'the enchantment of technology that grips even the most critical work in the field' (Maxwell and Miller, 2008, p339). The interrogation of 'our own investments in the technological sublime' that is required (Maxwell and Miller, 2008, p347) will undoubtedly demand changes in behaviour that, according to one respondent to my call, 'very few people are prepared to contemplate'.

Lecturers perceive a number of obstacles relating to the take-up of sustainability-related issues and concepts in media, communications and cultural studies, some of which contrast directly with the 'opportunities' outlined above. These range from perceptions of a fundamental incompatibility between a sustainability-related HE curriculum and the industry it feeds to institutional and practical barriers. One respondent suggests that a lack of demand from industry and potential students is inhibiting the growth of new courses; a lecturer in new media and magazine journalism commented that 'programme level changes seem to be much more difficult to implement because of the necessary economic and reputational aspects of doing things that will a) attract an audience and b) deliver high quality.' For another, the 'commercialisation of the education system means that environmental sustainability can only be embedded if financially appropriate.' This observation is set alongside a 'commercialised media' that 'does not see environmental sustainability embedded in its feeder education courses as an essential element of its success'.

A further barrier is related to a perceived lack of expertise. Respondents refer to a 'lack of awareness around what sustainability actually implies', 'little knowledge of these issues' and 'no expertise in the field'. For one, this lack of expertise is exacerbated by a 'university ... hostile to interschool collaboration'. For another, 'the swift growth of media studies in recent decades' has brought teaching staff into the discipline 'who ... often need to rely on immediately available canons and texts as they "learn on the job"'. This body of 'key' works and texts is held to exert considerable power over existing curriculum content with the potential to inhibit change: 'never underestimate the power of the canon, whether it's available texts or syllabus items, for such changes, especially in an area which has grown as media studies has grown in recent decades'.

Respondents also highlight some very practical barriers to embedding sustainability issues and concepts into their curriculum; these include the time to develop new materials and the time to deliver in an already crowded curriculum: 'it is jockeying for attention/time with other pressing issues'.

The current positioning of environmental sustainability in HE media, communication and cultural studies

Speaking in 1992 of education generally, David Orr concludes:

Sustainability is about the terms and conditions of human survival, and yet we still educate at all levels as if no such crisis existed. The content of our curriculum and the process of education, with a few notable excep-tions, is unchanged (Orr, 1992, p83).

This concern, as we have seen, is reflected in writings about media, communica-tions and cultural studies' engagement with eco-ethical issues. However, in spite of the perceived and the real challenges outlined, it is clear that HE opportunities for combining learning about and for environmental sustainability issues in this context do exist, at course, module and even 'lesson' level.

A search of the UK University and College Admissions Service website (UCAS, 2009) using the Course Search provision for 'courses starting in 2009' (all course types, all attendance types and all institutions) with the search terms 'media', 'communication' and 'cultural studies' in conjunction with the term 'environment' gives a good indication of the range of courses available and expecting to recruit in that year.[5] This search returned details of 13 universities where different aspects of media, communications and cultural studies can be studied alongside environmental science, environmental biology, environ-mental studies and the environment (UCAS, 2009). These courses are offered as combined degrees, with the different disciplines offered as joint, major or minor components.

However, of the institutions returned on the UCAS search only three make explicit links between the two course components in information about the combined programmes on the universities' websites. The University of Brighton's BA in Environment and Media Studies was a new programme that started in September 2009. The course information acknowledges the relationships between the science of environmental concerns such as climate change and the role of media in shaping understanding of and responses to these concerns. The course aims to 'encourage students to develop a broad understanding of the important connections between nature, culture and society which both politicians and academics alike argue are at the heart of tackling today's pressing environmental issues' (University of Brighton, 2009).

University Centre Hastings runs a BA in Environmental Biology and Media Production, with the degree awarded by the University of Brighton. The relation-ship between the strands of learning is less clear, but a link is made between learning about 'green issues' and taking action in a professional context: 'you'll be able to apply what you learn in the real world' (University Centre Hastings, 2009).

Finally, the University of the Arts London's BA in Graphic and Media Design – Design for Advertising sets the 'environmental' alongside the political, social and cultural issues that would usually form a key aspect of practice-based media programmes. The Design for Advertising programme examines and questions 'the ethics of advertising on both a global and local level' (University of the Arts London, 2009).

It is more difficult to obtain an accurate picture of current activity at grassroots or modular level. However, lecturers subscribing to the MeCCSA's JISCmail list provided some examples of ways in which they are developing relationships between environmental sustainability and curricula, teaching and learning. These 'developing relationships' span a broad range of established, but more often emerging, practices that include teaching, research and other types of individual or collaborative activities. There is some evidence of institutional support for these developments; one respondent reports that his background in environmental communication was 'seen as a real positive and something that could be put to use in developing new programmes based around environmental sustainability and communication within media and journalism.'

Several lecturers report research activity in this area, particularly in relation to media representation of climate change, environmentalism and environmental activism. One respondent mentions research concerned with the 'cultural construction of crisis in Anglophone literature' – an aspect of which would concern climate change as a cultural construction. A further research project concerned online representations of 'sustainability' itself.

A postdoctoral researcher cites work looking broadly at relationships between 'energy and audio-visual culture' and the 'role that new media forms play in radically reducing energy demand and effecting the kinds of cultural changes many analysts assert will be essential'. Another respondent refers to research exploring the environmental impact of educational practices themselves, in this instance a conference. In these latter cases we see a shift away from a focus on relationships between human systems and behaviours to considerations of the interactions between human systems and their ecological context, burgeoning questions akin to those posed by Maxwell and Miller:

What would happen to game studies if, rather than rehearsing the debates about ludological, narratological, and effects approaches, it confronted the fact that millions of cartridges of Atari's game adaptation of E.T.'The Extraterrestrial were buried in a New Mexico landfill? (Maxwell and Miller, 2008, p334).

Lecturers also report embedding their research (on media and politics and climate change) into aspects of their teaching, incorporating their learning into existing course modules. In a few instances, some of the opportunities highlighted by Maxwell and Miller are beginning to find their way into existing learning modules. They ask: 'What would it mean if film studies [was] required as an ordinary part of its work to evaluate motion picture production ecologically?' (Maxwell and Miller, 2008, p334). For example, of a BA Journalism, Film and Media programme at Cardiff University, a lecturer observes: 'I teach about Hollywood's environmental consequences as part of a third-year module, *Questions for Cinema Now*, and also show a small number of different kinds of films which represent that change.'

At the University of Sunderland, issues of environmental sustainability are 'injected' into a range of modules (International Journalism, Introduction to Media Studies, Social Media) via bought-in expertise: 'I am seen as our "environmental/media expert" and so I do a number of guest slots on other peoples' modules … where I provide an environment/sustainability lecture under the rubric of the overarching module direction.'

In two other cases, respondents refer to specific sustainability-related modules that illustrate ways in which sustainability issues are entering the HE curriculum on courses encompassing media creation and critique. A lecturer in Contemporary Media Theory at the University of Dundee is developing a 'sustainability module for the School of Design'. The School offers undergraduate programmes in creative design practice including Interactive Media Design and Graphic Design. As part of this, the third-year Design History, Theory and Practice programme aims to 'provide a cultural, social and political context to design activity.' The programme 'places a particular emphasis on sustainability', and exploration and understanding of 'what underlies our consumer and media culture, and what this implies for designers.'[6]

A Media Studies lecturer at the University of Brighton provides details of a Mediating the Environment module offered as part of an MA Creative Media programme. The programme aims to 'analyse the ways in which the environment is constructed and contested, by examining the role of science, media and culture in the communication of environmental issues'.[7]

These examples have provided an indication of courses, modules and additions or expansions to existing curricula, that is the ways in which sustainability issues and concepts are making their way into media, communications and cultural studies curricula. These burgeoning activities are building on a developing body of knowledge and 'teaching about' the environmental context of media, communications and cultural studies. The following section addresses the pedagogic strategies employed.

Pedagogies for sustainability

As we have seen, recent reports published in the UK emphasize an important role for HE relating to SD. Their impressions of the nature of this role differ however. According to the DIUS,

teaching about climate change and other sustainable development issues is relevant in academic and vocational disciplines and in professional and social science courses as much as the pure sciences. As the ramifications of climate change become more widespread, we can expect it to become a feature of courses in an increasing range of subjects, and new programmes arising that cross traditional boundaries between disciplines (DIUS, 2008, p14).[8]

The HEFCE, which resists a role in influencing HE curricula, emphasizes a more general function: 'the greatest contribution HE can make to sustainable development is through the values, skills and knowledge that students learn and put into practice' (HEFCE, 2009, p21).[9]

These UK policy statements illustrate two approaches to sustainability-related teaching and learning. The first emphasizes 'teaching about' SD, the second, 'teaching for' it. The distinction is important because 'teaching for' emphasizes praxis, the importance of putting, for example, DEFRA's principle of 'living within environmental limits' (DEFRA, 2005, p16) into practice. Dawe et al highlight the need for an 'action-oriented sustainability literate graduate body' while acknowledging that the skills and attributes that this would demand 'are not easy to teach in a traditional sense' (2005, p.4). The complexity of this task is indicated by a Film Studies lecturer: 'Sustainability is a mindset more than anything and it depends on understanding the situation of the self in the environment.'

However, Dawe et al also outline three prevailing approaches to teaching *for* sustainable development: 'educators as role models and learners', 'experiential learning' and 'holistic thinking' (Dawe et al, 2005, pp4–5). The following section explores the pedagogic approaches being employed in bringing sustainability issues and concepts into the fields of media, communication and cultural studies.

As we have seen, teaching *for* SD has a firm foundation in media, communications and cultural studies. This has been illustrated by the skills of critical, reflective and systems thinking that are fundamental to the disciplines and the bedrock of responsible professional practice. Across these disciplines, 'teaching about' is an important part of 'teaching for'. This is illustrated by Goldberg's model for 'social conscience' where 'consciousness', 'structure' and 'agency' combine to generate action. Goldberg describes 'agency' as 'a sense of personal power, as well as personal responsibility' (Goldberg, 2009, p107). 'Agency' is the part of sustainability literacy that, in the context of media, communications and cultural studies, is, to quote it again, 'not easy to teach in a traditional sense' (Dawe et al, 2005, p4).

The following examples emerge, however. The role of 'educator as role model' is not explicitly stated by respondents but can be discerned in the comments made by one tutor: '[I] think we should all be doing what we can in our workplaces and in reflecting on our practice. Video conferencing for example is not used nearly [often] enough.' Opportunities for experiential learning, that is 'learning by reconnecting to real-life situations', focusing on 'real and practical life issues and actual experiences as learning situations' (Dawe et al, 2005, p5) have traditionally played a key role on media practice programmes where opportunities for students to undertake live projects and work placements are common. For example, students starting the Environment and Media Studies programme at the University of Brighton will be able to undertake a module involving '50 hours of voluntary activities with local community, business and public sector organisations giving practical experience of working towards sustainable development' (University of Brighton, 2009).

This 'making real', however, can also be achieved in the context of the lecture theatre, as in this example provided by a tutor from the University of Dundee: 'I show a series of films. I also do an interactive event pacing out eco-footsteps in the lecture theatre – this is highly revealing with regards to how our behaviour impacts on e.g. CO_2 emissions.'

Dawe at al's 'holistic thinking' pedagogic approach is characterized by the active development and 'honing [of] critical thinking' (Dawe et al, 2005, p5) and a willing blurring of disciplinary boundaries and exploration of the interrelationships between subject fields. The emphasis on pedagogies for critical thinking is underscored by the QAA benchmarks, which state that these programmes are:

> committed to forms of pedagogy that place emphasis on developing critical and creative independence, flexibility, sensitivity to audience, and self-reflexiveness, across individual and group work and critical and production work (QAA, 2008, p8).

Media, communications and cultural studies programmes tend to be multidisciplinary and 'in many cases interdisciplinary' (QAA, 2008, p4), drawing theories, methods, concepts and knowledge from arts and humanities, social sciences, the media and communications industries, the applied arts and the sciences. Their study requires an holistic approach akin to Strachan's articulation of systems thinking, the 'ability to recognise and analyse the interconnections within and between systems' (Strachan, 2009, p84). Alongside this communication, media, film and cultural studies courses taken with other subjects on combined and joint honours degree programmes are commonplace. As one tutor puts it: 'Media studies is just another form of literacy ... [this] is essential in the world we live in and media is the word that is often attached' (Mallinder and Kent, 2008, p42).

This foundation of interdisciplinary (and interdepartmental) practices should provide a strong platform on which to build and address the problem of tutors reporting a lack of expertise on issues relating to environmental sustainability in their departments. Media, communications and cultural studies should be well positioned to share ways in which interdisciplinary learning is supported.

Conclusion

This chapter has explored some opportunities for, challenges to and the current positioning of curricula, teaching and learning for environmental sustainability in media, communications and cultural studies in HE. As Maxwell and Miller put it, 'understanding the ecological context adds a new level of complexity to the study of media and society' (Maxwell and Miller, 2009, p333). From their perspective, it adds another (vitally important) facet to the interrelationships between media production, distribution and consumption practices and their economic and social contexts. 'Understanding the ecological context' is even more complex than that, however. If research, teaching and learning for sustainability is to flourish, it has to be considered in the context within which learning takes place. This means that HEIs themselves will have to study (and perhaps work towards changing) the social, economic and cultural systems that impact their own institutional practices; the development of courses, the organization of departments and the pedagogic practices employed. Since many graduates from HE media, communications and cultural studies courses can expect to possess 'an understanding of the roles of ... cultural institutions in society' (QAA, 2008, p5), they can help with the task.

References

Bellamy, D. (2004) 'Global Warming? What a load of poppycock!', *Daily Mail*, 9 July

Curry, P. (2006) *Ecological Ethics: An Introduction*, Polity Press, Cambridge

Dawe, G., Jucker, R. and Martin, S. (2005) *Sustainable Development in Higher Education: Current Practice and Future Developments*, HEA, York, available at www.heacademy.ac.uk/assets/York/documents/ourwork/tla/sustainability/ sustdevinHEfinalreport.pdf, accessed 30 March 2009

DEFRA (2005) *Securing the Future – The UK Government Sustainable Development Strategy*, The Stationery Office, London, available at www.defra.gov.uk/sustainable/ government/publications/uk-strategy/documents/SecFut_complete.pdf, accessed 3 February 2010

DIUS (2008) *Investing in Our Future: Sustainable Development Action Plan 2008–09*, available at www.dius.gov.uk/about_us/~/media/publications/7/76-08-C_on, accessed 3 February 2010

Flint, D. (2008) 'Environmental sustainability and media, communications and cultural studies higher education', Email to the MeCCSA discussion list, 3 September, available at www.jiscmail.ac.uk/cgi-bin/webadmin?A0=meccsa, accessed 11 August 2009

Flood, R. (2001) 'The relationship of "systems thinking" to action research', In Reason, P. and Bradbury, H. (eds), *Handbook of Action Research*, Sage, London

Goldberg, M. (2009) 'Social Conscience', In Stibbe, A. (ed), *Sustainability Literacy: Skills for a Changing World*, Green Books, Dartington

HEFCE (2009) *Sustainable Development in Higher Education: 2008 Update to Strategic Statement and Action Plan*, HEFCE, Bristol, available at www.hefce.ac.uk/pubs/ hefce/2009/09_03/09_03.pdf, accessed 3 February 2010

Luna, H. and Stibbe, A. (2009) 'Introduction', in Stibbe, A. (ed.), *Sustainability Literacy: Skills for a Changing World*, Green Books, Dartington

Mallinder, S. and Kent, M. (2008) *Staff and Students in Media Education 2008 – Staff and Student Voice*, available at www.adm.heacademy.ac.uk/projects/adm-hea-projects/ media-comms-review, accessed 3 February 2010

Maxwell, R. and Miller, T. (2008) 'Ecological ethics and media technology', *International Journal of Communication*, vol 2, pp331–353, available at http://ijoc.org/ojs/index.php/ ijoc/article/viewFile/320/151, accessed 3 February 2010

MeCCSA (undated) *Media Programmes at University*, available at www.meccsa.org.uk/pdfs/Media-Programmes-brochure.pdf, accessed 30 March 2009

Monbiot, G. (2007) *Heat: How We Can Stop the Planet Burning*, Penguin, London

Orr, D. (1992) *Ecological Literacy: Education and Transition to a Postmodern World*, SUNY Press, Albany NY

QAA (2008) *Communication, Media, Film and Cultural Studies* (subject benchmark statement), QAA, Gloucester, available at www.qaa.ac.uk/academicinfrastructure/benchmark/statements/CMF08.pdf, accessed 13 August 2009

Stibbe, A. (2009) 'Communications and media studies: Curricula responding to a changing world', *Networks*, no 6, pp14–17

Strachan, G. (2009) 'Systems thinking', in Stibbe, A. (ed), *Sustainability Literacy: Skills for a Changing World*, Green Books, Dartington

UCAS (2009) *Course Search*, available at www.ucas.ac.uk/students/coursesearch, accessed 14 August 2009

University of the Arts London (2009) *BA (Hons) Graphic Design and Media Design – Design for Advertising* (course details), available at www.lcc.arts.ac.uk/courses/undergraduate/ba_graphic_media_design_advertising.htm#, accessed 14 August 2009

University Centre Hastings (2009) *BA (Hons) Environmental Biology and Media Production* (course details), available at www.uch.ac.uk/index.php?content=detail_c&id=56, accessed 14 August 2009

University of Brighton (2009) *Environment and Media Studies* (course details), available at www.brighton.ac.uk/set/courses/undergraduate/environment/environment_media.php?PageId=113, accessed 30 March 2009

Wayman, S. (2009) 'Futures thinking', in Stibbe, A. (ed.), *Sustainability Literacy: Skills for a Changing World*, Green Books, Dartington

Notes

1   David Bellamy is a British author, botanist and broadcaster. He was a popular TV presenter in the 1980s.

2   The QAA was established in 1997 to safeguard quality and standards in UK HE. For further information, see www.qaa.ac.uk/aboutus/default.asp (accessed 3 February 2010). The subject benchmark statement for *Communication, Media, Film and Cultural Studies* describes the nature, scope and characteristics of a bachelors degree with honours.

3   MeCCSA is the UK subject association for those that research and teach HE media, communication and cultural studies higher education. For more information, see www.meccsa.org.uk (accessed 3 February 2010).

4   The HEA is an organization funded by the UK HE funding councils to enhance the student learning experience. See www.heacademy.ac.uk (accessed 3 February 2010).

5   UCAS processes student applications to UK HE courses. A search on 14 August 2009 using the terms 'media', 'communication' and 'cultural studies' in conjunction with the term 'sustainability', by contrast, returned no course matches.

6   The module details are not available online. Details of the School of Design at Dundee (the Duncan of Jordanstone College of Art and Design) can be found at www.dundee.ac.uk/design/programmes.php (accessed 3 February 2010).

7   Further information about the Mediating the Environment module can be found at http://staffcentral.brighton.ac.uk/CLT/ESD/vignette/ma_creative_me.html (accessed 3 February 2010).

8 DIUS was the UK Government department responsible for HE. In June 2009 it was disbanded, and HE now falls under the auspices of the Department for Business, Innovation and Skills.

9 More details of HEFCE are available at www.hefce.ac.uk (accessed 3 February 2010).

Chapter 12

Sustainability in the Theology Curriculum

Katja Stuerzenhofecker, Rebecca O'Loughlin and Simon Smith

Introduction

The word 'theology' derives from the Greek to mean 'discourse about God', and refers to the systematic study of the divine and the nature and implications of belief about the divine. In UK HE, the teaching of theology is predominantly Christian in focus, with other faiths usually examined under the discipline heading of 'religious studies'.

Our focus in this chapter is on theology, the academic study of which has a strong tradition of delivering what can be seen as sustainability-related curriculum by preparing students for critical engagement with contemporary social and ethical issues. Theology has the potential, which is already realized in the areas we discuss in this chapter, to bring to ESD a critical understanding of the role of humanity in relation to creation. This can be done through uncovering the complex interconnections between ecology, society and economics that give rise to ethical questions of the inherent dignity and worth of the person in conflict with the needs and aspirations of other persons and the environment, where such a conflict arises. In this way, theology can make a significant contribution to the development of holistic alternative visions for the future that inspire action at the personal, grassroots and institutional levels.

In this chapter we will examine the relationship between theology and sustainability, considering historical developments while focusing on those particular qualities that theology possesses which enable it to critically encounter sustainability in an academic setting. We will argue that while there is something of a discontinuity between theology and dominant SD discourses, this provides theology with the opportunity to step back and critically assess the latter. We will further suggest that theology is in a position to do this because of the potential affinities it has with other disciplines, and that it is therefore able to make a valuable contribution to an holistic multidisciplinary approach. We further propose that theological education is well placed to fulfil this function partly because it has an affinity with, and tends towards, pedagogical approaches that themselves reflect the ethos of sustainability as something that should be inclusive, transformational, empowering and democratic; we also argue how these ideas are being put into action. As we develop this argument, we also consider the potential pitfalls of constructing orthodoxies around sustainability by emphasizing the need to critically reflect on both the content and delivery of curricula. First, however, we will set out how religious organizations have been active in the development of the sustainability movement and how this underlines theology's potential importance in contemporary debates and approaches.

Theology and sustainability

Christian organizations such as the World Council of Churches (WCC),[1] an international ecumenical fellowship of Christian churches, claim to have been among those who introduced the concept of sustainability back in the early 1970s. David G. Hallman (2001, p126) traces the WCC's first official use of the concept of sustainability to their 1974 consultation - responding to the Club of Rome's report, *The Limits to Growth* (Meadows et al, 1972). This consultation led to the WCC's inception of a programme on 'Just, participatory and sustainable societies' that linked socio-economic justice to ecological sustainability.[2] Scharper (1999) goes even further back to Sittler's presentation, 'Called to Unity' (1962), at the WCC assembly in 1961, in which he brought together environmental concerns and justice with Christian faith. The WCC has participated in and observed many major international sustainability initiatives and continues to be involved in critical discussions of the challenge of sustainability as an evolving concept.[3]

Explicit evangelical theological engagement with environmental concerns has been traced back to Shaeffer's *Pollution and the Death of Man: The Christian View of Ecology*, published in 1970, by Cheek (2002), who acknowledges the ongoing work of evangelicals[4] in this area (e.g. Bouma-Prediger, 2001),[5] but criticizes them for their limited impact outside evangelical circles. He also suggests that their understanding of 'creation care'[6] is too narrowly focused on scientific approaches to ecology at the expense of the theological dimensions and an holistic view. Whether this critique is justified or not, it is interesting to note that some prominent evangelical academics, such as McGrath[7] in the UK and Calvin de Witt[8] in the USA, have a background in both theology and science – hence their emphasis on the physical aspects of sustainability should not come as a surprise.[9]

Another example of the combined pursuit of science and theology in the quest for an ecological theology can be found in the work of the Jesuit paleontologist and geologist Pierre Teilhard de Chardin (1881–1955). His vision of a future worthy of the Earth and the human community is sustained by the British Teilhard Association and those of other nations, and by many academic theologians and scientists who interpret his thought in the light of the current challenges and contexts (e.g. Fabel and St. John, 2003). Teilhard's scientific understanding of evolution brought him into repeated conflict with his superiors in the Jesuit order and the Vatican.

Indeed, the environmental concerns of Roman Catholics have not been sufficiently and continuously reflected at the highest level. It was as late as 1990 that Pope John Paul II's *World Day of Peace* address focused on the 'ecological crisis [as] a moral problem' (John Paul II, 1990). This still stands as an isolated effort by the Vatican. For example, Hallman (2001, p129; 2005, p31), on behalf of the WCC, laments the lack of the Vatican's engagement in ecumenical work on climate change. He is especially disappointed since 'the Holy See is represented within the UN as a state, [and therefore] it has more direct access to the climate change negotiations than does the WCC, which participates in the category of non-governmental organizations' (Hallman, 2001, p129). Notwithstanding this unrealized potential for international policy-making, there are now an increasing number of organizations[10] and publications dedicated specifically to Roman Catholic engagement with ecology (see also Scharper, 1999).

The preceding is a short survey of key contributions to theological thinking about sustainability to illustrate the wider context of theology as a subject area in HE and its relationship to ESD. Although theology's strong tradition of engagement with sustainability issues seems to be clear to some commentators who assess theology's contribution to ESD from outside the discipline (e.g. Wylie et al, 1995), many theologians not directly involved in this discourse are less likely to recognize it.[11] This is a significant observation that highlights the discontinuity between an emerging dominant techno-scientific sustainability discourse and the ways in which theologians have come to define and address this contested complex of phenomena and concepts in their own terms. The common ignorance, be it witting or unwitting, resulting from this discontinuity of discourses poses a challenge for HEIs' efforts to make the integration of sustainability into curriculum design a requirement. There is a danger that such efforts, laudable as they are, might overlook existing provision if, for example, initial mapping exercises use criteria that are alien to theology – or for that matter to any other subject area.[12]

We therefore suggest a learning process both within and outside of theology, which will enable participants in the sustainability discourse in HE to become conversant across disciplinary boundaries. A possible alternative approach to disciplinarity, which also makes a practical contribution to the quest for solutions, is to make sustainability discourse truly multidisciplinary by allowing all disciplines to retain their identity and their unique means of approaching and articulating the issues. It is in this spirit that Wals and Jickling (2002, p229) 'seek more, not less diversity of thought' and 'less exclusive language'.[13] This can be enriching if theologians and other marginal participants[13] in this discourse are able to 'realise and exploit the relevance of their own disciplinary backgrounds, and the tools and dispositions they use' (O'Loughlin, 2008, p75). In other words, 'theologians ask *theologians*' questions' (O'Loughlin, 2008, p76) that are not usually considered relevant to ESD discourse, particularly when ESD is defined – erroneously – as education about the environment (see e.g. Roberts and Roberts, 2007, p4). Publications such as the one before you are one way of making the discourse more inclusive. The way forward lies in genuine collaboration through the provision of a greater number of opportunities for constructive dialogue through publications, events and networks.

For its part, theology has its distinctive tradition of thinking and teaching about *justice* as a discipline-specific way of engaging with sustainability-related questions without necessarily making explicit links to the sustainability discourse. Theological keywords in the discussion of social, ecological and environmental sustainability include 'eco-justice', 'creation care', 'stewardship' and the holistic formula 'justice, peace and the integrity of creation'.[14] It should not be assumed, however, that there is universal agreement among theologians about such terms and their meanings. For example the formula of 'justice, peace and the integrity of creation' was used as the name of one of the WCC's programmes until 2007 when it was relaunched as 'Justice, diakonia and responsibility for creation'. Note the shift from 'integrity' to 'responsibility', which signals a revised understanding of human participation in the ongoing process of creation (*creatio continua*, as opposed to a view of creation as a past event).[15] Whereas the former ascribes to human activity the responsibility for and the ability to save creation in a way that can be argued to constitute hubris for any creature who is not the creator/God, the latter limits human activity to co-operation in ongoing creation through for instance conservation activities and attention to sustainability (*Theologische Realenzyklopädie* [TRE] vol 30, 1999).

The understanding of human responsibility for creation care or stewardship follows from God's call for humans to 'have dominion' over all living things (*dominium terrae*) in Genesis 1, 26–28. The guiding principle of stewardship is justice with the aim of establishing peace. However, the traditional link of justice to legal systems in the Hebrew Bible/Old Testament can be seen as problematic for the development of creation care ethics. It has been suggested (*TRE* Band 30, 1999) that proposed social, economic and ecological interventions, what Butkus and Kolmes (2008, p45) call 'the *ought* of policies and actions', have to be assessed individually to ascertain their potential impact on the entire non-human and human worlds. This precludes the establishment of absolute legal codes.[16]

Biblical and theological concepts of justice and dominion raise the problem of anthropocentrism, which is certainly evident in theology in general and has been considered a weakness in theology's engagement with environmental sustainability (Berry, 2006, p5). Berry takes this as the starting point for introducing critical perspectives on environmental stewardship with reference to the ongoing[17] debate sparked off by White's paper 'The Historical Roots of our Ecological Crisis' first published in 1967. White, a cultural historian, accused Judeo-Christian anthropocentrism of being originally responsible for the ecological crisis. According to Scharper (1999), White's challenge led to wider Christian calls for the development of ecological theology and for critical and constructive engagement with stewardship and environmental sustainability. Following on from White, some commentators trace the cause of all practices of exploitation and destruction – environmental and otherwise – to Jewish and Christian *andro-centrism* and patriarchy. This forms the core of ecofeminists' critique and constructive response, being an important theme in the work of ecofeminist theologians such as Rosemary Radford Ruether (Ruether, 2000), Sallie McFague (McFague, 1987) and Heather Eaton (Eaton, 2002).

Curricula

What exactly is sustainability-related curriculum in theology? This question is still open to debate because it is not universally agreed what we mean by sustainability, and consequently what should be the content of appropriate curricula (Hopkins et al, 2003; Sterling, 1996). However, considerable work has been done to identify key areas where theology already contributes and where there is potential for further development. Dawe et al (2005) have compiled a list of 35 sustainability-related curriculum areas based on responses from HE practitioners in the UK. Although many of these areas seem to originate from science subject areas, some commentators have found 27 of them to have explicit or implicit relevance to theology.[18] Although it is beyond the scope of this chapter to discuss them all in detail, some further comments should clarify the emerging picture.

What surfaces is the relevance of theology's tradition of 'deep debate about normative, ethical and spiritual convictions' and 'the destination of humankind and human responsibility' that Wals and Jickling (2002, p227) regard as essential for teaching about sustainability. Not surprisingly, theology has a very strong affinity with social and economic curriculum areas like intergenerational and intragenerational equity, but also with issues around individual responses to uncertainty, threats to well-being and future-oriented ethics (Adam and Groves, 2007). What Dawe et al (2005) describe as 'techniques of *backcasting and forecasting*' have clear affinities with the study of historical and contemporary societies and their theological aspirations as well as the construction of 'the best we can imagine' in ecclesiology (the study of the Church itself), soteriology (the theological doctrine of salvation) and with eschatology (the study of the last things or 'what may be hoped for').[19] Where some theologians see significant gaps in current thinking about curriculum is in the critical study of sustainability discourse as reflecting contested and conflicting values, motivations and agendas within states and between cultural traditions.[20] Therefore, theological teaching might include reflection on the moral imperative for sustainability and on theological models of reconciliation. Further, a sustainability-related curriculum should prepare students to reflect critically on processes such as media responses to climate change and how to motivate different social groups to take action.[21]

There are also a number of issues specific to teaching and learning in theology that have a significant bearing on the discipline's engagement with ESD. These include the debate over 'insider'/'outsider' perspectives, the relationship between empiricism and reflection in disciplinary methodologies, the impact of the academic study of theology and religion on students' faith convictions and the challenge of managing the fall-out from the self-disclosure and emotion-arousing that occur in the theology classroom. These will now be considered.

One of the core skills to be acquired by theology students is 'an ability to understand how people have thought and acted in contexts other than ... [their] own' as the QAA subject benchmark statement on *Theology and Religious Studies* puts it (QAA, 2007, 3.2).[22] In the process of acquiring this skill, students face a fundamental challenge conceptualized in the literature as the insider/outsider problem. This problem relates to the question of which perspective should be given precedence in the study of religious phenomena and practices, that of the *subjective* religious believer or the *objective* academic researcher. More recently, this dichotomy has been criticized as untenable because both believers and researchers are insiders as well as outsiders in relation to religious experience (Knott, 2005). Instead, a more promising attitude is one of 'dialogical and reflexive engagement' (Knott, 2005, p255) between the scholar and the people they study.[23]

The significance of this debate for ESD lies first in the way it raises questions 'about the extent and limits of our knowledge and understanding' (Knott, 2005, p243). Bawden (2007) and Wals and Jickling (2002, p229) rightly emphasize the importance of epistemological debate for teaching about sustainability. More specifically, Dawe et al (2005, p58) identify that ESD needs to enable students to think critically about 'the ways in which knowledge is produced and validated'. Theologians consider truth to be contestable and regard argument as the route to knowledge. Although such a stance is by no means exclusive to theology, the insider/outsider debate shows how theology addresses the question of epistemology in a subject-relevant and self-reflexive manner.

Self-reflection is also identified by Dawe et al (2005, p58) as significant for ESD. This covers both professional as well as personal aspects. Personal self-reflection is a commonly used tool in formative and summative assessment in theology, especially in ministerial and professional doctorate training, but increasingly also as part of inquiry-based learning (IBL)[24] in undergraduate education (see *Approaches to Learning and Case Studies* sections below). The QAA's *Theology and Religious Studies* subject benchmark statement (QAA, 2007, 1.13) recognizes that many theology students' existing faith commitments and beliefs[25] can become destabilized by the critical analysis practised in the academic study of theology. The challenge that the academic study of theology presents to this fundamental aspect of an individual's identity can lead to a situation where students experience a faith crisis in the classroom. Constructive and structured self-reflection as a tool for learning can be used to prevent such students rejecting a critical approach in order to protect their faith and beliefs (see Crosby et al, 2003; cited in O'Loughlin, 2008, p101).

A variation of the faith crisis that is also highly relevant to ESD is what Turpin (2008) calls the 'luxury of despair' when teaching justice and peace in privileged contexts. She has identified five characteristic 'temptations' for theology students who encounter fundamental challenges to their 'self-understandings, historical understandings of their religious tradition and national context, and inadequate theological and faith formation shaped by dominant narratives that ignore social realities of oppression' (Turpin, 2008, p141). These five characteristics are namely the temptations to run, to defensive anger, to neutralize conflict, to 'fix it' and to despair (Turpin, 2008, p144). Although this research comes out of the disciplinary context of teaching theology, it will surely resonate with most ESD practitioners well beyond HE.

What Crosby et al (2003; cited in O'Loughlin, 2008, p101) as well as Turpin (2008) recognize to be at stake here is the potential for curriculum to enable transformative learning (Mezirow and Associates, 2000, O'Sullivan, 1999) that leads to action for social change. If students fall into Turpin's temptations without moving on to a constructive shift of perspective, or 'conversion' (Kennedy, 1984, p556) to use theological terminology, and to 'appropriate agency' (Turpin, 2008, p152) then this potential is lost.[26] However, the *Theology and Religious Studies* subject benchmark statement (QAA, 2007, 1.14) argues that the more desirable outcome for theology students is that this destabilization 'may also stimulate real engagement with contemporary concerns', thus echoing ESD's function as transformative learning (Dawe et al, 2005, p58). Teaching and learning in theology that actively acknowledges students' emotions in the learning process and engages students existentially through action–reflection has much to offer here (Glennon, 2004; O'Donovan, 2003; Haynes, 2001).[27]

To illustrate this point, a brief case study of religious education with adults is provided by Kennedy (1984) in the context of what he calls 'education for a just and peaceful world'. He describes a learning activity that begins with students sharing past experiences of their emotional responses to events that either confirmed or challenged their ethical criteria. What Kennedy (1984, p556) suggests is that 'we learn when our adrenalin runs'. This is confirmed by O'Donovan (2003, p161), who describes an innovative assessment task that requires the creative expression of a self-selected element of curriculum content in relation to students' personal or contemporary experience. O'Donovan describes the results of students' passionate engagement with this task as often fascinating, highly instructive and memorable due to the multi-sensory forms of their submissions.

Approaches to learning

It is outside the scope of this chapter to discuss the pedagogical underpinnings of ESD at a fundamental level. This has already been done in a number of publications, for example, in Gough and Scott (2007, especially chapters 15: 'Individual Learning in Higher Education' and 16: 'Collective Learning in Higher Education'), Scott and Gough (2003a and 2003b, especially chapters 8: 'Curriculum and Pedagogy' and 9: 'Measuring Learning: Aspects of Assessment' in both volumes), Leal Filho (2002) and Corcoran and Wals (2004), all presenting a range of international practitioner perspectives. Periodicals such as *IJSHE*[28] also keep the discussion open. However, the arts and humanities are not widely and systematically covered apart from a few chapters in Blewitt and Cullingford (2004), and none of the above sources address ESD specifically in relation to theology. It is not surprising given the lack of general pedagogical research by theologians (O'Loughlin, 2008), that pedagogical research which explores the very specific question of the pedagogical underpinnings of ESD in theology is virtually unheard of. We are therefore left with Dawe et al (2005), whose report is, to our knowledge, the only existing practitioner-led systematic study of ESD in HE that includes theology. Furthermore, while their data are restricted to the UK, this does not invalidate their findings, and it is to be hoped that the current gap in the literature will be filled by further research.

Following Dawe et al (2005), there seem to be four key pedagogic considerations in teaching sustainability-related curricula, namely critical thinking about the nature of, production and validation of knowledge, the empowerment of the learner, experiential learning, and learning for action. These four key considerations are reflected in four pedagogic approaches and methodologies that are widely used in teaching and learning in theology. They are first a variety of liberation pedagogies,[29] including Latin American (Freire, 1996) and feminist (hooks, 1994) pedagogies,[30] which envision and employ education as a means of helping learners to reflect on and change the oppressive situation in which they perceive themselves to be. Second, theological reflection is an inductive process of inquiry that emphasizes the primacy of lived experience. It utilizes theological and other sources to analyse and renew practice in a manner that echoes other models of the reflective practitioner (Graham et al, 2005). Interdisciplinarity, which is integral to theology as a multidisciplinary discipline, is harnessed to develop tools of inquiry that are appropriate to complex problems in order to shape ethical praxis and action (Butkus and Kolmes, 2008). Finally, IBL is a key method that is discussed in more detail below. Questions of epistemology have already been discussed earlier in the context of the insider/outsider debate. All four pedagogic approaches encourage critical engagement with epistemology; this is closely linked to the empowerment of the learner through the challenging of hegemonic classroom structures, which is a key political aim of all liberation pedagogies, and a key pedagogical method of IBL. Experiential learning through the critical analysis of real-life problems and actual experiences is also at the heart of IBL. Learning for transformation and action, a key concern of all liberation pedagogies, is supported by interdisciplinarity and the linking of knowledge with learners' experience.[31]

One of the chief advantages of IBL is that it has potential to promote inclusive teaching and learning, and this is something that is particularly important in the context of ESD (Wals and Jickling, 2002, p227). IBL works with a student–teacher model that is based more on mutuality and equality than that which underpins transmission teaching. The student and the tutor are reconceptualized in IBL as co-researchers rather than the tutor being regarded as the information-giver and the student as the receptacle. Furthermore, IBL employs non-traditional learning and assessment methods, such as joint research projects, assessed presentations and online assessment. To a degree, students decide how to do their research and they have a say in how, and by whom, they are assessed. IBL thus complements the widening participation and diversity agendas of HEIs in the UK.

Inquiry-based approaches share an affinity with the disciplinary culture, ethos and methods of theology and are well established in many university departments of theology. Since it endorses and enshrines each of the four key pedagogical considerations that Dawe et al (2005) have related to ESD, IBL may be viewed as a bridge between theology and ESD, allowing theologians to engage in discourse about ESD in ways that they experience as being appropriate to their discipline.

O'Loughlin (2008) explores the practice of inquiry-based pedagogies in theology departments in her case study of UK HEIs and argues that these practices are relatively common when they are named, and more so when they are not.[32] Her study suggests that two different types of IBL are being practised in theology departments: entire modules based on IBL; and 'hybrid' IBL, where discrete IBL exercises or resources are integrated into traditional curricula. It also includes reports from students that they feel valued as part of a research community and empowered as learners as a result of using inquiry methods. Students interviewed in the course of her research also said that IBL enables them to engage better with learning and retain more knowledge, primarily because their inquiries have developed in response to a desire to really know something or to solve a real problem, and are likely to be of genuine relevance to other people and their future careers. This has implications for ESD because it suggests that students are expressing a desire to engage, through their theological learning, with real-life problems and questions that have social, political, ethical and spiritual dimensions, and they have found that IBL has helped them to do this. This points to an affinity between theology and ESD discourse, since seeking effective ways to engage with real-life problems and questions is the essence of ESD. It is to be hoped that this affinity will be recognized by those disciplines that have heretofore dominated the debates, thus helping to make sustainability debates truly multidisciplinary.

According to O'Loughlin (O'Loughlin, 2008) epistemological and methodological affinities exist between IBL and theology that make IBL a particularly appropriate pedagogy for theology. O'Loughlin explored this in an earlier text (2008),[33] recalling that, in terms of methodology (according to Kolb's taxonomy as adapted by Becher and Trowler [2001]), theology and religious studies is a 'soft' discipline (Kolb, 1981, pp232–255). Colbeck explains: 'In high paradigm consensus or "hard" disciplines, knowledge is perceived as cumulative and concerned with universals, quantification, and discovery' (Colbeck, 1998, p651). Wareing develops this: '"hard" disciplines are characterized by widespread agreement about curriculum content, research collaboration, competition for recognition and funding, clearly defined intellectual boundaries, and the gatekeeping of those boundaries by a powerful elite' (Wareing, 2005, p11). To paraphrase Wareing, low paradigm consensus or 'soft' disciplines consider knowledge as recursive; scholars use new lenses to explore intellectual territory already mapped out by others. Knowledge is also concerned with particulars, qualities and understanding; she writes: '"Soft" disciplines are characterized by idiosyncratic curricula, weak boundaries, independent research efforts and tolerance for unusual ideas or methods' (O'Loughlin, 2008, pp72–73; citing Wareing, 2005, p11). The point here is that because it is a 'soft' discipline, theology has a greater potential affinity with IBL than 'hard' disciplines do because teaching and learning practices in theology are likely to be interpretative and constructive. Further to this, a culture of dialogue, inquiry, argument, critical reflection and, arguably, support for the practical application of learning,[34] characterizes theology and is similarly resonant in inquiry approaches. The point we can draw from this in relation to ESD is that the methods that IBL and theology have in common are common also in ESD, again giving rise to the conclusion that IBL offers theology a route into effective engagement with ESD.

In addition, the lack of an agreed methodology by which academics and students 'do' theology helps to make the discipline receptive to new methods of learning, teaching and researching, including IBL and, in turn, ESD. Fearn and Francis (2004, p61) make the point that the absence of core subject matter in theology may be causally related to the absence of a universally agreed methodology. As they note, linguists, historians, sociologists, archaeologists, philosophers and psychologists may all teach in theology departments. The QAA's *Theology and Religious Studies* subject benchmark statement affirms this: 'Much of the excitement of the discipline lies in its contested nature. What should or should not be regarded as belonging to the subject, what methods should be used, the different results that come from adopting different presuppositions – these are some of the issues.' (QAA, 2007, 2.2). The fluidity of the discipline of theology allows it to engage creatively with newer pedagogies, including IBL, and newer discourses, including ESD.

Although there is no *one* method for doing theology, it is nonetheless possible to narrow learning, teaching and research in theology down to a few key methods, which happen to correspond with many methods used in IBL and, in turn, ESD. These include documentary analysis, qualitative research (primarily used in practical theology), interpretative methods, phenomenology, action research and observational research. In addition, theology teaching is heavily seminar-based, thus suggesting that collaborative working – a central feature of both IBL and ESD – is an effective pedagogical approach for the discipline.

What we may refer to as the special issues unique to theology and religious studies – such as insider/outsider issues, potential challenges to faith engendered by the academic work in theology and religious studies, self-disclosure and emotion-arousing in the classroom and during unsupervised study, and encountering people from different religious and cultural backgrounds to one's own – give rise to three particular foci in IBL. These foci are also key in ESD approaches: experiential inquiry (reflecting on, and subjecting to scrutiny, one's own values, beliefs and practices), practical or active learning and a focus on the process of learning.

Active learning via practical theology may be one route into IBL – and from there into ESD – for theology tutors and students, since this form of *doing* theology is already established in the discipline and encapsulates many of the values at the heart of both IBL and ESD. Experiential learning via working with faith-based and voluntary organizations is also common practice in theology. Reflection on the process of learning is also built into many theology modules through the use of learning journals and self-evaluation questionnaires. The real-life reflective learning that is a key feature of both IBL and ESD is, then, already being practised to a considerable degree in theology.[35]

Case studies

The following three case studies are not representative but rather indicative of the range of sustainability-related provision in theology that demonstrates an holistic vision, future-oriented ethics, alternative visions for action and the critical study of human responses to global crisis. In the UK, there do not seem to be any single modules on theology and sustainability that give equal weight to all aspects of sustainability. However, we take the view that ESD in theology is currently delivered by a range of modules with specific foci that, taken together over the three years of undergraduate study, add up to an holistic form of provision. Sustainability-related curricula are more prevalent at postgraduate level, but to focus on this is beyond the scope of this chapter. Instead, the case studies and examples of existing undergraduate provision are intended as incentives for much-needed development and innovation.

For reasons of brevity, we were unable to include reference to modules on ecotheology, on other liberation theologies apart from feminist theology, and on public and political theology, political economy, globalization and ethics, but the reader should be made aware that these are well established in theology curricula. Space constraints mean that we have also been unable to focus on modules that reflect on the Bible through the lens of ESD, such as The Bible and Environmental Ethics taught at the University of Exeter (University of Exeter, 2008).

Provision at first year undergraduate level seems to be the most traditional in terms of curricula, pedagogy and assessment. Hence, the range of relevant modules for this case study was much more limited than at levels two and three. In addition to the case study below, other possible examples of sustainability-related curricula at level one can be found at the University of Gloucestershire (Christian Faith and the Environment),[36] at the Wesley Centre, Oxford Brookes University (Making Moral Choices and Liberation Theologies, both of which make links to students' own values and life in the UK), at the University of Wales Trinity St David (Christian Doctrine and Christian Ethics, both of which examine the links between theology and contemporary issues) and further modules at the Queen's Foundation (Introduction to Christian Theology, which assesses students' critical reflection on their own theological practice, and Black and Asian Christian Theology, which examines real-life contexts in the UK).

More research is required to understand fully why provision is so restricted at this level. In terms of pedagogy, there are no intrinsic reasons why assessment should follow the traditional format of essay and exam at level one, as it generally seems to do, before turning to more 'innovative' methods from year two. On the contrary, a research-based style of learning with frequent formative feedback should be introduced and nurtured right from the start when students are still adapting to HE (Pyne, 2008; Nelson, 2007). It seems that more innovative work needs to be done here both in terms of curriculum as well as teaching, learning and assessment.

It is impossible to give a comprehensive account of the three chosen modules in the short case studies that follow. Rather, the focus is on those elements that relate most closely to the four key pedagogical considerations in ESD discussed earlier. Of those, learning for action through interdisciplinarity is incorporated into all three modules.

Practical Contextual Theology for Mission and Ministry, Queen's Foundation, Birmingham

The level one module Practical Contextual Theology for Mission and Ministry (Queen's Foundation, 2006) delivered by David Hewlett introduces students to contextual theology as a mode of practical theology by collecting and studying ethnographic, sociological and narrative accounts of both congregational life and the communities in which they are set. This module helps students to explore an alternative approach to theology through experiential learning of the action–reflection model that challenges the dominance of theory over practice. It employs a broad understanding of research data and emphasizes feelings as well as facts that are seen as constructed and therefore contested.

Experiential learning through investigation of real-life problems and learner empowerment take on a specifically embodied character in the form of the IBL-based community engagement task. Students start the module on their own by 'walking the walk', an exercise that takes them outside the classroom to investigate a small geographical area of their own choice. This is the first stage in their congregational survey for the purpose of informing and advising 'a new minister moving to the church to take up appointment there' (1PT2 Module handbook, personal email). The emphases on giving advice and consideration of the context for practice are used as tools of learning for action beyond the classroom in students' professional practice. Questions of community cohesion, which are central to the social aspect of sustainability, are investigated by paying attention to the congregation's expression of identity, conflict handling and resolution, authority and power, and the character of the congregation.

Religion, Culture and Gender, University of Manchester

The level two module Religion, Culture and Gender (University of Manchester, 2009) taught by Elaine Graham and Katja Stuerzenhofecker is understood by the course team to contribute to ESD through the study of values of equity and equality, empowerment and inclusivity. It addresses issues of social and economic justice in relation to gender in Jewish and Christian religion and culture. There is some consideration of ecofeminist critiques to establish an holistic context.[37] The syllabus focuses on philosophical, ethical, moral and emotional interpretations of sustainability rather than on scientific ones.[38] Assessment offers students the opportunity to practice self-reflection, critical thinking, the application of theory to real-life problems and the development of a questioning attitude. The module encourages experiential learning of constructivist models of epistemology and existential engagement with the course topics.

The underlying feminist pedagogy emphasizes the active role of the learner in knowledge construction and highlights the link between theory and real-life experiences. To this end, seminars are IBL-based, student-led discussions that begin with a short presentation of academic analyses of case studies, followed by a student-run discussion of the leading group's own questions arising from their presentation.[39] Further, the experiences of the students and their peers are harnessed for knowledge construction in structured learning journals that assess increasing depth and breadth of reflection without being prescriptive about the outcomes.[40] Balanced analysis of a real-life issue of students' choice related to religion, culture and gender in a British context is assessed in the briefing guide, an IBL task that replaces the standard essay format. Briefing guides have covered issues such as links between marriage vows and domestic violence, homophobia in the Roman Catholic Church and Jewish masculinities.

Technology, Religion and Ethics, School of Divinity, University of Edinburgh

The level three module Technology, Religion and Ethics taught by Michael Northcott (University of Edinburgh, 2009) examines the ecological, cultural, moral and spiritual significance of technology. This includes an investigation of technology as religion and an exploration of the religious origins of technological innovation. According to the module director, Technology, Religion and Ethics is relevant to ESD because it enables students to learn about the interaction between technology and the environment and about how to critique the unthinking use of technology. The module also discusses how technology mis-shapes the human relationship with the environment, often making it less sustainable. Key ESD aspects of the module include thinking about wilderness, democracy, participation and the influence of technology.

The critical evaluation of real-life problems is practised through a number of case studies such as genetic engineering, electronic communication and intensive farming. Case studies of traditional religious communities – such as the Amish and some indigenous peoples –who have resisted the technological reshaping of life on spiritual grounds are also examined. E-learning technology supports assessment in the form of individual and joint blogs to give students the opportunity for active learning through reflection on their use of technology in education. The joint blog requires reflection on and critique of the readings, with students taking it in turn to initiate discussions.[41] The individual part of the blog is an autobiographical reflection by a student on their own use of particular pieces of technology during the semester.

Conclusion

While theology is perhaps not an area that one would immediately equate with having a significant contribution to make to ESD, we have sought to show here that there is considerable potential for this to occur. In order to claim a greater role for itself in ESD, we suggest that theology needs to move towards achieving that potential while ESD needs to be both reflexive and multidisciplinary to develop holistically within disciplines. We have sought to contribute to this process by highlighting the areas where theology can make this contribution, both in terms of curriculum content (especially, but not exclusively, around the concept of justice) and curriculum design (through such as IBL).

This is clearly not an easy outcome to achieve in practice. However, the very presence of this book suggests that disciplines are beginning to mature in their approach to ESD and the next step must surely be the development of a more integrated methodology in teaching ESD. On the one hand this requires disciplines, including theology, to reflect on how their approach can be contextualized more broadly, while on the other hand considering how the design of the curriculum, including assessment, can reflect the fundament values of ESD.

We argue, therefore, that by its very nature ESD should contain elements that are both vibrant and dynamic. Theology is well placed to contribute to this through both curriculum content and its affinity with pedagogic approaches that are inclusive, transformational, empowering and democratic. So by grounding ESD in this manner we may, in the longer term, achieve a shared approach that is in itself flexible and sustainable rather than being limited by any single discipline or methodology.

References

Adam, B. and Groves, C. (2007) *Future Matters: Action, Knowledge, Ethics*, Brill, Leiden

Arbuthnott, K.D. (2009) 'Education for sustainable development beyond attitude change', *IJSHE*, vol 10, no 2, pp152–163

Bawden, R. (2007) 'Pedagogies for persistence: Cognitive challenges and collective competency development', *International Journal of Innovation and Sustainable Development*, vol 2, no.s 3–4, pp299–314

Becher, T. and Trowler, P.R. (2001) *Academic Tribes and Territories*, Society for Research into Higher Education and Open University Press, Buckingham

Berry, R.J. (ed) (2006) *Environmental Stewardship: Critical Perspectives – Past and Present*, T&T Clark, London and New York NY

Blake, J. (2007) 'Missing links: Gender and education for sustainable development', *International Journal of Innovation and Sustainable Development*, vol 2, no.s 3–4, pp414–432

Blewitt, J. and Cullingford, C. (eds) (2004) *The Sustainability Curriculum: The Challenge for Higher Education*, Earthscan, London

Bouma-Prediger, S. (2001) *For the Beauty of the Earth: A Christian Vision for Creation Care*, Baker, Grand Rapids MI

Bouma-Prediger, S. (1995) *The Greening of Theology: The Ecological Models of Rosemary Radford Ruether, Joseph Sittler, and Jürgen Moltmann*, Scholars Press, Atlanta GA

Butkus, R.A. and Kolmes, S.A. (2008) 'Theology in ecological perspective: An interdisciplinary, inquiry-based experiment', *Teaching Theology and Religion*, vol 11, no 1, pp42–53

Cheek, D.W. (2002) 'Review' of *Earth Habitat: Eco-Injustice and the Church's Response*, *Journal of the Evangelical Theological Society*, vol 45, no 3, pp558–560

Colbeck, C. (1998) 'Merging in a seamless blend', *The Journal of Higher Education*, vol 69, no 6, pp647–671

Corcoran, P.B. and Wals, A.E.J. (eds) (2004) *Higher Education and the Challenge of Sustainability: Problematics, Promise, and Practice*, Kluwer Academic Publishers, Dordrecht

Crosby, K., Pattison, S., and Skilton, A. (2003) 'Project report: "Supporting questioning in theology and religious studies"', *The PRS–LTSN Journal*, vol 2, no 1, pp58–89

Dawe, G., Jucker, R. and Martin, S. (2005) *Sustainable Development in Higher Education: Current Practice and Future Developments*, HEA, York, available at www.heacademy.ac.uk/assets/York/documents/ourwork/tla/sustainability/sustdevinHEfinalreport.pdf, accessed 6 May 2009

Eaton, H. (2000) 'Response to Rosemary Radford Rueher: Ecofeminism and theology – challenges, confrontations, and reconstructions' in Hessel, D.T. and Ruether, R.R. (eds), pp113–124

Evangelical Environmental Network and *Creation Care Magazine* (2009) 'On the care of creation: An evangelical declaration on the care of creation', *CreationCare.org*, available at www.creationcare.org/resources/declaration.php, accessed 1 October 2009

Fabel, A. and St. John, D. (2003) *Teilhard in the 21st Century: The Emerging Spirit of the Earth*, Orbis, Maryknoll NY

Fearn, M. and Francis, L.J. (2004) 'From A-level to higher education: Student perceptions of teaching and learning in theology and religious studies', *Discourse*, vol 3, no 2 , pp58–91

Freire, P. (1996) *Pedagogy of the Oppressed*, Penguin, Harmondsworth

Garrard, G. (2007) 'Ecocriticism and education for sustainability', *Pedagogy: Critical Approaches to Teaching Literature, Language, Composition, and Culture*, vol 7, no 3, pp359–383

Glennon, F. (2004) 'Experiential learning and social justice action: An experiment in the scholarship of teaching and learning', *Teaching Theology and Religion*, vol 7, no 1, pp30–37

Gonzáles-Gaudiano, E. (2004) 'Complexity in environmental education', in Scott, W. and Gough, S. (eds), *Key Issues in Sustainable Development and Learning: A Critical Review*, Routledge, London, pp153–166

Goodwin, B.C. (2007) 'Science, spirituality and holism within higher education', *International Journal of Innovation and Sustainable Development*, vol 2, nos 3–4, pp332–339

Gough, S. and Scott, W. (2007) *Higher Education and Sustainable Development – Paradox and Possibility*, Routledge, London

Graham, E., Walton, H. and Ward, F. (2005) *Theological Reflection: Methods*, SCM Press, London

Gulwadi, G.B. (2009) 'Using reflective journals in a sustainable design studio', *IJSHE*, vol 10, no 1, pp43–53

Hall, D.J. (2004) *The Steward: A Biblical Symbol Come of Age*, Wipf & Stock, Eugene OR; previously published (1990) by Friendship Press, Cincinnati OH

Hallman, D.G. (2001) "Climate change and ecumenical work for sustainable community', In Hessel, D. and Rasmussen, L. (eds), *Earth Habitat: Eco-Injustice and the Church's Response*, Fortress Press, Minneapolis MN, pp453–472

Hallman, D.G. (2005) *Climate Change*, available at www.oikoumene.org/fileadmin/files/ wcc-main/documents/p3/Climate_Change_Brochure_2005.pdf, accessed 2 September 2009

Hansmann, R., Crott, H.W, Mieg, H.A. and Scholz, R.W. (2009) 'Improving group processes in transdisciplinary case studies for sustainability learning', *IJSHE*, vol 10, no 1, pp33–42

Haynes, S.R. (2001) 'Community happens: Anatomy of a remarkable teaching experience', *Teaching Theology and Religion*, vol 4, no 3, pp133–140

Hessel, D.T. and Ruether, R.R. (eds) (2000) *Christianity and Ecology: Seeking the Well-Being of Earth and Humans*, Harvard University Press, Cambridge MA

hooks, b. (1994) *Teaching to Transgress: Education as the Practice of Freedom*, Routledge, London and New York NY

Hopkins, C., Damlamian, J. and Ospina, G. (2003) 'Evolving towards education for sustainable development: an international perspective', in Scott, W. and Gough, S. (eds), *Key Issues in Sustainable Development and Learning: A Critical Review*, Routledge, London, pp137–145

Jickling, B. (2003) 'Why I don't want my children educated for sustainable development', in Scott, W. and Gough, S. (eds), *Key Issues in Sustainable Development and Learning: A Critical Review*, Routledge, London, pp131–137

John Paul II, Pope. (1990) Papal address for *World Day of Peace*, available at www.vatican.va/holy_father/john_paul_ii/messages/peace/documents/ hf_jp-ii_mes_19891208_xxiii-world-day-for-peace_en.html, accessed 4 February 2010

Kennedy, W. (1984) 'Education for a just and peaceful world', *Religious Education*, vol 79, no 4, pp550–557

Kolb, D.A. (1981) 'Learning styles and disciplinary differences', in Chickering, A. (ed), *The Modern American College*, Jossey Bass, San Francisco CA, pp232–255

Knott, K. (2005) 'Insider/outsider perspectives', in Hinnells, J.R. (ed), *The Routledge Companion to the Study of Religion*, Routledge, London, pp243–258

Kwok, P. (2005) *Postcolonial Imagination and Feminist Theology*, Westminster John Knox Press, Louisville KY

Kwok, P. (1994) 'Ecology and the recycling of Christianity', in Hallman, D. (ed), *Ecotheology: Voices from South and North*, Orbis, Maryknoll NY and WCC Publications, Geneva, pp107–111

Leal Filho, W. (ed) (2002) *Teaching Sustainability at Universities: Towards Curriculum Greening*, Peter Lang, Frankfurt

Meadows, D.H., Meadows, D.L. and Randers, J. (1972) *The Limits to Growth*, Potomac Associates, New York and Pan Books, London; republished 1994

McFague, S. (1987) *Models of God: Theology for an Ecological, Nuclear Age*, SCM, London

McKeown, J. (2007) 'Christianity and ecological sustainability', in Roberts, C. and Roberts, J. (eds), pp168–174

Mezirow, J. and Associates (2000) *Learning as Transformation: Critical Perspectives on a Theory in Progress*, Jossey Bass, San Francisco CA

Molderez, I. (2007) 'Spirits of ecological thinking', *International Journal of Innovation and Sustainable Development*, vol 2, nos 3–4, pp376–394

Nelson, J. (2007) 'Minding the gap: Employing formative assessment techniques', *Discourse*, vol 7, no 1, pp179–190

O'Donovan, T. (2003) 'Doing it differently: Unleashing student creativity', *Teaching Theology and Religion*, vol 6, no 3, pp159–163

O'Loughlin, R. (2008) 'Inquiry-based learning in theology and religious studies: An investigation and analysis', The Subject Centre for Philosophical and Religious Studies, available at http://prs.heacademy.ac.uk/view.html/PrsDocuments/398, accessed 6 May 2009

O'Loughlin, R. (2008) 'The relationship between pedagogical and discipline-specific research methods: Critical perspectives', *Discourse: Learning and Teaching in Philosophical and Religious Studies*, vol 7, no 2, pp67–120

O'Sullivan, E. (1999) *Transformative Learning: Educational Vision for the 21st Century*, Zed Books, London and University of Toronto Press, Toronto

Parvis, S. and Paterson, J. (2008) 'Use of blogs to enhance face-to-face learning at different levels' (abstract), *e-Learning in Dialogue*, PRS Conference, York, May, available at http://prs.heacademy.ac.uk/projects/elearning/abstracts.html, accessed 4 February 2010

Pyne, N. (2008) 'A report into the issues surrounding the progression of students to undergraduate studies with particular reference to GCE RS and undergraduate TRS', *Discourse*, vol 8, no 1, pp29–55

QAA (2007) *Theology and Religious Studies* (subject benchmark statement), QAA, Gloucester, available at www.qaa.ac.uk/academicinfrastructure/benchmark/statements/theology.pdf, accessed 6 May 2009

Queen's Foundation (2006) '1PT2 Practical contextual theology for mission and ministry', *Foundations for Christian Ministry – Pathway 1* (course details), available at www.queens.ac.uk/programmes/progs.php?_actID=2&grp=2&prg=37&mod=15, accessed 4 February 2010

Roberts, C. and Roberts, J. (eds) (2007) *Greener by Degrees: Exploring Sustainability through Higher Education Curricula*, Centre for Active Learning, University of Gloucestershire, available at http://resources.glos.ac.uk/ceal/resources/greenerbydegrees, accessed 26 August 2009

Ruether, R.R. (2000) 'Ecofeminism: The challenge to theology', in Hessel, D.T. and Ruether, R.R. (eds), pp97–112

Sauter, G. (1999) *What Dare We Hope? Reconsidering Eschatology*, Trinity Press, Harrisburg PA

Scharper, S.B. (1999) 'The ecological crisis', in Baum, G. (ed) *The Twentieth Century: A Theological Overview*, Orbis, Maryknoll NY, pp219–227

Scott, W. and Gough, S. (2003a) *Sustainable Development and Learning: Framing the Issues*, Routledge, London

Scott, W. and Gough, S. (eds) (2003b) *Key Issues in Sustainable Development and Learning: A Critical Review*, Routledge, London

Shaeffer, F. (1970) *Pollution and the Death of Man: The Christian View of Ecology*, Tyndale, Wheaton IL

Sitler, J. A. (1962) 'Called to unity', *Ecumenical Review*, vol 14, pp177–187

Sterling, S. (1996) 'Education in change', in Huckle, J. and Sterling, S. (eds), *Education for Sustainability*, Earthscan, London, pp18–39

TRE Band 30. (1999) 'Schöpfer/Schöpfung', Walter de Gruyter, Berlin and New York NY, pp348–355

Thomas, T. (2007) 'Education for sustainability: A double-edged sword?', *International Journal of Innovation and Sustainable Development*, vol 2, nos 3–4, pp453–465

Thompson, T.L. (2005) 'The role of faith in historical research', *Scandinavian Journal of the Old Testament*, vol 19, no 1, pp111–134

Turpin, K. (2008) 'Disrupting the luxury of despair: Justice and peace education in contexts of relative privilege', *Teaching Theology and Religion*, vol 11, no 3, pp141–152

University of Edinburgh (2009)

University of Exeter (2008) *Technology, Religion and Ethics 3/4 (U03407)* (course details), available at www.drps.ed.ac.uk/09-10/course.php?code=U03407, accessed 4 February 2010

THE3136 – The Bible and Environmental Ethics (module details), available at http://huss.exeter.ac.uk/theology/undergrad/module_description.php?code=THE3136&ayrc=2008/9, accessed 4 February 2010

University of Manchester (2009) *Course module – Religion, Culture and Gender* (course details), available at http://courses.humanities.manchester.ac.uk/undergraduate/module.html?code=RELT20121, accessed 4 February 2010

Volf, M. and Katerberg, W. (2004) *The Future of Hope: Christian Tradition Amid Modernity and Postmodernity*, Eerdmans, Cambridge

Wals, A.E.J. and Jickling, B. (2002) '"Sustainability" in higher education: From double-think and newspeak to critical thinking and meaningful learning', *IJSHE*, vol 3, no 3, pp221–232

Wareing, S. (2005) 'Discipline-specific professional development: Just branding?', *Educational Developments*, vol 6, no 1, pp11–15

White, L. (1967) 'The historical roots of our ecological crisis', *Science*, vol 155, no 3767, pp1203–1207

Worsley, H. (2005) 'Problem-based learning (PBL) and the future of theological education: A reflection based on recent PBL practice in medical training compared to emerging trends in residential ministerial training for ordination', *Journal of Adult Theological Education*, vol 2, no 1, pp71–81

Wylie, V., Watkin, G. and Wanklyn, M. (1995) *Taking Responsibility: Humanities and Social Sciences – Promoting Sustainable Practice through HE Curricula*, Pluto Press, London

Recommended reading

Freire, P. (1996) *Pedagogy of the Oppressed*, Penguin, Harmondsworth
A classic text on liberation pedagogy that is widely used by theologians, this book is foundational for the educational approaches discussed in this chapter. Freire's writing on the vital link between theory/knowledge and practice/action, on *conscientização*, an attitude of critical awareness required for authentic individual and social transformation, on problem-based learning and the dynamics of the teacher-student relationship is still inspiring and worth reading in the original rather than in often-used quotes.

Hallman, D. (1994) *Ecotheology: Voices from the South and North*, Orbis, Maryknoll NY and WCC Publications, Geneva
Originating from the WCC, *Ecotheology* is another collection of 26 papers that approach sustainability in an holistic, ecumenical and explicitly global manner. Questions of ortho-doxy and knowledge creation in the sustainability discourse are challenged by adding sections on 'Insights from Ecofeminism' and 'Insights from Indigenous Peoples' to the traditional disciplines of biblical witness, theological reflection and Christian ethics. However, there is overlap in contributors with Hessel and Ruether (2000; see below), which raises the question of whether theology should look for ways of throwing the net wider by keeping the discourse open.

Hessel, D.T. and Ruether, R.R. (eds) (2000) *Christianity and Ecology: Seeking the Well-being of Earth and Humans*, Harvard University Press, Cambridge MA

This large volume contains 28 papers and responses by a wide range of theologians in an ecumenical framework. It covers key concepts and issues in Christian doctrine and practice that need to be revisited in the light of current ecological challenges. The dialogic structure allows the reader to explore multiple, sometimes contradictory perspectives and to gain a sense of sustainability as process rather than as a fixed set of indicators. The extensive index allows for selective reading. As in Hallman (1994; see above), none of the papers address pedagogical questions.

Scott, W. and Gough, S. (2003b) *Key Issues in Sustainable Development and Learning: A Critical Review*, Routledge, London

This volume and its companion Scott and Gough (2003a) present a comprehensive overview of issues in ESD in different educational settings. Although many of the (older) texts collected in *A Critical Review* address 'environmental education' in a narrow sense, as a whole the collection charts the territory for critical discussions about ESD that need to be held in all subject areas. It is to be hoped that ongoing developments will be reflected in similar publications.

Notes

1   The current WCC programme that covers sustainability is Justice, Diakonia and Responsibility for Creation – see www.oikoumene.org/en/programmes/justice-diakonia-and-responsibility-for-creation.html (accessed 4 February 2010).

2   Hallman (2001) provides a timeline for the WCC's work on SD up to their recent contributions to the Earth Charter initiative.

3   More on sustainability as an evolving concept in the context of education can be found, for example, in Hopkins et al (2003).

4   Evangelicalism is an umbrella term that encompasses a number of Protestant Christian groups. Common beliefs that link these groups include: a commitment to the importance of a conversion experience for the Christian life (hence the term 'born-again Christianity'); a commitment to social action based on the Gospel (the books of Mark, Matthew, Luke and John in the New Testament); a high value placed on Biblical authority; and a focus on the crucifixion of Jesus. Baptists and Pentecostal Christians are amongst the most well-known evangelical Christian groups.

5   See also Bouma-Prediger's 1995 work *The Greening of Theology: The Ecological Models of Rosemary Radford Ruether, Joseph Sittler and Jürgen Moltmann*.

6   'Creation care' is the term preferred by evangelicals to refer to environmentalism. It is also the name of the Evangelical Environmental Network's publication – see www.creationcare.org/magazine (accessed 4 February 2010).

7   Professor of Theology, currently at King's College, London and previously at Wycliffe Hall, University of Oxford, McGrath holds degrees in the natural sciences and divinity. He is also a signatory of the Evangelical Environmental Network's declaration on the care of creation (Evangelical Environmental Network and *Creation Care Magazine*, 2009).

8   De Witt is Professor at the Nelson Institute for Environmental Studies, University of Wisconsin-Madison, with degrees in biology and zoology, and co-founder of the Evangelical Environmental Network.

9 It would be wrong, however, to suggest that evangelical thinking about sustainability lacks social and economic dimensions, as can be seen in the Evangelical Alliance's support for the holistic vision of the Millennium Development Goals through the Micah Challenge – www.micahchallenge.org.uk (accessed 4 February 2010).

10 For instance, the Justice, Peace and Integrity of Creation Commission, which is part of the Union of Superiors General and the International Union of Superiors General.

11 See, for example, Dawe et al (2005, p25), who report that the HEA Subject Centre for Philosophical and Religious Studies (PRS), which also includes support for learning and teaching in theology in its remit, has 'very high potential and a great enthusiasm for enacting ESD … but with little evidence of movement as yet'. Since this report was compiled, PRS has moved on significantly both in thought and action.

12 We are aware of anecdotal evidence in the humanities where faculty officers in charge of mapping existing ESD provision struggled to find any relevant teaching because the criteria they used are best described as pertaining to environmental education in a narrow sense.

13 Garrard (2007) seems to imply this for English as an HE subject area in the UK context.

14 For detailed and critical discussions of theologians' preferred terms such as 'eco-justice', 'creation care' and 'stewardship', see *Further reading*. See also Berry (2006) for critiques of Christian understandings of environmental stewardship. Hall (2004) provides a key exploration of the origins and past and present applications of the Biblical symbol of stewardship.

15 It seems that 'peace' has been replaced by 'diakonia' not as a response to theological debates about the appropriateness of the word in this context but because another WCC programme on 'Sharing and Service' (Greek: 'diakonia') has been merged with this one.

16 See also Bawden (2007, p306) on contingency.

17 Several authors in Berry (2006) make direct reference to White's challenge. As another example, Bouma-Prediger (2001) devotes an entire chapter to his apologetic response to this critique.

18 This is based on the response by the Subject Centre PRS (Philosophical and Religious Studies) as published in Dawe et al (2005) and by participants of the Teaching Justice in Theology and Biblical Studies Colloquium organized by the Subject Centre. The Colloquium took place at Woodbrooke Study Centre on 15 September 2008.

19 Out of the vast amount of available literature on these areas, we would like to highlight Volf and Katerberg (2004) and Sauter (1999) because they specifically address the question of hope from a Christian perspective.

20 See also González-Gaudiano (2004), who critiques essentialist tendencies in 'green discourse' (p122) and discusses alternative contextual paradigms. He specifically points to liberation pedagogies (pp125–126), including liberation theology, as providing open and fragmented proposals that have more potential for transformation than closed, essentialist ones. Another noteworthy contribution to this debate is made by Wals and Jickling (2002). Molderez (2007) suggests that ESD that is guided by principles of openness, inclusion and tolerance, and which problematizes potential solutions, requires spirit (*pneuma*). Since *pneumatology* is a core area of theological study, her thesis is worth further theological exploration.

21 See the case studies in this chapter for more details.

22 See QAA (2007); the QAA is an independent UK body that visits universities and colleges to check how well they are maintaining their academic standards. The QAA

produces subject benchmark statements for a range of disciplines, including theology and religious studies, which articulate the characteristics of each particular degree programme and the standards it should fulfill.

23 A variation of the insider/outsider debate concerns the relative authority and sincerity of believer academics, i.e. those who are members of the faith communities and religious traditions they study, over non-believer academics. For an example of this debate in Biblical Studies, see Thompson (2005).

24 IBL refers to a range of pedagogical approaches that have student-led research at their heart. The term IBL also accommodates the more widely known problem-based learning (PBL). Both IBL, and PBL within it, fall under the wider umbrella of 'active learning'. In its simplest expression, IBL is 'learning by doing'. Students learn by identifying and engaging with the questions and problems of their discipline, becoming participants in the research process. They direct their own lines of inquiry – which often means designing their own open-ended questions – and identify appropriate methods and resources with which to address them. The tutor acts as a 'walking resource', guiding the students' inquiries without undermining their autonomy, which is crucial in inquiry approaches. Entire modules or programmes can be designed along inquiry lines, or discrete IBL activities can be incorporated into more traditional curricula.

25 We would also consider secular and/or anti-religious positions as beliefs with reference to ESD in other disciplines where, for instance, ideological and technological beliefs have considerable influence. See also the third case study in this chapter on technology and religion.

26 Thomas (2007) discusses a similar counter-transformative process in his case study of student responses to awareness raising of corporate and executive environmental 'wrongdoing'.

27 Goodwin (2007) argues for the active fostering of intuition and feeling in science education.

28 *IJSHE* is available at http://info.emeraldinsight.com/products/journals/journals.htm? PHPSESSID=d2cjbep22t41a8rvkhn29jluq7&id=ijshe (accessed 4 Feburary 2010).

29 See Kolb (1981) and Wals and Jickling's (2002) discussion of what they call emancipatory views of education.

30 For an exploration of gender issues and ESD, see Blake (2007).

31 For a corresponding account of appropriate didactic orientation when integrating sustainability into the curriculum, see Wals and Jickling (2002, pp228–229).

32 A point about language helps to explain this situation. The term IBL is used in theology and religious studies communities with far less frequency than IBL itself is practised. This betokens a disciplinary suspicion of acronyms, particularly those related to teaching and learning, and perhaps also an unwillingness to bracket one's teaching practices off in this way.

33 By way of an explanation of what may appear to be an over-reliance on the work of O'Loughlin, we are unaware of any other work on pedagogical research in theology and on IBL specifically in its application in theology.

34 Theology can be taught as an applied subject, hence the development of the discipline of practical theology. Although not all theology is applied, where it is, the methodology of its praxis echoes the methodologies of both IBL and ESD.

35 The three case studies provide examples of all these approaches. For another example of PBL in theology, see Worsley (2005), who outlines two problem-based scenarios for use in ministerial theological education. In one, candidates assume the role of a vicar who has to solve the problem of low levels of attendance at their church, and in the

other, they assume the role of an inner city vicar who notices that a homeless project is attracting Christian volunteers who are meeting to pray, and that a local youth group is meeting for alternative worship (p76). For a detailed case study of the use of learning journals in sustainability-related teaching and learning, see Gulwadi (2009).

36 A case study of this module is already available; see McKeown (2007).

37 At the end of the module which has strong focus on social and cultural issues, students are confronted with the non-human world. They are asked to respond to Ruether's (2000) consideration of the compatibility of the preferential option for the poor, a key concept of liberation theologies, with an ethic of sustainability, in other words potentially conflicting concerns for human and non-human life. Ruether (2000, p97) defines ecofeminism as the examination 'of the interconnections between the domination of women and the domination of nature'. See also in the same volume the response by Eaton (2000). Ecofeminism and postcolonial perspectives are combined, for example, in the work of Kwok (1994 and 2005), which reflects recent developments in theology.

38 These interpretations are discussed by Dawe et al (2005, p31) as requirements of a generic ESD toolkit.

39 Hansmann et al (2009) describe issues of conformity in peer group processes that deserve further attention.

40 This is to make a clear distinction between assessing students' critical understanding of certain values and practices and requiring students to internalize and adopt them. For discussion of ESD as indoctrination, see Wals and Jickling (2002) and Jickling (2003). In contrast, Arbuthnott (2009) argues for ESD to support behavioural change more directly through specific mechanisms.

41 According to Parvis and Paterson (2008), this form of blogging has been found to enhance face-to-face teaching and discussion and it allows students to develop new skills while also gaining the core skill of close textual analysis in an innovative form.

Chapter 13

Sustaining Communities: Sustainability in the Social Work Curriculum

Andrew Whiteford, Viv Horton, Diane Garrard, Deirdre Ford and Avril Butler

Introduction

In this chapter, we offer a perspective on potentially transformative social work education that is responsive to the particular time and place in which our teaching is situated. One of the defining features of social work is its concern for the individual: their immediate needs and capacities in their unique social, geographical, economic and cultural environment. However, this individual focus is critiqued as encouraging a depoliticizing, even pathologizing, response to problems exacerbated by poverty, social exclusion and limited life chances. We therefore argue, in contrast, that the focus on the individual, the local and the uniqueness of each situation is social work's particular strength, in that it works with the local manifestations of global issues and has the capacity to support micro-level solutions that may be capable of macro-level impact. We celebrate the political nature of the personal and offer individual and community social work as powerful catalysts for sustainable development.

We situate our teaching within the serious global environmental challenges that already affect much of the world's population; a review of the literature indicates that this is a relatively new area for social work in the UK. In this chapter, we take a particular view of the meaning of environment that extends beyond psychosocial concerns to our relationship with the natural world (McKinnon, 2008, p256) and the necessity of teaching social work that is both responsive and sustainable at all levels. We define sustainability in a way that encompasses ecological factors such as climate change, and also consider the more subtle meaning of education or learning that is self-generative. In this way, we consider what kind of education will equip social workers to continue to be resource-rich professionals in an increasingly challenging environment for practice.

In order to prepare graduates for these demands, we employ a variety of methods where message and medium are congruent. Students are placed in situations that provoke 'disorientating dilemmas', but in a supportive and explicitly political structure (Jones, 2002, p4).

The chapter provides examples of teaching practices that illustrate the potential to reconsider existing theoretical frameworks, practice theories and models in the light of an imperative to work politically and in capacity-building ways. Each example has been developed within existing conventional academic structures and offers insight into the power of pedagogic innovation. We show that the use of transformative educational models for engaged teaching can effect significant change in both the content and quality of student learning.

What the literature tells us about sustainability and social work

For a definition of sustainability, Marlow and van Rooyen refer to Gilman (1990), who suggests that it involves 'developing human systems, technologies and lifestyles that can provide high quality and environmentally benign ways of life for all of humankind, now and many generations into the future' (cited in Marlow and van Rooyen, 2001, p242). To develop the concept in social work theory and practice, McKinnon (2008, p264) draws on the work of McKenzie (2004) to examine the 'interdependence of social, economic and environmental systems'. McKinnon calls for a new emphasis on 'social sustainability' that promotes healthy communities characterized by diversity, equity, active citizenship and intergenerational processes that can maintain these conditions (McKinnon, 2008, p265).

The widespread view of social work in the UK is unlikely to link its practice to sustainability, however (Thompson, 2000, p6). Social workers are called in when individuals have difficulty in managing their day-to-day lives. They respond when physical or emotional difficulties, loss or trauma, poverty and social isolation leave individuals, families and communities vulnerable, in need of support and protection. This view remains unchallenged by professional perspectives because of the contested nature of the definition of social work in the profession itself (Barnes and Hugman, 2002, p277). This diversity and lack of agreement in the profession may also be due to the inclusive nature of social work education as transdisciplinary. There are no limits to the disciplines that social work may draw on and so it is well placed to respond to research about climate change emerging from the natural sciences, for example, and to contribute to debates surrounding climate change and sustainability. The International Federation of Social Workers, for instance:

recognises that the natural and built environments have a direct impact on people's potential to develop and achieve their potential, that the earth's resources should be shared in a sustainable way. [It] calls on social workers and their representative bodies to recognise the importance of the natural and built environment to the social environment, to develop environmental responsibility and care for the environment in social work practice … to ensure that environmental issues gain increased presence in social work education (International Federation of Social Workers, undated).

Yet, as McKinnon (2008, p258) notes, English language articles on these subjects are largely authored by a small number of North American writers, while social work literature in the UK especially has been relatively slow to respond to this challenge. It might be conjectured that this is due in no small measure to the fact that, in general, prosperity in the UK has largely cushioned society against the impact of climate change. Moreover, a preoccupation with the individual in both health and social care has led to an undermining of collectivist approaches and a blinkered view that ignores the effects of climate change on some domestic groups and communities. The British Association of Social Workers (BASW) does make reference to the environment as a factor in the pursuit of social justice, in that 'social development and environmental management [are] in the interests of present and future human welfare' (BASW, 2002, p3), but to date has not engaged with the international debates surrounding climate change and social work practice.

In the UK, social workers mostly respond to people in difficulty by drawing on government resources to provide services intended to fix the problems. Issues publicly recognized as being the remit of social workers include supporting older people to remain independent, assessing the safety of children to remain with their families, providing community support and inclusion for people with mental health difficulties. However, demographic and economic shifts place increasing pressure on services that are unable to keep up with demand. Thus practitioners find themselves being forced to gate-keep diminishing resources, reviewing people's needs against ever-narrowing eligibility criteria with the inevitable consequence of reducing services (Tanner, 2003, p510). For example, people registered blind who had been receiving a domiciliary service to clean their homes following assessment under section 47 of the National Health Service and Community Care Act 1990 were reassessed and the service removed. This was not because people's capabilities had improved but because the cleaning service was no longer deemed to be an essential part of services to be provided (*In Touch*, 2008). Social workers find themselves constantly having to negotiate this narrowing gateway to provide services for people and avert crises that could involve more drastic and costly solutions. The culture of managerialism uses a cloak of evidence-based practice to demand compliance with targets that are imposed, unstable and politically driven (Jordan, 2001, p539). Nevertheless, as authors with a total of over 100 years of practice in the UK between us, we argue that social work offers a rich heritage that can support its professionals to work in conditions of environmental crisis and jeopardized ecosystems.

The impending disaster of climate change, exacerbated by environmental degradation, is well documented, and human services in England have been given glimpses of the scale of the unfolding crisis in Hull (Wainwright, 2008), Tewkesbury (Harris, 2008) and near misses along the east coast (Adam, 2007). Writers such as McKinnon (2008) and Muldoon (2006) have summarized the effects of climate change internationally. In the UK, it is possible to anticipate corresponding difficulties as, globally, populations are uprooted and migrate northwards as environmental refugees. For example, poor health conditions are exacerbated and communities under pressure experience rising crime rates. At present, however, relatively little attention is paid to the implications of environmental challenges for social work practice and there is scant evidence to suggest that the sustainability focus and approaches outlined in this chapter are mirrored elsewhere in the UK.

The people with whom social workers are mostly concerned are those who live in poverty. In the UK they pay the highest prices for utilities, as evidenced by the significantly higher cost of gas or electricity through pre-payment meters as compared to direct debit schemes (Riley, 2008). The rising cost of fuel, food and the insecurity of housing are affecting a larger section of the community and the poorest most severely (Johnson et al, 2008). It would seem that the government's response to the pressure on people's financial security and the potential increase in crime is to invest in building more and larger prisons (Bawden, 2008); this is in spite of the fact that England and Wales already have the highest rate of imprisonment in western Europe (Coyle, 2007, p14). It is clear, therefore, that we cannot continue to look to government to provide solutions to the social pressures that will result from peak oil and economic and climate change. Social workers are increasingly arriving empty-handed to individuals in need because the government resources are no longer available to draw on (Tanner, 2003, p500).

As educators, we are acutely conscious of the need to equip future professionals to look beyond local and national government for resources. This chapter describes some of the approaches we use to develop students' awareness of the potential for positive action by individuals and communities. Through these initiatives, we aim to promote a sustainable orientation in responding to the problems individuals have in their daily lives.

It is important to remember that social work has a rich legacy in supporting transformative intentions of this kind. Community-oriented social work was indeed a feature of 19th century settlements and community social work gained approbation through the report of the Barclay Committee, charged in 1980 by the government to inquire about the role and tasks of social workers (Stepney and Popple, 2008). The decline of community social work, however, was hastened by the ascendancy of managerialism and the conditions of modernity (Coates, 2003), so that contemporary practice focuses on individual casework rather than on community initiatives (Ungar, 2002). Muldoon is one of many writers who in arguing for ecological justice highlight the 'interdependence of community and ecology' (Muldoon, 2006, p2). Social work theory and practice have sought to integrate ecological principles (Jack, 1997) that offer potential for deep connections to be made.

Recommendations from the literature regarding sustainability can be divided into three categories: imperatives for social work education and training, implications for practising social workers and further research. Inevitably there are overlaps between the three. Here, our primary focus is on social work education, and writers' observations are wide-ranging, from 'a clear focus on social sustainability' in the curriculum (McKinnon, 2008 p257) to arranging student social work practice in 'environmental settings' (Muldoon, 2006, p5). The case studies presented later in the chapter give examples of how this might be achieved.

A number of authors assert that social work training should incorporate environmental issues in a variety of ways. These include 'making links between social and environmental justice' (McKinnon, 2008, p257) and exploring practice theories for their potential to inform 'environmentally effective social work practice' (Marlow and van Rooyen, 2001, p252). It is argued that not only should the ecological model be subject to further scrutiny but that other practice theories should be critiqued to broaden the practice paradigm (Muldoon, 2006, p4). Clear links will need to be made between society and the environment and the impact of modernity. Teaching a curriculum that is oriented towards environmental sustainability is proposed, which, for instance, would include dealing with the effects of environmental disasters (Muldoon, 2006, p5).

Practising social workers will need to have far wider roles than they do at present, including working with local communities on environmental issues such as clean-ups of localities and lobbying on pollutants and toxic waste (Marlow and van Rooyen, 2001). These are some of the ideas that inform our teaching and fieldwork development.

Our response

As authors, two of us are practice learning managers (or 'fieldwork educators') responsible for students' fieldwork throughout their study, while three of us are lecturers in social work. We work at Plymouth University, serving both urban and rural populations across the region. The practice described below takes place in a variety of locations to reflect the profile of the South West. The university supports two professional social work programmes, one at undergraduate and one at postgraduate level. What follows are three case studies of teaching and learning practices that illustrate the way we have sought to put our ideas into educational practice. The first describes a change to classroom-based teaching introduced a few years ago and now extended to second-year cohorts. The second case study outlines a community development approach to practice learning or fieldwork that is increasingly focused on education for sustainability. The third case study details an overseas placement opportunity for students, the aim of which is to promote global awareness. All three examples demonstrate how it is possible to apply sustainability-oriented methods in practice under existing programme and module structures.

Case study one: A pedagogic approach

The first year Foundations for Professional Practice module is a core strand of the undergraduate social work degree mentioned above, which has an annual intake of 100 students. Learners work in small groups of around 15 students with an academic teacher and a practice learning manager (fieldwork educator). Two hours of classroom activity per week are complemented by 40 days of learning in practice. This module carries the principal tasks of developing critical reflection, awareness of social injustices, professional identity and academic skills. Initially, sessions were framed by a detailed teacher guide, which ensured that the same programme of activities was followed in every group at the same time. Teacher dissatisfaction with this and a change of module leader presented an opportunity to develop the teaching practice from one of 'transmission' (giving information) or 'transaction' (exercises in which the teacher controls the intended learning outcome) to 'transformation' (in which new knowledge is constructed by learners and teachers together) (Miller, 2007, p11).

The principles that underpin the module are: an organic rather than linear curriculum structure; modelling engaged practice; working with strengths, and seeking and maximizing connections; the importance of reflection; and affirming the political nature of social work.

It is challenging to combine teaching that is responsive to current issues and trends with the demands of a curriculum and formal learning outcomes. In this module, a series of themes are specified that permit clear links to be made between practice and the environment and the impact of modernity. Each theme has four or five objectives articulated for it and lasts three weeks. The themes are as follows: developing the framework for learning; understanding groups and how to work in them; being a skilled learner; seeking and using feedback; interacting with the public; what is social work?; social justice; and critical reflection and identity. Themes are inter-linked, and this encourages groups to explore issues in different ways according to members' experience, strengths and learning needs. Critical incidents from practice or other experiences are brought to class when they are helpful to illustrate and promote learning. In this way the syllabus is taught in response to student experience rather than imposed through a teacher-led structure.

Social work education in England is bound by professional requirements and national occupational standards (DH, 2002; Training Organisation for Personal Social Services, 2002). Practice assessment throughout the programme is mapped to these standards and maintains an holistic approach in which multiple accounts are used to assess student performance as a whole rather than using a mechanistic, tick-box approach. This holistic approach enables students both to meet standards and to work in conditions of complexity. It gives them the confidence to work with professional integrity while remaining fully accountable.

This design assumes an engaged orientation to teaching (Askeland, 2006) that models the professional practice behaviours we are seeking to promote. Teachers are encouraged to use an interactive approach that combines exercises, readings, reflection on practice, input and role-play. This is to support *constructive* learning, rather than an approach symbolized by Freire's notion of the *banking* concept of education in which the teacher imparts knowledge to (or in the banking metaphor, *deposits* it in) students whose own knowledge, experience and skills of inquiry and critical reflection are of no account (Freire, 2000, p72). In contrast here, the combination of action, reflection, theorizing and planning is intended to support students in their development of self-directed learning. While this can produce feelings of anxiety and vulnerability for teachers as knowledge is constructed in the classroom (Fook and Askeland, 2007), it does give students the experience of working in creative and cooperative ways to explore issues and generate possibilities.

Students are recognized as resourceful people in transition (Butler, 2005) and are expected to bring their experience, knowledge and skills to enrich the wider group. This models an approach that works with strengths to draw on the diversity of social, economic and political backgrounds of students, permitting and encouraging connections to be made between difficulties experienced by individuals, local and national developments and global issues. Learning for students becomes a process of discovering the connections between environmental challenges and personal actions: for example, they are supported to question people's wishes for an improved *standard of living* to reframe expectations and enhance their *quality of life*.

Reflection is widely acknowledged to be an important aspect of professional learning. As a demonstration of the value we place on it, at least 15 minutes per session is devoted to students writing reflectively in their learning logs. The content of these is confidential to the student so as to encourage honesty in reflection. Teachers remain with the group during this time and undertake their own reflection.

In this teaching environment, the teacher's position cannot be neutral. We are required to be open about our own convictions whilst modelling that these are not fixed but emerging ideas. Social work is a situated and political activity requiring a critical position that seeks positive and sustainable solutions through action by individuals and communities. By the second term of the first year, the structure of classes is developed in collaboration with students and draws on their learning in practice. Explicit reference to diversity and values is integrated throughout, as is a developing emphasis on the relevance of globalization and sustainability to social work. Teachers and students use existing material and generate new resources for teaching as the year progresses. A team approach is promoted through regular meetings, in which individuals are encouraged to share materials and make them available to others. Through the module, we aim to promote transformative learning (Mezirow, 1995) and contribute to the wider goal of social transformation. As Jones (2002, p7) argues, the process demands a conscious pedagogy that places students in situations that:

- make explicit the process and goals of learning;
- intentionally create disorientating dilemmas for students;

- provide support for critical reflection;
- communicate the teachers' commitment to the wider purpose of social transformation.

All the changes identified have been possible without altering the module outline or the assessment. The fundamental change has been a change of principle and approach within existing frameworks (Kagawa and Butler, forthcoming). A similar development has informed a module in the second year and the responses from staff and students alike are positive.

Case study two: Practice learning

Before students can move into the second year, their readiness for social work practice is assessed. This is achieved through the Foundations for Professional Practice module described above. The practice learning then consists of a combination of individual work (Social Care Work Experience), where student responsibility is similar to that of a new volunteer, and group work (Community Development Project, or 'CDP').

All practice learning in the first year is in the voluntary and independent sector. This is to enable students to experience the enormous strength and resourcefulness of individuals and communities at a time when so many state services are being restructured and reduced. Students are encouraged to make the most of their own strengths and attributes while being helped to recognize the resources and potential of groups and individuals with whom they come into contact. Thus students have an opportunity to make a real contribution to people's lives through this period of practice learning.

The purpose of this practice learning in order of priority, therefore, is:

- to be of service to individuals and groups in the community;
- to learn and develop foundation skills for social work practice;
- to generate evidence for assessment.

The CDP

As stated, the degree programme is committed to a transformative approach to social work education that opens up possibilities for students, through their practice and in their lives, to advocate for sustainability in partnership with the communities in which they work and live.

Social work has a long-standing commitment to social justice and community development (Stepney and Popple 2008). While this has primarily been located in a social science rather than an environmental paradigm, social work has a strong tradition of working with the most marginalized and excluded individuals and communities, where the consequences of environmental degradation, climate change and globalization are experienced first and most harshly (Muldoon, 2006, p1). Services, support and development in these situations are increasingly being provided by community groups and voluntary agencies. These organizations are mostly small and under-resourced, run by service users, carers and committed individuals. A commitment to social justice has been the main driver in developing practice learning with a sustainability focus while also introducing and restoring community development principles to mainstream practice through student learning in, and for, practice.

It is becoming increasingly clear that social sustainability depends on broader ecological sustainability, and that ecological sustainability is equally dependent on social sustainability (Cook, 2004, p45). Social work's combination of values, knowledge and skills make it well placed to work with the interconnections between people and the environment, where the consequences of fracture and the potential for regenerating this interdependence is increasingly encountered. This learning context can be a resource in terms of continued collaborative projects, community-led initiatives and the broader greening of society.

Agencies respond to the programme's advertisement of students as a resource by offering projects for groups of three or four students to undertake. In return for the students' work, the agency provides a supervisor who oversees the work, supports students and gives them feedback to help their learning. The outcome of the work, including reports, is the property of the agency rather than the degree programme, while what the students have learned from the experience is assessed as part of the overall module.

CDPs in 2007–2008 were selected on the basis of their potential to help students explore sustainability and social justice by working across social networks. Examples of successful CDPs include: a feasibility study resulting in the establishment of a city food bank; the construction of a cob shelter for and with young people as their meeting place in a rural town; and the creation of a welcome pack for people seeking asylum in the UK and dispersed to Plymouth.[1] At the time of writing, CDPs are in place to develop sustainability-focused settings where there are particular concerns for the links between food production and supply. These include establishing a new allotment site, widening participation in existing allotments and exploring ways of promoting access to both urban and rural green spaces. Another example involves a permaculture teacher supervising a group of students who enable city residents to grow food in their own and surrounding public spaces.

The sustainability dimensions of projects are initially unclear to some students and moving from task-oriented to process-oriented learning proves to be a challenge. Viewing social work practice in the context of change-agency for sustainability is an emergent and at times difficult process (Blake, forthcoming). These factors clearly illustrate that learning for and about sustainability is an ongoing social learning process that is active, participatory and reflective, and not solely about awareness-raising (Tilbury, 2007, p120).

Case study three: Uganda placements

International placements are known to provide powerful and transformative learning opportunities for students from a wide range of disciplines (Shoughee, 1998, p56) and involve both tutor-led and independent (volunteering) experiences. Traditionally, these placements require high individual investment and a willingness to work outside conventional structures (O'Loughlin, 2007; Heron, 2005). In social work, there is little written from a UK perspective, although the rationale and benefits are clearly articulated elsewhere (Engstrom and Jones, 2007; Larson and Allen, 2006).

Social work education should raise awareness of international concerns for social justice and human rights. International placements in the majority world (the term used in preference to 'third world' or 'developing world'; see Thibeault, 2006, p159) offer rich learning opportunities for students in HE (JISC infoNet, 2009), and increasingly, students expect our own programmes to incorporate a global dimension.

In 2006, a group of first-year social work students undertook a CDP based in a local global education centre that examined the feasibility of setting up international practice learning opportunities, focusing their research on Uganda where the centre already had established links. Their findings strongly supported the relevance and desirability of such placements for students learning to practise in a rapidly globalizing world (Banwell, Hayes and Slee, 2006). Their work was followed up with a visit to Uganda by one of the authors, a practice learning manager, to explore and negotiate placement opportunities and potential academic partnerships. Five placements were identified, two in a residential training centre for young women affected by war in a post-conflict region in the north and three in a hospice in Kampala, the capital city.

The placements lasted six weeks early in the summer vacation. This allowed time for students to readjust and rest before the beginning of the new term in September. Students raised their own funds to participate, extending existing student loans, doing part-time work and seeking sponsorship.

In-country support and supervision was provided by the practice learning manager. Each student was assessed through direct observation of practice following normal programme practice guidelines, which garnered a wide range of feedback from practice supervisors, service users and other professionals.

Students' self-assessment, feedback and formal assessment demonstrated significant learning, as shown in Table 13.1.

While by no means exhaustive, this range and depth of learning held true for all students involved. In addition, they demonstrated considerable personal

Table 13.1 *Student learning derived from placements in Uganda*

Managing uncertainty	Identity – being stereotyped and in a visible minority
Reflexive practice; responding to emergent needs, and situations	Gender inequality and violence – how entrenched social attitudes undermine progress, particularly in relation to women's education and health
Recognizing the importance of planned endings	Physical and socio-economic effects of long-term war; strategies for conflict resolution at local, national and international level
Challenging established ideas and attitudes constructively	Development and international relations

growth and development from their individual experiences of travelling and living in a different country and culture in the majority world.

On their return, the students' learning has been widely and effectively disseminated through formal and informal mechanisms:

- Joining an international panel discussion with overseas practitioners working in Plymouth as a teaching session for social work students to promote international perspectives.
- Contributing to a global social work steering group set up to inform social work degree programmes in Plymouth about the community of the profession worldwide.
- Enriching group learning and academic teaching.
- Sharing experience with friends and colleagues, raising awareness of global issues and encouraging others to take up international opportunities.

A significant and valuable impact of the Uganda placements has been to highlight specific global themes and issues that interconnect and are the necessary concern of social work wherever it is practised, notably poverty, food production, climate change, sustainable practices and health.

While it is not essential for students to have such first-hand experience to engage with global issues, there is growing evidence to suggest that direct involvement can trigger a longer-term commitment to global activism (Green, 2008, p16). For example, concern with the £8 billion cost of food wasted in Britain each year (WRAP, 2008) is likely to be different if considered against an understanding of the impact of climate change on those countries where a significant proportion of the population live by subsistence farming. A realistic grasp of how degraded environments, high risks to health and extreme poverty limit life opportunities in the majority world is vital when considering the practice implications of global social justice. It also takes on Muldoon's argument for ecological justice (Muldoon, 2006, p1). This alternative comprehension is requisite to critical appraisal of the distorted picture provided by under-reporting, sensationalism and sentimentalism in the mass media. It is consistent with the concept of *conscientization*, which encourages the development of critical awareness or consciousness of reality through processes of dialogue, reflection and action (Freire, 2000, p35).

Through international fieldwork, social work students are exposed to models of development that use self-help and micro-credit, honed in parts of the majority world. These can offer readily transferable tools to equip them to be resource-rich professionals in the increasingly challenging environments in the west. The impact of the recent financial collapse is creating circumstances that urgently require such innovative solutions.

The placement opportunities stemmed from, and were sustained by, the initiative of students and their enthusiasm for learning. As outlined in Table 13.1, learning was achieved at micro (interpersonal) and macro (policy) levels. Students were faced with settings in which the social work role was not defined and they needed time to explore and identify a valid role rather than trying to fit what they found into a prescribed mode of intervention. They were encouraged to be creative, responding to the situations of human need before them rather than working to state-imposed bureaucracy and tasks, while discovering what social work has to offer. As state welfare recedes, this process increasingly mirrors the one in which students find themselves in the UK. A Zimbabwean social worker employed in Birmingham, however, observed:

At times people find it very difficult to think that someone coming from a third world country could actually bring some knowledge and input that might help. There was marginalization of ideas (Devo, 2006, p13).

In contrast, we argue that the integration of knowledge gained in the majority world through internationalization of curricula will inform the development of sustainable practice.

On the eve of his presidency of the International Federation of Social Workers, David Jones stated:

We need to connect social work with that basic humanitarian concern with helping and supporting people in need, and doing that globally is important for the national as well as the international agenda (Jones, 2006).

This chimes with our own experience, shared by students, that on returning to the UK it was the material excess and degradation of humanity in the west that truly shocked. In the face of accelerating globalization, social work education fails if it does no more than equip students for the narrowing remit of statutory bureaucracies.

At the time of writing, over 30 per cent of new entrants to the social work profession in the UK come from overseas, many from the global south, and UK social workers are increasingly going abroad to work. In UK HE, wider international experience is supported and encouraged and may be accepted as part of students' fieldwork.

Inevitably, concerns arise about international student mobility involving unsustainable modes of transport, notably aviation; this is incontrovertible (Bows et al, 2006). It could be argued, however, that this is a comparatively small footprint for a substantial outcome. The experience of an overseas placement can seed a lifetime of activism, setting in place changes in participants' attitude and behaviour that significantly influence their wider community of students, families and friends. Our experience has been that students return with a critical understanding of consumerism and global justice – put simply, about differentials between the *haves* and *have-nots*. Some returning students work to strengthen relationships with their host country organizations that build capacity and benefit local communities. With a changed awareness of their own privileges, students enter into a long-term engagement with the relevant issues; some have gone back to host countries after graduation for a protracted period of voluntary work and service.

Policy and process in the faculty currently support a range of students of different disciplines to undertake part of their fieldwork overseas, and at the time of writing plans are being made to enable Ugandan students to participate in reciprocal arrangements in the UK.

Conclusion: Learning for the future

This chapter has set out the authors' perceptions of the connections between sustainability and social work, giving examples of HE curricula and teaching practices to illustrate our position. These case studies show that it is possible to meet the national professional requirements for social work while concurrently promoting global and sustainable practices through education. Attention is paid equally to content, process and reflection as key elements in learning that together demand openness on the part of teaching staff to look for connections between ideas and to cross disciplinary boundaries. Social work has always been transdisciplinary and applied, and so many of the concepts and metaphors of sustainability have utility for social work practice. These metaphors of complex and diverse systems in which elements are mutually dependent, organic processes are sensitive to change and slow growth needs extended time scales contrast with short-term initiatives and responses that seek a quick fix, as favoured by the UK Government.

Education for social work needs to emphasize interconnections and ownership by everyone of the problems and the possible solutions. We recognize that social work is historically and contextually constructed and that knowledge and practice has to evolve to meet the demands of current conditions. Our understanding and teaching must be of causes and politics, not just social phenomena and individual reactions.

As teachers we seek to maintain our own openness to learning, recognizing that service users, students and practitioners are our allies in knowledge creation. Reliance on didactic methods alone will equip students for a world that no longer exists, and so knowledge should be shared in an environment that is reflective, challenging and constructive. Our case studies show what is possible in a traditional modular programme framework. Holistic models of teaching and assessment are recommended for practitioners who need to be able to work within policies and procedures proactively when responding to human distress. We emphasize the importance of communication skills, networking, negotiation and alliance-building, seeking solidarity with students and service users, with the wider purpose of achieving social, environmental and global justice.

References

Adam, D. (2007) 'Exceptional tidal surge puts east coast on emergency alert', *The Guardian*, 9 November, available at www.guardian.co.uk/uk/2007/nov/09/weather.world6, accessed 16 February 2009

Askeland, G.A. (2006) 'Turning a facilitator's critical incident into student learning', *Practice*, vol 18, no 2, pp103–116

Banwell, N., Hayes, L. and Slee, M. (2006) 'Social care work experience in Uganda', BSc undergraduate presentation, University of Plymouth

Barnes, D. and Hugman, R. (2002) 'Portrait of social work', *Journal of Interprofessional Care*, vol 16, no 3, pp277–288

BASW (2002) *The Code of Ethics for Social Workers*, BASW, Birmingham

Bawden, A. (2008) 'Time for a rethink on Titan jails?', *The Guardian*, 3 October, available at www.guardian.co.uk/society/2008/oct/03/titan.prisons.rehabilitation, accessed 16 February 2009

Blake, J. (forthcoming) *Sustainable Communities and Social Work Education: Reflections on Emergent, Learning Partnerships*

Bows, A., Anderson, K. and Upham, P. (2006) *Contraction & Convergence: UK Carbon Emissions and the Implications for UK Air Traffic*, Technical Report 40, Tyndall Centre for Climate Change Research

Butler, A. (2005) 'A strengths approach to building futures: UK students and refugees together', *Community Development Journal*, vol 40, no 2, pp147–157

Coates, J. (2003) 'Exploring the roots of environmental crisis: Opportunity for social transformation', *Critical Social Work*, vol 4, no 1, pp44–66

Cook, R. (2004) *The Natural Step: Towards a Sustainable Society*, Green Books, Dartington

Coyle, A. (2007) 'Does custodial sentencing work?', *Prison Service Journal*, vol 171, pp13–15

Devo, J. (2006) 'Out of Africa and into Birmingham', *Professional Social Work*, pp12–13, August

DH (2002) *Requirements for Social Work Training*, DH, London

Engstrom, D. and Jones, L.P. (2007) 'A broadened horizon: The value of international social work internships', *Social Work Education*, vol 26, no 2, pp136–150

Fook, J. and Askeland, A. (2007) 'Challenges of critical reflection: "Nothing ventured, nothing gained"', *Social Work Education*, vol 26, no 5, pp520–533

Freire, P. (2000) *Pedagogy of the Oppressed*, Continuum Books, New York NY

Gilman, R. (1990) 'Sustainability: The State of the movement', in *Context*, Spring, pp10–12

Green, C. (2008) *Learning that Global Rent is Due*, MSc thesis, University of Glasgow

Harris, J. (2008) 'Flooding: Once more unto the breach', *The Guardian*, 26 July, available at www.guardian.co.uk/environment/2008/jul/26/flooding.pollution, accessed 16 February 2009

Heron, B. (2005) 'Changes and challenges: Preparing social work students for practicums in today's sub-Saharan African context', *International Social Work*, vol 48, no 6, pp782–793

International Federation of Social Workers (undated) *International Policy Statement on Globalisation and the Environment*, available at www.ifsw.org/p38000222.html, accessed 5 February 2010

In Touch (2008) Transcript of radio broadcast, BBC Radio 4, 29 January, available at www.bbc.co.uk/radio4/factual/intouch_20080129.shtml#transcript, accessed 16 February 2009

Jack, G. (1997) 'An ecological approach to social work with children and families', *Child and Family Social Work*, vol 2, pp109–120

JISC infoNet (2009) 'Internationalisation', *JISC infoNet*, available at www.jiscinfonet.ac.uk/strategy-planning/challenges/internationalisation, accessed 16 February 2009

Johnson, V., Simms, A. and Cochrane, C. (2008) *Tackling Climate Change, Reducing Poverty: The First Report of the Roundtable on Climate Change and Poverty in the UK*, New Economic Foundation, London

Jones, D.N. (2006) 'David N Jones on the role of the International Federation of Social Workers', Interview with Valios, N., *Community Care*, 20 July, available at www.communitycare.co.uk/Articles/2006/07/20/55025/david-n-jones-on-the-role-of-the-international-federation-of-social.html, accessed 16 February 2009

Jones, P. (2002) *Education for Change: Transformative Learning and Progressive Social Work Education*, Higher Education Research and Development Society of Australasia

Jordan, B. (2001) 'Tough love: Social work, social exclusion and the Third Way', *British Journal of Social Work*, vol 31, no 4, pp527–546

Kagawa, F. and Butler, A. (forthcoming) *Pedagogies for Personal Transformation*

Larson, G. and Allen, H. (2006) 'Conscientization – The experience of Canadian social work students in Mexico', *International Social Work*, vol 49, no 4, pp507–518

Marlow, C. and van Rooyen, C. (2001) 'How green is the environment in social work?' *International Social Work*, vol 44, no 2, pp241–254

McKenzie, S. (2004) 'Social sustainability: Towards some definitions', Hawke Research Institute, Working Paper Series, no 27

McKinnon, J. (2008) 'Exploring the nexus between social work and the environment', *Australian Social Work*, vol 61, no 3, pp256–268

Mezirow, J. (1995) 'Transformation theory of adult learning', in Welton, M. (ed), *In Defense of the Lifeworld*, SUNY Press, New York NY

Miller, J. (2007) *The Holistic Curriculum* (2nd ed), University of Toronto Press, Toronto

Muldoon, A. (2006) 'Environmental efforts: The next challenge for social work', *Critical Social Work*, vol 7, no 2, pp1–7, available at www.criticalsocialwork.com/units/socialwork/critical.nsf/982f0e5f06b5c9a285256d6e006cff78/5882c9990dfda1e18525727700 2bd457?OpenDocument, accessed 5 February 2010

O'Loughlin, S. (2007) 'A South African placement', *Community Care*, 5–11 April pp32–33

Riley, A. (2008) 'NHF urges government action on prepayment fuel charges', *Community Care*, 23 September, available at www.communitycare.co.uk/Articles/2008/09/23/109512/nhf-attacks-1.35bn-fuel-penalty-for-prepayment-meter-customers.html, accessed 16 February 2009

Shoughee, M. (1998) *The Experiences, Meanings and Outcomes of Studying Abroad: A Qualitative Multiple-case Study*, PhD thesis, University of Toronto

Stepney, P. and Popple, K. (2008) *Social Work and the Community: A Critical Context for Practice*, Palgrave Macmillan, Basingstoke

Tanner, D. (2003) 'Older people and access to care', *British Journal of Social Work*, vol 33, pp499–515

Thompson, N. (2000) *Understanding Social Work: Preparing for Practice*, Palgrave Macmillan, Basingstoke

Thibeault, R. (2006) 'Globalisation, universities and the future of occupational therapy: Dispatches for the majority world', *Australian Occupational Therapy Journal*, vol 53, no 3

Tilbury, D. (2007) 'Learning-based change for sustainability: Perspectives and pathways', in Wals, A.E.J. (ed), *Social Learning Towards a Sustainable World*, Wageningen Academic Publishers, Wageningen

Training Organisation for Personal Social Services (2002) *The National Occupational Standards for Social Work*, TOPSS England, Leeds

Ungar, M. (2002) 'A deeper, more social ecological social work practice', *Social Services Review*, vol 76, no 3, pp480–497

Wainwright, M. (2008) 'Christmas is cancelled for Hull flood victims still waiting for a dry home', *The Guardian*, 24 December, available at www.guardian.co.uk/environment/2008/dec/24/hull-floods-christmas, accessed 16 February 2009

WRAP (2008) www.wrap.org.uk accessed 16 February 2009

Notes

1   For further information on this last project, please visit www.studentsandrefugeestogether.com (accessed 5 February 2010).

Chapter 14

Sustainability and Built Environment Professionals: A Shifting Paradigm

Judi Farren Bradley, Sarah Sayce and Amanda Lewis

Introduction

The importance of the built environment to society places a high level of responsibility on those professionals who plan, design, construct, manage and maintain that environment. The disciplines considered in this chapter include those of architecture, construction, landscape architecture, town and country planning, real estate, building and quantity surveying and urban design. In the UK, the majority of these have their own chartered professional institutions[1] and/or other regulatory bodies maintaining varying levels and forms of control over their educational programmes. They also monitor and regulate the performance of members and place considerable emphasis on ethical standards and the protection of the public interest. While graduates from engineering are an integral part of the professional teams that deliver and maintain our built environment, and are often co-located with other built environment courses at universities, this chapter focuses on those who envision, plan, detail, deliver, maintain and financially evaluate the physical fabric that provides both the envelope for the economy and the individual and intimate spaces we call home.

In the light of this, the chapter will cover current developments and future initiatives in built environment education in the UK, by exploring the influences on HEIs. It will appraise the ways in which graduates are being prepared to meet the challenge of building a sustainable future through the four stages at which sustainability is perceived to be advanced.

The construction industry receives extensive government attention in the UK (Banwell, 1964; Latham, 1994; Egan, 1998; Rogers, 1999). On average, 30 per cent of the industry's output involves government expenditure, it constitutes 10 per cent of gross domestic product (GDP) and in 2007 the export income for consultancy alone accounted for £1.2 billion. Several of the professional groups are also closely allied to other important sectors. Design professionals are included as part of the fastest-growing sector of the economy – the creative industries – and others, namely the valuers and real estate appraisers, form part of the financial sector – a very significant contributor to GDP, especially in the South East of England. As reported recently (Built Environment Strategic Alliance, 2009), construction and the built environment will continue to be critically important to the economy moving forward despite showing vulnerability during the economic downturn at the time of writing (Office for National Statistics, 2009).

Built environment professionals are required to respond to a plethora of policies, initiatives and changes in legislation. Since 1987 and the publication of the Brundtland Report (WCED, 1987), the majority of these fall under the widely used definition of sustainability – the triple bottom line of environmental, social and economic considerations. Policies on environmental protection and energy efficiency have been transformed into policies and targets devised in response to climate change and energy security. Action in relation to the built environment, which is cited as being responsible for 50 per cent of CO_2 emissions (UNEP, 2007), is crucial if the UK is to meet its targets for carbon reduction.

More recently, the emphasis in built environment practice has been refocused to incorporate matters of social well-being and wider concepts of value. Rogers (1999) provided a vision of urban regeneration that included social well-being, design quality and long-term sustainability. Policies to encourage brownfield development, promote mixed-use development and increase the density of new developments have now been introduced. Post-war planning policies for reconstruction and new town development have therefore evolved into regeneration policies, only to be revised again to address the need for sustainable communities (Office of the Deputy Prime Minister, 2003) and community cohesion, including proposals for Eco-towns. Based on local engagement with the planning, development and management processes, these demand new skill sets and participatory modes of working (Department of Communities and Local Government, 2008). However, despite the best endeavours of public policy, the most intractable problems have been encountered in the area of economic sustainability and the creation of business models that truly promote sustainability. Strategies are needed for new development and for the management of the 98 per cent of UK housing stock that predates current environmental standards (Association for the Conservation of Energy, 2007; Poel et al, 2007). The challenge includes developing selective and timely adaptation measures and appropriate upgrading so as to recognize our existing built environment as a significant material asset and ensure its continued role as part of the cultural heritage, giving character and significance to the places in which we live and work.

The critical realization in government and the professions is that an interdisciplinary approach to providing sustainable solutions is essential to making progress (Rogers, 1999). However, it has been widely acknowledged that built environment education has traditionally been founded on a silo mentality, which emphasizes competition and division between the contributing professions (Spence et al, 2001). This is the context in which the Centre for Sustainable Communities Achieved through Integrated Professional Education (C-SCAIPE) emerged, being one of 74 Centres of Excellence in Teaching and Learning (CETLs) funded by the HEFCE in 2005 (HEFCE, 2005; Gough and Scott, 2007, p51). As one of only two CETLs that specifically embody the principles of sustainability (the other being the CSF at the University of Plymouth; see p7), it can be regarded as an important educational response. It is also the only CETL that focuses on the relationship between sustainability and the built environment, actively working across disciplines and encouraging an exchange of ideas, embracing a multidisciplinary, inter-professional perspective through a variety of innovative teaching and learning initiatives.

Influences on HEIs

As professionally accredited and predominantly vocational courses, built environment programmes have a strong need to respond to external influences through the reframing of curricula so as to produce graduates equipped to work in an evolving and challenging context. Strong links with the professional bodies, reinforced through the use of practitioners to deliver and support subject areas, should ensure that graduate entrants to the professions are appropriately equipped. Further, many departments have strong industry-based research and consultancy, operating at the forefront of the discipline. Nonetheless, recent high-profile reports (e.g. Egan, 2004; Academy for Sustainable Communities [ASC], 2007) have identified that the skills base in the sector remains insufficient to meet the needs of the new sustainable communities agenda. While much had been done to increase the specialist knowledge base across the field of sustainability, the Egan report identified specific skills as lacking across the built environment professions, and challenged HEIs, professional bodies and continuing professional development providers to fill in the gaps (Egan, 2004).

Subsequently, a more focused report was commissioned by the ASC[2] (ASC, 2007). This study found that, although significant investment and progress had been made by organizations in tackling the issues the skills gaps in the built environment professions were widening, and it anticipated significant labour shortages in areas such as landscape architecture and urban design. The overall conclusion was that multidisciplinary working and the development of common generic skills remains a priority. Despite the job losses at the time of writing, this is likely to be a problem deferred rather than defrayed. More recent work entitled *Enabling Sustainable Communities* (Sayce et al, 2008) finds that not only were graduates seen to lack those skills that are key in terms of stakeholder engagement, but that many practitioners, reflecting on their own practice, acknowledge skill deficiencies. Sayce et al continue by identifying that the skills debate was not always about the acquisition of new skills but rather the reframing and application of existing skills in terms of sustainability to develop new working practices. The primary need is for the development of the attributes that contribute towards facilitation and empathetic practice.

It would be invidious, however, to imply that the relevant degree programmes are newcomers to the concepts and principles of sustainability, as the study and creation of the built environment is about the relationship of humans and nature. It is as much a social and economic act as it is one of applied technologies or asset management. In the first century BC, Vitruvius Pollio wrote *De Architectura*, known more commonly as the *Ten Books of Architecture* (Vitruvius, 1914), as a handbook for designers. Interestingly, the majority of the text deals with the practical problems of harnessing natural resources, land reclamation, sourcing and working with natural materials, city planning and understanding sea-level changes. All of these are issues common to current discussions and can be found in any text on 'green' buildings or the wider debate as to what constitutes SD. House builders are urged to 'take note of the countries and climate in which they are built' (Vitruvius, 1914, book VI, chapter 1, p198). Principles of natural venti-lation, rainwater harvesting, orientation and space are all included. However, such comprehensive capability has been compromised by our highly differentiated and professionally bounded disciplines, fragmenting an holistic approach. The modernist view has been to rely on progressive technical and social development to solve problems that we have created by ill-considered and regrettably short-term design and funding solutions. Partially in response to this, much of the recent research and innovation in learning, teaching and curriculum development has been to break down these professionally engendered divisions, reconfigure and perforate disciplinary boundaries and challenge professional paradigms (McIntosh and Bailey, 2004).

Study of the technical and environmental aspects of achieving SD has been an integral part of design and construction courses for nearly two decades – although, for those programmes of study primarily focused on management and valuation, SD concerns have played little if any part in the debate until very recently. Their dominant concern has been the alignment of building management with financial investment considerations and they have taken their lead from a market that has been reluctant to adopt sustainable practices. Following the Stern Review (2006), which provided clear evidence of the growing understanding of the economic impacts of climate change, all those involved with the built environ-ment have been challenged to devise financial and investment models that reflect the whole-life cost, long-term value and social benefits of what is built. In the same year, the largest built environment professional body, the Royal Institution of Chartered Surveyors (RICS), introduced a requirement that those seeking chartered status must reach a basic level of competence in sustainability as applied to their specific field of practice (RICS, 2006). Although competence in sustainability is assessed as part of the Institution's Assessment of Professional Competence once graduates are in subsequent employment, the requirement has given added impetus for the inclusion of sustainability across all RICS-recognized programmes, both at first degree level and in the increasingly popular postgraduate conversion courses.

A sustainable built environment is about sustainable place-making and there has been a significant shift from land-use planning to spatial planning (Royal Town Planning Institute [RTPI], 2001). The UK Government launched its communities plan with the publication of the *Sustainable Communities* review (Office of the Deputy Prime Minister, 2003), recognizing the importance of planning and spatial design as key to building and maintaining sustainable communities and promoting social cohesion. Subsequently, the independent *Barker Review of Land Use Planning* (2006), which focused on the link between planning and economic growth, emphasized the need for land to be seen as a resource that must be managed to promote economic as well as social and environmental well-being. In July 2009, RTPI launched its seven commitments on climate change, including a commitment to climate change education and skills (RTPI, 2009). The planning profession is recognized as making a major contribution to the knowledge base and stimulating innovative practice – as are the landscape architects, who are represented by the Landscape Institute, and have had sustainability at the forefront of their discipline for many years (Landscape Institute, 2008). These influences are leading to a revitalization of the core built environment curricula and an increasing recognition of the need for the development of new 'hybrid' disciplines.

These developments are not merely responses to government policy and professional pressure. More environmentally aware applicants have added to the pressure to more fully integrate sustainability into all programmes. In two recent surveys (Forum for the Future and UCAS, 2007 and 2008), applicants, students and recent graduates from built environment programmes considered that learning about SD was a key consideration in helping them obtain the job they wanted. The highest score was for applicants to architecture, building and planning courses, 74 per cent of whom stated that evidence of the opportunity to learn about SD was important or very important in helping them choose a course and an institution (Forum for the Future and UCAS, 2007, p17).

A longitudinal study of all surveying students (Cowling et al, 2007) has been undertaken at Kingston University in south London. It looked at students on entry to undergraduate and postgraduate programmes and then again at the point of graduation. The research covered three broad themes in relation to sustainability: interest and perceived importance; awareness and understanding; and behaviour and lifestyle. The respondents were taken from across the surveying disciplines, including real estate management, quantity and building surveying and town planning. The questions were framed in relation to SD as a topic, although when asked specific questions to ascertain their level of 'sustainability literacy' it became evident that there was a consensus that sustainability was important, even though there was a disparity in knowledge and awareness between disciplines and sustainability was understood as being predominantly an 'environmental' issue. The results demonstrate that, with the exception of real estate students, who saw little connection to their subject area, students recognized that sustainability was important to them, their courses and future careers; however, they had little understanding of sustainability from an holistic perspective (that is, one that considers the triple bottom line in all aspects of life).[3]

These findings correlate with an earlier study of the surveying profession, undertaken for the RICS Foundation by Upstream (2004), which showed that there was little evidence of consideration of sustainability during the initial development and investment phases of construction projects. This was despite a widely held recognition that this initial phase was crucial to achieving a sustainable construction project. Further work (Dixon et al, 2007) has also come to a similar conclusion, confirming that HEIs need to ensure that sustainability features more widely in built environment courses, implying that it remains insufficiently embedded.

Taken overall, the picture is moving increasingly towards embedding sustainability. In a recent review (Cade, 2008), built environment students and graduates showed the second highest indication of socially and environmentally responsible studentship, only marginally behind those studying education. In looking across built environment education, it is therefore possible to determine four levels at which sustainability is being addressed:

- Sustainability as *knowledge*.
- Sustainability as *practice*.
- Sustainability as *process*.
- Sustainability as *paradigm*.

Sustainability as knowledge

Environmental sustainability has had a lengthy pedigree, from the work of early environmentalists and the 'green' experiments of the 1960s and 1970s in housing and energy (Farmer 1996), through to the detailed analysis now possible using building information modelling software, the introduction of responsive materials and the development of intelligent building systems. This technical knowledge has tended to dominate the response of the built environment disciplines and has led to sustainability being viewed as something for which there is, or should be, a technological solution (Sayce et al, 2008). With the previous dominance of the environmental agenda over that of the social agenda, the introduction of sustainability onto the curriculum was focused on energy and resource efficiency. Sustainability in the curriculum at this stage was linked primarily to the supply of buildings, not to demand-side factors.

Over time, however, and particularly as the imperative of CSR has permeated the world of business, so a noticeable change has begun to take place. The narrow technical focus has been augmented by a much richer understanding of sustainability across the curriculum. The needs and aspirations of building occupiers and the impact of the built environment on society and the natural environment are under constant review. However, a truly critical understanding of sustainability as a cultural, social and economic phenomenon has been slow to emerge and remains relatively underdeveloped.

As part of research funded by the ASC and the Economic and Social Research Council[4] (Sayce et al, 2008), an analysis of how sustainability was being incorporated across built environment courses was undertaken by creating a matrix of various criteria. One criterion was the QAA subject benchmark statements,[5] while another was the educational requirements set out by the professional bodies at first degree and pre-registration stages. These were mapped against the 13 generic skills required for creating sustainable communities as defined by Egan (2004, pp103–105). Sayce et al confirm that a general knowledge and understanding of sustainability is necessary across academic and professional body requirements and is therefore being delivered, as verified by professional and academic accreditation and validation processes. However, to paraphrase George Bernard Shaw, the professions remain divided by a common language as far as sustainability is concerned. The terminology and the internalization of sustainability in the practice of each specific profession has resulted in everyone apparently saying the same thing but meaning and emphasizing very different things.

The challenge to curriculum providers is that sustainability is both a range of highly specialized knowledge sets and a cross-disciplinary endeavour synthesizing policy frameworks, social governance, ethics and concepts of equity. Few HEIs have the capacity to deliver the type of integrated programmes that are required to address such an holistic agenda. Different faculty and organizational structures favour different synergies and it would be difficult to find any built environment grouping that is fully comprehensive. Student numbers vary dramatically between disciplines: there are currently only 11 providers of landscape architecture programmes in the UK, with an annual graduation of less than 500, whereas surveying and construction courses are significantly larger. Programmes are not readily compatible. The length of study required varies from the minimum of a first degree to the four or five years of full-time academic study or postgraduate equivalent required for landscape architecture, engineering and architecture. The professional pathways are not readily compatible: the varying funding terms for different disciplines and entry points (undergraduate versus graduate) to the professions has previously been raised as a barrier to progress (Lewis et al, 2005). There are an increasing number of programmes jointly accredited by professional bodies such as architectural engineering, architecture and landscape, architecture and planning, and a range of surveying courses recognized by both the Chartered Institute of Building (CIOB) and RICS or the RTPI and RICS. However, joint honours programmes have proved to be less attractive and often require an additional year of study to meet all the required learning outcomes. Whether programmes that explicitly focus on sustainability command greater student attention has not been proven, although from the surveys conducted through C-SCAIPE (Cowling et al, 2007) this appears to be increasingly likely, especially at postgraduate level.

In terms of capacity, there are signs that some HEIs are developing widespread expertise in understanding education for sustainable built environment. A recent report (HEFCE, 2008) cited the Oxford Institute for Sustainable Development[6] at

Oxford Brookes University as being one of the major contributors to research in relation to sustainable built environment, while both the University of Plymouth (see p7) and Kingston University have been recognized by HEFCE for their developments in the field through their CETL programmes. In all these HEIs, sustainability is being infused into a range of professionally accredited and in some cases, multidisciplinary programmes at both undergraduate and postgraduate levels. These institutions may currently be in the minority, but the dynamic and significant curriculum changes that have taken place over little more than a five-year period indicate a definite direction of travel. Dissemination is assisted by the HEA's subject centre, the Centre for Education in the Built Environment (CEBE), which publishes a journal and case study material and supports special interest groups, including one on sustainability.[7]

Sustainability as practice

Built environment education is outcome and practice-oriented. Both curricula and the way they are delivered must adapt and respond to external pressures. In order to 'practise', graduates are required to have an applied and working knowledge of current legislation and must be aware of the wider political and cultural context in which they will be working. As the work of professionals has increasingly required greater management and interpersonal skills, so graduates are required to have developed a far wider range of generic skills including, for example, the ability to present and defend a case convincingly (Egan, 2004). The response of HEIs has been to develop methods of teaching that integrate project work and provide opportunities to present orally, engage in debate and solve problems. While such an approach has been fundamental to architecture and landscape education (being studio-based), for construction, surveying and planning, which have less generous funding, the introduction of such approaches has been more challenging. Nevertheless, there have been many innovative initiatives in this area where innovation has taken place using a combination of live projects or work simulations. One such example is the European Challenge, headed in the UK by Sheffield Hallam and Kingston Universities. This brings students from universities across Europe into a competition simulating a business relocation scenario (Nunnington and Eilander, 2005).

That sustainability has grown in the curriculum may have been slowed in part because this practice-led approach is a hallmark of built environment education. In sustainability, some areas of practice have not moved as fast as others. The driver for integrating sustainability as a modus operandi is not practice-led, as a study of graduate requirements demonstrates (Sayce et al, 2009). Instead, it has been led primarily by HEIs' endeavours and through partnerships with a limited number of organizations operating in the vanguard of change. An example of this is the MSc in Architecture: Advanced Environmental and Energy Studies offered by the University of East London in association with the Centre for Alternative Technologies in Machynlleth, Wales, one of the most established non-governmental organizations in the field (Harper, 2000; Smith, 2004).

In a limited number of cases, HEIs have led by example through their estates department. At the University of the West of England on the outskirts of Bristol, the Faculty of Environment and Technology's award-winning building (R Block)[8] has provided just such an opportunity. Constructed with prefabricated straw bale panels, co-designed by a member of staff, the building is an exemplar project. It incorporates a range of services and facilities that not only use 'green' technologies but also encourage sustainable behaviour. Using it as a living lab, students are able to assess the suitability and practicability of forms of sustainable construction. Post-occupancy studies being undertaken are providing useful data for other institutions and the wider community. The panel system that forms the external skin of the building is now commercially available and has been used on a range of projects. This too can be seen as an example of innovative practice where the boundaries between academic research, professional knowledge and commercial production have been transcended. The Centre for Efficient and Renewable Energy in Buildings,[9] meanwhile, is currently under construction at London South Bank University. This hands-on experimental technical laboratory will be jointly managed and used by London South Bank, Kingston and City Universities, enabling joint teaching and research and providing a space where industry can also engage through, for instance, short courses and events.

Sustainability as process

Progress towards producing 'sustainability literate' graduates depends on the approaches of teaching teams and the environment in which study takes place rather than the demands of practice. Sustainability is not just a matter of curricula; it goes far deeper. It is not just about the material taught but the *manner* in which it is delivered, debated and then applied. The development of teaching methods that encourage students to interrogate existing practices and instil a value-driven approach is crucial if graduates are to be empowered to challenge long-established patterns of behaviour, including professional norms. It is no longer a case, if indeed it ever was, of 'training' for competence to execute specific tasks. The primary reason for bringing the built environment disciplines into academic institutions rather than continuing with the traditional pupillage systems, was in recognition of the fact that the future of the professions depended on developing new knowledge through academic research liberated from the strictures and liabilities of professional practice. It may therefore seem ironic that much of the work being undertaken is about re-grounding the disciplines in the wider socio-economic context central to sustainable practice. However, as a great deal of education is about learning in a 'safe' environment where mistakes or errors of judgement are penalty-free educational experiences, if students are to develop 'soft skills', challenge accepted practice norms and discover new working practices, methods such as problem-based and action learning are key.

To encourage this attitudinal shift, course teams have introduced more inter-disciplinary project work, to help students think 'outside the box'. An example of such an innovation is the project undertaken at the University of Strathclyde's Department of Architecture and Building Sciences and the Department of

Psychology at the University of Surrey. This interdisciplinary collaboration, based on neighbourhood regeneration working with real clients in Glasgow, demonstrates both the educational benefits of working across disciplines but more importantly a way in which the 'soft skills', noted as crucial for community engagement, can be developed in an academic environment (Romice and Uzzell, 2005).

The provision of different learning environments, devised to promote peer discussion and more active learning styles, has also proved useful in stimulating staff and students to rethink both the way in which knowledge is created and transferred. Problem-based learning and action learning have always been integral to design disciplines such as architecture, landscape architecture and urban design. However, this methodology is being used increasingly across built environment education in order to broaden student perceptions, improve skills and give students the opportunities to gain in confidence. Coupled with digital technologies, staff and students are developing new ways of working and building and exchanging knowledge. The Landscape Interface Studio (LIS) at Kingston University[10] has been a pioneer of this 'open' working for several years, and is currently working on a Knowledge Exchange project funded by Westfocus, through which case study material including video presentations is provided on an open wiki.[11] A workshop held at Camley Street Natural Park in King's Cross, central London, with the London Wildlife Trust, Argent Group and Global Generation is now available to all through the LIS website.[10]

Sustainability as paradigm

Any agent of change knows that success is achieved when their role has been rendered redundant. For those involved with the development and delivery of built environment programmes, the same can be said for sustainability as a subject area. The inclusion of the term in a course title or in an individual module or unit of study seems at best a recognition that the principles are only an add-on and not an integral part of the approach. The use of the term 'sustainable' can act as a limiting condition – as in 'sustainable construction' or 'sustainable development'. If a paradigm shift has occurred then the adjective should be redundant. Does an explicit reference to sustainability suggest that it is not implicit across the rest of the curriculum? These questions are often raised by students and staff in informal debate.

Only a finely grained analysis of content, style of learning or teaching methodology and assessment techniques will verify the extent to which sustainability is infusing built environment education. Such a study has yet to be undertaken systematically across institutions and disciplines.

In lieu of an analysis of all student work, an indication of how far the paradigm has shifted can be gained through externally visible student work, as evidenced in competitions such as FutureVision, run annually by the Homes and Communities Academy and a range of public and private sponsors.[12] Another indicator is the contributions of academics: their journal papers, the nature of the journals to which they submit and the shifts in university governance and management. From this, there is tangible evidence of change. Most mainstream journals that service HE built environment work now regularly publish articles on sustainability-related topics. The launch in 2000 and subsequent success of the *IJSHE*[13] provides an outlet for work that previously would not have had a natural home. However, sustainability research, particularly that which relates to the pedagogy of sustainability, tends to be interdisciplinary and, until very recently, has been difficult to legitimize through both the government's research assessment processes and funding bodies. This is now changing, with interdisciplinary being systematically encouraged. Better funding for research helps to drive and embed change, and with this may come the development of new 'hybrid professions'. The challenge then will be one for the existing professions: whether they will embrace such diversity and modify their requirements, or whether these new practitioners will operate outside the framework of the existing professions, causing potentially greater fragmentation and duplication of effort.

The last locus of evidence for the start of a paradigm shift lies in change at HEIs themselves. The People and Planet Green League table (People and Planet, 2009)[14] is already proving to be an effective tool in raising awareness of environmental concerns, if not sustainability, as are the Green Gown Awards[15] (Environmental Association for Universities and Colleges, 2008). With the linked greening of the campuses, including changes to learning spaces, so the seeds are set for deeper organizational transformation.

Conclusion

There are those who would argue that HE is not the place to promulgate new irrefutable truths. Academic institutions are there to challenge, debate and contest. However, the disciplines included in this chapter bestride the boundaries of theory and practice, and their graduates need sufficient baseline skills to be able to practice, with a working knowledge defined by their respective profession. In referring to sustainability as a paradigm, or more precisely as requiring a paradigm shift, one of the key challenges presented by sustainability becomes evident.

If governments are to succeed in moving society to a low-carbon economy, lifestyle changes will be required and not just the introduction of more and better technology. Society will need to re-appraise, perhaps radically, its values in ways that challenge and redefine perceptions and accepted norms. This is already observable through local bottom-up initiatives such as the Transition Towns movement (Hopkins, 2008). Such shifts in power present enormous challenges to professionals in the field of the built environment, their institutional structures and their boundaries. Interdisciplinarity will become of increasing importance and this can be viewed as threatening to existing stakeholders, including established academic teams. Yet if academe does not rise to the challenge of truly embedding the values, skills and knowledge that can begin to transform society, sustainability will be destined to remain a bolt-on technical and legal addition to the curriculum, not a means of enabling our graduates to envision and deliver the built environment needed to support a low-carbon economy servicing sustainable communities.

References

Association for the Conservation of Energy (2007) *Communities and Local Government Committee Inquiry: Existing Housing Stock and Climate Change*, Association for the Conservation of Energy, London, available at www.ukace.org/publications/ACE%20Evidence%20(2007-09)%20-%20CLG%20Committee%20Inquiry%20into%20existing%20housing%20stock%20and%20climate%20change.pdf, accessed 12 August 2009

ASC (2007) *Mind the Skills Gap: The Skills We Need for Sustainable Communities*, ASC, Leeds

Banwell, G.H. (1964) *The Placing and Management of Contracts for Building and Civil Engineering Works*, Ministry of Building and Works, HM Stationery Office, London

Barker, K. (2006) *Barker Review of Land-Use Planning: Final Report – Recommendations*, HM Treasury, London

Built Environment Strategic Alliance (2009) *Towards a Construction and Built Environment Higher Education Strategy: Ensuring an Informed Conversation on Issues Faced by the Construction and Built Environment Sectors Where Higher Education Can Offer Solutions*, Proceedings of the Built Environment Strategic Alliance Conference, January, Built Environment Strategic Alliance, London

Cade, A. (2008) *Employable Graduates for Responsible Employers*, available at www.heacademy.ac.uk/assets/York/documents/ourwork/tla/sustainability/EmployableGraduates2008.pdf, accessed 13 August 2009

Cowling, E., Lewis, A. and Sayce, S. (2007) 'Towards Sustainability Literate Students: Results of an Ongoing Study', Built Environment Education Annual Conference, CEBE, Cardiff

Department of Communities and Local Government (2007) Eco-towns Prospectus, Communities and Local Government Publications, Wetherby, available at www.communities.gov.uk/documents/housing/pdf/ecotowns.pdf, accessed 5 March 2010

Department of Communities and Local Government (2009) *Communities in Control: Real People, Real Power*, Government response to the making and enforcement of byelaws Communities and Local Government Publications, London

Dixon, T., Colantonio, A., Shiers, D., Reed, R., Wilkinson, S. and Gallimore, P. (2007) 'A green profession? A global survey of RICS members and their engagement with the sustainability agenda', *Journal of Property Investment & Finance*, vol 26, no 6, pp460–481

Environmental Association for Universities and Colleges (2008) *Green Gown Awards 2008 – A Unique Sponsorship Opportunity*, available at www.eauc.org.uk/file_uploads/gga_2008_low_final.pdf, accessed 5 August 2009

Egan, J. (1998) *Rethinking Construction: The Report of the Construction Task Force on the Scope for Improving the Quality and Efficiency of UK Construction*, Department of the Environment, Transport and the Regions, London

Egan, J. (2004) *The Egan Review: Skills for Sustainable Communities*, Office of the Deputy Prime Minister, London

Elkington, J. (1994) 'Towards the sustainable corporation: Win–win–win business strategies for sustainable development', *California Management Review*, vol 36, no 2, pp90–100

Farmer, J. (1996) *Green Shift: Towards a Green Sensibility in Architecture*, Architectural Press, Oxford

Forum for the Future and UCAS (2007) *The Future Leaders Survey 06/07*, UCAS, Cheltenham, available at www.forumforthefuture.org/projects/future-leaders-survey-06-07, accessed 20 July 2009

Forum for the Future and UCAS (2008) *The Future Leaders Survey 07/08*, UCAS, Cheltenham, available at www.forumforthefuture.org/files/FutureLeaders0708.pdf, accessed 5 August 2009

Gough, S. and Scott, W. (2007) *Higher Education and Sustainable Development – Paradox and Possibility*, Routledge, London

Harper, P. (2000) 'The end in sight?: Some speculations on environmental trends in the twenty-first century', *Futures*, vol 32 no.s 3–4, pp361–384

HEFCE (2005) *Sustainable Development in Higher Education: Strategic Statement and Action Plan*, HEFCE, Bristol

HEFCE (2008) *Strategic Review of Sustainable Development in Higher Education in England*, HEFCE, Bristol, available at www.hefce.ac.uk/pubs/rdreports/2008/rd03_08, accessed 6 February 2010

Hopkins, R. (2008) *The Transition Handbook: From Oil Dependency to Local Resilience*, Green Books, Dartington

Latham, M. (1994) *Constructing the Team: The Latham Report*, HM Stationery Office, London

Lewis, A., Sayce, S. and Ellison, L. (2005) *Education for Sustainable Development in the Built Environment Disciplines*, CEBE Working Paper No. 9, CEBE, Cardiff

Landscape Institute (2008) *Landscape Architecture and the Challenge of Climate Change: Landscape Institute Position Statement*, Landscape Institute, London

McIntosh, S. and Bailey, N. (2004) *Higher Education, Professionalism and Skills in the Built Environment: The Impact of the New Urban Agenda on Teaching and Learning*, CEBE Working Paper No. 5, CEBE, Cardiff

Nunnington, N. and Eilander, H. (2005) 'The European Challenge', *CEBE Transactions*, vol 2, no 1, pp44–63

Office of the Deputy Prime Minister (2003) *Sustainable Communities: Building for the Future*, HM Stationery Office, London

Office for National Statistics (2009) 'GDP growth: UK output decreases by 0.8 per cent', *Directgov*, available at www.statistics.gov.uk/pdfdir/gdp0709.pdf, accessed 4 March 2010

People and Planet (2009) *Green League 2009: Rewarding UK Universities for Excellent Environmental Performance*, available at http://peopleandplanet.org/dl/gogreen/greenleague2009.pdf, accessed 5 August 2009

Poel, B., van Crutchen, G. and Balaras, C.A. (2007) 'Energy Performance Assessment of Existing Dwellings', *Energy and Buildings*, vol 39, no 4, pp393–403

RICS (2006) *APC/ATC: Requirements and Competencies*, RICS, London, available at www.rics.org/site/download_feed.aspx?fileID=3729&fileExtension=PDF, accessed 4 March 2010

RICS Foundation (2004) *Sustainability and the Built Environment – An Agenda for Action*, Upstream, London

Rogers, R. (1999) *Towards an Urban Renaissance: Final Report of the Urban Task Force*, Department of the Environment, Transport and the Regions, London

Romice, O. and Uzzell, D. (2005) 'Community Design Studio: A collaboration of architects and psychologists', *CEBE Transactions*, vol 2, no 1, pp73–88

RTPI (2001) *A New Vision for Planning: Delivering Sustainable Communities, Settlements and Places, Mediating Space – Creating Place: The Need for Action*, RTPI, London

RTPI (2009) *Planning to Live with Climate Change: Our Seven Commitments*, available at www.rtpi.org.uk/download/6440/Sevencommitments.pdf, accessed 5 August 2009

Sayce, S., Clements, B. and Cowling, E. (2009) 'Are employers seeking sustainability literate graduates?', Final Report, Higher Education Academy, York, available at www.heacademy.ac.uk/assets/York/documents/ourwork/sustainability/kingston_sayce_full.pdf, accessed 5 March 2010

Sayce, S., Morad, M., Farren-Bradley, J., Lewis, A., Harris, C., Cowling, E., Toogood, E. and Neenan, T. (2008) *Enabling Sustainable Communities: Supporting Effective Skills Development for Current and Future Core Built Environment Professions*, Kingston University, Kingston-upon-Thames

Smith, A. (2004) 'An R&D lab for Utopia? Alternative technology centres in the UK', *The Politics of Utopia: Intentional Communities as Social Science Microcosms* (The European Consortium for Political Research Joint Sessions Workshop), Uppsala University, April, available at www.sussex.ac.uk/sussexenergygroup/documents/aps_-_uppsala_-_final.pdf, accessed 12 August 2009

Spence, R., Macmillan, S. and Kirby, P. (2001) *Interdisciplinary design and practice*, Thomas Telford, London

Stern, N. (2006) *The Economics of Climate Change* ['The Stern Review'], HM Treasury, London, available at www.hm-treasury.gov.uk/stern_review_report.htm, accessed 10 February 2010

Vitruvius Pollio, M. (1914) 'De Architectura' (trans. Morgan, M.H.), *Vitruvius: Ten Books of Architecture*, Harvard Press, London

UNEP (2007) *Buildings and Climate Change: Status, Challenges and Opportunities*, UNEP, Paris

WCED (1987) *Our Common Future: The Report of the World Commission on Environment and Development* ['The Brundtland Report'], Oxford University Press, Oxford www.un-documents.net/wced-ocf.htm Accessed 29 January 2010

Notes

1   The main professional bodies considered here are the Royal Institute of British Architects, the Landscape Institute, the Chartered Institute of Building, the Royal Town Planning Institute and the Royal Institution of Chartered Surveyors.

2   The ASC was a national body established by the UK Government to address the demands of community building, and in this capacity it assigned the task of producing a report to Arup, which as a global, multidisciplinary and independent organization of designers, planners and engineers was well placed to undertake a national study of this nature. The ASC is now the skills arm of the Homes and Communities Agency and known as the Homes and Communities Agency Academy – see www.hcaacademy.co.uk (accessed 6 February 2010).

3   For the purpose of the research, holistic sustainability was defined by an appreciation of the interconnectedness of subject disciplines and economic, social and environmen-

tal issues. The inclusion of economic, social and environmental issues is frequently referred to as the triple bottom line, a term coined by Elkington (1994).

4   The Council is the UK's leading agency for research funding and training in economic and social sciences in the UK – see www.esrc.ac.uk/ESRCInfoCentre/index.aspx (accessed 6 February 2010).

5   The QAA subject benchmark statements provide expectations about standards of degrees, giving a discipline its coherence and identity, and define graduate abilities and skills – see www.qaa.ac.uk/academicinfrastructure/benchmark/default.asp (accessed 6 February 2010).

6   The Oxford Institute for Sustainable Development, based in the School of the Built Environment at Oxford Brookes University, was established in July 2004. It has six main research groups and is the largest academic research institute in the UK dedicated to research on SD in the built environment – see www.brookes.ac.uk/schools/be/oisd (accessed 6 February 2010).

7   The CEBE is part of the subject centre network of the HEA and provides discipline-based support to enhance the quality of learning and teaching in the UK HE built environment community – see www.cebe.heacademy.ac.uk (accessed 6 February 2010).

8   This award-winning building houses part of the School of Built and Natural Environment and provides a home for the Centre for the Study of Sustainable Building, a unit dedicated to the understanding of the relationship between design quality, building performance, environmental sustainability and conceptions of financial value – see www.uwe.ac.uk/et/rtblock2/design/sustainability.shtml and www.bne.uwe.ac.uk/cssb (both accessed 6 February 2010).

9   The Centre aims to provide a high-quality teaching resource in sustainable energy technology and building design, construction and management. It also plans to offer facilities to conduct research and to demonstrate specific sustainable energy technologies including solar photovoltaic, solar thermal, ground-source heat pumps and wind power – see www.lsbu.ac.uk/cereb (accessed 6 February 2010).

10 The Landscape Interface Studio is a unique environment at Kingston University where staff and students work on live proposals for real client communities in real local sites across the UK and throughout Europe – see www.landscapeis.org (accessed 6 February 2010).

11 The Landscape Interface Studio open wiki can be found at http://landscapeisffwd.wetpaint.com (accessed 6 February 2010).

12 The students' work can be accessed at www.futurevisionaward.com/About/Default.aspx (accessed 6 February 2010).

13 The *IJSHE* was the first scholarly publication to specifically address the need for the dissemination of information on sustainability matters at HEIs.

14 People and Planet is an organization for UK students campaigning on world poverty, human rights and the environment (see http://peopleandplanet.org, accessed 6 February 2010). Its Green League is the only such ranking of the environmental performance of UK universities (People and Planet, 2009).

15 The Green Gown Awards recognize positive actions to achieve sustainable HE and further education, with particular emphasis on environmental improvement. They are organized by the Higher Education Environmental Performance Improvement project, which is funded by HEFCE. The Awards are run in partnership with key sectoral bodies such as the Association of University Directors of Estates, the British Universities Finance Directors Group, College and University Business Officers, the

Environmental Association for Universities and Colleges, Guild HE, the Learning and Skills Council, the Energy Consortium and Universities UK.

Chapter 15

Costing the Earth: The Economics of Sustainability in the Curriculum

Anthony Plumridge

Introduction

Economics as a discipline has been concerned with some of the major elements of sustainability from at least the 18th century.[1] However, this concern has been tacit rather than explicit and despite this fundamental resonance, sustainability has remained at the margins of the discipline. Even here, a significant rift has emerged between traditional economists applying established principles to the environment and those with a deeper understanding of the complexity and unpredictability of ecological systems. The former have evolved a body of work referred to as 'environmental economics', while the latter tend to identify with an approach known as 'ecological economics'. In spite of these developments, there is a surprising lack of formal engagement with sustainability in much core teaching of economics. While there are increasing instances of specialist teaching that fully embrace sustainability, either in optional modules or interdisciplinary programmes, it must be admitted that these are more concerned with environmental sustainability than with the socio-cultural aspects.

The discussion below will explore the deep relevance of many long-established economic concepts to sustainability. Some reasons why this relevance is not often explored in teaching will be suggested and ways of overcoming this shortcoming investigated. Specialist programmes and module provision that specifically address sustainability will be considered. Finally, some brief case studies will be presented.

It is assumed that some readers will not be economists and thus the concepts relevant to SD are presented in a non-technical way. It is hoped that the positioning of economics as having much to offer in disseminating a deeper understanding of the implications of sustainability for individual behaviour, markets and policy-making will encourage those engaged in introducing interdisciplinary sustainability programmes to include economics as a core element in their planning. Observations on the extent to which SD is included in the economics curriculum are based on practice at the author's own institution, telephone interviews with the heads of department in five other institutions and an examination of the latest editions of first and second year undergraduate economic texts.

Economic concepts and sustainability

The use of resources

It is common practice for the first lecture of an economics undergraduate programme and the first chapter of introductory economics texts to introduce a simple grouping of productive resources into three basic categories: land, labour and capital, or in more contemporary nomenclature natural resources, human resources and man-made resources (see, for example, Sloman, 2006, p4). A typical definition of the scope of the discipline used by the author is as follows:

The use of resources to create wealth and the subsequent distribution of that wealth.

By creating wealth, economists refer to the production of goods and services, and much of the discipline is concerned with the allocation of resources – how they are combined and used to produce goods and services. There is thus an immediate resonance with the resource-based view of sustainability:

Sustainable development is development that meets the needs of the present without compromising the ability of future generations to meet their own needs (WCED 1987, p54).

If this Brundtland Report definition is reformulated as: 'Future generations should inherit a stock of resources such that they can enjoy a quality of life at least equal to that enjoyed by present generations',[2] it then becomes apparent that economics has at its heart the study of processes and behaviours that are also of paramount importance to moving towards sustainability. However, it is rare that a link with sustainability is explicitly made.

The introductory seminar exercise (see Box 15.1) offers an example of the way in which this aspect of introductory economics is taught at the author's institution. The exercise reinforces some of the concepts of wealth creation and resource use. This example features stronger links with sustainability than is the case with much introductory teaching of these concepts, and clearly even here there are opportunities to go much further. For example, introductory lectures could address sustainability directly by giving the resource-based definition

Box 15.1 An example of teaching materials on the use of resources

This seminar exercise has been used by the author at the University of the West of England (UWE), Bristol, for the last 15 years and allows reflection and discussion of concepts introduced in lectures. Specifically, questions 1, 2, 3, 4 and 10 have particular relevance to the resource-based definition of sustainability. The remaining questions are concerned with the allocation of resources to the production of alternative combinations of goods and services. The way in which markets perform this allocation is a preoccupation of much of introductory economics.

Seminar sheet 1: Resource Problems and Economic Systems

Prepare notes to enable you to supply an answer to the following questions during the seminar:

1 List, with examples, at least five categories of resources.
   This question includes the concept of natural resources as an input into the economic system, together with man-made and human resources, entrepreneurship, technology and financial resources. This categorization of resources can be compared with the 'Five Capitals' approach to sustainability (Porritt, 2007, p137).

2 What might be included in a Resource Audit of these countries: The Netherlands, Australia, Japan, Ethiopia?
   This allows discussion of how the endowment of these resources in the nations listed has influenced their historical development trajectories, resulting in trade, labour migration, colonialism and foreign direct investment. It sets national resource endowment in a global resource stock context.

3 Differentiate between finite and renewable resources. Give three examples of each.
   Examples such as oil and natural gas and the imminent arrival at the mid-point of depletion ('peak oil') can be discussed in some depth. Discussion of water as a renewable resource offers opportunities for considering local scarcity.

4 Describe the difference between the stock and flow approaches to drawing up an account of the wealth of a nation. How might the widely used flow method distort the development of a nation?
   The importance of offsetting the depletion of resource stocks against the output of goods and services can be emphasized.

5 What are the opportunity costs of being a student? What are the opportunity costs of building the Channel Tunnel?

6 Make one *positive* and one *normative* statement about the state of the UK economy.

7 List at least three advantages and three disadvantages of the free market system over the centrally planned economy.

Box 15.1 continued

8 Plot a production possibility curve based on the data in Table 15.1:

Table 15.1 *Production of food versus production of clothing exercise*

Food (million units)	Clothing (million units)
8.0	0.0
7.0	2.2
6.0	4.0
5.0	5.0
4.0	5.6
3.0	6.0
2.0	6.4
1.0	6.7
0.0	7.0

9 Explain why the production possibility curve is concave to the origin in shape. What does this signify?

10 Sketch a new production possibility curve to show how economic growth may occur.

   This allows discussion of how the growth in output is constrained by the availability of resources.

11 As a result of economic growth, will everybody be equally better off? Can anybody be worse off?

Meeting needs and the allocation of resources

As discussed above, economics is concerned with the use of resources to produce wealth. Much emphasis is given to the efficiency of this process, whether it is achieved through markets or the intervention of the state. The efficiency in the use of resources must be related to the impact of a particular use on the well-being of the population. In introductory micro-economics,[3] where the market is almost the only means of allocating resources considered, the rather dubious concept of utility (broadly, satisfaction) is introduced. Consumers seek to maximize their total utility by adjusting their selection of products and the quantities of each purchased. In many economics programmes, it is not until level two that the more empirically testable concept of indifference is introduced. With indifference, the consumers being analysed are seen as being presented with a range of combina-

quoted above and questions could be asked of students regarding how resource stocks might be monitored. This could lead to discussion of the degree of substitutability of resources that should be allowed, and this in turn could present an opportunity to introduce strong and weak views of sustainability.

tions of quantities of products. Some of these combinations are clearly preferable to others but there are some combinations to which they are indifferent. Relative prices based on resource costs determine which combinations are affordable and one combination emerges as just affordable and preferable to all other affordable combinations. Producers follow a similar process. The same quantity of a product can be made using different combinations of resources and the choice of production method is made on the basis of resource costs. This approach is used to analyse the behaviour of consumers and producers at the individual or unit level or at the market or industry level and is known as neoclassical micro-economics.[3] Very similar analysis is applied at the international level and is known as neoclassical trade theory (see, for example, Appleyard et al, 2006, chapter 5).

The outcome of such producer and consumer behaviour in markets can be shown to produce an efficient[4] and optimal outcome under a rather unrealistic set of assumed pre-conditions.[5] It can be characterized as a system in which producers compete to provide goods and services according to consumer needs at the lowest possible prices. At a global level, countries specialize in producing those products in which they have a competitive edge because of the resources with which they are endowed. The outcome, in theory, is one in which societies enjoy the range of goods and services they value most highly at the lowest possible resource cost.

Much attention is given to *market failure* in introductory texts, that is, the failure to attain this desirable outcome as a result of one or more of the assumed pre-conditions not being met. There is a particular concern about the structure of the market, especially where there are only a few producers (oligopoly) or just one (monopoly). Under such circumstances, producers are able to prevent competitors entering the market, restrict supplies, drive up the price and thereby make excessive profits. This concern has led to a regulatory framework designed to limit market dominance by firms and such anti-competitive behaviour. The relationship between various market structures, the outcome for consumers and the impact of regulation is a significant element of the curriculum of an economics degree (see, for example, Sloman, 2006 chapter 11). Other causes of market failure are usually given less emphasis. This is unfortunate, because two in particular have the potential to contribute greatly to an understanding of SD. These are externalities and imperfect information, which are considered below.

Externalities

As discussed above, the allocation of resources results from consumers and producers making decisions with the aim of maximizing utility and profits respectively. Decisions are based on consumers' and producers' consideration of their respective self-interests; this can be referred to as the private realm. Private costs and benefits are taken into account when deciding purchases and organizing production. The interests of wider society, the social realm,[6] are usually ignored. Social costs and benefits include the costs and benefits for consumer and producer but also costs borne by those who are not participating in that particular market. These are known as external costs and benefits or externalities. Thus:

- Social costs = private costs + external costs
- Social benefits = private benefits + external benefits.

External costs and benefits can arise through both consumption and production. From an SD perspective, external costs are most significant and arguably account for the failure of individuals, communities and nations to follow a sustainable path (Tietenberg and Lewis, 2009, p607). For example, pollution is often perceived as an externality of production and can cause costs for communities and environments at a great distance from the source at the production site; it can also impose costs on future generations. As a result of this separation in distance and time, producers do not generally take the pollution cost into account when deciding how much to produce and how to produce. If these external costs associated with the pollution were internalized and set against the benefits of production, profits would be lower and production of the product less attractive to firms. As a result, either fewer of the product would be manufactured and/or investment in cleaner technology would be adopted. The result would be a re-allocation of resources, achieving a social rather than a private optimum. If firms had to face the full costs of their carbon emissions in terms of climate change, economic theory suggests they would reduce their carbon footprints and global warming would be reduced (see, for example, Tietenberg and Lewis, 2009, chapter 8).

A common expression of production externalities and policy interventions to achieve internalization is contained in the 'polluter pays' principle. This simple concept is used in the discussion of green taxes (Sloman, 2007, p327) but can also apply to the other market measures to combat pollution, such as capping and trading and property rights (see below). Imperfect information may be mentioned here, but it is still rare for the precautionary principle to be introduced. In the absence of full information on the impacts of pollutants on complex ecosystems that are imperfectly understood, the precautionary principle would dictate that a large safety margin is allowed when designing policies to combat pollution.

There are also significant external costs of consumption. Internalization of these could lead to more sustainable lifestyles. For example, if private motorists had to face the full external costs of their motoring, such as carbon emissions, other pollution, wear and tear on roads and congestion, they might limit car use to the most essential trips (for a full discussion of this topic, see Fullerton et al, 2008 and Tietenberg and Lewis, 2009, chapter 18).

Externalities are, in the majority of cases, mentioned at level one in HE economics teaching but are considered at some depth in level two micro-economics courses. The external benefits of health services and education, for example, are discussed as a justification for government intervention in the supply of these services, as the private sector would under-provide these so called 'merit goods'. Pollution is usually discussed as an external cost and some anti-pollution policies are briefly examined, usually taxes and cap-and-trade regimes. However, the connection with sustainability is not often made. This is evidenced by the fact that sustainability and SD are absent from the indexes of even the latest editions of economic texts.[7] A brief format for a level-two tutorial

---

Box 15.2 A tutorial on externalities

Think about the questions below and prepare some answers:

1   What is an externality?

2   (i) List five actions that *you undertake on a daily basis* that produce negative externalities.

     (ii) Note one action that produces no externalities.

     (iii) Note one action that produces positive externalities.

3   From your list in 2(i), rank these from most significant to least significant.

     What factors did you consider in order to do this?

4   Define pollution in your own terms.

5   Public goods and merit goods – how do they relate to externalities?

---

discussion helping students to appreciate the pervasiveness of externalities is shown in Box 15.2.

As with so much economic analysis that is highly relevant to SD, the concept of externalities has been current for the 120 years since it was formulated by Alfred Marshall (1890). Policies to combat pollution began to be considered some 40 years later when a pollution tax was proposed by Arthur Pigou (1932). A generation later, Ronald Coase suggested what has become known as the property rights approach to pollution, whereby the perpetrator and sufferer negotiate a reduction in pollution (Coase, 1960).

Imperfect information

The efficient allocation of resources assumes perfect information is available to assist both producers and consumers in their decision-making. The consequences of imperfect information and uncertainty are considered superficially in core micro-economics at level two but only considered in depth in specialist modules. One of the key problems in achieving sustainability is that finite resource costs do not necessarily reflect scarcity. This has been most evident in the case of oil and metals – it is arguable that this failure of the price of these resources to reflect scarcity is due to a combination of a lack of information about remaining reserves and a degree of monopoly power combined with short-termism on the part of certain producers and speculation (Krugman, 2009).

In the case of oil, this has resulted in long periods of relative stability at historically low prices (1985–2006) with shorter periods of extreme volatility (1972–1985 and 2007 to the present). The predictions of economic models of finite resource depletion are at odds with this reality. They assume perfect information and suggest a steadily increasing price path up to the point at which the resource is depleted and an alternative technology takes over (see, for example, Hotelling, 1931). Information also has an important role in the sustainable harvesting of renewable resources (see, for example, Clark, 1990). If those exploiting the resource act in their mutual long-term self-interest and have full information of the impact of various levels of harvesting on stock levels, then the risk of over-exploitation is removed and the maintenance of carrying capacity is more likely. It is fascinating that traditional hunter-gatherer societies often had such information systems embedded in their cultures, reinforced by a system of beliefs and rituals.

Cost–benefit analysis (CBA)

It is common practice for level two and three micro-economics to devote some time to exploring CBA, usually in the context of major public sector infrastructure projects such as road schemes, airport expansion or the Channel Tunnel.[8] The theoretical basis for the methodology rests on the work of Kaldor (1939) and Hicks (1939).[9] Essentially, applying CBA to a proposed project entails listing all of the positive and negative impacts on all individuals in the population in each time period, monetizing them as costs and benefits, aggregating them to give net benefits in each time period and then discounting future net benefits to give a net present value for the project.[10] Various tests are then applied to determine whether the project should proceed.[11]

CBA as a methodology brings into focus many issues that are critical to sustainability. The choice of discount rate effectively involves taking a position on inte-generational equity. Arguably, the Brundtland definition of sustainability implies a zero discount rate so that the interests of future generations are weighted equally to those of the current generation. As indicated above, economists have much to offer in refining concepts such as intergenerational equity (see Rawls, 1972) and introducing this issue offers an opportunity for a tutorial debate that goes to the heart of SD. The choice of discount rate is considered in the curriculum but usually in relation to the rate of interest and is rarely debated from the perspective of intergenerational equity and sustainability.

The monetization of environmental impacts is also a critical issue in SD and is sometimes briefly referred to in levels two and three. The direct use value of environmental assets may be included where market prices exist. However, techniques for evaluating the non-marketed services derived from environmental assets are usually only dealt with in depth in specialist modules.

The potential contribution of CBA to deciding policy priorities has been illustrated recently in the Stern Review (Stern, 2006), in which it was the key methodology for assessing the benefits of intervening to reduce carbon emissions and thus to reduce the likelihood of further global warming.

The circular flow of income

This simple model of the economy shows the major transactions between the productive and household sectors. The supply of human and other resources by households in return for wages, salaries and other incomes allows producers to supply goods and services. Households are able to purchase these goods and services with their incomes. An addition to the circular flow diagram to represent the relationship between this economic activity and the environment is given in

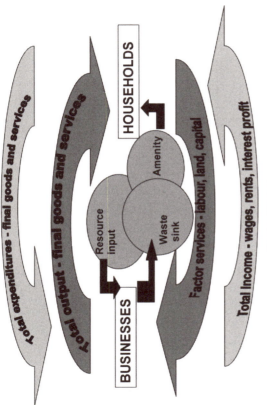

Figure 15.1 *The circular flow of income and the natural environment*

Figure 15.1 above. When introducing macro-economics at level one, the use of this diagram offers an ideal opportunity to raise discussion concerning sustainability issues.

Macro-economic objectives

Much of the economics curriculum is concerned with the approaches that governments have made to influence the state of their national economies. A typical list of economic objectives would include:

- full employment;
- price stability;
- long-term fiscal balance;
- long-term current account balance;
- elimination of poverty;
- economic growth.

Of these, economic growth is the most contentious objective for SD. Ever since the limits to growth hypothesis was put forward in 1972 (Goldsmith et al, 1972), economic growth has been seen as the enemy of sustainability by most in the green movement. The hypothesis is easier to support now than it was 35 years ago and makes an ideal platform for discussing sustainability at the national level. An opposing view is centred on the environmental Kuznets curve hypothesis, which suggests that as nations become wealthier a point is reached where environmental

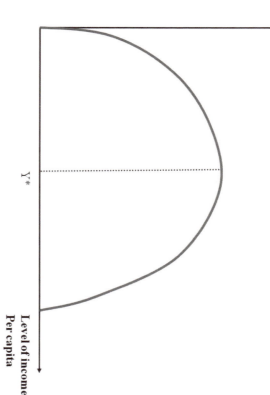

Environmental
Impact eg
Pollution
Per capita

Y*

Level of income
Per capita

Figure 15.2 *Environmental Kuznets curve*

damage *decreases* with further economic growth and increases in wealth (Grossman and Krueger, 1995). There are many critiques of this hypothesis. One of the most telling is that the finite resources of the planet constrain the ability of all nations to reach the level of wealth that represents the point of transition from a direct relationship between income growth and environmental damage to an inverse one. The most damning critiques challenge the empirical evidence for the relationship and show that few damage indicators reveal a turning point across those nations for which data are available. Furthermore, the hypothesis does not appear to apply to carbon emissions (Bradford et al, 2005).

One response to the need for sustainable economic growth has been to use an alternative to conventional output measures such as GDP that reflects negative externalities. Such a measure is the index of sustainable economic welfare (ISEW) which takes a more holistic view of the factors involved than does GDP A simplification of the formula is:

ISEW = personal consumption + public non-defensive expenditures − private defensive expenditures + capital formation + services from domestic labour − costs of environmental degradation − depreciation of natural capital.[12]

Another approach to judging the efficacy of individual economic measures is to submit them to CBA (see above). Classroom discussion of such an approach allows an examination of the impact of various policies from the SD perspective. Mainstream macro-economics modules consider various macro-economic objectives, and here an opportunity exists to introduce SD targets as policy objectives.

For example, carbon emission targets could be given an economic dimension by formulating objectives in terms of the carbon intensity of output. It may be appropriate to consider other output resource-intensity measures, for instance an ecological footprint-related measure such as GDP per global hectare. The water-intensity of output would also be relevant to some economies. Some interesting coursework could be designed around comparative analysis using measures such as these. REAP[13] software provides an ideal tool for making UK regional comparisons of this type.

International trade

There is little reference to sustainability in the teaching of international trade. Neoclassical trade theory still holds a dominant position in the economics curriculum in spite of its limited application to the real world. It fails to account for (or assumes away) many of the realities of trade between nations such as imperfect markets, transport costs, intra-industry trade, foreign direct investment, migration and remittances (see Appleyard et al, 2006, chapters 8 and 10). Later theories such as Dunning's eclectic theory are more empirically based (Dunning, 1980). However, the free trade policies of the World Trade Organization remain firmly rooted in the neoclassical paradigm. From the perspective of sustainability, three aspects of reality fail to be taken fully into account by trade theory taught at undergraduate level: market imperfections (especially externalities), transport costs and resource scarcity.[14] However, it is a valuable exercise for students to consider how the predictions of theoretical models might change if restrictive assumptions are relaxed. There is a tradition in economic analysis of putting forward simple abstract models bearing little relationship to reality and then progressively introducing real-world complexities (see Demeulemeester, 2009).

In some cases, free trade could give rise to sub-optimal outcomes. This might arise if externalities are not reflected in resource, transport or production costs, where resource costs are based on imperfect information and where migration may lead to the abandonment of highly sustainable lifestyles. Once again, issues such as these give ample scope for introducing sustainability into classroom discussions of trade theory. A useful critique of trade policies from an environmental perspective is provided by Gallagher and Werksman (2002).

Social capital

The dimensions of sustainability other than the environmental one are largely ignored in the economics curriculum, although they should be given attention in the consideration of social costs and benefits. A platform for the discussion of socio-cultural sustainability is the concept of social capital, rooted in sociology but given some consideration in comparative economics. Knack and Keefer (1997) investigate social capital as one of the factors explaining the differential economic performance of nations. At a micro-economic level, in institutional economics and the economics of law, social capital has some influence on the way in which trust plays a part in relational contracting (Williamson, 1985). Socio-cultural sustainability is more apparent in the contribution economics makes to interdisciplinary programmes. In business economics, the triple bottom line of environmental, social and economic considerations has a socio-cultural dimension (see Elkington, 1998, pp1–16). In sustainable tourism programmes, the economics of tourism recognizes the potential destruction of social capital through the commodification of indigenous culture.

Opportunities for embedding SD

It is clear from this discussion that sustainability does not feature prominently in many areas of the typical single honours curriculum. This is in spite of the strong relevance that a number of key economic concepts have for SD, as has been argued above. The reason for this oversight is most probably the increasing need to devote resources to teaching quantitative methods and research skills to enhance vocational skills for employment as professional economists. This has emerged as a constraint in the author's own institution and has added to the difficulty in covering the benchmarked components of a sound economics degree. [15] Furthermore, the curriculum only reacts to the contemporary context after a period of delay. There are some signs that sustainability is beginning to be more formally addressed in reaction to the prominence of sustainability as a government policy priority and this has been reinforced by attention given to ESD by the HEA. Further, a rush by HEIs to be seen as green has led some to adopt institution-wide initiatives to increase the prominence of SD in the curriculum.

There are two complementary approaches to overcoming this lack of an explicit treatment of sustainability in the curriculum. Firstly, SD can be used as a context for illustrating many concepts in the economics curriculum. A number of examples have been given in the discussion of concepts above. It is largely a matter of rebalancing the way in which these concepts are applied to topical issues and the examples used to illustrate them. This is a process that is already underway. It will be given greater impetus as HEIs attempt to fortify their green credentials. Secondly, specialist modules can be offered as is already the case in a number of institutions. While this allows those interested in sustainability to pursue their interests, it cannot achieve the same breadth of exposure to sustainability among students as can be achieved through altering the emphasis of core modules. The provision of specialist modules is discussed below.

Specialist modules

There are three main sub-disciplines within economics in which SD is central to the curriculum, namely environmental economics, natural resource economics and ecological economics. There is considerable overlap between these territories and all three might be represented in a module on environmental economics.

Environmental economics

An optional module in environmental economics is offered in a significant number of economics programmes, although it is difficult to conduct any comprehensive survey of availability because detailed module information is not usually accessible online. In the case of the HEIs consulted,[16] environmental economics is only available at level three, if at all. A typical module might include the following content:[17]

- Ecological and economic systems concepts.
- Sustainability: values, views and definitions.
- Externalities and public goods; an analytical framework.
- Policies to combat pollution.
- CBA.
- Valuation of environmental assets.

Ecological and economic systems concepts introduce the key aspects of an ecosystem including materials balance, laws of thermodynamics and entropy, assimilative capacity, threshold effects, irreversibility, stability, resilience, biodiversity and keystone species. The limits to growth and environmental Kuznets curve debates can be introduced at this early stage.

The sustainability views of academics, policy-makers and activists range from the very weak, entertaining full substitutability of natural capital, to the very strong, based on Daly's four principles (1991).[18] This range leads to debate about the fundamental relationship between humankind and the planet, including reference to the position of the natural world in various religions and cultures currently and historically. It finds formal expression in the schism between neoclassical economics and ecological economics referred to below.

Externalities provide the starting point for introducing the optimum level of pollution and the optimal level of abatement cost. Policies to combat pollution include the property rights approach discussed above, systems of regulation backed up by sanctions, taxes and marketable permits.

CBA, also discussed earlier, leads into the various approaches to valuation including the contingent valuation method, hedonic pricing and the travel cost method. These can be judged by their ability to capture the components of total economic value. As mentioned above, environmental economics modules often also include some material on natural resource economics.

Natural resource economics

It is common practice to include the analysis of both renewable and non-renewable resources in modules focusing on this area of the discipline.

In the case of renewable resources, the focus might be harvesting a renewable resource such as marine fisheries under different access conditions. The threat to the fish population from over-exploitation will be considered. Other renewable resources such as water may be the subject of similar analysis. The depletion of oil and the peak oil hypothesis (see Pesaran and Samiei, 1995) are often used as an example of a finite resource. A family of depletion models such as that of Harold Hotelling, mentioned above, might be included. The analysis is likely to be extended to other mineral resources.

Ecological economics

Ecological economics is a somewhat younger branch of the discipline. Neoclassical theory, the basis of much environmental economics, is challenged or given little attention. The focus is more on approaching ecological processes that form an economic perspective. Two names are particularly prominent in ecological economics: Herman Daly and Robert Constanza. They demonstrated the immense value of natural systems by attempting a monetary valuation of them, and the total value they derived dwarfed the value of other inputs into economic systems (Costanza and Daly, 1991). Daly also proposed a steady-state economy in the sense that it operates so as to avoid further ecosystem degradation but rather enables natural systems to recover (Daly, 1991). To achieve this, he put forward four operating principles to which economic policy-makers should conform.[18] Costanza's research has meanwhile focused on the relationship between ecological and economic systems, particularly at the long-term macro level and especially on energy and material flows through economic and ecological systems and impacts on biodiversity, carrying capacity and natural capital. He also considered dysfunctional incentive systems and ways to correct them.

There is considerable overlap in the subject matter of ecological and environmental economics. The key difference is one of orientation: environmental economics tends to embrace the neo classical paradigm as an analysis of the economic system and seeks to incorporate environmental assets and services into that behavioural model. The objective is to maximize economic welfare. Ecological economics gives priority to the health of complex interrelated ecological systems and considers how economic behaviour can be modified to that end.

Specialist programmes

Very few environment-oriented economics undergraduate programmes are available in the UK. There were just two examples of a sustainability-oriented programme in economics listed on the UCAS website for 2009: Environmental Economics at York College and at the University of York (see case study below). UCAS lists no additional programmes for 2010 entry. A UCAS subject search shows Environmental Economics as forming part of degrees in Building Surveying at Birmingham City University, Environmental Science at the University of Sussex and Business Economics at Nottingham Trent University. Ecological economics is listed under Sustainable Development at the University of St Andrews. In reality, all these programmes are interdisciplinary awards with environmental or ecological economics modules representing a small part of study.

Case studies

The institutions that are the subject of the case studies below were chosen for their strong research profile in areas associated with SD or for their institution-wide green credentials. The studies were assembled from telephone interviews with departmental heads. These are not divided by level as there is little formal teaching of sustainability at levels one and two in any of the institutions investigated.

University of Bath

The Economics Department at Bath is divided into an Economics Group and an International Development Group. A concern with sustainability is prominent in research and some staff have international reputations in environmental and natural resource economics. There is an interdisciplinary research centre concerned with sustainability, namely the Institute for Sustainable Energy and the Environment.

These research interests are reflected in undergraduate teaching. There are two optional modules concerned with SD offered at level three: Environmental Economics and Natural Energy and Resource Economics. The latter is actively underpinned by research by teaching staff. In the case of these specialist modules, tutorial discussions revealed that, initially, students did not have much familiarity with the concept of sustainability or with areas of economic analysis that were relevant to the concept.

University of York

The University hosts part of the Stockholm Environment Institute and it might be anticipated that this would spill over into a general embedding of sustainability in undergraduate teaching. However, this is not particularly the case in economics. There are no modules offered in Environmental or Resource Economics at the undergraduate level and no initiatives to include sustainability explicitly in other modules.

There is a joint undergraduate award in Environment, Economics and Ecology offered by the Economics and Biology Departments. However, the economics modules are standard modules from the single honours award. Some ten credit modules explore the common ground between the two disciplines. Unfortunately, these modules do not appear to be available to students of economics degrees.

As this is one of the most ambitious interdisciplinary programmes combining economics with sustainability offered by a UK university, the full award structure is shown in Table 15.2 on page 288.

Table 15.2 *Environment, Economics and Ecology award,*
Environment Department, University of York

Year 1	Year 2	Year 3
Ecology and economics: a global perspective. (C) 10 credits	Environmental management. (C) 20 credits	Research project. (C) 40 credits
Tools and techniques for studying the environment. (C) 20 credits	Environmental management project. (C) 10 credits	Coastal zone management. (O) 10 credits
Quantitative methods for studying the environment. (C) 20 credits	Economics of ecological resources. (C) 10 credits	Current issues in atmospheric science. (O) 10 credits
Environment field project. (C) 20 credits	Economics of environmental policy. (C) 10 credits	Forest management. (O) 10 credits
Ecology for environmental scientists I. (C) 10 credits	Micro-economics. (C, E) 20 credits	Wildlife conservation and management. (O) 10 credits
Ecology for environmental scientists II. (C) 10 credits	Introduction to environmental law. (O) 10 credits	Environment and health. (O) 10 credits
Principles and applications of ecological economics. (C) 10 credits	Applied ecology and environmental management. (O) 10 credits	Sustainable use of soil and water resources. (O) 10 credits
Economics I. (C, E) 20 credits	Geographical information systems. (O) 10 credits	Environmental policy and valuation. (O) 10 credits
	Applied ecology project. (O) 10 credits	Economics of social policy. (O, E) 10 credits
	Cost–benefit analysis. (O, E) 10 credits	Industrial economics. (O, E) 20 credits
	Econometrics for economists. (O, E) 20 credits	International economics. (O, E) 20 credits
	Macro-economics. (O, E) 20 credits	Nutrient acquisition and cycling. (O, B) 10 credits
	Economics of population. (O, E) 10 credits	Conservation biology and biodiversity. (O, B) 10 credits
	Population and community ecology. (O, B) 10 credits	Behavioural ecology. (O, B) 10 credits
	Population, resources and the environment. (O, B) 10 credits	Global change ecology. (O, B) 10 credits
	Environmental issues. (O, B) 10 credits	

C: Core module; O: Optional module; E: Taught in Economics Department; B: Taught in Biology Department
Source: University of York website (University of York, 2009)

UWE, Bristol

UWE aspires to be highly rated as a green university (UWE, 2008) and there are initiatives to embrace ESD in all faculties. This is likely to take many forms including multidisciplinary provision. Some economics module leaders are responding to this context by introducing sustainability issues. A level two module, The Economics of Fun and Games, includes applications of economic analysis to the sports and tourism sectors. In the latter, there is consideration of sustainable tourism. At level three, there has been a long history of teaching environmental economics as an optional module. The recent move of economics into the Bristol Business School resulted in this module being repositioned as Sustainable Business. Some 60 per cent of the content is common to the previous environmental economics module. There is some pressure from students to introduce a module in sustainable business at level two.

Conclusions

Economics includes concepts and methodologies that are valuable and relevant to the pursuit of sustainability. This relevance is not made explicit in much of the teaching in the institutions investigated apart from in specialist modules at level three and in interdisciplinary awards. An easy step towards embedding sustainability in the general economics curriculum would be to illustrate more economic concepts by referring to SD and associated issues. A number of suggestions as to how this could be done are given in the discussion of concepts above. Demonstrating the relevance of economics to sustainability is also likely to encourage more students to take optional modules in environmental economics, natural resource economics or ecological economics. This would have a beneficial impact where such modules are offered but rarely run through lack of student numbers. Finally, champions of economics and sustainability should be able to exploit the growing green movement amongst HEIs to campaign for interdisciplinary awards with a significant contribution from economics.

Further reading

Common, M. and Stagl, S. (2005) *Ecological Economics: An Introduction*, Cambridge University Press, Cambridge.
Provides a different perspective to texts on environmental economics. One of the challenges in teaching sustainability in economics is the need to enable students to understand some essential elements of ecosystems and the nature of human economic activity's impact. This text is very helpful in achieving this.

Field, B.C. and Field, M.K. (2006) *Environmental Economics*, McGraw Hill, Maidenhead
A clear introductory text to environmental economics, this still omits resource economics and is written for the US regulatory context. This would be a good text to use in multidis-

ciplinary awards where economics is only a subsidiary part of the curriculum and could be used at level two.

Perman, R., Common, M., McGilvray, J. and Ma, Y. (2003) *Natural Resource and Environmental Economics*, Pearson, London
A more comprehensive theoretical approach suitable for economics students with extensive use of mathematical notation. For the less numerate readers there are clear verbal explanations of concepts and relationships. It does include resource economics and is written in a UK context. This text would be ideal for use to support an option in environmental economics at level three.

References

Appleyard, D., Field, A. and Cobb S. (2006) *International Economics*, McGraw Hill, Maidenhead

Bradford, D., Fender, R., Shore, S. and Wagner, M. (2005) 'The environmental Kuznets curve: Exploring a fresh specification', *Contributions to Economic Analysis & Policy*, vol 4, no 1, available at www.bepress.com/bejeap/contributions/vol4/iss1/art5, accessed 7 February 2010

Clark, C.W. (1990) *Mathematical Bioeconomics: The Optimal Management of Renewable Resources* (2nd ed), Wiley-Interscience, New York NY

Coase, R. (1960) 'The problem of social cost', *Journal of Law and Economics*, vol 3, no 1, pp1–44

Costanza, R. and Daly, H. (1991) 'Valuation of ecosystem services and natural capital', In Costanza, R. (ed), *Ecological Economics: The Science and Management of Sustainability*, Columbia University Press, New York NY

Daly, H. and Cobb, J. (1989) *For the Common Good*, Beacon Press, Boston MA

Daly, H.E. (1991) *Steady-state Economics* (2nd ed), Island Press, Washington DC

Demeulemeester, J. (2009) Letter to *The Economist*, vol 392, no 8643, 8 August, pp15

Dunning, J. (1980) 'Toward an eclectic theory of international production', *Journal of International Business Studies*, vol 11, no 1, pp9–31

Elkington, J. (1998) *Cannibals With Forks: The Triple Bottom Line of 21st Century Business*, New Society Publishers, Stony Creek CT

Fullerton, D., Leicester, A. and Smith, S. (2008) *Environmental Taxes: Report to the Mirlees Committee*, Institute for Fiscal Studies, London

Gallagher, K. and Werksman, J. (eds) (2002) *The Earthscan Reader on International Trade and Sustainable Development*, Earthscan, London

Goldsmith, E., Allen, R., Allaby, M., Davoll, J. and Lawrence, S. (1972) 'A blueprint for Survival', special issue of *The Ecologist*, vol 2, no 1

Grossman, G. and Krueger, A. (1995) 'Economic growth and the environment', *Quarterly Journal of Economics*, vol 110, no 2, pp353–377

Hicks, J. (1939) 'The foundations of welfare economics', *Economic Journal*, vol 49, no 196, pp696–712

Hotelling, H. (1931) 'The economics of exhaustible resources', *Journal of Political Economy*, vol 39, no 2, pp137–175

Kaldor, N. (1939) 'Welfare propositions in economics and interpersonal comparisons of utility', *Economic Journal*, no 49, vol 195, pp549–552

Knack, S. and Keefer, P. (1997) 'Does social capital have an economic payoff? A cross-country investigation', *Quarterly Journal of Economics*, vol 112, no 4, pp1251–1288

Krugman, P. (1980) 'Scale economies, product differentiation, and the pattern of trade', *The American Economic Review*, vol 70, no 5, pp950–959

Krugman, P. (2009) 'Oil Speculation', *New York Times*, 8 July

Mishan, E. (1971) *Cost–benefit Analysis*, George Allen and Unwin, London

Malthus, T. (1823) 'Population', *Encyclopaedia Britannica*, A and C Black, Edinburgh

Marshall, A. (1890) *Principles of Economics: An Introductory Volume*, The Macmillan Company, New York NY

Nordhaus, W. and Tobin, J. (1972) *Is Growth Obsolete?* Columbia University Press, New York NY

Pesaran, M. and Samiei, H. (1995) 'Forecasting ultimate resource recovery', *International Journal of Forecasting*, vol 11, no 4, pp543–555

Pigou, A. (1932) *The Economics of Welfare* (4th ed), Macmillan, London

QAA (2000) *Economics* (subject benchmark statement), QAA, Gloucester, available at www.qaa.ac.uk/academicinfrastructure/benchmark/honours/economics.pdf, accessed 7 February 2010

Porritt, J. (2007) *Capitalism as if the World Mattered* (Revised ed.), Earthscan, London

Rawls, J. (1972) *A Theory of Justice*, Clarendon Press, Oxford

Scitovsky, T. (1941) 'A note on welfare propositions in economics', *Review of Economic Studies*, vol 9, no 1, pp77–88

Smith, A. (1766) *An Inquiry into the Nature and Causes of the Wealth of Nations*, W. Strahan and T. Cadell, London

Stern, N. (2006) *The Economics of Climate Change* ['The Stern Review'], HM Treasury, London, available at www.hm-treasury.gov.uk/stern_review_report.htm, accessed 10 February 2010

Sloman, J. (2006) *Economics*, Pearson, Harlow

Tietenberg, T. and Lewis, L. (2009) *Environmental and Natural Resource Economics*, Pearson, Boston MA

University of York (2009) 'Courses Offered', Department of Economics and Related Studies, available at www.york.ac.uk/depts/econ/prospective/ugrad/courses/tables.htm, accessed 14 September 2009

UWE (2008) *Sustainability Strategy 2008/2012*, available at www.uwe.ac.uk/environment/documents/Strategy.pdf, accessed 14 September 2009

WCED (1987) *Our Common Future: The Report of the World Commission on Environment and Development* ['The Brundtland Report'], Oxford University Press, Oxford www.un-documents.net/wced-ocf.htm Accessed 29 January 2010

Williamson, O. (1985) *The Economic Institutions of Capitalism*, Free Press, New York NY

Notes

1 Early theories of specialization and exchange implied a relationship between wealth and resource endowment (see Smith, 1766). Thomas Malthus was concerned with the sustainability of growing populations (see Malthus, 1823).

2 The concept of intergenerational equity was developed by the philosopher and economist John Rawls in 1972. This concept lies at the heart of the Brundtland definition of sustainability.

3   The synthesis of earlier economic principles into the framework of neoclassical micro-economics was predominantly the result of the work of Alfred Marshall (Marshall, 1890).

4   Economists describe this as an efficient allocation of resources or 'allocative efficiency'. It is based on the concept of Pareto optimality, in which it is not possible to make any adjustments to the system to make someone better off without making someone else worse off.

5   The assumptions lead to a state that is known as 'perfect competition.' The assumptions are that for each market there is:

- a large number of producers and consumers;
- ready access to resources for producers;
- perfect information for consumers about products available and for producers about the best available production technology;
- action by producers to maximize their profits;
- no externalities;
- no economies of scale.

6   The use of 'social' refers to the impact on society as a whole and includes environmental, socio-cultural and economic impacts.

7   This surprising omission may be due to a crowding-out effect: the scope of the discipline and the range of policy contexts in which it is applied are so wide that there is stiff competition for space in introductory texts (and in the curriculum). In addition, the QAA subject benchmark statement (2000) makes no mention of sustainability. However, the most recent statement, December 2006, does refer to sustainable development in the context of the use of resources.

8   For a full description of the methodology, see Mishan (1971).

9   The original Pareto condition for optimality was amended by Hicks and Kaldor, such that optimal resource allocation is attained where no adjustment is possible once the benefits to those who gain exceed the costs to those who lose. Hicks and Kaldor both published papers in the *Economic Journal* in 1939 that were reconciled by Tibor Scitovsky in 1941.

10   There are complex rules that need to be followed to give a fair evaluation of the impact of the projects. For example, the opportunity cost of the resources employed should be used, only additional benefits should be ascribed to the project, other benefits displaced by the project should be subtracted and taxes and subsidies allowed for.

11   A favoured test is the internal rate of return, the discount rate that brings the net present value to zero. However, this tends to favour those projects that bring most net benefits in the short term.

12   ISEW is based on the work of Nordhaus and Tobin (1972) and was proposed by Daly and Cobb (1989).

13   Teaching licences for Resources and Energy Analysis Programme (REAP) are available from the Stockholm Environment Institute at the University of York.

14   Krugman's Nobel Prize-winning work includes transport costs and market imperfections but not resource scarcity (see Krugman, 1980).

15   The QAA attempts to maintain standards of provision by setting the minimal (threshold) and average (modal) content expected of an economics degree; See QAA (2000).

16   The HEIs consulted included the three case study institutions (Bath, York and UWE) plus Bradford and UCL. See the case studies for details of specialist modules. Bradford offers Environmental Economics at level three but it has not run because an

insufficient number of students have opted to take the module. UCL only offers specialist modules at masters level.

17 This brief outline is based on the author's level three module on the economics programme at UWE.

18 Daly's operating principles are:

1 Renewables: rate of harvest ≤ population growth rate.

2 Pollution: waste discharges below assimilative capacity – cumulative pollutants set at zero (or as close as possible).

3 Non-renewables: benefits should be split between Y (Income) and I (Investment) such that a renewable substitute is available at depletion.

4 Macro-economic controls: minimize matter/energy throughput in the economy, control population growth.

Chapter 16

Translating Words into Action and Actions into Words: Sustainability in Languages, Linguistics and Area Studies Curricula

John Canning

Introduction

What has been lost sight of is that business, science and engineering are all carried out through the medium of language (Stibbe, 2007, p74).

Commentators may disagree on the precise details of what a sustainable future might look like and how it could be achieved. However, all would agree that the challenges we face are global ones that transcend physical, cultural, political and linguistic boundaries. It is perhaps surprising, therefore, that language, the means by which we communicate with each other, has played such a marginal role in discourses about SD. Moreover, while the future of the physical environment is among the key challenges facing a linguistically diverse global society, academics in languages, linguistics and area studies do not appear to be at the forefront of debates about SD. However, an understanding of the language we use to talk about SD and its relationship with our culture is a critical attribute of the graduate who is literate in sustainability.

While teaching about sustainability is widespread in languages, linguistics and areas studies, much of it is discrete and disconnected and most certainly cannot be viewed as a key disciplinary concern. This chapter aims to sketch out a map of current practice in these disciplines and identify potential for further development, including the study of literature, culture, English as an additional language, the emerging field of ecolinguistics, translation studies and language death. Language programmes are not only concerned with the acquisition of language skills, but also understanding the nature of language itself and the cultures and societies in which the language is spoken: 'The intercultural nature of the subject represents one of its key characteristics and is inherent in the discipline. The intercultural nature of the subject includes learning to reflect upon aspects of one's own culture' (QAA, 2007a, p2). Linguistics concerns the study of language in all its forms, whether spoken, written or signed (QAA, 2007b, p1). Area studies are meanwhile explicitly concerned with the interdisciplinary or multidisciplinary study of a country or a global region, and although language learning is often a substantial part of this (as in Middle Eastern studies or European studies), this is not always the case, for example, in American or US studies (QAA, 2008, p1). Comprehension of our own languages, cultures and societies, as well as those of others, is critical to thinking about how we understand environmental issues. Crucially, our understandings affect our responses and reactions to these concerns.

Literature

Literature offers many opportunities for discussing sustainability, particularly through approaches based on ecocriticism, a term used in literary studies to describe 'an interdisciplinary approach to the study of nature, environment, and culture' (Levin, 2002, p172). Garrard recognizes that although his book *Ecocriticism* deals primarily with British and North American literature, 'the principles of ecocriticism would of course admit of more general application' (Garrard, 2004, p5).

Although the Association for the Study of Literature and Environment has internationalized in recent times, this has 'relied on the interest of Americanists in other countries far more than experts on those countries' own languages and cultures' (Heise, 2006, p297). Garrard suggests that the absence of indigenes in the UK vis-à-vis the USA and Australasia is a contributory reason for a relative lack of interest in ecocriticism among UK academics (Garrard, 2007, p362). The Association's website hosts a database of syllabi from US-based American studies programmes and includes such courses as 'Ecological issues and American nature writing' and 'Landscape and American culture'. As a footnote, Garrard speculates that a lack of interest from continental Europe may have been affected by the ecological sensibilities of German Nazism (Garrard, 2007, p378).

However, German studies is the modern language field that has had the most engagement with ecocriticism and environment–literature relationships and the study of the 'nature poem' (*naturgedicht*) has brought about opportunities for embedding sustainability-related concepts into the curriculum (Goodbody, 1994). Other Germanists have reread traditional texts through the lenses of present-day environmental concerns, for example, Brecht's *Life of Galileo* (1943, 1998) and the responsibilities of scientists (Arons, 2004) and Goodbody's (2006) examination of apocalypse, idyll and utopia in the work of Arno Schmidt (see also Box 16.1, Nabham, 2001). Examples in other language areas include Watts on water in French Caribbean literature (Watts, 2007) and the work of Brazilian poet Márcia Theóphilo on the Amazon Forest, including its people, animals, trees, flowers, rivers and myths (Theóphilo, 2008).

Area and cultural studies

Area and cultural studies offer opportunities to examine environmental issues in wider multidisciplinary contexts. 'The Greening of Germany' (Phipps, 2005) is a particularly innovative example in which students examine the nature of 'rubbish' and waste and consider differences between British and German cultural attitudes towards recycling, litter and the idea of 'rubbish'. Students talk to German residents of Glasgow to explore their attitudes to waste. These attitudes are conditioned by very strict controls on packaging and waste disposal in Germany, the absence of which can be surprising to Germans living in the UK. Waste disposal is not a trivial concern in the study of culture; 'Our definitions of rubbish are fundamental of our relationship with nature and the environment' (Phipps, 2005).

Through a multidisciplinary approach to the study of some countries, environmental issues inevitably arise as central concerns. In the study of Canada, the experiences of indigenous peoples offer opportunities to discuss the idea of nature, linguistic rights and responsibilities, the protection of indigenous cultures, laws, practices and knowledges (see Patrick, 2005; Canning, 2005), as does the philosophy of National Parks in US history and the national imagination (Coates, 1996).

At the University of Manchester, a module based on Latin America examines fair trade, moral responsibility and the effects of globalization on indigenous peoples. Also at Manchester, an assignment of an enquiry-based learning module called *La invasión de Posadas* is concerned with the development of a new tourist resort and enables students to take on a variety of roles including a housing developer, a local resident and a representative of an environmental group (see Lorenzo-Zamorano, 2007). Latin Americanists at the State University of New York (SUNY) Plattsburgh run a study visit to southern Mexico, which requires the study of Spanish language and a course on sustainable communities (SUNY Plattsburgh, 2009).

Humanities and social science-based courses in environmental history are increasingly commonplace and many of these feed into multi- or interdisciplinary area studies programmes. Available to students of both American studies and history, John Wills's course (see Box 16.2) addresses themes as diverse as architecture, the atomic bomb, environmental protest, Disney, racism and ecofeminism. Although over a decade old, Peter Coates's article in *History Today* (1996) offers a very accessible overview of environmental history studies.

English as an additional/foreign language

Almost all UK universities teach English to speakers of other languages. These learners come from a wide variety of linguistic, cultural and disciplinary backgrounds. SD is a topic that can form the basis of class assignments, discussions and intercultural exchange. In his study of English language textbooks written for Japanese learners, Stibbe identifies a prevailing 'shallow environmentalism' in the way that environmental concerns are addressed in these publications, concentrating on the 'immediate physical symptoms' rather than 'underlying cultural factors such as consumerism' (Stibbe, 2004, p244). Stibbe also identifies a lack of a two-way intercultural dialogue in the teaching of English: 'If deep ecology were taught in English classes, then intercultural communication would be two-way, with the values behind ecological destruction challenged, and alternatives from traditional [in this case Japanese] sources considered' (Stibbe, 2004, p243). In the Japanese context, such intercultural dialogue would include the concept of *naikan*, 'a cultural value [that] in contrast to consumerism encourages the use of the minimum necessary resources with gratitude and simplicity' (Stibbe, 2004, pp253–254). A lack of two-way communication is brought about by a tradition of monoglot English teachers using textbooks that make no reference to the language and culture of the people being taught. In these contexts, English 'operates only in its own presence' (Pennycook, 2008, p44).

Ecolinguistics

Discussions about the relationship between language and environment date back at least to the beginning of the 20th century. Edward Sapir's paper 'Language and Environment' was first published in 1912 and reprinted in 2001. *The Ecolinguistics Reader* (Fill and Mühlhäusler, 2001) has usefully brought this and a wide collection of other papers in this emergent field together, although the subject has yet to gain prominence in the discipline of linguistics, while the term 'ecolinguistics' is absent from the most recent QAA benchmarking statement for linguistics (QAA, 2007b).[1] The field's most visible presence in the UK is the University of Gloucestershire-based journal *Language and Ecology* and the *Language and Ecology Research Forum*. However, at the time of writing only 2 of the 18 listed members of the forum are based in the UK. The University's module Discourse and Sustainability (formerly Language and Ecology) contributes to the degree course in English Language, the study of which has taken off in both secondary education and HE in recent years (see Box 16.3). The increasing popularity of English language degrees (as opposed to traditional literature degrees) has left many practitioners feeling betwixt and between the more established fields of English (literature) and linguistics (Baxter, 2009). If ecolinguistics is to grow as a field of study, it will be interesting to see whether it will be as a sub-field of linguistics or English language studies, or both.

Exploring definitions of the term 'sustainable development' itself is a good starting point for thinking about sustainability. The best-known definition, that sustainable development 'meets the needs of the present without compromising the ability of future generations to meet their own needs' (WCED, 1987), is not uncontested (see Leal Filho, 2000). We can, for instance, explore the meanings of 'development' – is it about economic prosperity, technological advancement or cultural change?:

Almost every article, paper or book on sustainability bemoans the fact that the concept is broad and lacks a broad consensus; this is usually followed by the author's own preferred definitions which in turn add to the lack of consensus! (Bell and Morse, 1999, p9).

Examining the language we use to describe environmental problems is another good starting point. The term 'global warming' can easily lead us to perceive such an outcome as desirable (in the UK at least) – what could possibly be wrong with warmer temperatures? Selby prefers the term 'global heating' in order to avoid what he calls 'the palliative effect of euphemism' (Selby, 2007, p267), while Schultz proposes the term '(human-induced) climate dislocation' as a more accurate reflection of what is really happening; 'the future can be won or lost in the language adopted today', she argues (Schultz, 2001, p113). She identifies a number of other euphemisms: 'a development' (why not call it a factory, houses, a mine, an office building or whatever else it is?), 'land reclamation' (why not 'wetland drainage'?), 'remnant native vegetation' – the '(last) remaining (patches of) original vegetation.'

Ecofeminist Tzeporah Berman argues that language is 'a cultural artefact invented by humans in the interest of the dominant male paradigm' (Berman, 2001, p259). This leads us to consider the gendered metaphors for describing the earth and impact of human beings on it. While human impact is still described in masculine terms e.g. man-made [disaster], feminine metaphors are used to describe the Earth, such as Gaia, Mother Earth and virgin [forest], with verbs such as 'rape' being employed to describe environmental damage. These terms, she argues, 'continue to objectify women and nature' (Berman, 2001, p258), which has an impact on our attitudes:

Within patriarchal society women have been traditionally associated with motherhood, and therefore responsible for nurturing, caring and giving. Mother's work in turn is unpaid and often unrecognized and devalued in capitalist society. In patriarchal culture it is our mother who satisfies all our needs, takes away waste, cleans and feeds us without any cost to us (Berman, 2001, p263).

A greater consciousness of the ways in which we use language to talk about the environment is an important part of changing our unsustainable behaviours into sustainable ones. If the language we use suggests neutral or positive outcomes for actions that are actually unsustainable, then we will continue to behave unsustainably. Language use is also critical to communicating scientific knowledge about environmental problems in a way that empowers people to take necessary actions for more sustainable lifestyles. Stibbe outlines the need to 'discover discourses which encode worldviews that inspire people into action for sustainability', as well as acknowledging that 'different discourses motivate different audiences' (Stibbe, 2009, p4). The UK Government is conscious of using different 'languages' for different audiences, for example, the general public, public sector and business. The general public is often appealed to through the money-saving potential of sustainable living – 'save money, save energy', whereas SD is promoted to NHS staff, for instance, as an aspect of the Service's 'corporate citizenship' (Ashley-Cantello, 2009).

Translation

Translation of sustainability concepts into other languages is an important challenge that can be addressed by students of those languages. Do *développement durable* (French) and *nachhaltigkeit* (German) embody the same sorts of meanings? On a superficial level, both words are generally accepted translations of 'sustainable development'; Jucker notes that *zukunftsfähigkeit* (literally 'future-proofing') has also been used in German (Jucker 2005). The Agenda 21 document *Glossaire pour le développement durable* notes the role of English as 'la principale langue de travail internationale' and the importance of developing a terminology, in the French language, of the most appropriate translations for English words (Agenda 21, 2002, p1). However, many French speakers prefer to use the term *développement soutenable* instead. Genuit, writing for Les Amis de la Terre (Friends of the Earth) views *développement soutenable* not only as a more literal French translation of 'sustainable development' but also one that better embodies the changes necessary to put 'sustainable development' (she uses the English here) into action (Genuit, undated). On the other hand *durable* places more emphasis on the balance between long-term global needs and resources rather than the idea of seeking to discover the limit of the Earth's carrying capacity without damage (Genuit, undated). Complexity can be even greater in the case of non-European languages. *Naikan* (Japanese), explored by Stibbe in an environmental context, literally means 'inside looking' or 'introspection', yet this translation alone cannot convey the depth of the concept or the deeper nature of the philosophy (if philosophy is the right word). A learner of the Japanese language needs to acquire this cultural knowledge in addition to the language (Stibbe, 2004, pp253–254):

Those of us who speak more than one language know that precise transla-
tion between languages is not always possible ... As a result international
documents, which are written in five languages, cannot convey the

richness of the concepts brought to the UN body [World Commission on Environment and Development]. However, when local cultures interpret and implement the international agreements, they develop a local interpretation and a fuller meaning. The term sustainable development does not translate well; the same is true of education for sustainable development (McKeown and Hopkins, 2003, p125).

The ability to understand and translate these nuances is not achievable through language skills alone. Being able to speak, read or write a language does not in itself equip a person with the cultural knowledge necessary to be an intercultural individual in a country where that language is spoken. Of speakers of 'heritage' languages in the USA, Kramsch contends, 'the meanings their language conveys are not necessarily those conveyed in their country of origin. The cultural worldview of American heritage speakers has become American, even if their words are Korean, Chinese or Arabic' (Kramsch, 2006, pp102–103). It is essential to have sustainability literate graduates who are able to understand and negotiate these diverse meanings.

Language death

Speaking two or more languages can give us two or more perspectives on life. The death of a language is a 'serious loss of inherited knowledge' (Crystal, 2000, p34) and some of this knowledge may provide vital insights into sustainable living. Language 'unifies everything, linking environmental practice with cultural knowledge, and transmitting everything synchronically among the members of a community, as well as diachronically between generations' (Crystal, 2000, p49). These knowledges include understandings of plant and animal life that may prove difficult to come by through observation alone. For example, the Kunwinjku have long understood that different wallaby species are best identified by focusing on their movement rather than on their static appearance, but western zoologists have only recently begun to understand this (Crystal, 2000, p49). Similarly, languages transmit knowledge about agriculture, animal management and medicine in ways which are much more difficult in translation (Crystal, 2000, p49). The death of a language causes 'a serious loss of inherited knowledge', which in turn lessens the pool of knowledge in the world from which we can draw (see Crystal, 2000, p34). Nabhan observes that minority language communities are 'reservoirs of considerable knowledge about rare, threatened, and endemic species that has not to date been independently accumulated by Western-trained conservation biologists' (Nabhan, 2001).

Box 16.1 Case study 1

Module title: German National Option: Mensch–Natur–Technik
(Human–Nature–Technology)

Year: 4 (students will have spent Year 3 abroad)

Institution: University of Bath

Lecturer: Axel Goodbody

Degree: Modern Languages/European Studies (options with German).

Summary

This module (taught in German) investigates the role of literature and film in posing
practical and ethical questions about relationships between humans and the natural
environment.

Course plan

The first meeting provides an introduction to the course and a workshop/discussion on
Kubus's video *Gentechnik und Ethik* (Genetic engineering *and ethics*). The second session
begins with a lecture on the ideas of *fortschritt* (progress) and *aufklärung* (enlightenment),
the *moderne* (modern) and the *postmoderne* (postmodern), cultural counter-movements
to modernization such as *zivilisationskritik* (criticism of civilization), ecology and environmentalism, and the environmental movement in West (and East) Germany. This is
followed by student presentations on set texts:

- Peter Bekes's introduction in Mensch und Technik on attitudes towards technology.
- Anon (1995) 'Angst vor der Endzeit. Umwelthysterie und Aktionismus – die
  Deutschen im Öko-Fieber' (a critique of exaggerated responses to environmental
  'crisis') Die Spiegel 39, pp.40–62.
- Sections from Goodbody (1997) on the scope of literary works to shape environ-
  mental attitudes; arguments and writing strategies.
- Model interpretation of Sarah Kirsch, 'Bäume' and Volker Braun, 'Verfahren
  Prometheus'.

Assessment

Assessment of the module comprises the presentation in groups of two or three (16.5
per cent), individual write-up based on the group presentation (16.5 per cent) and an
essay on a topic relating to at least two authors or directors (67 per cent).

Seminars

The remainder of the course consists of a series of seminars on the literary texts and
films. For example:

- Seminar on Max Frisch, Homo Faber – On the engineer's approach to life as an
  extension of Enlightenment rationalism, Faber's understanding of nature, the gender-
  ing of nature, the change in Faber's attitudes (the green bildungsroman), his guilt and
  Frisch's use of Greek myth.

- Seminar on Metropolis (1927) – On science fiction and 'city film' as genres, Expressionism, attitudes towards modernization in the 1920s, the plot, Lang's career, the reception of the film, technological advances, imagery and the representation of machines/technology and women.

Selected module readings

General introductions to the subject

Bekes, P. (ed) (2002) *Mensch und Technik, Arbeitstexte für den Unterricht*, Reclam, Ditzingen

Goodbody, A. (1997) 'Introduction', in *Umwelt-Lesebuch: Green Issues in Contemporary German Writing*, Manchester University Press, Manchester

Literary texts

Brecht, B. (1998) *Leben des Galilei [Life of Galileo]*, Text und Kommentar, Suhrkamp, Frankfurt am Main

Duve, K. (1999) *Regenroman [Rain Novel]*, Eichborn Verlag, Frankfurt am Main

Frisch, M. (1957) *Homo Faber: Ein Bericht [Homo Faber: A report]*, Kommentar von Walter Schmitz, Suhrkamp, Berlin

Haushofer, M. (1963) *Die Wand [The Wall]*, Deutscher Taschenbuch-Verlag, Munich

Films

Aguirre, oder der Zorn Gottes [Aguirre, or the Wrath of God] (1972). Director Werner Herzog

Metropolis (1927). Director Fritz Lang

Residence abroad

A year (or sometimes a semester) spent studying or working abroad is widely regarded as a seminal experience for the student of languages or area studies. This period abroad is important for developing intercultural competence as well as language skills. Students will usually write a dissertation on a topic of their choice, providing opportunities to address sustainability even if the core curriculum does not. Local planning disputes concerning the location of wind farms and nuclear energy planning have, for instance, been topics of student year-abroad dissertations.

Obstacles

Common arguments for not embedding SD into existing curricula are probably little different from those that arise in many other disciplinary contexts, for instance, that it is not seen as a core disciplinary concern, or that there is a lack of knowledge of the subject or a concern about interference in the curriculum. In reality, there is a lot of practice that could be construed as 'education for sustainable development', but this term is not widely used in practice.

Box 16.2 Case study 2

Module title: Inviting Doomsday: US Environmental Problems in the Twentieth Century

Year: 2, 3 or 4

Institution: University of Kent

Lecturer: John Wills

Degree: American Studies/History

Summary

This module introduces students to the field of environmental history in a modern (20th century) North American setting. Environmental History considers the changing relationship between humans and the rest of the natural environment from a critical and analytical perspective. Environmental historians take interest not just in human involvement with the material landscape but also in questions relating to popular attitudes, environmental determinism and 'natural agency'.

The module follows a broadly chronological format, commencing with an introductory session on US environmental history as a discipline (referencing formulative historic attitudes toward the American wilderness, agriculture and industry) before moving on to consider the birth of conservationist (and later, environmental) thinking in response to fears of vanishing resources, ecological collapse and nuclear catastrophe. The course ends by reflecting on contemporary ruminations over whether nature as a category endures given our proclivity for celebrating fake mementoes of the outdoors (such as pink lawn flamingos and plastic plants). Over the 12 weeks, the module will construct a comprehensive map of the USA as a country under transformation, in ecological, geographical and psychological terms. Consideration will be given to the interaction between nature (natural resources) and national identity, the evolution of environmental thinking and protest strategies, and changing verdicts on what constitutes 'progress'.

Assessment

Students are required to produce two essays of 3,000 words each (totaling 40 per cent of the overall module mark) plus one examination for (50 per cent). The final 10 per cent will be examined by one seminar presentation per student alongside contributions to seminar debate over the course of the module by each candidate.

Selected module reading

Abbey, E. (1975) *The Monkey Wrench Gang*, Penguin, London

Carson, R. (1963) *Silent Spring*, Penguin, London

Jones, K. and Wills, J. (2005) *The Invention of the Park: Recreational Landscapes from the Garden of Eden to Disney's Magic Kingdom*, Polity Press, Cambridge

Merchant, C. (1993) *Major Problems in American Environmental History*, DC Heath, Lexington MA

Nash, R. (1989) *American Environmentalism: Readings in Conservation History*, McGraw Hill, London

Opie, J. (1998) *Nature's Nation: An Environmental History of the United States*, Harcourt Brace College Publishers., Fort Worth TX

Price, J. (1999) *Flight maps: Adventures with Nature in Modern America*, Basic Books, New York NY

Rothman, H. (1998) *The Greening of a Nation: Environmentalism in the United States since 1945*, Harcourt Brace College Publishers, Fort Worth TX

Steinberg, T. (2002) *Down to Earth: Nature's Role in American History*, Oxford University Press, New York NY

Wasko, J. (2001) *Understanding Disney*, Polity Press, Cambridge

Box 16.3 Case study 3

Module title: Discourse and Sustainability
Year: 1
Institution: University of Gloucestershire
Lecturer: Arran Stibbe
Degree: English language, but available to students of other disciplines

Summary

Discourse and Sustainability is a 15-week module taught in the Humanities Department. It begins with a description of what happens when oral languages, fine-tuned to local ecological conditions, are displaced by the global spread of written languages. This is followed by sessions that investigate the potential ecological harm caused when certain discursive constructions of progress, economic growth, material consumption, success and convenience are spread on a global scale. The module then looks at discourses such as environmentalism, ecology and wildlife conservation, asking whether they can provide genuine alternatives to destructive discourses or whether they are based on similar assumptions. The last part of the module involves exploration of a range of very different discourses, from the lyrical science writing of Rachel Carson to Romantic poetry, haiku and documentary films in a search for alternative discourses that have the potential to contribute to a more sustainable society.

Course plan

Students meet in 12 weekly sessions covering topics ranging as widely as language death, the representation of animals in the animal product industry, haiku poetry, and transcendentalist and Native American literatures. Students study the use of language in these contexts and explore the ways in which this can enable varying perspectives on environmental and ecological issues.

Assessment

Assignment 1: Students read a selection of articles from the journal *Language & Ecology* and the other journal articles available online. What discourses do these articles analyse? What impact do they claim that the discourses have on the environment and/or sustainability? 1,000 words (30 per cent).

Assignment 2: Finding their own original data from TV, magazines or the internet (e.g. fashion advertisements, zoo websites, newspaper descriptions of the 'gloomy' economy), students write a mini-article of a similar style to the articles they examined in their first assignment. They are required to describe how the kind of language used could have a potential impact on sustainability or the environment. The essay should include analysis of specific features of the data (such as pronoun use, levels of certainty, metaphor or visual features). 2,000 words (70 per cent).

Selected module reading

Carson, R. (1956) *A Sense of Wonder*, HarperCollins, New York NY
Chawla, S. (1991) 'Linguistic and philosophical roots of our environmental crisis', *Environmental Ethics*, vol 13, no 3, pp253–262.
Fill, A. and Mühlhäusler, P. (eds) (2001) *The Ecolinguistics Reader: Language, Ecology and Environment*, Continuum, London
Goatly, A. (2002) 'The Representation of Nature in the BBC World Service', *Text*, vol 22, no 1, pp1–27
Harré, R., Brockmeier, J. and Mühlhäusler, P. (1999). *Greenspeak: A Study of Environmental Discourse*, Sage, London
Stibbe, A. (2004) 'Environmental education across cultures: beyond the discourse of shallow environmentalism', *Language & Intercultural Communication*, vol 4, no 4, pp242–260
Stibbe, A. (2004) 'Language, Health and Ecology', *Language & Ecology*, vol 1, no 3, available at www.ecoling.net/summer0.htm, accessed 13 August 2009
Stibbe, A. (2004) 'Masculinity, health and ecological destruction', *Language & Ecology*, vol 1, no 3, available at www.ecoling.net/summer1a.htm, accessed 13 August 2009

'Sustainable development' or related terms are notable for their absence from the UK benchmarking statements for languages, linguistics and area studies. While traditional sub-fields (e.g. phonetics, sociolinguistics) are present in the linguistics statement (QAA, 2007b), ecolinguistics does not feature. This lack of an explicit recognition of sustainability as a key issue in the study of these subjects may be an obstacle.

In an interdisciplinary context, the convenors of a module involving students of medicine, geography, education and Spanish report that students in the other disciplines often found it hard to see what the Spanish language student might be able to contribute to a cross-disciplinary project. Using an enquiry-based learning approach to a specific environmental or societal issue, four out of the seven multi-disciplinary teams of students employed the strategy of situating the problem in a Spanish or Portuguese-speaking country (Woods et al, 2006, p13). This situation may be the result of a disconnect between student experiences of languages at school, which emphasize language skills, and languages at university, in which 'content' courses on literature, culture and politics, for example, form the basis of modern language degrees.

A further obstacle is the lack of engagement of modern languages with the academic field of tourism, and especially the growing market for ethical and ecotourism. Despite having common interests in travel and 'foreign' places, linguists have written surprisingly little about tourism (although see Phipps, 2007). Cheap flights between the UK and other European destinations not only have an impact on the physical environment but may also affect the ability of students to embed themselves in the local culture given that return trips to the UK are so readily available; fee-waivers for students participating in the EU-based ERASMUS scheme may also make study outside Europe less financially attractive.

Conclusion

Obstacles to embedding sustainability in the curriculum can be overcome if lecturers identify ESD in their existing teaching and research. As interdisciplinary fields of study, languages and area studies curricula are broad and diverse and offer ample opportunity to explore SD through politics, literature, language, cultural studies and history – this is illustrated in Boxes 16.1 to 16.3. Residence abroad projects offer opportunities for interested students to explore sustainability issues, even if explicit opportunities do not exist in a particular curriculum. While the breadth of languages and area studies as disciplines offer many opportunities for embedding sustainability concepts, it is not really possible to identify core disciplinary concerns that encompass all languages and area studies. The emerging sub-field (if that is the correct term) of ecolinguistics offers exciting opportunities in linguistics and related language studies, which could bring about an increasing consideration of the relationship between languages and environmental issues in both teaching and research.

This chapter has provided a sketch map of current and potential sustainability practice. While by no means a compete picture, it illustrates the importance of an understanding of language and culture to long-term SD for students of all disciplines. The language we use to talk about the environment affects our responses to the challenges we face. Understanding how our own language is used to discuss sustainability, and how sustainability is discussed in other languages is critical to ensuring that actions taken on an individual, local and global scale are beneficial and not detrimental to long-term sustainability.

Acknowledgements

I would like to thank Shoshannah Holdom and Angela Gallagher-Brett for their comments on an earlier draft of this chapter, and Axel Goodbody, Arran Stibbe and John Wills for allowing me to use their courses as case studies.

References

Agenda 21 (2002) *Glossaire pour le développement durable*, Agenda 21, Johannesburg, available at www.francophonie-durable.org/documents/Glossaire.pdf, accessed 23 March 2009

Arons, W. (2004) 'Interdisciplinarity, performance, power: "Galileo" in the academy', *Theatre Topics*, vol 14, no 1, pp275–291

Ashley-Cantello, W. (2009) 'A policy maker's perspective', *The Language of Sustainability: Shouting but Not Being Heard* conference, April 1, available at www.ies-uk.org.uk/resources/eventresources/languageofsustainability/Will_Ashley_Cantello.doc, accessed 11 August 2009

Baxter, J. (2009) 'Undergraduate English language: A subject in search of an identity?', *Liaison*, vol 2, pp35–37

Bell, S. and Morse, S. (1999) *Sustainability Indicators: Measuring the Immeasurable*, Earthscan, London

Berman, T. (2001) 'The rape of mother nature? Women in the language of environmental discourse', in Fill, A. and Mühlhäusler, P. (eds)

Brecht, B. (1998) *Leben des Galilei* [*Life of Galileo*], Text und Kommentar, Suhrkamp, Frankfurt am Main

Canning, J. (2005) 'Global issues, local responses: Engaging with environmental issues through Languages and Area Studies curricula', available at www.llas.ac.uk/resources/paper/2433, accessed 23 March 2009

Coates, P. (1996) 'Clio's new greenhouse', *History Today*, vol 46, no 8, pp15–22

Crystal, D. (2000) *Language Death*, Cambridge University Press, Cambridge

DEFRA (2000) *Towards a Language of Sustainable Development*, available at http://collections.europarchive.org/tna/20061023111737/, www.defra.gov.uk/environment/sustainable/educpanel/language/index.htm, accessed 22 February 2010

Fill, A. and Mühlhäusler, P. (2001) *The Ecolinguistics Reader: Language, Ecology and the Environment*, Continuum, London

Garrard, G. (2004) *Ecocriticism*, Routledge, London

Garrard, G. (2007) 'Ecocriticism and education for sustainability', *Pedagogy: Critical Approaches to Teaching Literature, Language, Composition, and Culture*, vol 7, no 3, pp359–383

Genuit, H. (undated) *Le développement soutenable*, available at www.amisdelaterre.org/Le-developpement-soutenable.html, accessed 23 March 2009

Goodbody, A. (1994) 'Es stirbt das land sienen zwecken: Writers, the environment and the green movement in the GDR', *German Life and Letters*, vol 47, no 3, pp325–336

Goodbody, A. (2006) 'Postwar dystopia and rural idyll: Arno Schmidt's early novels and the context of ecocriticism and cultural ecology', *Anglia- Zeitschrift für englische Philologie*, vol 124, no 1, pp70–100

Heise, U.K. (2006) 'Greening English: Recent introductions to ecocriticism', *Contemporary Literature*, vol 47, no 2, pp289–298

Jucker, R. (2005) personal communication with author.

Kramsch, C. (2006) 'The traffic in meaning', *Asia Pacific Journal of Education*, vol 26, no 1, pp99–104

Leal Filho, W. (2000) 'Dealing with misconceptions on the concept of sustainability', *IJSHE*, vol 1, no 1, pp9–19

Levin, J. (2002) 'Beyond nature? Recent work in ecocriticism', *Contemporary Literature* vol 43, no 1, pp171–186

Lorenzo-Zamorano, S. (2007) 'The potential of language: Sustainability in the curriculum', Teaching and Learning Forum, March, available at www.humanities.manchester.ac.uk/hummet/tandl/teachingandlearningpractice/curriculumdesign/sustainabledevelopment/fileuploadmax10mb,10624 7,en.ppt, accessed 12 August 2009

McKeown, R. and Hopkins, C. (2003) 'EE ≠ ESD: Defusing the worry', *Environmental Education Research*, vol 9, no 1, pp117–128

Nabhan G.P. (2001) 'Cultural perceptions of ecological interactions: An "endangered people's" contribution to the conservation of biological and linguistic', in Maffi, L. (ed) *On Biocultural Diversity. Linking Language, Knowledge and the Environment*, Smithsonian Institution Press, Washington & London, pp145–156

Patrick, D. (2005) 'Language rights in Indigenous communities: The case of the Inuit of Arctic Quebec', *Journal of Sociolinguistics*, vol 9, no 3, pp369–389

Pennycook, A. (2008) 'English as a language always in translation', *European Journal of English Studies*, vol 21, no 1 pp33–47

Phipps, A. (2005) 'Real and virtual rubbish: Keeping things tidy in modern languages', Enhancing environmental awareness workshop, London, September, available at www.llas.ac.uk/events/archive/2383, accessed 11 August 2009

QAA (2007a) *Languages and Related Studies* (subject benchmark statement), QAA, Gloucester, available at www.qaa.ac.uk/academicinfrastructure/benchmark/statements/languages07.pdf, accessed 23 March 2009

QAA (2007b) *Linguistics* (subject benchmark statement), QAA, Gloucester, available at www.qaa.ac.uk/academicinfrastructure/benchmark/statements/Linguistics07.pdf, accessed 23 March 2009

QAA (2008) *Area studies* (subject benchmark statement), QAA, Gloucester, available at www.qaa.ac.uk/academicinfrastructure/benchmark/statements/areastudies08.pdf, accessed 23 March 2009

Sapir, E. (2001) 'Language and environment', in Fill, A. and Mühlhäusler, P. (eds)

Schmidt, A. (1994–7) *Collected Early Fiction, 1949–1964*, Dalkey Archive Press London, 4 volumes, translated by John E Woods.

Schultz, B. (2001) 'Language and the natural environment', in Fill, A. and Mühlhäusler, P. (eds)

Selby, D. (2007) 'As the heating happens: Education for sustainable development or education for sustainable contraction?', *International Journal of Innovation and Sustainable Development*, vol 2, nos 3–4, pp249–267

Stibbe, A. (2004) 'Environmental education across cultures: Beyond the discourse of shallow environmentalism', *Language and Intercultural Communication*, vol 4, no 4, pp242–260

Stibbe, A. (2007) 'Developing critical awareness language skills for sustainability: A trans-disciplinary approach', in Roberts, C. and Roberts, J. (eds), *Greener by Degrees: Exploring sustainability through Higher Education Curricula*, University of Gloucestershire, Cheltenham, pp74–80

Stibbe, A. (2009) Keynote address, *The Language of Sustainability: Shouting but not being heard* conference, April, available at www.eauc.org.uk/file_uploads/language_of_sustainability_-_arran_stibbe.pdf, accessed 12 August 2009

SUNY Plattsburgh. (2009) *Sustainable Development and Cultural Studies in Southern Mexico* (course details), available at www.plattsburgh.edu/academics/studyabroad/latinamerica/sustainabledevelopment.php, accessed 6 April 2009

Theóphilo, M. (2008) *Márcia Theóphilo*, available at www.theophilo-amazonia-e-poesia.info, accessed 23 March 2009

Watts, R. (2007) 'Contested sources: Water as commodity/sign in French Caribbean liter-ature', *Atlantic Studies*, vol 4, no 1, pp85–101

WCED (1987) *Our Common Future: The Report of the World Commission on Environment and Development* ['The Brundtland Report'], Oxford University Press, Oxford, avail-able at www.un-documents.net/wced-ocf.htm, accessed 29 January 2010

Woods, C., McMorrow, J., Braidman, I., Lorenzo-Zamorano, S. and Bowsher, C. 'Embedding interdisciplinarity: Developing a generic EBL team project module for undergraduates', Centre for Excellence in Enquiry-Based Learning First Annual Symposium, University of Manchester, June, available at www.campus.manchester.ac.uk/ceebl/projects/casestudies/9.pdf, accessed 23 March 2009

Recommended reading

Coates, P. (1996) 'Clio's new greenhouse', *History Today*, vol 46, no 8, pp15–22
A very accessible, albeit now slightly dated, overview of environmental issues in a histori-cal (US) context.

Crystal, D. (2000) *Language Death*, Cambridge University Press, Cambridge
Well-researched and very accessible work on the consequences of language death and the importance of cultural and linguistic sustainability.

Fill, A. and Mühlhäusler, P. (2001) *The Ecolinguistics Reader: Language, Ecology and the Environment*, Continuum, London
This collection gives a good insight into the possibilities for embedding sustainability concepts into language and linguistics curricula, as well as being an accessible key text for students. In my view, Mühlhäusler's *Language of Environment: Environment of Language:*

A Course in Ecolinguistics (2003), Battlebridge Publications, London, is a useful text for students of linguistics, but is possibly too specialist for a wider audience.

Garrard, G. (2004) *Ecocriticism*, Routledge, London
Although focusing on Anglophone literature, the principles in Garrard's book can and have been applied to literature in other languages.

Goodbody, A. (2002) (ed) *The Culture of German Environmentalism: Anxieties: Visions: Realities*, Berghahn, Oxford
A range of essays on German environmentalism from literary, cultural and historical perspectives. A very useful overview for students of German.

Riordan, C. (2002) 'Environment, landscape and culture in Germany', In Phipps, A. (ed), *Contemporary German Cultural Studies*, Arnold, London, pp65–81. A helpful starting point for students of German and European Studies.

Weblinks

The Association for the Study of Literature and the Environment (UK) www.asle.org.uk is the UK affiliate of the US-based Association for the Study of Literature and the Environment, www.asle.org (both accessed 7 February 2010). The US site includes links to syllabi in humanities subjects.

The European Association for the Study of Literature, Culture and Environment has a multilingual website. Member interests encompass a broad range of language fields including English. See www.thermaldegree.com/designs/easlce/index (accessed 7 February 2010).

The journal *Language and Ecology* and its website are run by Arran Stibbe, University of Gloucestershire. See www.ecoling.net/journal.html for more on the journal and www.ecoling.net/courses.html for the university module on Discourse and Sustainability (both accessed 7 February 2010).

The Journal of Ecocriticism is a new open-access peer reviewed journal based in North America – http://ojs.unbc.ca/index.php/joe (accessed 7 February 2010).

Agenda 21's *Glossaire pour le développement durable*, www.francophonie-durable.org/documents/Glossaire.pdf, is a glossary in French with English equivalents of terms (accessed 7 February 2010).

The website of Nature and Environment in Modern German Literature, an AHRC-funded project, contains a useful bibliography and provides a strong sense of the possibilities for embedding ESD into German Studies; see http://research.ncl.ac.uk/nemgl (accessed 7 February 2010).

Márcia Theóphilo's website has English and Italian translations of her writing as well as a biography and commentary on her work www.theophilo-amazonia-e-poesia.info/ (accessed 7 February 2010).

Notes

1   The QAA benchmarking statements are written by groups of academics and describe the nature and content of an undergraduate degree in the subject. They provide guidance for creating new programmes but they are not detailed programme descriptions, neither are they intended to be prescriptive. See QAA, 2007a, piii for more details.

Chapter 17

If Sustainability Needs New Values, Whose Values? Initial Teacher Training and the Transition to Sustainability

Robert Cook, Roger Cutting and Denise Summers

Introduction

In a scene from the film *Monty Python's Life of Brian* (1979), the People's Front of Judea have just concluded a meeting agreeing on the need for direct action when Judith (the girlfriend of the eponymous Brian) runs in to say that Brian has been arrested. 'Right!' says Reg (their leader), 'This calls for immediate discussion!'

The frustration felt by Judith (and not least by Brian on hearing the result – a message of support delivered during 'what must be a difficult time', namely his crucifixion) must exemplify similar but less comedic frustrations felt by many of us who are involved in the broad area of sustainability. We have our own Judiths in the science community who rush to tell us with undisputed certainty and ever-increasing alarm that our actions are leading to catastrophe. Yet in the face of this environmental crisis, we seem to react like Reg, apparently drifting into immediate discussions concerning definitions, metaphors, paradigms, all taking place during what we realize to be 'this difficult time'.

Arguably, one of the few areas of academic study that vies with sustainability in terms of the multiplicity and plurality of definitions is education. It is unsurprising, therefore, that the attempts to combine these two fields into ESD, or education for sustainability (EfS), have, over the last two to three decades, produced a significant body of discursive literature centred on definitions, perhaps even to the point of occasional bouts of what Shallcross and Robinson (2007, p138) describe as 'definition dementia'. These debates concerning definitions are undoubtedly important but are they in reality mere entertaining diversions for the academic mind, and is this institutionalization of environmentalism (Rootes, 2003) largely responsible for the subject losing its radical edge? Given this context, this chapter considers a number of ways forward and reports on examples of how 'sustainability' may be applied directly to initial teacher training programmes.

We need action.
But what sort of action?

In the *Life of Brian*, the procrastination of the People's Front was due to their recognition that while their inflated egos could not admit it, the scale of the problem was beyond their limited abilities to remedy. But if *they* couldn't do it, then who would? So they pretended that they could. Similarly, environmental educationalists have spent much time discussing whether there really has been a change from environmental education to ESD and what the nature of the change has been (Blewitt and Cullingford, 2004). Meanwhile, any innovation in getting children into the outdoors, 'connecting' with others or being active citizens is celebrated as another bold step towards sustainability. But are these contributions really being effective in our drive for sustainability or, like the note sent to Brian, are we merely trying to reassure ourselves that we are actually doing something? Are we spending too much time agreeing on bold statements and strategies while actually coming up with no more than token actions because we cannot accept that formal education, as it is currently organized, is incapable of ever really getting to grips with the problem?

There is, at least, a growing consensus amongst educationalists and educators that there is a need for us not just to promote an understanding of the problem, but also to promote the appropriate personal values needed for a population that will behave in an environmentally and socially benign manner. This is recognized in England's National Curriculum, which speaks of enabling the development of 'knowledge, skills, understanding and values' that will improve our quality of life 'without damaging the planet' (Qualifications and Curriculum Authority [QCA], 2007). Similarly, the UK DCSF's *Sustainable Schools Strategy* identifies values in eight 'doorways' or themes for sustainability that include, 'a respect for human rights ... corporate citizenship' and understanding 'the impact of [students'] personal values and behaviours' (DCSF, 2009). It is increasingly accepted that mere knowledge and conceptual understanding of the environment and its problems does not necessarily effect behavioural change (Sterling, 2001). If that is the case, then we need to identify strategies and pedagogic approaches that challenge and even change our values and ethics if we are to bring about behavioural change. However, there is little clarity on the nature of what those 'values' must comprise, although they are normally presented as the vaguely agreeable standards of behaviour that we would want from any civilized individual. However, any attempt to change our values and ethics is beset with difficulties.

Selby (2006) uses an intriguing narrative concerning people trying to find their way out of a forest and setting off down a broad and easy path – and, because it is easy, setting off without a thought as to where the path might be leading. Think carefully about that. You don't know where any of the paths lead, but one is broad and bright and easy-going. The others are dark and difficult. No contest, after all; hard roads are just that. This is an important metaphor. In the West, many of us enjoy lifestyles unparalleled elsewhere, we have access to affordable consumer goods and food, we benefit from uninterrupted power supplies, sophisticated communications networks, heat, water supply, sanitation, universal healthcare and education, political stability and security and, although subject to constant attrition, human rights. Not a bad list; yet, while many of us in the developed world have a clear and rational understanding of what such privilege is based on (Bonnett, 2002), we choose to turn away, safe and secure as we are on the easy road. We could take the harder road towards sustainability and in moments of lucidity we probably know we should, but not only are we hesitant of the sacrifices that we will need to make along the way, but so unknown is our destination we are also unsure if we will even know it when we get there. The problem is that we have little idea of what sustainability looks like (Shallcross and Robinson, 2007). Given the option of stumbling down the painful path, making significant economic and social sacrifices accompanied by recalcitrant chants of 'Are we nearly there yet?', is it any wonder we take the easy route? We need to consider where this easy path is leading. While we have no examples of sustainable societies in the industrialized world, we do have plenty of examples of *de facto* sustainability in primitive ('traditional' or 'primal') human systems. However, these are not seen as exemplars for obvious reasons. Some paths are too hard, even for the most zealous. However, the general scepticism about the possibility of ever getting a 'technological fix' for our environmental woes has led to a growing acceptance that profound personal lifestyle change, based on reductions of consumption and a new relationship with our environment, will be necessary.

The 'hard' path implies that we cannot reduce our demands on the environment unless we accept that we may have to live with fewer possessions, with reduced choice, reduced mobility and reduced physical ease and comfort. This path demands that teachers will need to confront the reality that, if we are really going to try to do something useful, we are likely to have to move out of our comfortable quality of life into circumstances that will be potentially difficult. However, are we as professional teachers qualified to take up such a challenge? Indeed, we may also ask whether we have a remit or even the right. Are we and should we be really preparing the next generation of educators to do so? The 'hard path' will undoubtedly need greater focus and attention from educationalists. So it is here that we need to direct our energies.

Before we look at some contemporary developments in teacher training, it may be worthwhile to consider where we are in the UK in relation to delivering education that promotes sustainability. The following points are the key findings of a review of teaching about sustainability based on a sample of 41 schools in England and Wales in 2008:

- In most of the schools there was little emphasis on SD and limited awareness of national and local government policies for this area.
- In the large majority of schools, promoting SD through National Curriculum subjects was inconsistent and uncoordinated.
- In many of the schools, SD was a peripheral issue, often confined to extracurricular activities and involving only a minority of pupils.
- A small number of the schools placed considerable emphasis on SD. In these cases teaching was good, lessons were stimulating and pupils took an active part in improving the sustainability of the school and the wider community (Ofsted, 2008a, p6).

With the exception of the last point, these findings make fairly damning reading, particularly in the context of its authorship, the UK Government's inspectorate of all things educational the Office for Standards in Education (Ofsted). This, then, is the official state of EFS in UK schools: uncoordinated, peripheral, involving only a minority. So much for the mainstream, state sector. However, one group of schools in the UK interestingly seem to do very much better. A cursory glance through the Ofsted reports for Steiner-Waldorf schools (the periodic reviews carried out by the inspectorate[1]) yields a very different set of results. Here, in relation to spiritual, moral and social development, 10 of the 27 schools reviewed are described as 'outstanding', two are 'good with outstanding qualities' and the others are described as 'good'. HM Inspectorate of Education, (the Scottish equivalent to Ofsted[2]) describes two Scottish Steiner Schools as 'very good' and 'good' and identifies 'outdoor education in all weathers' and 'stimulating outdoor activities' as two key strengths in the these schools.

Therefore, we have mainstream schools seemingly approaching sustainability in a piecemeal way, with little coordination and cross-curricular planning and only 'new school buildings' needing to be carbon-neutral by 2016 (DfES, 2006). The Government aim for universal 'sustainable schools' by 2020 (DfES, 2006) seems a very long way off. On the other hand, according to the inspectorates, the Steiner-Waldorf schools seem to have achieved exactly what recent Government pronouncements have called for, namely the 'commitment to care', the 'integrated approach' and the use of the so-called 'eight doorways' to sustainability (Ofsted, 2008a).

The holistic model used in Steiner-Waldorf education appears to offer a way of achieving this ambitious goal. If schools are to be sustainable, this must mean sustainability beyond the simple physical construction of the building. It is simply not sufficient to place EfS into a traditionally delivered curriculum as another subject; we have tried that for 30 years while nearly every environmental indicator you could choose shows further (and frequently more rapid) deterioration. For nearly a decade, ESD has been in the National Curriculum, and Ofsted's own report acknowledges its poor delivery. How long do we continue with a failed model? Perhaps now we need to try something else and, in the absence of contrary evidence, borrow from Steiner–Waldorf education to make the environment, environmental values and human relationships the central focus of the curriculum. The transformation of education, however, would also require new teaching and learning methods, and specifically trained educators to enable, focus and consolidate learning. The traditional linear, cognitive models of learning that are based on artificial subject divides, where the teacher has 'ownership' of the knowledge, would no longer be appropriate. Affective learning (Bloom, 1956) not only requires new methods but needs teachers to be cognisant of its dangers. History has frequently shown that changing views and values to affect behaviour may not be the sole reserve of liberal thought (Bruggemeier et al, 2005). We need therefore commensurately radical changes in teacher education if we are to produce the new skills and approaches for transformation that ESD requires.

Ideas in action: Some examples and implications

In the initial teacher training (ITT) programme at the University of Plymouth, we have attempted to introduce some appropriate new teaching techniques. For example, since 2008 modules for science education students have been taught exclusively through PBL (Cutting and Kelly, 2008). The problems are often based on school teaching and do not just involve environmental issues (although this is an important source for some of the units) but also include issues of ethical science (through discussion of topical ethical debates) and holistic science (again, by considering the validity of such wider approaches to science understanding). One session, for example, involves collating and discussing emotional responses to quiet meditation and contemplation in a woodland setting. Such attempts to actively involve science education students in wider holistic approaches are admittedly limited but have tended to result in a greater appreciation of both the limitations and strengths of reductionism. Any critique of holistic approaches to science is at least better informed from such experiences of practice. Certainly, PBL approaches – after some degree of transitional angst – have elicited exceptionally positive responses from student cohorts (Cutting and Kelly, 2008). Furthermore, ecological fieldwork now regularly includes so-called 'Gaian' meditations based on those provided by Harding in *Animate Earth* (2006), now a key text for these students. In addition, students are taken out at least fortnightly on these modules and are introduced to Forest Schools work (Davis and Waite, 2005). They also have the additional opportunity to join a formal Forest Schools training programme should they wish. The environment is no longer seen as the subject for science education but rather the reason, and the space in which it takes place.

While these units are examples of activities and approaches that are included in an ITT programme, they still remain additional to the core curriculum. Elsewhere, however, the entire nature and approach of the programme has been adapted. An illustration of how this might be achieved may be found in the example of Somerset College.

Since 2005, one member of Somerset College's ITT team had been introducing ESD informally into the teacher training programme offered with the University of Plymouth and other further education colleges in South West England to teachers in the lifelong learning sector (i.e. post-compulsory, adult and community education and work-based learning). However, as it was not an assessed part of the curriculum it was not essential for the student teachers to engage with it and therefore was unlikely to have had much effect on their teaching practice. To explore this further, data were collected from the students involved and out of 20 surveyed, 15 responded. Of these, seven felt their understanding had been enhanced 'a lot', eight 'a little' and three felt it had not influenced them at all professionally, although one mentioned greater understanding of global issues and would share this with students when appropriate. Other responses ranged from being more aware of the subject and not wasting paper and turning off lights in classrooms to feeling more confident about exploring ESD in a deeper way to develop their curriculum. Four respondents were actually developing ESD within their curriculum, three others wanted to do so, one was not and one 'didn't know' whether they would do so.

When asked what might support them in this, the majority needed more suggestions and resources to help them move from theory to practice. When asked about barriers to including ESD, seven mentioned 'time', four mentioned 'concern about lack of knowledge' and one mentioned 'reluctance and prejudice from students'. The majority of the respondents felt more time could be devoted to ESD in the programme, some wanted more suggestions and others felt it should be a formal part of the curriculum. Twelve of the students felt the introduction had affected them personally while three didn't know. Overall, the message seemed to be that the introduction had affected the majority to various extents, although only a minority had actually started to integrate it in their own curriculum and the majority felt they needed more guidance.

Due to changes in UK Government policy (DfES, 2003 and 2004) requiring a fully qualified teaching profession in the lifelong learning sector, the ITT programmes had to be rewritten in 2007 to meet the standards required for Qualified Teacher Status in the Lifelong Learning Sector. This coincided with the sustainability strategy of the UK Learning and Skills Council (2005), the body responsible for funding post-compulsory education and training, which stated that all providers should embed 'sustainable development skills' in education and training programmes by 2010 (Learning and Skills Council, 2005). Therefore, it was an opportune time to suggest that there should be an ESD learning outcome in one of the modules and that sustainability should become an underpinning theme of the programme. This was agreed and plans and resources developed so far were shared with colleagues across the University of Plymouth partnership.

At that stage, ESD had only been introduced into one module and so the Somerset College team began to consider how to thread it throughout the whole teacher training programme. The team were keen to do this but there was a lack of confidence and understanding as to how ESD could be integrated in a way that would not be perceived as a 'bolt-on' extra. Each member of the team had varying experience, knowledge and values relating to ESD and they needed to consider how to share this and support each other in their own development as well as the necessary curriculum development. It was decided that an appropriate way forward was through a cooperative inquiry (Heron and Reason, 2001). This approach involved each member of the team acting as co-researchers and co-subjects moving through a series of cycles of action and reflection. This participatory and democratic approach was particularly appropriate in meeting the aims of embedding ESD in the team's practice. In regular meetings, the team shared ideas, experiences and resources and drew up action plans, and each member reflected on their progress to inform the following meeting. During the first year of the project, the team developed session plans and resources to be used in four of the six modules that were subsequently reviewed. Additional developments during the following year were informed by reflections on previous attempts and feedback from students. Plans and resources were also developed for the final two modules.

In the first module, alongside the usual session in which the development of teaching and learning resources was explored, students were encouraged to consider the sustainability of their resources, adapting an activity from the *Linkingthinking* resources for teachers (Sterling et al, 2005). They were also introduced to the concept of sustainable communities of practice (Stuckey and Smith, 2004) to encourage student teachers to identify colleagues from whom they could receive support, and as they developed, provide mutual support to avoid the isolation that new teachers often experience (Summers, 2005). In the second module the concept of sustainable assessment (Boud, 2000) was introduced, in which students are encouraged to develop self- and peer-assessment among other strategies outlined. In the third module, students consider the use of Bloom's (1956) Taxonomy in relation to ESD values, which is followed up by encouraging them to consider how they might use this model with their students to explore values relevant to their own subject specialism. Also, alongside a session on classroom management in which behaviourist strategies are discussed, the concept of non-violent communication (Rosenberg, 2003) is considered as an alternative, humanist approach to behavioural concerns. The fourth module includes the ESD learning outcome, which entails students having to show their understanding of ESD principles and research this in their own subject specialism. This work provides the foundation for students to design a session plan and resources to introduce sustainability to their own students. They are encouraged to consider 'linkingthinking' approaches to explore the bigger picture in relation to issues of concern (Sterling et al, 2005). The fifth module investigates curriculum ideologies and design and considers Sterling's (2001) transformative approach and Miller's (2007) holistic curriculum. In the final module, the introduction to non-violent communication is developed in relation to community cohesion and cultural diversity, which is recognized by Ofsted (2008b) as an area requiring development. Students are also guided to David Orr's chapter on 'Rating colleges' in *Earth in Mind* (2004) to consider how they might develop their quality procedures (which is the focus of this final module) and evaluate the environmental and social impact, as well as the economic impact, that their students will have on their communities following the completion of their programmes of study.

At the time of writing, two groups have experienced ESD right through the programme and will provide the basis for further evaluation data to inform future developments. Comments from the majority of students were very positive and included feedback on their gaining knowledge and developing resources to introduce sustainability to their students, demonstrating that as teachers they are able to bring about change in a professional and educational context. However, a few of the comments were less positive and suggested there was too much focus on ESD, whereas some felt they needed more practical support in developing plans for their own practice. The team considered student reaction to all developments throughout the cooperative inquiry, which enabled them to adjust and refine their practice.

The process of staff development continued through regular cooperative inquiry meetings over a two-year period to enable the team to further develop the knowledge, values and skills base to confidently embed ESD in their practice. This included a member of the CSF, the centre with the remit of transforming Plymouth into a sustainability university (Dyer et al, 2009), who plays a critical 'devil's advocate' to the team's cooperative inquiry. This way, the team is able to consider approaches in greater depth, which helped the programme develop still further. Having trialled the programme, it is now providing the basis for a number of regional and national staff developments to promote not only the embedding of ESD/EfS into teacher training programmes but also to encourage the appropriate staff team cooperative learning mechanisms that have worked so well. The process by which this ITT course has been redesigned and developed through a team-based cooperative learning process is an example of how not only the curriculum needs to change along with teaching/learning methods, but also how the teacher's own epistemology also needs to be challenged. It is perhaps only when the teaching population is sensitized to the environmental and sustainability crisis in outlook and approach that there will be the required shift towards a core of sustainability in the taught curriculum. Other sustainability-related models of ITT courses can be found at Nottingham University (Firth and Winter, 2007) and Hertfordshire University (Huckle, 2006), to name just two.

There seem to be two approaches to the teaching of EfS or ESD in schools. The first argues for a multidisciplinary method, which in practice is frequently not quite what it appears to imply. Rather than breaking down or even abandoning the historical divides between subjects, it generally entails attempting to embed ESD into existing subject areas, perhaps by using ESD-based examples for some part of an individual subject's teaching. When described, the methods used are frequently interactive and engaging, often involving group work, problem-solving and critical review. However, environmental or sustainability educators cannot claim these characteristics solely for themselves, as they are simply good teaching methods. To illustrate this, the Sustainable Education Development Panel as early as 1998 published specifications relating to teacher education (Ali Khan and Sterling, 1998). The specifications are presented in three parts: sustainability concepts, sustainability solutions and effective sustainability teaching. The section on methods calls for a balance of learning approaches, the use of direct experience and pupils' knowledge to explore and clarify values. Indeed, if references to ESD are edited from the remaining points it would instruct students to do the following:

- Use a range of participative techniques to facilitate the development and exchange of viewpoints.
- Consider uncertainty and controversy.
- Critically reflect.
- Consider both problems (cause and effect) and possible solutions.
- Refer to and encourage participation in responsible practices at school and at home.
- Foster community, regional and global links.
- Use interdisciplinary approaches where appropriate.

This tendency of appropriating certain values to sustainability is contentious and open to enormous debate as to their interpretation and weighting (Leiserowitz et al, 2004). The fact that they are generally not unique to ESD is perhaps indicative of the area becoming so broad a concern that it is being interpreted as all things to all people (Cutting and Cook, 2009). However, while it may be possible to embed subject materials and topics across curricula, it is not always a welcome addition. For example, in 2009 the QCA, the Government's examination agency in England, proposed a new mathematics A-level, 'The Use of Mathematics'. A more applied approach to 16-plus mathematics was suggested and the specimen papers included maths questions based on issues such as population growth, germination of seeds, geographical variation in women's income and statistics relating to the health issues of the newly born. What could therefore be seen as an example of bringing ESD into the maths curriculum was met with a well-publicized storm of protest in the UK, with the media seemingly using the topics to denigrate the qualification. Eventually, 64 university professors wrote to oppose the proposal, calling the new examination 'mindless' and 'not a preparation for university courses' (Curtis, 2009). Resistance to change is evidently strong even at subject level and the inclusion of such materials or applied examples is seen as extra content, or is evidently perceived to undermine the academic integrity of the subject.

In contrast to this cross-curricular approach, the second identifies subjects that are best placed to deliver the appropriate ESD outcomes. Given the existing content of many subjects' curricula it is questionable how far the inclusion of ESD would be beyond the propaedeutic, however, when examples are provided of how sustainability may be linked to existing subject areas, geography and, to a lesser extent, science consistently appear as the predominant vehicles (Huckle, 2006). Orr (2004) has discussed the many issues relating to ESD and EE being taught separately from the wider curriculum, but the priority use of a subject such as geography is further compounded by the regrettable reality of the significant decline geography has experienced as a subject in the UK. Beyond the point when the subject ceases to be compulsory, student numbers have continued to fall throughout the last decade (Curtis, 2008).

The question of introducing values relating to sustainability into some disciplines is always likely to be problematic. The form that those values should take, however, must remain a primary concern of teacher-trainers, and they must be predicated on what are seen as the defining characteristics of sustainability. Metaphors have commonly, and usefully, been used to help define these characteristics, and the example of ecosystems has tended to predominate (Capra, 1996), the efficient fluxes and cycles of which stand as perfect exemplars of sustainable systems. The problem here is that ecosystems are dynamic and in a constant state of readjustment whereas populations are subject to what may be catastrophic dependent and independent controls. Furthermore, ecosystems are unemotional in their functioning; we are not. The principle of the ecosystem has moreover been widely recognized since the concept was first developed in the 1930s and there is general acceptance of the interconnected nature of the environment. However, this knowledge appears to have been used at best to evaluate our impact on the environment and at worst to more efficiently exploit it.

Challenging their values and questioning our values

David Orr has (2004) called for a change in the metaphors we use in environmental education, so let us move away from the parallels drawn with the natural world and look at those which are inclusive of the frailty and vulnerability of human communities. Let us see ourselves in the industrialized world as estranged from the wider global community. We have a collective and chronic behavioural problem that allows us to continue tearing out resources, spraying toxic pollutants and throwing our waste across the face of the Earth. An appropriate analogy is of global-scale vandals engaged in the worst forms of antisocial behaviour. Behaviour aside, we certainly have a collective hearing impairment that means we cannot hear the cries from the poorest, and this seems combined with a collective visual impairment as we cannot, or do not, see the hungry, the poor and the dispossessed. We turn away to face the wall like a disturbed adolescent; secure perhaps, but deeply troubled. How then, can we as educators, change our behaviour to promote our inclusion as responsible and responsive members of a global community?

The first step in rectifying antisocial behaviour is to encourage dysfunctional individuals to confront the effects of that behaviour. The problem with modern society is that the effects of our behaviour, on other people and the planet, are obscure, uncertain, with indeterminate links between cause and effect and seemingly far removed from us. Developing an intellectual understanding of the full range of problems that our consumption currently leads to would strain the abilities of the most committed environmentalist. From a teaching point of view, it would suffice to ensure that students are made aware that in a world dominated by a global trading system we can rarely know what effects our actions have and so we are inevitably acting 'irresponsibly'; that is to say that such a system demands that we abrogate our responsibility to others. The morality of this needs to be questioned. Secondly, troubled adolescents must recognize that their behaviour does not ultimately serve *themselves* well. Encouraging empathy for others may convince a few to adjust their behaviour, but self-interest, as ever, is the greater motivator. In the environmental field, we can turn to recent research into the nature of personal happiness (Layard, 2005), as well as to ancient philosophies and psychologies, which show that increases in material wealth either have no effect on our personal sense of well-being or actually diminish it (Douthwaite, 1992; Wilkinson and Pickett, 2009).

This idea of focusing on our current environmentally dysfunctional behaviour rather than on identifying 'sustainable' modes of action could be a useful and significant one. If we apply the same idea to 'values', we need to make a subtle but important shift from our current concern with identifying values for future sustainability to identifying and questioning the values that underlie modern life and have led us to live so *unsustainably*. This approach is, of course, potentially subversive and transformative of the social norms and the economic and political structures on which society is currently based. It is highly contentious ground in which education has conventionally been very wary of becoming bogged down. For this reason, such deep questioning of current norms must avoid any suggestion of prescription or promotion (to a greater degree than in most other areas of study). To achieve this, we will need teachers who see a capacity for radical and provocative questioning to be at the forefront of their skills. We live in an age when rapid global socio-economic changes are in any case making traditional conceptions of responsible citizenship redundant (Falk, 2000). New forms of social identification and cultural norms will appear, and are doing so already, in the international milieu of the internet age. At the same time, there are powerful ideological forces in processes such as international trade, religion, politics and marketing that are actively seeking to manipulate the values of future generations. For current generations to have the skills to identify the subtle and often insidious processes that mould their opinions and behaviour will be even more vital in the future, if they are to be able to identify and move away from the values of *un*sustainability.

At Plymouth, this shift in emphasis has been utilized by the authors in discussing sustainability matters with undergraduates in Faculty of Education courses. A conventional explanatory and exploratory approach to the nature of SD and its potential transmission in a school environment has often been met with a degree of bored familiarity. However, when the subject is approached with Socratic inquiry as to the motivations students feel for their personal behaviour and how they believe it will influence their future happiness, the class is transformed. Once the class has become engaged with questions of the nature of perceived pressures to conform, unthinking patterns of behaviour and consumption and the nature of their underlying ('real') needs, they are then much more ready to question the nature of conventional SD concepts and assess their value, potential development and application. Also, by focusing on questioning personal values rather than encouraging the adoption of 'appropriate' ones for sustainability, staff have felt that they are also actually working in a way that is more fitting and plays to their strengths as academics.

While this approach militates against focusing on developing a set of 'appropriate values' for sustainability, there are practices that promote reflection, self-containment and self-reliance and that strengthen an individual's capacity to question personal motivations and actions. These are affective rather than cognitive skills and, perhaps because of this, they are likely to be invaluable tools in developing a self-motivated and self-directed population resistant to the destructive values foisted on them by other interests. Thus it may be crucial that trainee teachers become skilled in the arts of self-actualization (Maslow, 1943), meditation and mindfulness (Kaplan, 2001) or at least to be able to teach students skills for deep experience of quietude and tranquillity such as 'active silence training' (Angelotti et al, 2009). Of course, if we are successful in this we may find that future environmental education and ESD see themselves as being conceptually opposed to the ethic of ever-increasing economic production, or even high levels of consumerism and material wealth, as being desirable from a personal, let alone an environmental, perspective. They may even come to consider students who decide to seek a quieter, simpler, more frugal existence based on close community structures and self-reliance as the 'successful', 'enterprising' and exemplary pupils.

Conclusion

Like the characters in the Monty Python film, we must also accept that our powers are limited. Wider social education is far more important in generating our personal values than is the classroom. Our family, our need to belong and our peer-group values are all far more influential. It is all too easy to ignore the processes of education that go on outside the classroom. How can we promote sustainability in a culture that encourages ever-greater amounts of consumption and an advertising industry that tries to convince credulous young minds that possessions are the route to personal fulfilment and contentment? If we are to embody the principles of sustainability as educators then we must see it as part of our individual and institutional remits and responsibilities to engage with the wider community and its educational needs. If we see wider social concerns as being beyond our remit then we fail to embed sustainability in our educationalist practice. Widening participation (of academia in society as much as society in academia) should not just be a transient government policy; it should be a major driver of ESD.

Thus, as teachers and trainers of teachers we must strive to develop a culture of sustainability, which means more than reducing the school heating bill or encouraging recycling, as worthy as these are. At the very least, schools must become public information beacons for the basic values of sustainability, but they must also entertain and explore the more radical values of self-reliance, economic localization, environmental activism, 'doing less and being more', frugality, and communalism, as well as the vast range of methods for finding personal fulfilment and happiness within as much as, or more than, from the external world. Consequently, teachers and institutions need to be retrained and redirected if we are to teach sustainability effectively. The culture of educational institutes must support the sustainability ethic as enthusiastically as they have previously supported the business ethic. Whatever metaphors and imagery we adopt in order to conceptualize our sustainability target, environmental educationalists must now 'walk' our sustainability 'talk'.

References

Ali Khan, S. and Sterling, S. (1998) *Sustainable Development Education: Teacher Education Specification*, HE21 Project, Forum for the Future, London

Angelotti, M., Perazzone, A., Tono, M., Bertolino, F. and Barbiero, G. (2009) 'Educating the educators: Primary teacher education', in Gray, D., Colucci-Gray, L. and Camino, E. (eds) *Science, Society and Sustainability: Education and Empowerment for an Uncertain World*, Routledge, London

Blewitt, J. and Cullingford, C. (eds) (2004) *The Sustainability Curriculum: The Challenge for Higher Education*, Earthscan, London

Bloom, B.S. (1956) *The Taxonomy of Educational Objectives, The Classification of Educational Goals*, Longmans Green, New York

Bonnett, M. (2002) 'Education for sustainability as a frame of mind', *Environmental Education Research*, vol 8, no 1, pp9–20

Boud, D. (2000) 'Sustainable assessment: Rethinking assessment for the learning society', *Studies in Continuing Education*, vol 22, no 2, pp151–167

Bruggemeier, F., Cioc, M. and Zeller, T. (2005) *How Green Were the Nazis? Nature, Environment and Nation in the Third Reich*, Series in Ecology and History, Ohio University Press, Athens OH

Capra, F. (1996) *The Web of Life: A New Scientific Understanding of Living Systems*, Anchor Books, New York NY

Curtis, P. (2008) 'Popularity of "boring" geography on the wane', *The Guardian*, 17 January, available at www.guardian.co.uk/uk/2008/jan/17/schools.ofsted, accessed 2 October 2009

Curtis, P. (2009) 'New maths A-level "not of A-level standard"', *The Guardian* 10 July, available at www.guardian.co.uk/education/2009/jul/10/new-maths-a-level-criticised, accessed 20 July 2009

Cutting, R.L. and Cook, R. (2009) 'The world environmental education conference 2007: A critical appraisal', *Environmental Education Research*, vol 15, no 2, pp177–187

Cutting, R.L. and Kelly, O. (2008) 'Going up alleys to see if they're blind: The use of problem solving as a basis for teaching undergraduate science programmes', *Proceedings of the 13th IOSTE Symposium on The Use of Science and Technology Education for Peace and Sustainable Development*, Kusadasi, September, pp944–952, available at www.ioste.org/pdf/proceed13.pdf, accessed 9 February 2010

Davis, B. and Waite, S. (2005) 'Forest School: Opportunities and Challenges in Early Years', University of Plymouth, available at www.edu.plymouth.ac.uk/oelresnet/documents/Forestschoolfinalreport2.doc?page=17736, accessed 21 September 2009

DCSF (2009) *Sustainable Schools Strategy*, available at www.teachernet.gov.uk/sustainableschools/index.cfm, accessed 18 July 2009

DfES (2003) *The Future of Initial Teacher Education for the Learning and Skills Sector: An Agenda for Reform*, DfES, Sheffield

DfES (2004) *Equipping Our Teachers for the Future: Reforming Initial Teacher Training for the Learning and Skills Sector*, DfES, Sheffield

DfES (2006) *Sustainable Schools*, available at www.sustainableschools-ne.org.uk/Documents/SustainableSchoolsA4leaflet.pdf, accessed 22 September 2009

Douthwaite, R. (1992) *The Growth Illusion: How Economic Growth has Enriched the Few, Impoverished the Many, and Endangered the Planet*, Resurgence, London

Dyer, A., Selby, D. and Chalkley, B. (2009) 'A centre for excellence in education for sustainable development', in Chalkley, B., Haigh, M. and Higgit, D. (eds), *Education for Sustainable Development: Papers in Honour of the United Nations Decade of Education for Sustainable Development (2005–2014)*, Routledge, London, pp155–60

Falk, R. (2000) 'The decline of citizenship in an era of globalization', *Citizenship Studies*, vol 4, no 1, pp5–17

Firth, R. and Winter, C. (2007) 'Constructing education for sustainable development: The secondary school geography curriculum and initial teacher training', *Environmental Education Research*, vol 13, no 5, pp599–619

Harding, S. (2006) *Animate Earth: Intuition and Gaia*, Green Books, Dartington

Heron, J. and Reason, P. (2001) 'The practice of co-operative inquiry: Research "with" rather than "on" people', in Reason, P. and Bradbury, H. (eds), *Handbook of Action Research*, Sage Publications, London

Huckle, J. (2006) *Education for Sustainable Development: A Briefing Paper for the Teacher Training Resource Bank* (revised ed), available at http://john.huckle.org.uk/publications_downloads.jsp, accessed 19 July 2009

Kaplan, S. (2001) 'Meditation, restoration and the management of mental fatigue', *Environment and Behaviour*, vol 33, no 4, pp480–506

Layard, R. (2005) *Happiness: Lessons from a New Science*, Penguin, London

Learning and Skills Council (2005) *From Here to Sustainability: The LSC's Strategy for Sustainable Development Supporting Document*, available at http://readingroom.lsc.gov.uk/lsc/2005/ourbusiness/strategy/from-here-to-sustainability-lsc-strategy-for-sustainable-development.pdf, accessed 9 February 2010

Leiserowitz, A., Kates, R.W. and Parris, T.M. (2004) *Sustainability Values, Attitudes, and Behaviors: A Review of Multi-national and Global Trends*, Center for International Development Working Paper no 113, Harvard University, Cambridge MA

Maslow, A.H. (1943) 'A theory of human motivation', *Psychological Review*, vol 50 no 4, pp370–396

Miller, J.P. (2007) *The Holistic Curriculum* (2nd ed), University of Toronto Press, Toronto

Monty Python's Life of Brian (1979), Director Terry Jones

Ofsted (2008a) *Schools and Sustainability: A Climate for Change*, available at www.eauc.org.uk/file_uploads/schoolsandsustain.pdf, accessed 20 July 2009

Ofsted (2008b) *Schools to Promote Community Cohesion and Ofsted to Inspect*, available at www.culturaldiversity.org.uk/docs/255.pdf, accessed 22 July 2009

Orr, D.W. (2004) *Earth in Mind – On Education, Environment and the Human Prospect* (10th anniversary ed), Island Press, Washington DC

QCA (2007) *Education for Sustainable Development*, available at http://curriculum.qcda.gov.uk/key-stages-1-and-2/learning-across-the-curriculum/education-for-sustainable-development/index.aspx

Rootes, C. (2007) 'The transformation of environmental activism', in Rootes, C. (ed) *Environmental Protest in Western Europe*, Oxford University Press, Oxford, pp3–13

Rosenberg, M. (2003) *Nonviolent Communication: A Language of Life* (2nd ed), Puddle Dancer Press, Encinitas CA

Selby, D. (2006) 'The firm and shaky ground of education for sustainable development', *Journal of Geography in Higher Education*, vol 30, no 2, pp351–365

Shallcross, T. and Robinson, J. (2007) 'Is a decade of teacher education for sustainable development essential for survival?', *Journal of Education for Teaching*, vol 32, no 2, pp137–147

Sterling, S. (2001) *Sustainable Education: Re-Visioning Learning and Change*, Schumacher Briefing, Green Books, Dartington

Sterling, S., Irving, D., Maiteny, P. and Salter, J. (2005) *Linkingthinking: New Perspectives on Thinking and Learning for Sustainability*, WWF Scotland, Aberfeldy

Stuckey, B. and Smith, J.D. (2004) 'Building Sustainable Communities of Practice', In Hildrethand, P.M. and Kimble, C. (eds) *Knowledge Networks: Innovation Through Communities of Practice*, IGI Publishing, Pennsylvania PA, pp150–164

Summers, D.B. (2005) *Becoming a Teacher in the Post-compulsory Sector: Student Teachers' Perceptions of Influences on the Development of their Professional Identities*, EdD thesis, University of Exeter

Wilkinson, R. and Pickett, K. (2009) *The Spirit Level: Why More Equal Societies Almost Always Do Better*, Penguin, London

Notes

1 Ofsted reports are available online at www.ofsted.gov.uk (accessed 9 February 2010).

2 HM Inspectorate of Education reports are available at www.hmie.gov.uk/Default.aspx (accessed 20 July 2009).

Endword

Paula Jones, David Selby and Stephen Sterling

Some emails are really interesting: the one reproduced below is from a communication that the editors received recently. As it happens, it came from an American mathematics teacher – an area not covered in this book – but it reflects a questioning process in which more and more academics appear to be involved, as the big issues of how to ensure a liveable, peaceful and secure future impact on everyday experience and consciousness:

My original research focused on a narrow area of math education ('teaching logarithms'); it has progressively broadened ('why teach logarithms?') to 'why teach math?' and to 'why teach?' Again and again, I had to confront questions of purpose in my field. I have also become acutely aware that the work that math teachers do in their classes has very little to do with the real problems of society, most notably issues of sustainability.

This 'progressive broadening' of concern and horizon is the essence of sustainability, looking critically not just at our immediate work but at the context of our work, and then the wider contexts of contexts, which in turn inevitably raises questions about the local and the immediate and how they affect the bigger picture. There is no neutral and justifiably isolated position here, or if there is, it's probably rare. Teaching and learning, whether concerned with the student experience, innovative pedagogy, e-learning, employability or internationalization (or anything else), take place in the context of and affect the real world: one which is increasingly characterized by uncertainty, loss of boundaries, complexity and unsustainable patterns of economic and social life. But the real world is also a place of innovation, energy, and potential opportunities to achieve more sustainable communities and lifestyles as we peer, with some unease, into an unclear and endangered future. Nicholas Stern, who authored the influential 2006 UK report on climate change (Stern 2006), writes in the foreword to the HEFCE action plan on sustainable development in HE that the world 'needs minds capable of creating new possibilities', and that we need to 'transform our current ways of thinking and operating', and that the HE sector offers a 'vital platform' for undertaking the transition necessary to 'safeguard a secure future' (Stern, 2009, p1). It's quite a challenge. It requires learning *within* educational systems, not just learning *through* educational systems, as the chapters of this book demonstrate. And as our correspondent above suggests, it raises questions of purpose.

Sustainability requires HEIs to become less centres of transmission and delivery and more centres of transformation and inquiry, less teaching organizations, more learning organizations critically engaged with real-world issues in their community and region. It requires, too, that they be less engaged in 'retrospective education', following on from past practice, and more involved in 'anticipative education'; that is, in Scharmer's words, 'learning from the future as it emerges' (Scharmer, 2009). For now, there is a difference between those who see ESD as a necessary add-on that leaves most current practices otherwise unaffected, and those who see it as representing a shift of culture that changes policy and practice at a whole institutional level. The two are not exclusive: one can, in time, lead to the emergence of the other, although there is the ever-present danger that adding on reform could be used to buttress resistance to more fundamental, cultural change. There is evidence of a strong upwelling of interest in sustainability in HE that manifests both perceptions, but given the insistence and dynamism of this movement, we think deeper change has a winning chance. It will need to win if Stern's challenge is to be met, and we hope this book contributes to that end.

References

Scharmer, O. (2009) *Theory U: Learning from the Future as it Emerges*, Berrett-Koehler Publishers, San Francisco CA

Stern, N. (2006) *The Economics of Climate Change* ['The Stern Review'], HM Treasury, London, www.hm-treasury.gov.uk/stern_review_report.htm, accessed 10 February 2010

Stern, N. (2009) 'Foreword', in HEFCE, *Sustainable Development in Higher Education: 2008 Update to Strategic Statement and Action Plan*, HEFCE, Bristol, www.hefce.ac.uk/pubs/hefce/2009/09_03/09_03.pdf, accessed 10 February 2010

List of Contributors

John Blewitt is Director of Lifelong Learning at Aston University, UK. Formerly Director of the MSc Sustainable Development at University of Exeter, he is author of *The Ecology of Learning* (Earthscan, 2006) and *Understanding Sustainable Development* (Earthscan, 2008) and editor of *Community, Empowerment and Sustainable Development* (Green Books, 2008). His most recent project involves working with *Wildscreen* on the use of film, television and new media in conservation education and lifelong learning. He is a member of the Commission for Education and Communication of the IUCN, the UK Sustainable Development Panel and a Fellow of the Royal Society of Arts.

Jennifer Blumhof has enthusiastically supported her discipline of Environmental Science for the past 20 years. She was Principal Lecturer in the Division of Geography and Environmental Science and then Assistant Director for Learning and Teaching (in the Learning and Teaching Institute) at the University of Hertfordshire. Since the inception of GEES she has been its Senior Advisor for Environmental Science and has worked with academics across the UK. Her special interests are skills development, problem-based learning and Education for Sustainable Development (she is a member of the Higher Education Academy's Planning Group for ESD). More recently, particularly through her work with the Committee for the Heads of Environmental Science and the Institution of Environmental Sciences, she has promoted and supported stronger links with the professional bodies as a way of enhancing career potential and progression. In 2007 she was awarded a National Teaching Fellowship and in 2009 became a Visiting Research Fellow at the University of the West of England. jrblumhof@googlemail.com

Avril Butler is Senior Lecturer in Social Work, Practice Learning Coordinator and a Fellow of the Centre for Sustainable Futures, University of Plymouth. She is also a 2008 National Teaching Fellow.

John Canning is Senior Academic Coordinator in the Subject Centre for Languages, Linguistics, and Area Studies at the University of Southampton. As well as sustainable development, his interests include interdisciplinary teaching and learning, professional identities and student employability. j.canning@soton.ac.uk

Brian Chalkley is currently Director of Teaching & Learning at the University of Plymouth. From 2000–2008 he was the Director of the Higher Education Academy GEES Subject Centre (which is based at the University of Plymouth) where he is also Professor of Geography. Although a human geographer by background, in recent years he has concentrated on learning and teaching in the GEES disciplines. He is a former member of the editorial board of the *Journal of Geography in Higher Education* and for several years was a council member of the Royal Geographical Society. His main current interests lie in the field of graduate employability and Education for Sustainable Development. Brian is a National Teaching Fellow and a Senior Fellow of the Higher Education Academy.

Robert Cook is a lecturer in Education Studies at Plymouth University. His doctoral thesis was concerned with the nature of 'sustainable development' processes and purposes within a remote region of northern India. He subsequently left education for a time and lived amongst 'low impact' communities in Britain that seek high levels of self reliance, frugality and sustainability. Since joining the University of Plymouth he became a fellow of the Centre for Sustainable Futures and has promoted student involvement with 'low impact' communities both through formal teaching programmes and through informal, student union based, volunteering. His research is generally focused on the personal and social change aspects of education for sustainable development. The transformation of sustainable development into a method for personal well-being through the identification and fulfilment of true 'needs', rather than merely a necessary environmental duty, remains his particular motivation. robert.cook@plymouth.ac.uk

Debby Cotton received a DPhil in Environmental Education from St Anne's College, Oxford, and currently has a cross-institutional role in supporting higher education research at the University of Plymouth. Her research interests include environmental education and education for sustainable development (both in school and higher education contexts) and e-learning. She has published widely in education research journals, including the *Journal of Curriculum Studies*, *Studies in Higher Education* and *Environmental Education Research*, and she is on the editorial board of the *Journal of Geography in Higher Education*, where she heads up the pedagogic research team.

Roger Cutting is a widely published author in environmental sciences. In particular his science-based research evaluates the contribution that ancient and dynamic forms of landscape may offer us today in relation to both biodiversity and environmental management. More recently his interests have turned to education and in particular pedagogical approaches related to promoting sustainability and he has co-authored a number of publications in this area. He presently works at the University of Plymouth where he teaches science and environmental education on initial teacher training courses and is a research fellow in the Centre for Sustainable Futures. roger.cutting@plymouth.ac.uk

Judi Farren Bradley is a Chartered Architect by profession. She was a principal in practice for over ten years and ran the architectural section of a management consultancy company. She is Director of Research in C-SCAIPE and a Principal Lecturer and Course Director in the School of Architecture and Landscape at Kingston University. She has researched and published in the area of architectural education and the professions, and researches and lectures on sustainability and heritage. She is actively involved with the profession, being an Examiner for the Architects Registration Board and a member of the RIBA Validation Committee, as well as an active Validation Board member. She is a member of the current QAA Benchmark group for Architecture.

Debbie Flint is an Academic Developer at the Art Design Media Higher Education Academy Subject Centre based at the University of Brighton. She has taught Cultural Studies on a range of practice-based art and design programmes. Alongside education for sustainable development, her interests include museology, relationships between museums and higher education, and higher education in a further education context. d.flint@brighton.ac.uk

Deirdre Ford is a Lecturer in Social Work and Fellow of the Centre for Sustainable Futures at the University of Plymouth. She teaches a range of subjects in social work and social care programmes with a commitment to social justice, human rights and the future of professional practice in the context of climate change. deirdre.ford@plymouth.ac.uk

Diane Garrard lectures in Social Work and is a Fellow of the Centre for Sustainable Futures, University of Plymouth. She has a range of responsibilities within the Social Work programme and a keen interest in international social work and the implications of global challenges and shortages for social work. dgarrard@plymouth.ac.uk

Benny Goodman is a Lecturer in Health Studies (Nursing) in the Faculty of Health at the University of Plymouth. A registered nurse, and nurse teacher since 1993, he has been involved in education at both pre and post registration levels. Alongside clinical teaching, his main teaching interests are Evidence Based Practice and Substance Abuse. He is a Centre for Sustainable Futures Fellow at the university. He has an internationalization role for the University which involves addressing student experience and curriculum implications. He regularly contributes to the *Nursing Standard* and has just completed, with Ruth Clemow, a nursing textbook. benny.goodman@plymouth.ac.uk

Viv Horton is an Associate Lecturer in Social Work and a Fellow of the Centre for Sustainable Futures at the University of Plymouth. She works closely with colleagues to integrate global perspectives in teaching and learning and has helped to negotiate and sustain international practice learning opportunities for social work students. Now semi-retired, she is a regular volunteer in a vibrant NGO in Uganda that trains subsistence farmers in sustainable organic agriculture and fosters community development through adult education. Her special interests are self-help group methodology, its potential to achieve transformative and sustainable development, and the wider application of social work knowledge and skills to support communities challenged by the impacts of poverty, conflict, climate change, land degradation, scarcity of resources, displacement and marginalization. viv.horton@gmail.com

Paula Jones is a Research Assistant at the Centre for Sustainable Futures at the University of Plymouth. She has been involved in a number of research projects with a focus on sustainability and institutional change at the university since 2006. Paula has a background in teaching and experiential environmental education, previously having worked as an education officer for the Westcountry Rivers Trust, developing educational resources for schools, and as a primary school teacher. Prior to this she volunteered with the Groundwork Trust, a UK wide environmental regeneration charity, working specifically on projects involving schools and the local community. paula.jones@plymouth.ac.uk

Paul Kleiman is Deputy Director of PALATINE, the Higher Education Academy Subject Centre for Dance, Drama and Music, based at Lancaster University. He trained as a designer, and had a successful career in the theatre using drama as an agent of social, political and educational change. He was a member of the team that created and then led the Liverpool Institute for Performing Arts (LIPA). LIPA's unique inter-disciplinary curriculum placed a strong emphasis on the notion of providing graduates with the skills and experiences to forge sustainable careers in an uncertain field of work. His current work and research interests include creativity in higher education, and the development of innovative approaches to curriculum design and assessment.

Amanda Lewis qualified as an architect working in practice for ten years before joining Kingston University' School of Surveying & Planning in 1994 following successful completion of her RICS accredited masters. As an academic she has worked as a researcher, senior lecturer, Course Director of postgraduate studies and is now the Director of C-SCAIPE which is Kingston University's Centre of Excellence in Teaching and Learning (CETL.) During this time she gained her PG Certificate in Teaching & Learning in Higher Education leading to Fellowship of the Higher Education Academy.

Amanda has extensive experience in pedagogic issues. She co-directed the HEFCE funded project *Learning to Work:Working to Learn* (LWWL) which was a built environment, cross-disciplinary investigation into graduates' professional assessment experience. Simultaneously she was an original member of the steering group for *Better Together*, a multi-institution, FDTL project exploring interdisciplinary education in HE. Subsequently her personal research *Where's the Fun in Surveying?* has impacted on the School's students. She was made a University Teaching Fellow in June 2006.

In her C-SCAIPE role over the past four years, Amanda has worked with other individuals, universities and professional organisations concerned with education for sustainability, in the UK and internationally.

Jason Lowther is a Senior Lecturer in Law at the University of Plymouth and a Fellow of the University's Centre for Sustainable Futures. Jason's research interests concern environmental law and regulation, with a specific interest in sustainable development, civil liability and conservation. He is an assistant editor with an environmental law journal and has published widely on environmental law, on issues relating to sustainability and the law of torts. Current projects include writing a student text for OUP on environmental law; legal protection of cultural heritage; and ongoing research into the sustainability literacy of the higher judiciary. jason.lowther@plymouth.ac.uk

Rebecca O'Loughlin is Academic Coordinator for Theology at the Higher Education Academy Subject Centre for Philosophical and Religious Studies. She was awarded a PhD in Theology from the University of Leeds in 2006. Rebecca's research interests lie primarily in the field of Christian theology and theological ethics. She is also interested in discipline-specific models and methods of pedagogical research, particularly in relation to Theology and Religious Studies. She has tutored on a range of Theology and Religious Studies modules at the University of Leeds. R.M.O'Loughlin@leeds.ac.uk

Simon Payne is Professor of Law at the University of Plymouth and a Fellow of the Centre for Sustainable Futures. He is also Head of the Law School at the University of Plymouth. His research interests are in environmental law and sustainable development. He is well known as a commentator and writer on UK and EU environmental and planning law and is a member of the University's Marine Institute undertaking research and consultancy on comparative environmental law for international institutions. Simon has co-authored and contributed to a number of books on environmental law. simon.payne@plymouth.ac.uk

Anthony Plumridge read for the Economics Tripos at Cambridge and then entered marketing with a leading multinational, now Reed Elsevier. He obtained a second degree in Environmental Studies at University College London and worked at the Centre for Alternative Technology in Wales. After starting and growing a number of small businesses, he entered academic life in 1990. He is a Principal Lecturer in economics at the Bristol Business School, University of the West of England, teaching modules in Environmental Economics, Law and Economics, International Trade and Multinational Business and Sustainable Tourism and Local Economic Development. He has published in regional and spatial economics and has undertaken many consultancy projects in economic regeneration for clients ranging from Local Authorities in the UK to the World Bank. Anthony is married with two children and lives on 12 acres of wilderness in rural Monmouthshire

Kristin Vala Ragnarsdottir studied geology in Iceland, she gained a PhD in Aqueous Geochemistry from Northwestern University in Evanston, Illinois in 1984. After working in Chicago, Paris and Evanston she moved to the UK and was at the Department of Earth Sciences of the University of Bristol from 1989–2008 where she became interested in sustainability. Her personal Chair was named Professor of Environmental Sustainability in 2005. Vala worked closely with the Schumacher Society in Bristol, becoming its Chair in 2007. In 2008 she took up the post as Dean of Engineering and Natural Sciences at the University of Iceland where sustainability is at the forefront of her policies.

Janet Richardson is Professor of Health Service Research in the Faculty of Health and Social Work at the University of Plymouth. A registered nurse and chartered psychologist she has been researching patients' views of healthcare, and evaluating health service effectiveness since 1989. Much of this work has focused on engaging staff and users in the development and commissioning of services using participatory approaches. She has made a significant contribution to the development of the evidence-base in complementary therapies including the NHS National Library for Health Complementary and Alternatively Medicine Specialists Library. Janet has a particular interest in teaching and evaluating health services responsiveness to climate change, supported by a Fellowship with the Centre for Sustainable Futures at the University of Plymouth.

Sarah Sayce is a Chartered Surveyor by profession. After spending some years in practice as a valuer and commercial property manager she became an academic and she is now Head of the School of Surveying & Planning at Kingston University, a position she has held for a number of years. She undertook a PhD by research investigating the emergence of the new leisure property sector as an institutional investment vehicle but since then she has developed an extensive research portfolio based on the operation of the commercial property markets including the rise of the sustainability agenda as it impacts on and influences property appraisal. She has also researched and published in the field of professional education and she is the Chair of the University's Centre for Sustainable Communities Achieved through Integrated Professional Education (C-SCAIPE) which aims to promote in graduates the skills and value sets to assist in the move towards a more sustainable society. Outside the University she continues to be very actively involved with the RICS (Royal Institution of Chartered Surveyors), involved with professional assessments and currently sits as an elected member of their Governing Council.

David Selby is Adjunct Professor in the Faculty of Education, Mount St. Vincent University, Halifax, Nova Scotia, Canada, and Founding Director of Sustainability Frontiers, an international non-governmental organization concerned with global sustainability and climate change education. He was previously (2005–2009) Professor of Education for Sustainability and Director of the Centre for Sustainable Futures at the University of Plymouth, United Kingdom, and, before that (2003–2005), Professor of Continuing Professional Development in the Faculty of Education, University of Plymouth. From 1992–2003 he was Professor of Education and Director of the International Institute for Global Education at the Ontario Institute for Studies in Education of the University of Toronto, Canada. He has directed UN-funded national curriculum development projects in some ten countries in South East Europe, the Middle East and Central Asia, and has lectured or facilitated workshops and seminars on global education, environmental education and education for sustainability in some 30 countries. He has (co)written and (co)edited some 20 books and over 100 book chapters. His recent books include: *Weaving Connections: Educating for Peace, Social and Environmental Justice* (2000); *Green Frontiers: Environmental Educators Dancing Away from Mechanism* (2008); *Education and Climate Change: Living and Learning in Interesting Times* (2010). He was co-recipient of the Canadian Peace Education Prize in 2003 and is a Fellow of the Royal Society of Arts. He is a British and Canadian national. dselby@sustainabilityfrontiers.org.

Simon Smith is Director at the Higher Education Academy Subject Centre for Philosophical and Religious Studies, and also leads the Academy's Education for Sustainable Development project. Simon's academic background is at the meeting point of Buddhist Studies and social theory where his research has included the role of Buddhism in the deep ecology movement. Prior to his work for the Subject Centre, Simon was a lecturer in Religious Studies at the University of Leeds. s.g.smith@leeds.ac.uk

Delyse Springett is Director of the Programme for Business and Sustainable Development in the College of Business at Massey University, New Zealand, and Director of the consultancy, Business and Sustainable Development Training and Consulting (BSDNZ). Her doctoral thesis, awarded by Durham University, provided a critical analysis of corporate conceptions of sustainable development in New Zealand. She is an affiliate lecturer in Business and Sustainable Development at The University of Hong Kong. She taught English to university scholarship level in the UK before moving to New Zealand. Her broad interests in education then focused on social education and education for the environment. As Senior Fellow in Education at Massey University, she developed a social and human development education programme for schools, introducing action research and action methods of teaching and learning to teachers. In 1987, following the Brundtland Report, she became co-founder and director of a charitable education trust, based at Massey University, where the focus was on education for sustainability from early childhood to tertiary levels of formal education as well as education in the community. She has developed and taught master's level courses in the College of Education and the College of Business at Massey University. Her key interests are in critical perspectives on sustainability and sustainable development. She works as a consultant with companies and government departments in New Zealand, and the workshops with these groups are driven by an educational agenda. Since 1999, she has administered the New Zealand Survey of Corporate Environmental and Social Responsiveness with New Zealand companies. She was the founding editor of *The International Journal of Innovation and Sustainable Development* (Inderscience, 2005–2009), is a board member of the International Sustainable Development Research Society (ISDRS) and a member of the Advisory Board of the Green Economics Institute. D.V.Springett@massey.ac.nz

Simon Steiner is a chartered engineer, who originally worked for ten years in the aerospace industry before moving into academia, firstly at the then Coventry Polytechnic and latterly since 1989 at the University of Birmingham. He was responsible, as Programmes Manager at Birmingham, for the development and evolution of established degree programmes in mechanical and manufacturing engineering for both undergraduates and postgraduates. This included topics such as sustainable development, team skills, ethics, health and safety – as well as more technologically advanced engineering topics like robotics and automation, integrated manufacturing systems, CADCAM and intelligent systems. He is currently Academic Advisor with the Higher Education Academy Engineering Subject Centre, working with academic departments in facilitating pedagogic change, and is also responsible for leading on the Centre's work in sustainable development. He retains a Visiting Lectureship at the University of Birmingham and is a Visiting Fellow with IRIS at the University of Gloucestershire. simon@engsc.ac.uk

Stephen Sterling, Professor of Sustainability Education, Centre for Sustainable Futures (CSF) at the University of Plymouth, UK and Senior Advisor to the Higher Education Academy Education for Sustainable Development (ESD) Project. He is also a Visiting Research Fellow at the Centre for Research in Education and the Environment at the University of Bath, and has worked as a consultant in environmental and sustainability education in the academic and NGO fields nationally and internationally. He was a founder of the Education for Sustainability Programme at London South Bank University, where he retains an academic role. His research interest is in the interrelationships between ecological thinking, systemic change, learning, and sustainability in moving forward the educational response to the sustainability agenda. His key publications include *Education for Sustainable Development in the Schools Sector* (Sustainable Development Education Panel1988), *Education for Sustainability* (Earthscan 1996), *Sustainable Education: Re-visioning Learning and Change* (Green Books 2001), his doctoral thesis *Whole Systems Thinking as a Basis for Paradigm Change in Education – Explorations in the Context of Sustainability* (CREE/U of Bath 2003), and *Linking Thinking – New Perspectives on Learning and Thinking for Sustainability* (WWF Scotland 2005). His work at CSF involves leading the research team, whilst his work for the Academy centres on advising the ESD Project on programmes and strategy in supporting curriculum change across the HE sector. stephen.sterling@plymouth.ac.uk

Katja Stuerzenhofecker is currently working as a part-time lecturer in Religions and Theology at the University of Manchester, and as an Associate Lecturer in Religious Studies at the Open University. Katja is commissioned by the Higher Education Subject Centre for Philosophical and Religious Studies to research into the pedagogies underpinning approaches to ESD in HE Theology in the UK. She is also taking part in a collaborative pedagogical research project in Religions and Theology at the University of Manchester to develop a progression model for enquiry-based learning in undergraduate education. katja.stuerzenhofecker@manchester.ac.uk

Denise Summers has taught in the further and community education sectors for over 25 years; ranging from teaching student teachers, adults, 16–19 year olds and students with learning difficulties and disabilities. She studied for her MEd at the University of Birmingham specializing in teaching students with additional needs. This led to Denise managing and teaching the Cert Ed/PGCE programmes at Somerset College, in partnership with the University of Plymouth. To further support this role, she completed her doctorate at the University of Exeter in 2006. Developments in ESD at Somerset College since 2006 have led to Denise's current research interest in using co-operative inquiry to support the professional and curriculum development required to embed ESD in the College's initial teacher education provision within the Lifelong Learning Sector.

Tracey Varnava is Associate Director of the UK Centre for Legal Education, the Higher Education Academy Subject Centre for Law based at the University of Warwick. Prior to joining the University of Warwick in 1997, Tracey was a Lecturer in Law at the University of Leicester specialising in Criminology, Criminal Law and Justice. She has taken the lead for the UKCLE on education for sustainable development and, with Hugh Brayne, has published a survey and discussion paper on the topic as part of UKCLE's project on Developing Global Citizens through Legal Education, funded by the Higher Education Academy's ESD project. T.Varnava@warwick.ac.uk

Arjen E. J. Wals is a UNESCO Chair and Professor in Social Learning and Sustainable Development within the Education and Competence Studies Group of Wageningen University in The Netherlands. He has (co)published and (co)edited over 150 articles, chapters, books and professional publications on topics such as: action research & community problem-solving, whole school approaches to sustainability, biodiversity education, and sustainability in higher education. He is the editor of *Social Learning Towards a Sustainable World* published by Wageningen Academic Publishers (2007) and serves on the editorial boards of a number of environmental education research journals. arjen.wals@wur.nl

Andrew Whiteford is a Practice Learning Manager working with the under-graduate Social Work programme at the University of Plymouth, with responsibility for developing, supporting and managing student practice learning. He became a Fellow of the Centre for Sustainable Futures in 2007 working with 1st year Social Work students' practice experience of networking and community with a sustainability focus. This work was developed further the following year, seeing students engaged directly in working with individuals and communities establishing allotments and accessing nature. His interest is driven by a desire to see creative, emancipative social work restored to mainstream practice whilst advocating for sustainability awareness within the profession. andrew.whiteford@plymouth.ac.uk

Jennie Winter completed her PhD in Geography at the University of Plymouth. She remains at the university as a Research Fellow in the Teaching and Learning Directorate and an associate lecturer in Geography. Her research interests include education for sustainable development, individual responses to sustainability, e-learning, research-informed teaching and progression pathways from further to higher education. jennie.winter@plymouth.ac.uk

Recommended Publications and Websites

Publications

Adomssent, M., Godemann, J., Leicht, A. and Busch, A. (2006) *Higher Education for Sustainability: New Challenges from a Global Perspective*, VAS, Frankfurt

Blewitt, J. and Cullingford, C. (2004) *The Sustainability Curriculum: The Challenge for Higher Education*, Earthscan, London

Bartlett, P.F. and Chase, G.W. (2004) *Sustainability on Campus: Stories and Strategies for Change* Massachusetts Institute of Technology, Cambridge MA

Corcoran, P.B. and Wals, A.E.J. (eds) (2004) *Higher Education and the Challenge of Sustainability. Problematics, Promise, and Practice*, Kluwer Academic Publishers, Dordrecht

Chalkley, B., Haigh, M. and Higgit, D. (eds) (2009) *Education for Sustainable Development: Papers in Honour of the United Nations Decade of Education for Sustainable Development*, Routledge, London

Dawe, G.R., Jucker, R. and Martin, S. (2005) *Sustainable Development in Higher Education: Current Practice and Future Developments*, Higher Education Academy, York, available at www.heacademy.ac.uk/assets/York/documents/ourwork/tla/sustainability/ sustdevinHEfinalreport.pdf, accessed 23 January 2010

Gough, S. and Scott, W. (2007) *Higher Education and Sustainable Development – Paradox and Possibility*, Routledge, London

HEFCE (2009) *Sustainable Development in Higher Education: 2008 Update to Strategic Statement and Action Plan*, HEFCE, Bristol, available at www.hefce.ac.uk/pubs/hefce/2009/09_03/09_03.pdf, accessed 3 February 2010

Kaivola, T. and Rohweder, L. (eds) (2007) *Towards Sustainable Development in Higher Education – Reflections*, Ministry of Education, Department for Education and Science, Finland, available at www.minedu.fi/export/sites/default/OPM/Julkaisut/2007/liitteet/ opm06.pdf?lang=e, accessed 10 February 2010

M'Gonigle, M. and Starke, J. (2006) *Planet U: Sustaining the World Reinventing the University*, New Society Publishers, Gabriola Island

Scott, W. and Gough, S. (2003) *Key Issues in Sustainable Development and Learning: A Critical Review*, Routledge, London

Websites

Association for the Advancement of Sustainability in Higher Education www.aashe.org accessed 10 February 2010

UN DESD www.desd.org accessed 10 February 2010

Education for Sustainable Development and Global Citizenship, Wales www.esd-wales.org.uk accessed 10 February 2010

HEFCE www.hefce.ac.uk/susdevresources/curric accessed 10 February 2010

IAU www.unesco.org/iau/association/index.html accessed 10 February 2010

The Environmental Association for Universities and Colleges www.eauc.org.uk/home accessed 10 February 2010

HEA www.heacademy.ac.uk/ourwork/learning/sustainability accessed 10 February 2010

Second Nature www.secondnature.org accessed 10 February 2010

ULSF www.ulsf.org/programs_talloires.html

UNESCO www.unesco.org/en/higher-education accessed 10 February 2010

This book was supported by:

Centre for Sustainable Futures (CSF) University of Plymouth

The CSF is a Centre for Excellence in Teaching and Learning funded by the HEFCE. Opened in 2005, it works to embed sustainability throughout the University in curriculum, campus, community and culture, by means of whole institutional change and support, and thereby also encourages and informs national and international initiatives towards the 'sustainable university'. See http://csf.plymouth.ac.uk (accessed 10 February 2010). It will be relaunched as an ESD research centre in 2010.

The Higher Education Academy Education for Sustainable Development (HEA ESD) Project

The purpose of this project is to help institutions and subject communities develop curricula and pedagogy that will give students the skills and knowledge to live and work sustainably. Programmes are being developed in three areas: research and support, building capacity, and coordination and dissemination. See www.heacademy.ac.uk/ourwork/learning/sustainability (accessed 10 February 2010).

Index